שער איסור והיתר

הלכות בשר בחלב

חכמת אדם

הלכות
בשר בחלב

עם תרגום אנגלי והערות
מאת
יהושע ירוחם הלוי כהן

יודאיקא פרעסס
ניו יורק • תשנ"א

ENGLISH TRANSLATION & COMMENTARY

by Dr. Yehoshua Cohen

Judaica Press

New York • 1991

932 East 23rd Street
Brooklyn, New York 11210
718 258-2125

LIBRARY OF CONGRESS CATALOG NUMBER: 90–091918
ISBN: 0–910818–91–6

Typography by
Simcha Graphic Associates
4311 15th Avenue
Brooklyn, N.Y. 11219
(718) 854–4830

Manufactured in the United States of America

Rabbi Avraham Asher Zimmerman
Congregation Khal Shaarei Tefillah
4407 12th Avenue
Brooklyn, New York 11219

I wish to extend my most sincere blessings and good wishes to Dr. Jeffrey Cohen שליט"א for his ספר dealing with הלכות בשר בחלב that he will publish in the near future. Dr. Cohen has written a most comprehensive and accurate English translation of the famous ספר חכמת אדם on הלכות בשר בחלב and has added a commentary of his own. I believe that this ספר can be of great benefit to anyone who wishes to learn these important דינים.

It is not my custom to give הסכמות on ספרים. May *Hashem* bless you that you continue to learn and teach, and spread Torah—ויפוצו מעינותיו חוצה.

בברכת ידידו המוקירו

אברהם אשר צימערמאן

Rabbi Avigdor Miller
Bais Yisroel Torah Center
1821 Ocean Parkway
Brooklyn, New York 11223

Dr. Cohen's translation and commentary are carefully composed, and they constitute a valuable aid for aspiring Torah students.

Rabbi Avigdor Miller

Dedication

This work is dedicated by the translator
in memory of his father

יצחק בן יעקב מאיר הלוי ע״ה

Isidore Cohen

on the occasion of his seventh yahrzeit

ג׳ כסלו

His memory is continually with
his wife, children, and grandchildren

Table of Contents

Table of Contents

Introduction

1. The חָכְמַת אָדָם

The publication of the *Chochmas Adam* in the year 5574 (1812) was hailed by the rabbinical authorities of that era as a landmark event. Why was the appearance of this volume considered to be of such great significance? It is because a much needed reference work had now become available for the first time—a concise yet comprehensive review of the rulings contained in the *Yoreh Deah* section of the *Shulchan Aruch*.

The *Chochmas Adam* was composed with two purposes in mind: Firstly, it was geared to provide the layman with the means to learn almost the entire contents of the *Shulchan Aruch-Yoreh Deah*. This was indeed an important goal, since many of the laws contained in *Yoreh Deah* affect the daily conduct of the ordinary person. It would no longer be necessary to spend inordinate amounts of time delving through the text of the *Shulchan Aruch* and its sometimes lengthy commentaries. By learning through the text of the *Chochmas Adam* one could gain an authoritative synopsis of all of this material.

Moreover, it was designed to furnish the advanced Torah scholar who had already studied this section of the *Shulchan Aruch* with an accurate, terse review of the subject matter. Even today, there is no other published work which provides such a complete yet succinct review of these *halachot*.

The *Chochmas Adam* is divided into several sections which are known as שְׁעָרִים (literally, "gateways"), each of which provides a "gateway" to those who desire to enter into the study of that respective topic. They are named as follows:

שער איסור והיתר—Laws concerning the "forbidden and permissible"

Many topics are covered in this section including: Laws of slaughtering an animal; laws of *terefot*; salting meat to remove its blood; laws of meat and milk; regulations pertaining to forbidden mixtures; the food and wine of a gentile; and finally, laws pertaining to vows and oaths.

שער בית הנשים—Laws pertaining to women

This portion of the work deals with the laws of the *niddah*. It also includes regulations relating to marriage which are summarized from the *Even Ha'ezer* section of the *Shulchan Aruch*.

שער משפטי צדק—Laws regarding righteousness in money matters

The regulations relating to the prohibition of taking interest on a loan are covered in this section, as well as the laws concerning the giving of charity.

שער רינה וישועה—Laws relating to "joyous song and redemption"

This relatively short section deals with circumcision and the redemption of the first-born son.

שער השמחה—Laws of "happiness"

The title is a euphemism, as this section deals with the laws of mourning, and concludes with regulations relating to excommunication *(cherem).*

We are pleased to present a translation and commentary of this very important work to the English speaking public, commencing with the laws which relate to mixtures of meat and milk. With the help of *Hashem,* additional volumes will continue to appear in the near future.

2. Rabbi Avraham Danzig—Author of the חָכְמַת אָדָם

The renowned author of the *Chochmas Adam,* Rabbi Avraham ben Yechiel Mich'l Danzig, was born in 5508 (1748) in the city of Danzig, located in northern Poland. (The Polish name of this city is Gdansk.) While a young man, he learned in the Yeshiva of Rabbi Yosef Lieberman in Prague, and in the Yeshiva of Rabbi Yechezkel Landau, better known as the *Noda BiYehudah.*

Rabbi Avraham has become famous for composing two very important works which deal with Jewish law: His first publication was the *Chayei Adam,* which covers all of the laws contained in the *Orach Chayim* section of the *Shulchan Aruch.* This work, first published in the year 1810, became so extremely popular that it has appeared in almost one hundred editions. It was published together with the *Nishmas Adam,* which provides sources and explanations for many of his *halachic* decisions.

The *Chayei Adam* proved to be an eminently useful work, providing an easy to follow summary of the laws contained in the *Shulchan Aruch—Orach Chayim.* It was so successful in making the study of Jewish law accessible to the populace that Rabbi Avraham was approached by the Torah scholars of his generation with a request to publish a similar volume dealing with the laws contained in the *Yoreh Deah* section of the *Shulchan Aruch.*

This led to the publication of Rabbi Avraham's second important work, entitled the *Chochmas Adam*, approximately three years later, which indeed provides a summary of the *halachos* that are covered in the *Shulchan Aruch—Yoreh Deah*. The *Binas Adam*, which contains more detailed discussions and source material, was appended to it. It should be noted that the laws in *Yoreh Deah* which relate to agricultural produce are not covered in the *Chochmas Adam*, but they are dealt with in a separate volume by Rabbi Avraham entitled *Shaarei Zedek*. This work also covers other laws which relate primarily to the land of Israel.

Rabbi Avraham suffered a great tragedy when his son *Moshe*, passed away on Purim of the year 5574 (1814). Rabbi Moshe was only twenty years old at the time, yet he had already become known as an exceptional Torah scholar. In his memory, Rabbi Avraham published the *Matzeves Moshe* which deals with laws of mourning, and this was appended to the *Chochmas Adam*. In addition, the work *Zichru Toras Moshe*, dealing with the laws of the Sabbath, was published in memory of his son.

During most of his lifetime, Rabbi Avraham declined to receive a salary for serving as a rabbinical leader. Rather, he earned his livelihood as a merchant, frequently traveling to trade fairs in Germany. During his travels he always took with him a *Tanach, Mishnayos*, and *Gemara*; he learned a minimum of one and a half folios (*dafim*) of *Gemara* each day, in addition to a number of *Mishnayos*. Nevertheless, as he aged and became too weak to carry on his business, he accepted money to serve as a judge and leader of the Jewish community in Vilna.

Rabbi Avraham Danzig passed away soon after *Rosh Hashanah* of the year 5581 (1820). Now, 170 years after his passing, he continues to be remembered by Jews throughout the world who constantly learn and relearn his published works.

3. The Present Edition of the חָכְמַת אָדָם

The primary goal in producing this edition of the *Chochmas Adam* is to provide a clear, literal English translation of this important classic. It should be noted, moreover, that many other useful features have been incorporated into the present edition as well. Most important, a comprehensive English commentary entitled *Yad Adam* has been included, which serves to clarify and explain the entire text. The commentary contains all background material necessary for understanding the text, and includes relevant *halachic* decisions found in later sources, such as the *Aruch Hashulchan*. Comments from contemporary authorities, including Horav Moshe Feinstein זצ״ל, are also mentioned in the commentary. For ease of reference, the statements in the commentary are printed underneath the text, and are referred to by numbers which have been inserted into the English translation and into the Hebrew text as well.

Another important feature of this edition is a change in the text format which will make it easier to follow. All previous editions of the *Chochmas Adam* contain parenthetical notes which consist primarily of references and detailed technical discussions. Some of these are rather long and may serve to distract the reader from his train of thought. In order to facilitate learning from the text, all of these notes have been removed from the main body of the text and placed in the outer margins of the pages. A full English translation of these notes has been provided on the facing page in the corresponding margin. These marginal notations (and their translations) are referred to by inserting Hebrew letters in the appropriate places in the text. Supplementary information has been added into the translation of these marginal notes; these informative notations have been placed in square brackets [ ].

A third important aspect of this work involves revision of the Hebrew text. A great deal of effort was expended to clear up the many inaccuracies which abound in the current available editions of the *Chochmas Adam*. The methods used to provide the reader with an accurate Hebrew text are mentioned below.

In order to assist the reader, each *halacha* in the text has been given a title which is printed in the appropriate place in the English commentary. These titles will help one locate the subject matter he desires to learn, and will also help to distinguish between rulings which involve closely related circumstances.

At the end of this work, the Hebrew text of the appropriate sections of the *Binas Adam* is included. Two additional appendices have also been provided. One consists of biographical information relating to each of the authorities quoted in the text of the *Chochmas Adam* as well as those cited in the English commentary. Separate listings are made of the *rishonim* (early authorities), *achronim* (later authorities), and contemporary sources. The second appendix is a complete alphabetical guide to all of the Hebrew abbreviations used in this work.

4. The Text of The חָכְמַת אָדָם

It is noteworthy that the current published texts of the *Chochmas Adam* differ significantly from those of the early printed editions. The manner in which these changes came about is rather intriguing, and is recounted to us by Rabbi Yisroel ben Eliezer of Vilna, in his preface to the *Chochmas Adam*. Rabbi Yisroel relates that after publication of the first edition of the *Chochmas Adam*, Rabbi Avraham prepared a list of corrections and additions to the text which were to be incorporated into future editions. Furthermore, shortly before his death, Rabbi Avraham accumulated a large number of unsorted papers which contained material relevant to the topics covered in the *Chochmas Adam*. Rabbi Avraham personally appealed to Rabbi Yisroel to review all of these papers and to insert their contents directly into the relevant places in the text. Rabbi Yisroel worked very diligently to fulfill the wishes of the *Chochmas Adam*, and, with the help of Rabbi Avraham Abbale of Vilna, finally completed the task. Rabbi Yisroel ben Eliezer then went even further—he incorporated relevant statements from contemporary rabbinical authorities into the text which the *Chochmas Adam* failed to mention, each one being stated together with the author of that respective statement. The editions of the *Chochmas Adam* which are currently in print contain these textual changes.

All of the above revisions, which were completed in the year 1848, certainly represent valuable additions to the work. Unfortunately, however, there are several instances where they cause ambiguity of the text and serve to confuse the reader. When preparing the translation of the *Chochmas Adam*, it was noted that such difficulties in interpreting the text could often be resolved by referring to the early editions which were published before these textual changes were made. The old texts also proved helpful in resolving seemingly contradictory rulings.

Furthermore, it is not surprising that many printers' errors have crept into the various editions which are in use today. Whenever a textual problem suggested that a printer's error might be present, the old editions of the *Chochmas Adam* were perused in order to elucidate the proper wording in each instance. All such printers' errors were corrected, based on the wording found in the early editions. In addition, a number of the current editions of the *Chochmas Adam* contain appendices which list printers' errors which have crept into the text. These appendices have been carefully reviewed and where appropriate, the proper changes in the text have been made. Finally, the text of the first edition of the *Chochmas Adam* was reviewed in its entirety and compared with the current editions, and this resulted in further revisions of the text.

Whenever there is a major deviation in the text of this edition of the *Chochmas Adam* from the others which are currently in print, the difference is recorded in the English commentary or in the marginal notes. As a result of the efforts which have been described, it is hoped that the text in the present edition of the *Chochmas Adam* is significantly more accurate and easier to follow than that of its predecessors.

5. Acknowledgments

I have many people to thank who have provided their assistance to help bring this work to fruition. First and foremost, I would like to thank Rabbi Avraham Asher Zimmerman. His clear, incisive lectures on the *Shulchan Aruch*, the *Tur*, and the *Bais Yosef* helped provide me with the basic knowledge which led to the publication of this volume. Moreover, his complete review of my manuscript was vital to insure accuracy of the text.

I next wish to thank the staff of Simcha Graphic Associates who devoted a great deal of time and effort to insure production of an accurate yet easy-to-follow text. Mr. Jack Goldman of Judaica Press deserves special mention for his enthusiastic support and assistance in producing this work. I am also grateful to Mrs. Devora Weitzman for creating the cover design. Special thanks are due to Rabbi Eliyahu Meir Cohen for obtaining copies of the old editions of the *Chochmas Adam*.

I must express my gratitude to my wife Yosefa (Josie) for her constant support, and her readiness to assist in all aspects of this publication. Finally, I wish to show my appreciation to my daughter Meira, who spent many hours of her summer vacation proofreading the Hebrew text and reading over the English translation to insure a clear presentation of the material.

I have recently been saddened by the passing of my wife's mother, מאשא בת יוסף ראובן—Mrs. Marcia Sebrow. Her generosity has resulted in the establishment and expansion of Yeshiva libraries, and in the publication of several valuable *seforim*.

Notes for using this sefer

Most works dealing with Jewish law are divided into chapters, usually denoted by the Hebrew term סימן or פרק. The *Chochmas Adam*, however, uses a different terminology:

The Hebrew word כלל (English translation: **topic**) is used to denote a chapter. Each chapter is divided into several numbered paragraphs, and each one of these is called a סימן (English translation: **section**).

The parenthetical notations written by the *Chochmas Adam* (and their translation) have been removed from the main body of the text and are printed in the outside margins of the page. These notations are "footnoted" in the text using Hebrew letters.

The notes provided in the translator's commentary are printed underneath the text and are indicated by numbers inserted into both the Hebrew text and English translation. Any words or phrases added into the text of the translation (whether to form proper English sentences or to make the text easier to comprehend) are placed in square brackets [ ].

Please note that the subject matter of every numbered paragraph is indicated by a title placed in the English commentary.

See the introduction for a full discussion of the many features incorporated into this edition of the *Chochmas Adam*.

Notice to the reader:

The commentary in this work is not meant to serve as a primary guide for making *halachic* decisions. A competent rabbinical authority should be consulted whenever a practical *halachic* question arises.

כלל מ
הלכות בשר בחלב
(סימן פ״ז פ״ח פ״ט)

א. כתיב בתורה לא תבשל גדי[1] בחלב אמו ג׳ פעמים[2] וקבלו חז״ל[3] אחד לאיסור אכילה ואחד לאיסור בישול ואחד לאיסור הנאה[4] ועוד קבלו דאע״ג דכתיב גדי לאו דוקא אלא הוא הדין כל בשר בהמה טהורה אסור[5] אלא שדיבר הכתוב בהווה שכן היה דרכם לבשל גדיים בחלב.[6]

והוציא הכתוב איסור אכילה בלשון בישול[7] ללמד דאינו אסור מה״ת באכילה אלא אם כן דרך בישול[8] אבל אם נבלע בו[9] על ידי

יד אדם

1. Meat and Milk—The Basic Prohibition

1. The word גדי (kid) denotes a young nursing animal.

2. *Shemos* (Exodus) 23:19, *Shemos* 34:26, *Devarim* (Deuteronomy) 13:21.

3. I.e., the following *derasha* (exposition) explains why the Torah mentions this ruling three times.

4. It is forbidden to derive any benefit whatsoever from a mixture of meat and milk which has been cooked together. See section 2 for further discussion.

Thus, the threefold repetition implies to us that there are three different Torah prohibitions which apply to meat and milk.

5. I.e., the Torah forbids cooking the meat of any kosher species of animal with milk. Eating such meat which has been cooked with milk or deriving benefit from it is forbidden by the Torah as well. See also note 24.

6. Furthermore, the Torah does not mean to imply that it is forbidden to cook an animal only in the milk of its own mother and that it is permitted to cook it in other milk. Rather, the Torah is again speaking in an ordinary situation: When a young nursing animal is present, its mother will be producing milk. We can then apply the following reasoning: Since the Torah forbids one from cooking an animal in the milk of its own

Topic 40
Laws of Meat and Milk–
[Basic Principles, Laws and Customs]
(based on *Shulchan Aruch–Yoreh Deah* chapters 87, 88, 89)

1. In the Torah, [the phrase]: "You shall not cook a kid[1] in its mother's milk," is written three times,[2] and our sages (of blessed memory) have received [the following tradition]:[3] One is for the prohibition of eating, one is for the prohibition of cooking, and one is for the prohibition of [deriving] benefit.[4] And they have also received [a tradition] that even though "A kid" is written [in the Torah, the prohibition] is not limited [to a young nursing animal]. Rather, the rule is the same with regard to any meat of a kosher animal, that it is forbidden.[5] Nevertheless, the Torah [specifically mentions the kid because it] is speaking of an ordinary situation, as such was the practice [of gentiles] to cook kids in milk.[6]

And the Torah expresses the prohibition of eating in terms of cooking[7] in order to teach that [a mixture of meat and milk] is not forbidden to be eaten according to Torah Law except by means of cooking.[8] However, if it is absorbed into it[9] by soaking meat with milk for

Yad Adam

mother from whom it nurses and derives its nourishment, then certainly it should be forbidden to cook it in the milk of any other animal. (*Aruch Hashulchan* 87:1)

7. The Torah does not state, "You may not eat meat with milk." Rather, the prohibition is implied by the Torah's repetition of the prohibition to cook meat and milk together.

8. If the mixture of meat and milk is not first "cooked" together, then it is not forbidden to eat it by Torah law. The term "cooking" (*bishul*) used in the Torah generally denotes cooking in a pot of liquid. Other methods of food preparation are discussed below.

9. If the taste of milk is absorbed into meat, or vice versa.

א. פ״ז.
ב. פ״ח.
ג. סי׳ ל״ד.
ד. ש״ך ס״ק ב׳.

[Additional information pertaining to the marginal notations are included in their English translation.]

שנכבש בשר בחלב מעת לעת או שנמלחו יחד מותר מן התורה[10] אלא מדרבנן אסור בכל ענין.[11]א אבל צלי וטיגון[12] הוא כבישול ואסור מן התורה.[13]ב

ב. ולפיכך[14] בשר וחלב שנאסר ע״י בישול צריך לזרוק לבית הכסא[15] ואסור ליתנו לעכו״ם או אפי׳ לכלב שאינו שלו אבל הקדירה[16] מותר להשתמש בו פירות ודברים יבישים[17] ולהחם בו מים לחוף ראשו[18] דבזה אינו נהנה מן האיסור ג אבל אם אינו אסור אלא מדרבנן כגון בשר עוף בחלב[19] או אפילו בשר בהמה על ידי כבישה ומליחה[20] מותר בהנאה דעל הנאה לא גזרינן.[21]ד

יד אדם

10. Soaking for twenty four hours or salting are indeed considered to be like cooking with regard to other forbidden mixtures, but this is not the case with regard to the Torah prohibition of meat and milk.

11. For example, if a piece of cold meat falls into cold milk and remains there for 24 hours, the meat will be completely forbidden. The milk will also be completely forbidden unless the amount of milk present is at least sixty times the meat. (When sixty is present, the taste of the meat will not be detectable and the milk will therefore be permitted. See topic 44, beginning of section 1.)

What will be the rule if the meat and milk were together less than 24 hours? It is certainly forbidden to eat the mixture, since there is a rabbinical prohibition to eat any mixture of meat and milk, even if they were not cooked, or soaked together for 24 hours, or salted together. Nevertheless, if the meat is removed from the milk, then they may, under certain circumstances, be eaten. Since both of them are cold, they do not absorb each other's taste and they will be permissible if the meat and milk will be completely separated from each other. (See topic 42, sections 1 and 6 for further details.)

The laws concerning salted mixtures of meat and milk will be discussed in detail in topic 43.

12. For example, placing butter on meat while it is broiling, or frying meat in butter.

13. However, some authorities (including *Rashi* and *Tosafot*) rule that this is not so, and broiling meat and milk together or frying them together is forbidden only by rabbinical decree. (See *Aruch Hashulchan* 87:10-11.)

2. The Prohibition to Derive Benefit from a Mixture of Meat and Milk

14. Since it is forbidden to derive any benefit from meat and milk which have been cooked together.

15. I.e., the mixture should be disposed of in a toilet, or in any other manner which will prevent one from deriving benefit from the forbidden mixture.

א. [*Shulchan Aruch*] chapter 87 [See *Shach* paragraph 2.]
ב. *Pri Chadash* [87:2].
ג. *Shulchan Aruch*, chapter 94 [paragraph 3].
ד. *Shach*, [chapter 87], paragraph 2.

twenty four hours or if they are salted together, [the mixture] is permitted by the Torah[10] but it is rabbinically forbidden in any case.[11א] However, broiling or frying[12] is like cooking and is forbidden by the Torah.[13ב]

2. Therefore,[14] meat and milk which have become forbidden by being cooked [together] must be thrown into a bathroom,[15] and it is forbidden to give it to a gentile, or even to a dog which is not his own. However, the pot[16] is permissible to be used for fruits and dry food items,[17] and for warming water to groom one's hair,[18] for in this way he does not benefit from the prohibited matter.[ג] Nevertheless, if the [mixture] is only rabbinically prohibited, such as the meat of a bird [cooked] with milk[19] or even the meat of an animal [which became forbidden] by soaking or salting,[20] it is permitted to derive benefit [from the mixture], because [the rabbis] did not decree that deriving benefit [is forbidden].[21ד]

Yad Adam

16. The pot in which the forbidden mixture was cooked may no longer be used for cooking. This is because the taste of meat and milk has been absorbed into the pot, and this forbidden taste will be emitted into any food that will subsequently be cooked in the pot. However, the pot still can be used for other purposes, as noted here by the *Chochmas Adam*.

Most pots used at the time of the *Chochmas Adam* were made of clay or earthenware. Since such pots cannot be made fit for use by kashering, the *Chochmas Adam* rules that one can no longer cook in these pots. If, however, the pots were made of metal, they could certainly be used again for cooking after kashering them. The laws relating to kashering are explained in topic 74.

17. However, to heat up something edible in this pot will be forbidden, as noted above. It will also be prohibited to leave any liquid or moist food in the pot in accordance with the rulings mentioned in topic 42, sections 1 and 2.

18. Since he is heating water only to groom his hair, no benefit is derived from the taste of meat and milk that is emitted into the water, and it therefore will remain permissible to use.

19. We will learn in the next section that the Torah prohibition of meat and milk applies only to domesticated animals: the bull (or cow), goat, and sheep. Eating meat from a chicken cooked in milk is forbidden only by rabbinical decree.

20. For example, meat from a cow was soaked in milk for 24 hours, or was salted together with milk.

21. Rather, the rabbis decreed only that eating such mixtures is prohibited.

ג. מדכתיב ג׳ פעמים[22] גדי קבלו חז״ל דאתי למעוטי חיה[23] ועוף ובהמה טמאה.[24] ודוקא בחלב טהורה דומיא דגדי בחלב אמו שהוא טהור בחלב טהורה. אבל בשר טהורה בחלב טמאה[25] או בשר טמאה בחלב טהורה מותרים בבישול ובהנאה ואפילו לענין אכילה לא גזרו בהם חז״ל איסור של בשר וחלב דכיון שהם אסורים בלאו הכי משום טמא לא גזרינן.ה

וכן בשר חיה ועוף אפילו בחלב טהורה מותר בבישול והנאה[26] ומ״מ בזה גזרו חכמים שאסור באכילה דשמא יטעה ויאמר מאי שנא בשר חיה ועוף או בשר בהמה אבל דגים וחגבים[27] אין בהם שום איסור אפילו מדרבנן.

והרוצה לאכול בשר אפילו של עוף עם חלב שקדים[28] צריך שיניח שקדים בתוך החלב משום מראית עין[29] דאע״פ דעוף בחלב

ה. וכ״מ דל״א חכ״נ* וגם לא הוי חתיכה כר״ל** עיין ש״ך ס״ק ג׳.

יד אדם

3. Meat and Milk—Which Animals Are Included in the Prohibition?

22. The word גדי is mentioned three times to imply to us that three categories of animals which do not include the גדי are excluded from the prohibition. The sources are noted above in note 2.

23. The word *chaya* denotes nondomesticated animals, and the Torah lists seven species of them which are kosher (*Devarim* [Deuteronomy] 14:5). Animals such as the deer, antelope, and buffalo are in this category. The word *beheimah*, on the other hand, denotes domesticated animals. The bull (cow), sheep and goat are the kosher animals in this category (*Devarim* 14:4).

24. Such as pigs or horses. It should be noted that if the meat of a kosher species of animal is *nevelah* (it has become forbidden because the animal was not slaughtered properly), then the Torah prohibition of meat and milk will still apply. The same holds true for the meat of a *terefah* (an animal which is forbidden due to an abnormality of one of its internal organs.)

25. For example, cooking meat from a bull in pig's milk.

26. This is in accordance with section 2 above, that the rabbis did not extend their decree to prohibit cooking or deriving benefit from such mixtures. It is similarly permissible to cook or derive benefit from meat of a *beheimah* with milk of a wild animal (*chaya*). (*Aruch Hashulchan* 87:15) However, in all cases where cooking meat and milk is permissible, it should nevertheless be avoided except when cooking them to make a medicine, as noted in section 4 below. (See also *Aruch Hashulchan* 87:17.)

ה. The practical importance [of this ruling] is that we do not say [according to some authorities] that the piece becomes inherently forbidden,* nor do we apply [the status of] a piece which is fit to honor [guests].** See *Shach* [chapter 87] paragraph 3.

*For example, a kosher piece of meat was cooked in a small amount of pig's milk. Then this piece fell into a pot of kosher food. If the prohibition of meat and milk would apply to the piece, then it would be considered *nevelah* (inherently forbidden), and the entire pot of food would become forbidden unless it contains sixty times the entire piece. However, since we say that the prohibition of meat and milk does not apply, then according to some authorities (the *Bais Yosef*—see topic 44, section 7), it is sufficient for the pot to contain sixty times the pig's milk in which the meat had been cooked.

**For example, a piece of kosher meat which is fit for a guest was cooked in pig's milk. If the piece would become forbidden as a mixture of meat and milk, then the stringencies of "a piece fit for a guest" would apply, and we would say that it cannot become nullified. If that were the case, then even if the forbidden piece became mixed up with a thousand other pieces, all of them would be forbidden. However, since the prohibition of milk and meat does not take effect, the stringencies of "a piece fit for a guest" will not apply. This is because the piece is not forbidden due to its own nature. See topic 44, section 5.

3. Since [the word] "kid" is written three times,[22] our sages (of blessed memory) have received [the tradition] that this comes to exclude [three groups of animals from the prohibition]: wild animals,[23] birds, and unkosher animals.[24] And [the prohibition applies] only to milk of a kosher animal, in accordance with [the phrase]: "A kid in its mother's milk," which [is dealing with] a kosher [animal] in kosher milk. As such, kosher meat in unkosher milk[25] or unkosher meat in kosher milk are permissible with regard to cooking and deriving benefit. And even with regard to eating, our sages (of blessed memory) did not apply the prohibition of meat and milk to them, for since they are [already] forbidden [to be eaten] without this [prohibition] because they are unkosher, they did not apply the prohibition [of meat and milk to them].[ה]

The meat of a wild animal or a bird even [together] with kosher milk is permissible with regard to cooking and deriving benefit.[26] Nevertheless, the sages decreed that such [a mixture] is forbidden to be eaten, for perhaps one will err and say, "What is the difference between the meat of a wild animal or a bird and that of a domesticated animal?" However, fish and locusts[27] have no prohibition whatsoever [to be cooked or eaten together with milk] even according to the rabbis.

And one who desires to eat meat, even [meat] of a bird, with the "milk of almonds,"[28] is required to leave almonds inside the "milk" because of *maris ayin*.[29] For even though [meat of] birds [mixed] with milk is [prohibited] only by the rabbis, nevertheless, even with respect

Yad Adam

27. There are four species of kosher locusts which are mentioned in the Torah. (*Vayikra* [Leviticus] 11:22)

28. A white liquid extracted from almonds which has the appearance of milk.

29. Literally, appearance of the eye. This term refers to certain actions which have been forbidden by the rabbis in order that people should not suspect that a prohibition is being performed. In this case, one who eats "milk of almonds" with meat might be suspected of eating meat and milk together. By keeping pieces of almonds in the mixture, it will be obvious to everyone that the white liquid is not real milk.

ו. ס״ק ו׳.
ז. ס״ק ז׳.
ח. ט״ז וש״ך.

אינו אלא מדרבנן מ״מ גם באיסור דרבנן גזרו משום מראית עין.[30] [ו]

ד. אע״ג דמותר לאכול חלב אשה כדלעיל כלל ל״ז מ״מ אסור לבשל כדי לאכול בשר בחלב אשה משום מראית עין[31] ומ״מ אם נפל חלב אשה לתוך התבשיל בטל ואין צריך שיעור.[32] אבל אם רוצה לבשל שלא לצורך אכילה אלא שצריך להניח על מכתו וכיוצא בו וכן אם צריך לבשל בשר טהורה בחלב טמאה או בשר טמאה בחלב טהורה לרפואה אפילו לחולה שאין בו סכנה מותר כיון דאינו מבשל לאכילה ליכא משום מראית עין[33] [ז] אבל שלא לרפואה כגון שמבשל להאכיל לנכרי אסור מפני מראית העין בין בטמאה ובין בעוף בחלב.[ח]

ה. ביצים הנמצאים בעופות[34] אם הם גמורות דהיינו שיש להם גם הקליפה הקשה לכתחילה[35] נוהגין הנשים שלא לבשלן בחלב אבל מדינא מותר ואלו שאינן נגמרים אלא בחלבון וחלמון וקליפתן רכה[36] אסור לכתחלה[37] ובדיעבד[38] מותר[39] אבל אלו שאין

יד אדם

30. Thus, *maris ayin* applies even when the suspected prohibition is mandated only by rabbinical decree.

4. Milk of a Nursing Woman

31. People may think he is cooking meat in an animal's milk.

32. No matter how much milk happens to fall into this pot of meat, the food remains permissible.

33. It is implied here that to cook such a mixture is permitted only for placing it on a wound, but not for the purpose of ingesting the medication. Nevertheless, some authorities rule that a mixture such as a woman's milk with meat (where the prohibition is due only to *maris ayin*) may be cooked and ingested. (*Madanei Hashulchan*, introduction, paragraph 22 citing *Shach* 87:7 in the name of the *Maharshal; Badei Hashulchan* 87:43.)

5. Cooking Eggs With Milk

34. The rabbinical prohibition against eating birds with milk does not apply to their eggs, and it is therefore permissible to cook and eat eggs with milk. As such, if one slaughters a chicken or other kosher bird and eggs are found inside it—if the eggs are well developed, then technically speaking they may be cooked and eaten with milk (although it is customary not to do so).

ו. [*Shach* there,] paragraph 6.
ז. [*Shach*, chapter 87] paragraph 7.
ח. *Taz* and *Shach*.

to a rabbinical prohibition, [the rabbis have] decreed because of *maris ayin*.[30ו]

4. Even though it is permissible to partake of the milk of a [nursing] woman as noted previously in topic 37 [section 3], nevertheless, it is forbidden to cook meat with a woman's milk in order to eat [them], because of *maris ayin*.[31] However, if a woman's milk has fallen into a cooked food, it is nullified and there is no required measurement.[32]

On the other hand, if one desires to cook [a woman's milk with meat] not for the purpose of eating but because he has to place [the mixture] on his wound or for similar needs; or else, if he has to cook kosher meat in unkosher milk or unkosher meat in kosher milk for a medication—even for a sick person whose life is not in danger—it is permissible, for since he is not cooking in order to eat [the mixture], there is no [prohibition of] *maris ayin*.[33ז] However, if it is not for medication, such as one who cooks to feed a gentile, it is forbidden because of *maris ayin*, whether [he cooks the meat of] an unkosher animal or a bird in milk.[ח]

5. If eggs are found inside birds[34]—if they are completed, that is, they also have a hard shell, the preferred practice[35] which women are accustomed to follow is not to cook them with milk; however, according to the letter of the law it is permissible [to do so]. And those [eggs] which are not completed except for their white, their yolk, and their soft shell[36]—to begin with,[37] they are forbidden [to be cooked with

Yad Adam

However, if the eggs are not well developed, then they are to be regarded as if they were the meat of the bird itself. The criteria necessary for an egg to be well developed will now be discussed.

35. More literally, "to begin with."

36. But the hard shell has not yet formed.

37. The word לכתחלה (translated "to begin with") denotes the preferred practice that **should** be followed in any given case, whereas the expression בדיעבד (translated "after the fact") denotes the situation that exists if the proper practice was not followed. In many situations where the preferred practice was not observed, the food involved might still be permissible.

(Note: לכתחלה is sometimes used in a different way, referring to a practice that **could** be followed without any reservation.)

ט. סס בס״ך.

להם אלא החלמון לבד[40] דינן כבשר עצמו ואסורין לאכלן בחלב.[41] ובהפסד מרובה[42] יש להתיר אפילו אם לא נגמר רק החלמון לבד ומעורה ג״כ בשדרה[43] ומ״מ אם אכלם בפני עצמו מותר לאכול אחריהם גבינה וחלב.[44]ט

ו. המעושן[45] והמבושל בחמי טבריה[46] והמבשל בשר במי חלב[47] דהיינו אחר שעושים גבינות מבשלים הנסיובי והאוכל צף

יד אדם

38. If they have already been cooked together with milk.

39. And one will not be required to avoid eating the eggs nor the milk in which they were cooked.

40. And the other parts have not yet developed.

41. And if they are cooked in milk, the mixture should not be eaten.

42. For example, these eggs were cooked in a large amount of dairy food. In such a case, we rely on *Rashi's* opinion to be lenient and permit the mixture.

See also the additional note, where the term "great loss" will be discussed.

43. The eggs generally remain attached by a stalk to the ovary (which lies alongside the birds's spine) until the white of the egg is formed. (See *Aruch Hashulchan* 87:20.)

44. And it is not necessary to wait the accustomed six hours. The laws concerning the six hour waiting period are discussed below in sections 12 and 13.

Additional Note—הפסד מרובה

There are many instances where we are taught that a certain food or mixture of ingredients is forbidden, but in cases involving a great loss (הפסד מרובה) it is permitted. The *Rama* (in the introduction to the *Toras Chatas*) explains such rulings as follows: When there is a disagreement among the *halachic* authorities with regard to a certain ruling, where many authorities permit a certain mixture but some forbid it, we are often scrupulous to follow the more stringent opinions. This is frequently the case even when it is felt that the correct practice is reflected by the opinion of the more lenient authorities. Nevertheless, in a case where a "great loss" will be suffered, it may be appropriate to rely on the many authorities who are lenient and permit something which we might otherwise rule as being forbidden.

What exactly is meant when we say that something is permitted in cases of "great loss"? It does not mean specifically that a great monetary loss must be involved to allow for a lenient ruling. Rather, we may be lenient in any situation where there would be a significant loss or great inconvenience. For example, if the person who would sustain the monetary loss is poor, we would classify the case as involving a "great loss" even if a relatively small monetary loss is involved. We will also say that a "great loss" is involved if it is shortly before the Sabbath, such that if we declare that a pot of food is

ט. *Shach, Ibid.* (87:10)

milk], but after the fact[38] they are permitted.[39] However, those that have only the yolk[40] are to be regarded as the meat itself and it is forbidden to eat them with milk.[41] But in case of a great loss[42] there are grounds to be lenient even if only the yolk is completed and [even though the eggs] are also attached to the spine.[43] In any case, if one ate them by themselves, it is permissible to eat cheese or milk afterwards.[44ט]

6. [If meat and milk have been] smoked;[45] or have been cooked in the hot springs of Tiberias;[46] or if one cooked meat in *mei chalav*[47]— that is, after making cheese the whey is cooked and the solid portion floats to the top and only watery liquid (the *mei chalav*)

Yad Adam

forbidden there will not be sufficient time to prepare additional food for the Sabbath meals. Accordingly, it is necessary to assess each individual situation which involves monetary loss or extenuating circumstances to determine if a lenient decision is warranted.

See the *Igros Moshe* (*Yoreh Deah* part 1, section 17) where again it is stated that there need not be a great monetary loss to rule leniently, but each case should be decided by taking all of the circumstances into account.

In certain instances, we will learn that a "great loss" is not enough grounds to allow for a lenient ruling, but we may be lenient only if there is a great loss and in addition, the food is required for a סעודת מצוה (a meal involving a precept). When is this the case? This is where a recognized authority has put forth a lenient ruling in a specific case, but many others disagree and rule more stringently. Since many authorities rule that the correct practice is reflected by the more stringent opinions, there are less grounds to be lenient. As such, the suffering of a "great loss" does not warrant a lenient decision unless, in addition, the food is needed for a סעודת מצוה. Examples of meals which are considered to be סעודת מצוה include a Sabbath or *yom tov* meal, the meal preceding the *Yom Kippur* fast, and the meal served following a circumcision. A meal which has been prepared for guests has the same status as a meal prepared for the Sabbath (*Rama* 69:6, 11).

6. Mixtures of Meat and Milk Which Are Rabbinically Forbidden

45. Meat was first immersed in milk and was then hung up in smoke. This smoking is not real cooking and is not forbidden by the Torah. Nevertheless, smoking meat and milk together is forbidden by the rabbis.

The *Chochmas Adam* now goes on to list a number of other mixtures of meat and milk (or their derivatives) which are not forbidden by the Torah but are rabbinically forbidden to be cooked together.

46. Or in any other naturally heated spring.

47. When cheese is being made, the liquid

י. שקורין סירלוויטקי.
יא. דהי של אדם דינו כחלב אשה.
יב. סעיף ו׳ ובש״ך.
יג. סעיף ז׳.

מלמעלה ולא נשאר בו אלא מים[48]י׳ וכן חלב של בהמה שחוטה מה שנמצא בכחל (ר״ל דדי בהמה) או חלב מתה[49] וכן דם בחלב וחלב זכר של בהמה[יא] כל אלו אסורין בבישול מדרבנן וכן האוכלן[50] אין לוקין משום בשר וחלב מן התורה[51] אלא מדרבנן[52] ואם נפלו לתבשיל[53] אוסרים התבשיל כשאר איסור דרבנן.[יב]

ומי חלב המתמצה מקפאון גבינה (ר״ל כשעושין גבינות נוטף המי חלב)[54] יש אומרים דאינו בכלל מי חלב[55] ואסור מן התורה לבשלן עם בשר.[56]

ושליל דינו כבשר וחייב על בישולו ואכילתו מן התורה אבל שליא[57] ועור וגידים ועצמות ועקרי קרנים וטלפים הרכים אסורים בבישול ובאכילה מדרבנן.[יג]

ז. טוב ליזהר מלחתות אש תחת קדרה של נכרי[58] לפי שמבשלים בהם פעמים בשר ופעמים חלב ונמצא שנבלע בו בו״ח[59] וכן

יד אדם

that separates from the curds of cheese is called whey. If one cooks meat in this whey, then (according to many authorities) he transgresses the Torah law, since it is as if he cooked meat in milk. If one will remove the whey from the curds and cook the whey, then only a watery liquid will remain behind, and the term *mei chalav* (literally, water of milk) used here denotes this watery liquid. The *Chochmas Adam* is now explaining that one who cooks meat in this *mei chalav* does not transgress a Torah prohibition.

48. The term *mei chalav* can also refer to the whey itself as noted below.

49. The milk was found inside an animal that died by itself, without being slaughtered. (Even though the animal is forbidden by the Torah because it died without being slaughtered, this Torah prohibition does not extend to the animal's milk. The reason is that the milk was produced while the animal was still alive. *Derisha* 87:5)

50. He partakes of the mixture after it was cooked.

51. One who eats a real mixture of meat and milk which have been cooked together is liable to receive the Torah penalty of lashes, similar to one who transgresses most of the prohibitions stated in the Torah. (*Devarim* 25:1-3)

52. He is liable to receive a different type of lashes which are given to those who transgress rabbinical prohibitions.

53. If one of the above mixtures which are forbidden by the rabbis falls into a pot of food.

י׳. Which we call *seravitky* [in the vernacular].
יא. Milk of a male person, [on the other hand,] has the same status as milk from a woman. [See section 4 above.]
יב. Paragraph 6 [in chapter 87 of the *Shulchan Aruch*] and in the *Shach*.
יג. Paragraph 7 [there in the *Shulchan Aruch*].

remains from it;[48][י׳] and similarly, [cooking meat in the] milk of a slaughtered animal which is found in the *k'chal* (that is, the udder of the animal); or [cooking meat with] milk [which is found inside] a dead animal;[49] and similarly [cooking an animal's] blood with milk; and [cooking meat in the] milk of a male animal[יא]—all of these [mixtures] are forbidden to be cooked according to the rabbis. And similarly, one who eats them[50] will not receive the Torah [penalty of] lashes for [eating] meat and milk,[51] but only according to the rabbis.[52] And if they fall into a cooked food,[53] they render the cooked food forbidden as with any other food which is prohibited by the rabbis.[יב]

And [with regard to] *mei chalav* which is drained from the curds of the cheese (that is, when they make the cheeses the *mei chalav* floats upward)[54] some say that this is not in the category of *mei chalav*[55] and it is forbidden by the Torah to cook it with meat.[56]

A fetus is regarded to be like meat and one is liable for cooking and eating it [with milk] by Torah law. However, *shilya*,[57] and hide, and ligaments, and bones, and the roots of the horns, and the soft hooves are forbidden to be cooked or eaten [with milk] according to the rabbis.[יג]

7. It is a good practice to avoid stirring the fire under the pot of a gentile[58] because sometimes they cook meat in them and sometimes milk, and it is found that [the tastes of] meat and milk are absorbed into it.[59] And similarly, the vessel which they use to make

Yad Adam

54. The *Chochmas Adam* is now discussing the status of the whey itself.

55. I.e., it is not in the same category of the *mei chalav* discussed above in note 47.

56. Others, however, rule that even cooking meat in whey is also only a rabbinical prohibition. (This is the opinion of *Rashi* and *Tosafot*. See *Aruch Hashulchan* 87:27.)

57. The protective membranes that surround the fetus (including the amniotic sac).

7. Practices Which Resemble Cooking Meat and Milk

58. Stirring the coals or wood will increase the heat coming from the fire and will cause the food in the pot to cook faster. We are dealing with a case where there is no mixture of meat and milk in the pot at the present time. If such a mixture were present there would be a definite prohibition to assist in the cooking.

59. Although there is no real prohibition to

יד. סס.
טו. סעיף ט' ובש"ך ס"ק כ"ה.

הכלי שעושין בו מים לחפיפת הראש אין לשמש בו שעושין בו מאפר שע"ג כירה ורגילות הוא להתערב שם בו"ח[60] וכן טוב ליזהר שלא להשתמש מן הקדרות של תנורי בית החורף[61] שמבשלים בתוכו דלפעמים ניתז עליהם מהקדרות שמבשלים בתנור[62] אבל אם הם של מתכות אין לחוש שמתלבנים[63] וכ"ז אינו אלא זריזות וחומרות והמיקל לא הפסיד.[64]יד

ח. חלב הנמצא בקיבה[65] לכתחלה אסור לבשל בו בשר[66] אפילו בחלב הקרוש שבו משום מראית עין[67] ובדיעבד[68] מותר אפילו אם בישל בצלול שבו כן פסק הב"י[69] אבל אנו נוהגין דאפילו בדיעבד אסור אפילו אם בישל בקרוש שבו[70]טו ובהפ"מ יש להתיר בקרוש.[71]

יד אדם

cook what has been absorbed into the wall of a pot, it is still best to avoid doing so. See *Aruch Hashulchan* 87:31.

60. The burnt residues from both dairy and meat foods have been heated in this pot and the pot absorbs their taste. However, since all the moisture had been removed from the residues of the meat and milk (thereby making them inedible before they were mixed together), and because they also impart a bad taste, the pot does not become forbidden when absorbing their tastes. (*Aruch Hashulchan* 87:33) Nevertheless, it is best to avoid heating food in such a pot.

61. These ovens were furnaces which were used to heat their houses, and they contained earthenware "pots" which were filled with water. (It appears that these pots of water had to be present for the furnace to function properly.) Sometimes vessels of dairy food and sometimes vessels of meat food would be placed into these furnaces in order to cook there. (*Badei Hashulchan* 87:92.)

62. And it is possible that both hot meat and hot dairy food have splashed onto the "pots" of water in the oven. It is therefore best not to use anything that has been heated in these "pots." (*Badei Hashulchan* 87:92) Nevertheless, if one did heat food or liquid in these "pots" it does not become forbidden. The reason is that we are unsure whether any milk and meat actually splashed there, and even if they did, the splashed material may well have been burned up. (*Madanei Hashulchan* 87:60)

63. And since these metal compartments are inside a hot furnace, any forbidden matter in them will be burned up and this will serve to kasher them. The concern is only regarding the use of earthenware compartments.

64. I.e., he is not performing any prohibition.

יד. *Ibid.* (*Rama* 87:6)
טו. [*Shulchan Aruch*, chapter 87] paragraph 9, and in the *Shach* paragraph 25.

water for grooming the hair—one should not use it, since they use some ashes from the stove in it and it is customary to mix meat and milk there.[60] And similarly, it is good to be careful not to use what is in the "pots" in the ovens of a winter residence[61] in which people cook, for sometimes [liquid] from the pots [of food] which have been cooking in the oven splash on them.[62] However, if they are metal there is no concern [at all about using them] since they become "white-hot."[63] And all of these [rules] are only for diligent and strict practice, and one who is lenient does not lose out.[64]יד

8. If milk is found in an [animal's] stomach[65]—to begin with, it is forbidden to cook meat in it,[66] even in the curdled milk that is in it, because of *maris ayin*.[67] But after the fact[68] [the meat] is permissible, even if he cooked in the clear (uncurdled) portion of it. Such is the decision of the *Bais Yosef*.[69] However, we are accustomed that even after the fact, [the meat] is forbidden even if one cooked in the curdled portion of it.[70]טו Where a great loss [is involved, the meat] can be permitted [if one cooked] in the curdled portion.[71]

Yad Adam

8. Cooking with Milk Found in the Stomach of a Slaughtered Animal

65. The term *keivah* refers to the fourth stomach of the bull (or cow). This stomach resembles the human stomach more than the three others, as digestion of food occurs within it. The glands in its wall produce the enzyme known as rennet which curdles milk into cheese. As such, any milk found in this stomach will contain curds of cheese.

66. If one slaughters a young calf which nurses from its mother and milk is found inside its stomach, this milk is permissible, as it has not absorbed taste from the stomach (in accordance with section 10 below). Nevertheless, it is forbidden to cook meat in this milk.

67. See note 29 above.

68. If meat was cooked together with this milk.

69. This is because any milk in the stomach is not regarded to be milk but as waste material, similar to the waste found in the animal's intestine. This represents the opinion of the *Rambam*. (*Aruch Hashulchan* 87:35)

70. This ruling is in accordance with *Rashi* and other authorities who rule that the milk in the cow's stomach, whether curdled or not, is to be regarded as real milk.

71. In cases of great loss (see additional note on section 5), we can rely on the opinion of *Rabbenu Tam* who rules that curdled milk is like waste matter, but the clear liquid portion is to be regarded as real milk.

טז. ס"ק ל"ג.

ט. עור הקבה או שאר בני מעיים שמייבשין אחר שנמלחו עד שנעשין כעץ וממלאין אותן חלב מותר[72] דמאחר שנתייבש כ"כ הוי כעץ בעלמא ואין בו לחלוחית בשר כלל ומ"מ לכתחלה לא יעשה כןט"ז ונ"ל דה"ה להעמיד בו גבינות[73] דלכתחלה אסור ובדיעבד[74] מותר.[75]

י. חלב הנמצא בקבה לכתחלה אין להניחו בקבה עד שיצטנן החלב בתוך הקבה שחלב הקבה חריף וחמוץ שהרי מעמידין בו[76] אבל בדיעבד אין לחוש[77] עד שנמלח בקבתה כשיעור שיתן על האש ויתחיל להרתיח[78] ויהיה נמלח כ"כ שלא יהיה נאכל מחמת מלחו.[79]

ואפילו להנמשכין אחר רמ"א דקיי"ל דאפילו נמלח מעט ולא שהה כלל אסור מחמת מליח כרותח[80] מ"מ הכא כיון דהרבה פוסקים סבירי להו דאינו אלא כפרש בעלמא אפילו הצלול[81] וגם

יד אדם

9. Using an Animal's Stomach Lining As a Container For Milk or to Produce Cheese

72. It is implied here that the milk remains permissible even though its container is derived from meat and the milk remains in it for 24 hours. (This corresponds to the *Aruch Hashulchan* 87:43. The *Pri Megadim*, however, rules that the milk becomes forbidden after 24 hours.)

73. One should not place milk on the dried out stomach lining in order to curdle the milk into cheese.

74. If cheese was already made with it.

75. Nevertheless, the *Aruch Hashulchan* (87:43) mentions that they were accustomed to use the lining of an animal's stomach to make cheese after it had been thoroughly dried out and then crumbled into dust.

10. Leaving Milk Inside an Animal's Stomach

76. Milk which is found in the stomach of an animal is a very sharp substance, as it can be added to other milk in order to curdle it into cheese. It is therefore proper to be strict and avoid letting it remain in contact with the wall of the stomach for even a short period of time. We are concerned here that if we leave the milk in the stomach long enough for the milk to cool down, then due to its sharpness it might absorb some of the taste of the stomach. (*Aruch Hashulchan* 87:40) It is therefore proper to remove the milk while it is still warm, i.e., very soon after the animal is slaughtered.

77. The milk left in the stomach will not become forbidden, and it may be added to other milk to curdle it into cheese.

טו. *Shach* [chapter 87] paragraph 33.

9. If the lining of the stomach or other intestinal structures are dried out after they are salted until they become like wood and we fill them with milk, it is permissible,[72] for since they are dried out so much, they are like ordinary wood and there is no moisture of meat at all. Nevertheless, to begin with, one should not do this.[טו] And it is my opinion that the same rule applies regarding making cheese with it,[73] that to begin with it is forbidden but after the fact[74] it is permissible.[75]

10. If milk is found inside [an animal's] stomach—to begin with, one should not leave it in the stomach until the milk inside the stomach cools down, since the milk of the stomach is sharp and fermented, as one can curdle with it.[76] However, after the fact, there is no concern[77] unless it was salted while in the stomach [and left there] for the amount of time such that if it were placed on the fire it would begin to boil,[78] and it was salted so much such that it would be inedible because of its saltiness.[79]

And even those who follow the opinion of the *Rama*, who rules that even when [meat is] salted a little and [the salt] does not remain on at all, [then the meat can become] prohibited as a result of [the principle that] salted food is as if it were boiling hot[80]—nevertheless, here, since many authorities rule that [the milk found in the stomach] is like mere waste matter even [with respect to] the clear portion,[81] and also it

Yad Adam

78. I.e., the salt must remain together with the milk and the stomach for this amount of time in order that the stomach and its contents become forbidden. This ruling is in accordance with the opinion of the *Bais Yosef* as mentioned in topic 32, section 14. Although we generally follow the opinion of the *Rama* who is more strict (and rules that there is no minimum time requirement), in this case we rely on the more lenient opinion of the *Bais Yosef*, as the *Chochmas Adam* will go on to explain.

What is the period of time that it would take for a liquid to boil? The *Tiferes Yisroel* on *Terumot* 10:10 states that this time period is equal to 18 minutes. Others rule that the period is ten minutes. (See *Darkei Teshuvah* 105:42.)

79. If these two criteria are met, then we view the stomach and the milk as if they were being "pickled" together (*kavush*), and the entire mixture becomes forbidden. (*Nekudos Hakesef* 87:6) See topic 58, section 3.

80. This is indeed the ruling which we follow if salted meat is left in contact with its own forbidden blood. As a result, one might think that here also, if a little salt has been added, the milk and the stomach would become forbidden immediately. (Compare topic 43, sections 1 and 2.)

81. This is the *Bais Yosef's* and *Rambam's* opinion. (See section 8 and note 69.) Accord-

הוא מילתא דרבנן דאינו דרך בישול[82] יש להתיר בדיעבד אלא א״כ נמלח שאינו נאכל ושהה כדי שיעור כבישה בציר[83] או אפילו לא נמלח כלל אלא ששהה בתוכו מעת לעת דהוי כבוש[84] ואסור להעמיד בו[85]יז ולענין אם העמיד גבינות עיין כלל נ״ג סימן ל״ד עד סופו.[86]

יא. כיון דבו״ח מותר כל א׳ וא׳ בפני עצמו והאדם רגיל בהם תמיד חששו חכמים שאם יהיו שניהם לפניו יאכל משניהם יחד[87] ולא עוד אלא שלפעמים יטעה מסדר השלחן שיצטרך להעלות על השלחן לזה בשר ולזה גבינה ויניח הגבינה באותו אלפס רותח שמונח בו הבשר ונמצא דנתבשלו יחד ואסור מה״ת[88] ולכן גזרו חז״ל דאסור להעלות על השלחן בשר וגבינה כאחת[89] ואגב בשר בהמה[90] גזרו גם אפילו על בשר עוף אע״ג דגם אכילתו אינו אלא מדרבנן מ״מ לא פלוג רבנן בזה.[91]יח

וגזרו דאפילו ב׳ בני אדם המכירים זה את זה אפילו הם מקפידים זה על זה[92] אסורים לאכול על שלחן אחד זה בשר וזה גבינה אא״כ עשו היכר ביניהם כגון שכ״א יאכל על מפה אחרת או

יז. סי׳ פ״ז סעיף י׳.
יח. ומש״כ בפ״ע שלא יבא לאכלם וע״ש בט״ז תמוה שהרי בגמרא מוכח דטעמא כמו שכתבתי.

יד אדם

ing to their opinion, milk found in the stomach, regardless of the amount of salt and the time they were together, will not cause milk curdled with it to become forbidden. (See topic 53, section 34.)

82. We have learned above in section 1 that meat and milk which were salted together are not prohibited by the Torah but only by rabbinical decree.

83. This is the same as the amount of time that it would take to boil if it were placed on a fire (*Chochmas Adam* topic 32, section 14). As explained above, if the milk were so heavily salted and it remains with the stomach for this amount of time, then this milk should not be used to curdle other milk into cheese.

84. As noted previously in section 1, food which is *kavush* (soaked in a liquid for 24 hours) is to be regarded as if it were cooked in that liquid. As such, the stomach will be regarded as if it were cooked with the milk and they will become forbidden.

85. The use of this milk to curdle other milk, as well as the use of the stomach, will be forbidden.

86. It is explained there how to determine whether or not the resulting cheese is forbidden.

11. Milk and Meat Should Not Be Placed Together on a Table Where One Is Eating

87. This would involve transgressing a rabbinical ruling, as the Torah prohibits eating milk with meat only if they have been cooked together. See section 1.

יז. *Shulchan Aruch*, 87:10.

יח. In the *Shulchan Aruch* (88:1) it is written [that the reason for the decree is] lest one come to eat them, and refer there to the *Taz*. This is puzzling, for in the *gemara* it is demonstrated that the reason is in accordance with what I have written.

is a rabbinical matter because it is not the normal manner of cooking,[82] it is proper to permit [the milk] after the fact. [This will apply] unless it is salted [so much] that it could not be eaten and [the salt] stayed on the amount of time needed for pickling in brine.[83] Or else, [the milk will become forbidden] even if it was not salted at all but it remained inside it for twenty four hours so that is *kavush* ("soaked"),[84] and it will [then] be forbidden to curdle with it.[85][יז] Regarding [the situation] where one curdled cheeses [with this milk that had become forbidden], see topic 53, section 34 until the end [of that topic].[86]

11. Since meat and milk are permissible [to be eaten when] each one is by itself, and a person is accustomed to [eat] them all the time, the sages were concerned that if both of them will be in front of him he might eat both of them together.[87] And not only this, but sometimes someone setting the table might err when he will have to place meat on the table for one [person] and cheese for another, and he will [mistakenly] come to place the cheese in the same hot pot in which the meat has been placed. This would result in their having been cooked together, which would be a Torah prohibition.[88] Therefore, our sages (of blessed memory) decreed that it is forbidden to place meat and milk on the table together.[89] And while [decreeing this prohibition] for the meat of an animal,[90] they also decreed [likewise] regarding the meat of a bird, for even though eating it is not [forbidden] except by the rabbis, nevertheless, the rabbis did not differentiate in this matter.[91][יח]

And they even decreed that if two people recognize each other, even if they are particular about each other[92]—it is forbidden [for them] to eat on one table [if] one eats meat and the other [eats] cheese, unless they devise a reminder between them, such as each one eating on

Yad Adam

88. The Torah prohibits cooking meat and milk together, and eating the mixture once it has been cooked.

89. This prohibition applies only to the table where one is eating. Storing the foods near each other is permitted, as explained in topic 42, section 3,

90. I.e., meat from a bull (or cow), sheep, or goat, which is forbidden to be cooked with milk according to Torah law.

91. And it applies to the meat of birds just as it applies to the meat of animals.

92. I.e., they normally would not eat food from each other's portion.

יט. סי' פ"ח.
כ. כו"פ דלא כפ"ח.

שיניחו דבר המפסיק ביניהם ואפילו פת או כלי עם משקין הוי היכר אם אינן אוכלין ושותין מאותו פת ומאותו כלי דאל"כ אין כאן היכר וכן כל דבר שאין רגיל להניחו על השלחן כגון מנורה ביום הוי היכר וכ"ש אם אוכל בפני עצמו[93] או עם ב"ב שצריך היכר[94] ויזהרו שלא יאכלו מפת א'[95] ולא ישתו מכוס א' שהמאכל נדבק בהם ויבואו לידי איסור וכן צריכין ליחד כלי של מלח לכל א' כי לפעמים מטבילין מאכלם במלח[96] וזה אפילו באינן מכירין זא"ז אסור.

אבל ב' בני אדם שאינם מכירים זא"ז כגון ב' אכסנאים מותר לאכול כ"א בפ"ע זה בשר וזה חלב[97] וכן מותר לישראל לאכול עם נכרי אע"פ שהוא אוהבו ומכירו זה בשר כשר וזה בשר טרפה כיון דישראל בדיל תמיד מטריפות לא חיישינן.[יט]

יב. עוד גזרו חז"ל שאם אכל בשר אפילו של חיה ועוף שאין איסורן אלא מדרבנן מ"מ לא פלוג באיסור בשר וחלב ואסרו לאכול אחריו חלב עד סעודה אחרת ונחלקו הפוסקים בפירוש הדבר י"א דר"ל זמן סעודה[98] דהיינו שש שעות בין בקיץ בין בחורף[99][כ] והטעם לפי שהבשר מוציא שומן ומושך טעם עד זמן זה שאז כבר נתעכל לגמרי ולכן אפי' אין בשר בין שיניו צריך להמתין

יד אדם

93. With both meat and milk on the table.

94. Some authorities rule that if one is eating by himself, placing a reminder on the table will not help. (See *Kaf Hachayim* 88:16.)

95. If, however, each one washes his hands before cutting the bread and uses a clean knife, then it is permitted. (*Aruch Hashulchan* 88:11)

96. It would certainly be improper to dip meat and cheese into the same dish of salt. Nowadays that we used saltshakers which are covered, it would appear that the same salt could be used by both of them.

97. Since they are strangers, there is no concern that they will eat from each other's plates.

12. Waiting Six Hours to Eat Dairy After Eating Meat; Laws Which Apply to One Who Eats Meat Soon After Eating Dairy

98. I.e., the normal time interval between

יט. *Shulchan Aruch*, chapter 88 [paragraph 2].
כ. *Kreisi u'pleisi*, not in accordance with the *Pri Chadash*.

another tablecloth, or [unless] they place something that serves as a separation between them. Even bread or a vessel with liquid is a [valid] reminder as long as they do not eat or drink from that bread or from that vessel, for if this were not the case there is no reminder. And similarly, anything that they are not accustomed to place on the table, such as a candelabra during the daytime, is a [valid] reminder; and certainly, if one eats by himself[93] or with the members of his family a reminder is required.[94] And they should be careful not to eat from one loaf of bread[95] and they should not drink from one cup, as food will cling to them and they will come to [eat] what is forbidden. And also, it is necessary to set aside a vessel with salt for each one because sometimes they will [each] dip their food into [the same] salt,[96] and this is forbidden even if they do not recognize each other.

However, [regarding] two people who do not recognize each other, such as two lodgers [in an inn], it is permissible [for them] to eat, each one by himself, where one [eats] meat and the other [eats] milk.[97] And similarly, it is permissible for a Jew to eat with a gentile, even though he is friendly with him and he recognizes him, where one [eats] kosher meat and the other [eats] unkosher meat, for since the Jew separates [himself] all the time from unkosher meat, we are not concerned [that he will eat it by mistake].[יט]

12. Our sages (of blessed memory) have also decreed that if one ate meat, even [if it was meat] of a wild animal or a bird which is only rabbinically prohibited [to be eaten with milk], in any case there is no difference between the [Torah or the rabbinical] prohibitions of meat and milk, and it is prohibited to eat milk after [the meat] until there is "another meal." The authorities disagree as to what is meant by this term—some say that it means the time of a meal[98] which is six hours, whether in the summer or in the winter.[99][כ] And the reason [for this] is that meat exudes fat and its taste lingers for this amount of time, for by then [the food] has been completely digested. Therefore, even if there is no meat [remaining] between one's teeth he must wait.

Yad Adam

the morning and evening meals. (*Aruch Hashulchan* 89:1)

99. Thus, these hours are sixty minutes long and do not vary with the length of the day.

כא. פ״ט.
כב. ש״ך ס״ק י׳.
כג. סי׳ פ״ט.

ולפ״ז הלועס לתינוק[100] א״צ להמתין שהרי אינו מושך טעם[101] (טור) וי״א (הרמב״ם) דהטעם לפי שכל זמן זה יש בשר בין שיניו ועדיין נקרא בשר ולפ״ז אפי׳ לועס לתינוק צריך להמתין וגם אפילו אם כבר המתין ו׳ שעות אם יש בשר בין שיניו צריך להסירו[102] ואנו קבלנו לחומרא כשני הטעמים.[103]

ואם מצא אח״כ בשר בין השינים ומסירו א״צ להמתין דחשבינן ו׳ שעות מאכילתו אך צריך קינוח והדחת הפה והקינוח הוא שילעוס פת[104] ויקנח בו פיו יפה והדחה הוא שידיח פיו במים או בשאר משקין ואין קפידא אם מקדים הקינוח או ההדחה. ושומן של בשר או אפי׳ של עופות דינם כבשר.[105]כא

ואם אכל גבינה א״צ להמתין ומותר לאכול אחריו בשר ובלבד שיעיין בידיו שלא יהא שום דבר מהגבינה נדבק בהם ובלילה שאינו יכול לעיין היטב צריך לרחצם במים דוקאכב וגם צריך הדחה וקינוח וכן אם אוכל בשר או תבשיל של בשר[106] אחר תבשיל של גבינה צריך נטילה בינתים כן סתם הב״י.[107]כג

יד אדם

100. This was done to soften the food in order that an infant will be able to eat it.

101. The taste does not linger since he did not actually swallow it.

102. This last statement is not the *Rambam*'s opinion. Rather it is the *Tur's* opinion that one must remove what is left between the teeth even after six hours. The *Rambam* rules that what remains after six hours may be left there, since it is no longer called "meat." (It appears that this last statement of the *Chochmas Adam* [starting with the word וגם] belongs before the word טור in the text.)

103. We therefore are required to remove all meat that remains between the teeth, and to wait six hours after chewing meat which is not swallowed. If, however, the teeth are cleaned well after chewing it, then one need not wait the six hours after chewing for an infant, even according to the *Rambam*. Rather, waiting one hour will be sufficient. (Rabbi Akiva Eiger. See *Aruch Hashulchan* 89:4)

If one places meat in his mouth to taste it and he then spits it out without chewing it or swallowing any of it, then he need not wait six hours. (See *Darkei Teshuvah* 89:22.) Since he does not chew it, we are not concerned that pieces remain between his teeth. Furthermore, since he does not swallow any

כא. [*Shulchan Aruch*, chapter] 89, paragraph 1.
כב. *Shach* [chapter 89, paragraph] 10.
כג. [*Shulchan Aruch*] chapter 89 [paragraph 2].

And according to this [reason], one who chews [food] for an infant[100] is not required to wait, because its taste does not linger.[101] (This is the opinion of the *Tur*.) But others (the *Rambam*) say that the reason [for waiting] is that during this period of time there is meat [remaining] between the teeth and [for six hours] it is still called "meat." According to this [reason], even one who chews [food] for an infant must wait. And also, even if one already waited six hours, if there is meat between his teeth he must remove it.[102] And we have accepted the stringencies of the two reasons.[103]

If one later found meat between the teeth and he removes it, he need not wait [any longer], as we calculate the six hours from his eating. However, wiping and rinsing the mouth is required—the "wiping" is that he should chew bread[104] and [thereby] wipe out his mouth well, and the "rinsing" is that he should rinse his mouth with water or another liquid, and it does not matter if the wiping or the rinsing is first. The fat of meat and even [the fat] of birds is to be regarded as meat.[105]כא

And if one ate cheese, he need not wait and he is permitted to eat meat after it, on condition that he will examine his hands [to make sure] that no particles of cheese are stuck to them. And during the night when he is unable to examine well, he must wash them specifically in water.כב Also, he requires rinsing and wiping [of the mouth]. And similarly, if one eats meat or a cooked food made with meat[106] after [eating] a cooked food made with cheese, he requires washing [of the hands] between them. So concludes the *Bais Yosef*.[107]כג

Yad Adam

of it, there will not be a lingering taste while it is being digested. However, rinsing and wiping the mouth is required. (*Kaf Hachayim* 89:56)

104. Or any other food which will not stick to the palate. (*Shulchan Aruch* 89:2)

105. And the six hour waiting period will be required.

106. Such as beans or potatoes which had been cooked in a pot with meat.

107. The generally accepted practice is mentioned below in the second paragraph of section 13—that it is customary to wait six hours after eating certain hard cheeses.

כד. עיין כו״פ.
כה. ע״ז ס״ק ד׳.
כו. ש״ך ס״ק י״ט.

יג. וי״א דמה שאמרו בגמרא בסעודה אחרת מותר אינו ר״ל זמן סעודה[108] אלא סגי בהמתנת שעה א׳[109] דזה הוא זמן התחלת עיכול[כד] ובלבד שלא יאכל בסעודה אחת קודם בהמ״ז אפי׳ המתין כמה שעות לא מהני אלא דוקא שיברך מקודם בהמ״ז וגם שיהיה שעה אחת לאחר שאכל הבשר בין שהמתין קודם בהמ״ז או לאחר בהמ״ז ואם אכל בשר בלא סעודה[110] לא מיקרי סילוק[111] עד שיברך ברכה אחרונה[112] ואם מצא בשר בין שיניו אחר השעה צריך הדחה וקינוח[113] ואם לא מצא א״צ הדחה וקינוח.

והמנהג הפשוט במדינות אלו להמתין שש שעות כדעת הב״י. ועוד אנו נוהגין להחמיר שאפי׳ אם אכל גבינה קשה דהיינו שהיא מתולעת או שישנה ששה חדשים[כה] אין אוכלין אחריה אפי׳ תבשיל של בשר[114] וכן אם אכל אפי׳ תבשיל של בשר אין אוכלין אחריו מאכל של חלב אלא בהמתנת שש שעות ולאחר בהמ״ז[115] והמיקל בזה עובר משום אל תטוש תורת אמך[116] ומ״מ אם אין בשר בתבשיל רק שנתבשלו בקדירה של בשר[117] אע״פ שלא הודחה יפה[כו]

יד אדם

13. Further Discussion of the Waiting Period After Eating Meat; Waiting Six Hours After Eating Hard Cheese; Washing the Hands between the Handling of Dairy and Meat Foods

108. These authorities explain that the *gemara* does not mean that one must wait six hours as noted above in section 12.

109. This is the opinion of *Rabbenu Tam.*

110. He had no bread so that he need not recite the grace after meals.

111. He has not "removed himself" from eating the meat.

112. Even though he has already waited an hour since eating the meat, he may not eat dairy until he recites this blessing.

113. As described in the previous section.

114. I.e., even eating such items as beans which have been cooked with meat, or a meat soup (whether or not pieces of meat are now present) would be forbidden until six hours have elapsed. Regarding whether it is permissible to eat wormy cheese, see topic 38, section 29.

115. The *Aruch Hashulchan* rules similarly (89:4). However, the *Dagul Mei'revava* (on

כד. See *Kreisi u'pleisi.*
כה. *Taz,* [chapter 89] paragraph 4.
כו. *Shach,* [chapter 89] paragraph 19.

13. Other [authorities] rule that when the *gemara* stated [that after one eats meat and waits] for "another meal" it is permitted [to have milk]—it does not refer to waiting the time for a meal.[108] Rather, it is enough to wait one hour,[109] as this is the time of the beginning of digestion,[כד] but on condition that he will not eat [both meat and milk] during one meal before [reciting] the grace after meals. Even if he waited many hours it will not help unless he specifically will recite the grace after meals beforehand, and also there should be one hour since he ate the meat. [There is no difference] whether he will have waited [the hour] before [reciting] grace after meals or after grace after meals. And if he ate meat without a meal,[110] it is not called "removing"[111] until he will recite the final blessing.[112] If he found meat between his teeth after the hour, he requires rinsing and wiping [of the mouth],[113] and if he does not find [meat there] he does not require rinsing and wiping.

The widespread custom in our lands is to wait six hours in accordance with the opinion of the *Bais Yosef.* And furthermore, we are accustomed to be stringent that even if one ate hard cheese, that is, which was wormy or was aged for six months,[כה] one may not eat even a cooked food made with meat after it.[114] And similarly, if one ate even a cooked food made with meat, he may not eat a dairy food after it except by waiting six hours following the grace after meals.[115] And one who is lenient regarding this transgresses: "Do not forsake the teaching of your mother."[116] Nevertheless, if there was no meat in the cooked food, but it only was cooked in a meat pot,[117] even though it was not thoroughly washed,[כו] it is permissible to eat cheese after it and there is

Yad Adam

the *Shach* 89:3) rules that in any case one need not wait six hours after reciting the grace after meals. Rather, the established custom is that the six hours begins from the time that one finishes eating the meat.

116. *Mishlei* (Proverbs) 1:8, 6:20. If one fails to observe any well established custom, he transgresses what is written in this passage.

117. One has eaten pareve food which was cooked in a meat pot (a pot which had been used for cooking meat). The *Chochmas Adam* goes on to mention that he may eat dairy shortly afterwards, even though the pot was not thoroughly cleaned. Similarly, if one has eaten meat and shortly thereafter he desires to eat pareve food cooked in a dairy pot, he may do so.

כז. ש״ך ס״ק כ״ח.

מותר לאכול אחריו גבינה ואין בו מנהג להחמיר וכן נוהגין לאכול בשר אחר תבשיל שיש בו גבינה או חלב,[118] מיהו יש ליטול ידיו ביניהם אפי׳ ביום ואפילו לא יאכל בשר ממש רק תבשיל של בשר אחר תבשיל של גבינה אם נגע בהם בידיו[119] ואפי׳ שמש המשמש בסעודה אע״פ שאינו אוכל אלא שנוגע באוכל צריך נטילה בין מאכלי חלב למאכלי בשרכ״ז ומ״מ לצורך חולה קצת נ״ל פשוט דיש להתיר אפי׳ אכל בשר בהמה לאחר שימתין שעה ויחטט שיניו לאחר בהמ״ז.

יד • האוכל גבינה רכה וחמאה ורוצה לאכול אח״כ בשר צריך לבער מן השולחן שיורי פת שאכל עם הגבינה[120] ואסור לאכול גבינה על מפה שאכל בשר וכן להיפך וכ״ש שאסור לחתוך גבינה אפילו צוננת בסכין של בשר וכן להיפך[121] מיהו ע״י נעיצה בקרקע קשה מותר בשעת הדחק שאין לו סכין אחר[122] וה״ה בסכין של איסור[123] דינא הכי כמו שנבאר לקמן אי״ה כלל מ״ז אבל לחתוך הלחם לא בעינן נעיצה[124] אלא סגי בקינוח יפה שלא יהא שום

יד אדם

118. And he need not wait six hours even though cheese is mixed into it.

119. In addition, if one does eat meat soon after eating dairy, he is required to chew bread (or another similar food) to wipe out his mouth and rinse it with liquid. (This ruling has been mentioned at the end of section 12.) It is not necessary for him to recite the grace after meals before eating the meat. (*Mishnah Berurah* 494:16.)

14. Preparation of the Table and Utensils for One Who Eats Meat After Dairy

120. This rule applies to individual pieces of bread on the table which had been sliced in order to eat them together with meat or cheese. However, what remains from a large loaf of bread may be used at a dairy meal and then at a meat meal (or vice versa), if care was taken that the loaf should not come into contact with meat or with dairy substances. (*Igros Moshe—Yoreh Deah*, part 1, section 38). See also topic 42, section 5 and note 20 thereon.

121. Even though the knife and the food are cold and therefore the knife will not emit the taste of the meat or dairy food that is absorbed into it, it is still not proper to use such a knife. The laws pertaining to cold food which was cut with the wrong type of knife are discussed in topic 47, sections 3 and 4.

כו. *Shach*, [chapter 89] paragraph 21.

no established custom to be strict in this matter. We are also accustomed [to allow one] to eat meat after [he eats] a cooked food which contains cheese or milk.[118] However, it is proper to wash one's hands between [eating] them, even during the daytime. And even if one does not eat real meat but [he eats] only a cooked food made with meat after [eating] a cooked food made with cheese, [he should wash] if he touches them with his hands.[119] And even a servant who serves during the meal, even though he does not eat but he touches the food, he is required to wash [his hands] between [handling] dairy foods and meat foods.[כו] Nevertheless, for the sake of one who is [even] slightly ill, it appears obvious to me that one can permit [eating dairy food], even with regard to one who has eaten the meat of an animal, after he waits an hour and cleans out his teeth, [and] after reciting the grace after meals.

14. If one eats soft cheese or butter and he desires to eat meat afterwards, he must remove from the table the leftover pieces of bread that he ate with the cheese.[120] And it is forbidden to eat cheese on the [same] tablecloth on which he ate meat, and it is also [forbidden] the other way around. And certainly it is forbidden to cut cheese, even cold, with a meat knife, and it is also [forbidden] the other way around.[121] However, by inserting [the knife first] into hard ground it is permitted in cases of necessity where he has no other knife.[122] And so is the ruling regarding a forbidden knife[123]—the law is the same as we will explain later on, God willing, in topic 47 [section 8]. However, to cut bread it does not require insertion [into ground].[124] Rather it is enough to wipe [it] well so that there will not be any grease stuck to it,

Yad Adam

122. The knife must be inserted at least ten times into hard ground in order to clean off any remaining grease on it, and to remove any absorbed taste that is in the outer surface of the knife. See topic 47, section 8. Rubbing a knife with steel wool is considered equivalent to inserting it into the ground. (Horav Avraham Asher Zimmerman)

123. I.e., a knife which is forbidden to use because, for example, it was used to cut hot unkosher meat. Such a knife can be prepared for use in the same manner.

124. A meat or dairy knife will not require insertion into the ground to cut bread.

כח. שם. שמנונית דבוק בו ואף שלא בשעת הדחק (ל״ח)[125] ומנהג כל ישראל להיות להם סכינים מיוחדים לבו״ח והמנהג לרשום של חלב.[כח]

כלל מא
דין כחל
(סימן צ׳)

א. פ׳ כחל של בהמה.

א. הכחל[א] בין של קטנה שלא הניקה ובין של גדולה מה״ת מותר לבשלה בין בפ״ע ובין עם בשר שאין בשר שנתבשל בחלב שחוטה אסור מה״ת[1] אלא שחכמים אסרוהו דדמי לבו״ח. וכן הדין אם קרע והוציא את החלב שבו מותר לצלותו[2] ולאכלו אבל לבשלו אפי׳ בפ״ע אסור דאע״פ שהוציא החלב מ״מ נשאר עדיין חלב בגומות.[3]

ב. ואם קרעו שתי וערב וטחו בכותל[4] עד שלא נשאר בו לחלוחית חלב מותר לבשלו אפי׳ עם בשר ואפי׳ לכתחלה[5] ואם קרעו וחתכו כמה פעמים שו״ע על פני כולו עדיף ומהני יותר מטיחה בכותל וכן אם נתנו תחת המכבש[6] הוי כטיחה בכותל וכל זה מדינא.

יד אדם

125. It is explained there that it is permitted to use a clean meat knife to cut bread even if the bread will be eaten with cheese. Nevertheless, many authorities mention that it is proper for each household to have one knife which is not used for meat nor dairy, but only for cutting bread. (*Aruch Hashulchan* 89:16)

1. Cooking an Udder—The Basic Principles

1. This has been mentioned in topic 40, section 6. As such, there is no Torah prohibition to cook and eat the udder together with the milk which is present inside it.

2. He may broil the udder on a spit. Broiling requires less preparation than cooking in a pot, since milk will drip off and fall away from the meat while it is being broiled.

3. And during the cooking process, the milk will flow out from the pores of the udder and then be reabsorbed into its meat.

כח. *Ibid* (*Shulchan Aruch* 89:4 and the *Rama* there.)

and [this is permissible] even when it is not a case of necessity. (See *Binas Adam*, section 38.)[125] The custom of all Israel is to have separate knives for meat and milk, and the custom is to mark those which are dairy.[כח]

Topic 41

Laws Concerning the Udder

(based on *Shulchan Aruch—Yoreh Deah* chapter 90)

א. [The word *k'chal*] denotes the nipples of the animal.

1. The udder,[א] whether from a small [animal] which has never nursed [a calf] or from a grown animal, is permissible to be cooked according to the Torah, either by itself or with [other] meat, as meat which is cooked with the milk [found inside] a slaughtered animal is not forbidden by Torah law.[1] However, the sages prohibited it because it is like [a mixture of] meat and milk. And the rule is as follows: If one cut [the udder] and removed the milk that is in it, it is permissible to broil it[2] and eat it, but to cook it [in a pot] even by itself, is forbidden, for even though he has removed the milk, nevertheless, milk still remains in the pores.[3]

2. But if one cut across the length and width [of the udder] and pressed it on a wall[4] until there is no moisture from the milk remaining in it, it is permissible to cook it [in a pot], even with [other] meat, and even to begin with.[5] And if he cut it and slit it many times in the length and the width across all of it, it is proper, and this helps [remove the milk even] better than pressing on a wall. And similarly, if one placed it under a press,[6] it is like pressing on a wall. And all of this is according to the letter of the law.

Yad Adam

2. Preparing the Udder for Cooking

4. The meaning is: He squeezed the udder with a great deal of force to wring out the milk. He can do this by pressing it against a wall or by any other method of accomplishing this.

5. I.e., this method complies fully with the all the requirements. Nevertheless, the custom is not to permit cooking it in the same pot with other meat, as described below.

6. He used a type of pressing machine to wring out the milk.

ב. סעיף ג'.
ג. ס"ק ג'.

ג. ומ"מ נהגו שלא לבשלו עם בשר כלל[7] אפילו על ידי קריעת שו"ע וטיחה בכותל ולבשלו בלא בשר בטיגון או בפשטידא[8] אפילו במחבת מותר ע"י קריעת שו"ע וטיחה בכותל דוקא ולצלותו על השפוד סגי בקריעת שו"ע בלא טיחה בכותל.[9]ב

ד. ובדיעבד אם עבר ובשלו בלא בשר אפילו בלא קריעה אע"פ שבשלו עם ירקות או שאר דברים מותר לאכלוג ומכ"ש אם צלאו אבל אם בשלו שם בשר אחר צריך ס' נגד כל הכחל[10] שהרי אין אנו יודעים כמה חלב נפיק מיניה[11] ומ"מ בדבר זה הקילו חכמים בכחל אע"ג דבשאר איסורים צריך ס' חוץ מן האיסור אבל בכחל מצרפין גם הכחל עם הבשר[12] ולכן אם יש נ"ט פעמים בשר ושאר דברים שבקדירה נגד הכחל הבשר והתבשיל מותר שהרי הכחל עצמו הוא בשר וא"כ יש ס' נגד החלב[13] ונתבטל טעם החלב ולפיכך מותר.

אבל הכחל אפ"ה נשאר באיסורו מפני שיש גומות בכחל

יד אדם

3. Customs Which Apply to Cooking, Frying, and Broiling the Udder

7. The reason we are stringent about cooking the udder with other meat is that during the cooking, milk will flow out from the udder and be absorbed into the other meat. This will affect the flavor of the other meat and thereby resemble a forbidden mixture of milk and meat.

8. Such a pudding is made by mixing the meat of the udder with dough, and no other meat is added. (*Aruch Hashulchan* 90:9)

9. The customary practices mentioned here follow the opinion of the *Bais Yosef* in the *Shulchan Aruch*. However, the accepted practice is in accordance with the more stringent rulings of the *Rama* which are mentioned below (beginning with section 6).

4. Rules Regarding an Improperly Cooked Udder and Food Cooked with It

10. In general, when a forbidden substance becomes mixed into permissible food, the resulting mixture is permitted only if the amount of permissible food is sixty times the forbidden substance. This is because the taste of the forbidden substance will not be noticeable in such a large amount of other food.

11. We assume that the udder was filled with milk and we therefore require that the pot contain sixty times the entire udder. Consequently, if there is so much meat and

ב. *Shulchan Aruch*, [chapter 90] paragraph 2.
ג. *[Shach*, chapter 90] paragraph 3.

3. Nevertheless, it is customary not to cook it with [other] meat at all,[7] even by [first] cutting across the length and width and pressing on a wall. And to cook it without [other] meat by frying or in a pudding,[8] even in a pan, is permissible [but] only by cutting across the length and width and pressing on a wall. But to broil it on a spit, it is enough to cut across the length and width without pressing on a wall.[9]ב

4. After the fact, if one transgressed and he cooked it without [other] meat without even cutting [open the udder], even though he cooked it with green vegetables or other things, it is permissible to eat it.ג And certainly [it is permitted] if he broiled it. However, if he cooked it [in a pot] with other meat he needs sixty times the entire udder,[10] for we do not know how much milk came out of it.[11] Nevertheless, in this matter the sages were lenient regarding the udder—even though with other forbidden food we require [the pot to contain] sixty [times the forbidden food] in addition to the forbidden food [itself], with regard to the udder, however, the udder also is to be combined with the [other] meat.[12] Therefore, if the meat and the other ingredients in the pot are 59 times [the size of] the udder, the meat and the other cooked ingredients are permissible. Since the udder itself is [permissible] meat, as such, there will be sixty times the milk[13] and the taste of the milk will be nullified; and therefore [the mixture] is permissible.

However, even though this is so, the udder remains in its forbidden state, because there are pores in the udder into which the milk is

Yad Adam

other ingredients in the pot such that together they equal sixty times the size of the udder, we would then be certain that we have sixty times the quantity of milk that had been present in the udder, and the mixture will be permitted.

12. The udder is not intrinsically forbidden, but only the milk inside it. Therefore, we are able to add the size of the udder to the other permissible ingredients in the pot when determining how much permissible food is present.

13. If the udder is combined with other ingredients which are 59 times its size, the total will be at least 60 times the volume of the milk. (The volume of milk present can be no more than the size of the udder itself.)

ד. ש"ך ס"ק כ'.
ה. עיין ט"ז ס"ק ד'.
ו. סעיף ח'.

שהחלב כנוס בתוכן ויש באותו חלב טעם מן הבשר שנתבשל עמו[14] ואותו חלב שבגומות א"א להפרישה מן הבשר דלא מהני קריעה לאחר הבישול ואע"ג דבגמר בישולו יוצא כל החלב מ"מ קודם גמר בישולו נאסר בשביל חלב שבגומות[15] ותו לא משתרי דחיישינן שמא יאכלנו קודם גמר בישולו[16] א"נ משום מראית העין.[17]ד

ואם לא הי' בין הכל ס' הכל אסור מדרבנן ומ"מ מותר בהנאה.

ה. ואע"פ שהיה ס' נגד הכחל[18] אם נפל לקדירה אחרת דינו כקדירה ראשונה ומשערינן בו בס' והכחל מן המנין[19] ואפילו לא היה בקדירה ראשונה ס' נגד הכחל ונאסר מדינא[20] אפ"ה מצטרף למנין ס'[21] שלא יהא סופו חמור מתחלתו[22]ה כל זה הוא לדעת הב"י בש"ע ולדעת רמ"א אם לא היה בו ס' בקדירה הראשונה ונפל אחר כך לקדירה אחרת אין הכחל מצטרף לס' דכיון דנ"נ[23] איך יצטרף להתיר.[24]ו

יד אדם

14. The taste of the other meat cooked in the pot is emitted into the other ingredients of the pot (including the udder and any milk inside it), as a result of their being heated together.

15. The milk inside the udder became forbidden because it had been mixed with the taste of other meat in the pot.

16. While the forbidden milk is still in the pores.

17. (This term has been defined in note 29 on topic 40.) People will think he is performing a transgression when he eats an udder that was cooked with other meat.

5. An Improperly Cooked Udder Which Was Mixed into a Second Pot of Food

18. We have learned above that if an udder is cooked in a pot with other meat and sixty times the udder was present in the pot, the udder becomes forbidden (even though the remaining meat in the pot is permissible). The reason for the prohibition is *maris ayin*, or because one might eat the udder before it is fully cooked, as noted above.

19. As such, the ingredients in the second pot must be 59 times the size of the udder.

20. The entire pot of food became forbidden because it is regarded as a mixture of meat and milk which is rabbinically prohibited.

21. And only 59 times the udder need be present in the second pot.

ד. *Shach*, paragraph 5.
ה. See the *Taz*, [chapter 90] paragraph 4.
ו. *Shulchan Aruch*, [chapter 90] paragraph 1.

gathered, and there is in that milk the taste of the meat that was cooked with it,[14] and that milk which is in the pores is impossible to separate from the meat [of the udder], as cutting [the udder] after cooking [has begun] does not help. And even though by the completion of the cooking all of the milk goes out [of the udder], nevertheless, before the completion of its cooking it had [already] become forbidden because of the milk that is in the pores,[15] and it can no longer become permissible [for the following reason]: we are concerned lest he will eat it before the completion of its cooking;[16] or else, because of *maris ayin*.[17]ד

And if there was not among everything sixty [times the udder], everything is rabbinically forbidden. Nevertheless, it is permissible to derive benefit [from the mixture].

5. Even though there was sixty times [the size of] the udder,[18] if it has fallen into another pot, the rule is that it is like the first pot and we measure it by sixty with the udder included.[19] And even if there was not sixty times [the size of] the udder in the first pot and it became forbidden according to the law,[20] even so, [the udder still] combines [with the other contents of the pot] towards the tally of sixty[21] so that its end should not be more stringent than its beginning.[22]ה All of this is according to the opinion of the *Bais Yosef* in the *Shulchan Aruch*. According to the opinion of the *Rama*, if there was not sixty times [the udder] in the first pot and [the udder] has fallen afterwards into another pot, the udder does not combine towards the sixty, for since it has been made inherently forbidden,[23] how can it combine to make [itself] permissible?[24]ו

Yad Adam

22. I.e., the udder in the second pot should not be regarded as more stringent than in the first pot.

23. Since the udder and the rest of the pot became completely forbidden, the udder must now be regarded as if it were an ordinary piece of unkosher meat.

24. Thus, the remaining ingredients in the second pot must be sixty (not 59) times the size of the udder.

ז. ס״ק י״ח.

ו. מנהגינו ע״פ הכרעת רמ״א[25] דלצלי בפ״ע בלא בשר לכתחלה צריך קריעת שו״ע וטיחה בכותל[26] ובדיעבד אם נצלה לחוד בלא בשר אפילו לא קרע כלל מותר.

ואם נצלה עם בשר אם נקרע שו״ע וטחו בכותל שניהם מותרין אפי׳ ידוע שנתהפכו על השפוד[27] דכיון שנקרע שו״ע וטחו בכותל חשוב כבשר ממש לענין זה.ז

ואם לאו העליון מותר והתחתון אסור[28] ולא חיישינן שמא נתהפך השפוד ונעשה העליון תחתון[29] דבדיעבד לא מחזיקינן איסורא[30] וכן אם ידוע ששניהם היו תחובין בשוה בשפוד[31] ולא היה שום אחד מהם עליון או תחתון שניהם מותרים[32] אבל לכתחלה אין לצלותו עם בשר כלל משום שרגילות להתהפך השפוד לפעמים זה עליון וזה תחתון[33] וכ״ז בצלי על השפוד אבל במחבת דינו כמבושל בקדירה.

ז. ולקדירה בלא בשר נוהגין בו איסור לכתחלה אפילו ע״י קריעת שו״ע וטחו בכותל דגזרינן שמא יבא לבשלו עם בשר

יד אדם

6. Broiling an Udder—the Accepted Practice

25. The rulings we have learned above in sections 1-4 regarding cooking and broiling an udder represent the opinion of the *Bais Yosef* in the *Shulchan Aruch*. In this section and in the ones that follow, we are learning the more stringent rulings of the *Rama*, which represent the accepted practice.

26. The *Rama* is thus more stringent than the *Bais Yosef* (mentioned at the end of section 3) who does not require pressing on a wall.

27. If, for example, both the udder and other meat were on a horizontal spit, perhaps we should be concerned that sometimes the portion of the spit with the udder will be elevated, and the milky fluid dripping from the udder will drip onto the other piece of meat and make it forbidden. Also, if the half of the spit which holds the other piece of meat were elevated, juices from it would drip onto the udder and make the udder forbidden (since the taste of these juices would be absorbed into the pores of the udder and be mixed with the milk there). Nevertheless, we are not concerned about these possibilities here, because after the fact, even if one of them were placed directly above the other they would still be permissible, as the *Chochmas Adam* goes on to explain (since the udder was cut and pressed). (See *Aruch Hashulchan* 90:11-13.)

28. Here we are dealing with a case in which a vertical spit was used, and one piece

ı. *Shach*, [chapter 90] paragraph 11.

6. Our custom is according to the decision of the *Rama*[25] that for broiling [the udder] by itself without [other] meat, to begin with, it requires cutting in the length and width and pressing on a wall.[26] But after the fact, if it is broiled by itself without [other] meat, even if he did not cut [it] at all, it is permissible.

And if it is broiled with [other] meat—if it is cut in the length and width and pressed on a wall, both of them are permissible, even if it is known that they were overturned on the spit,[27] for since it was cut in the length and width and pressed on a wall it is considered like ordinary meat in this case.[ı]

And if it was not [cut and pressed on a wall], the upper one is permissible and the lower one is forbidden.[28] And we are not concerned that perhaps the spit was overturned and the upper one became the lower one,[29] because after the fact, we do not presume [a permissible substance has become] forbidden.[30] And similarly, if it is known that both of them were attached onto the spit on the same level,[31] so that neither one of them is upper or lower, both of them are permissible.[32] However, to begin with, one should not broil it with [other] meat at all, because it is customary to turn over the spit, [such that] sometimes this one is upper and [other times] it is lower.[33] And all of this is with broiling on a spit, but in a pan, the ruling is [the same] as cooking in a pot [which is discussed below].

7. And regarding [cooking] in a pot without meat, we are accustomed to prohibit it to begin with, even with cutting in the length and width and pressing on a wall, for we decree [that it is forbidden]

Yad Adam

was broiling above the other. Since the udder was not cut and pressed on a wall, the lower piece will become forbidden, based on the concerns mentioned in the previous note.

29. In which case both pieces would be forbidden.

30. We will not presume that the spit was overturned unless this was seen to have occurred.

31. With the spit held horizontally.

32. However, in this case, if one side of the spit is elevated, the lower piece will become forbidden.

33. And the concerns mentioned in note 27 apply.

7. Cooking an Udder in a Pot—the Accepted Practice

ח. רמ"א סעיף ג'.
ט. שם.
י. ס"ק י"ז.
יא. כמו שאופין לחם ממולא בבשר.
יב. רמ"א סעיף ג'.

וה"ה לטגן אפילו בלא בשר דאין חילוק בין טיגון לבישול. ואפילו נתייבש כבר הכחל. ואם עבר ובשל בקדירה לבדו[34] בדיעבד אם נקרע שו"ע וטחו בכותל מותר אפילו בלא ס'[35] אבל אם לא קרעו שו"ע או לא טחו בכותל אפי' בדיעבד אסור עד שיהא ס' נגד הכחל וכחל עצמו מן המנין.[36]ח

ח. ולבשלו עם בשר אפילו קרעו שו"ע וטחו בכותל אסור ובדיעבד במקום הפ"מ יש להתיר[37] אבל לא בלא"ה.ט

ט. ואם אנו רואין שנתייבשה הכחל או לאחר ל' יום דמסתמא כבר נתייבשה' אם עבר ובשלה אפילו עם בשר מותר בדיעבד אפי' בלא קריעה כלל דכיון שכבר נתייבשה אינה נותנת טעם ולכתחלה אסור אפי' בנתייבשה.

י. לעשות פשטידא מן הכחל דהיינו שמניחין אותו בעיסה[יא] בלא בשר נוהגין בו היתר אם אין אופין אותה במחבת אלא בתנור[38] אבל במחבת דומה ממש לבישול בקדירה[39] ואם נתייבשה תחלה מותר בפשטידא אפילו במחבת ויש נוהגים איסור אפילו בנתייבשה אם אופין במחבת.[יב]

יא. ולאפות הפשטידא שבו הכחל בתנור קטן עם מאכלי חלב דינו כשאר בו"ח שנאפה בתנור א'[40] ומבואר דינם כלל ס"ב.

יד אדם

34. I.e., without other meat in the pot.

35. Even though all the ingredients in the pot (with the udder included) are less than sixty times the size of the udder.

36. If the ingredients are at least sixty times the udder (with the udder included), the udder together with the other ingredients in the pot will be permissible. *(Pri Megadim)*

This ruling of the *Rama* is more stringent than that of the *Bais Yosef* which is cited in the beginning of section 4, as the *Bais Yosef* permits the udder without sixty, even if the udder was not cut and pressed.

8. An Udder Cooked in a Pot with Other Meat

37. We can rely on lenient authorities who permit the mixture if the udder had been cut and pressed on a wall. (See *Shach* 90:8.)

Regarding the term **הפסד מרובה**, see the additional note on topic 40, section 5.

9. A Dried Out Udder

ח. *Rama*, [chapter 90] paragraph 2.
ט. *Ibid.*
י. *Shach*, [chapter 90] paragraph 17.
יא. As we bake bread filled with meat.
יב. *Rama*, [chapter 90] paragraph 2.

lest he will come to cook it with [other] meat. And so is the law regarding frying even without [other] meat, as there is no difference between frying and cooking. [The prohibition to cook applies] even if the udder has dried out. And if one transgressed and cooked it in a pot by itself[34]—after the fact, if it had been cut in the length and width and pressed on a wall it is permitted, even without sixty.[35] However, if he had not cut it in the length and width or he had not pressed it on a wall, even after the fact it is forbidden unless there is sixty times the udder, with the udder itself included.[36ח]

8. And to cook it with [other] meat, even if he cut it in the length and width and pressed it on a wall, is forbidden. And after the fact, in case of a great loss there are grounds to permit it,[37] but otherwise not.[ט]

9. If we see that the udder has dried out, or after it is thirty days old in which case it has probably dried out[י]—if one transgressed and cooked it even with [other] meat it is permissible after the fact, even without having been cut at all, for since it has already dried out, it does not impart any taste. But to begin with, it is forbidden [to cook it] even if it has dried out.

10. To make a pudding from the udder, that is, to place it in dough[יא]—without [other] meat we are accustomed to allow it if we do not bake it in a pan but in the oven.[38] However, in a pan it is exactly like cooking in a pot.[39] And if it has dried out first it is permissible even [to bake] the pudding in a pan. But some are accustomed to forbid this, even where it had been dried out, when baking [it] in a pan.[יב]

11. And to bake pudding which contains the udder in a small oven with dairy foods, the ruling is the same as with other meat and milk which is baked in one oven[40] and their rules are explained in topic 62.

Yad Adam

10. Preparing an Udder Pudding

38. Where it is placed on the oven floor.

39. And we should avoid doing this in accordance with section 7 above.

11. Baking an Udder Pudding in an Oven with Dairy or Meat Food

40. Since the udder is essentially meat, it should not be baked together with dairy food.

יג. שם.
יד. שם סעיף ג׳.

ועם מאכלי בשר מחמירין שלא לאפותם יחד אלא יש להניח הפשטידא בפי התנור[41] ויש ליזהר לכתחלה אע״פ שאינה אלא חומרא.[יג]

יב. כל כחל שקרעו שו״ע וטחו בכותל דמותר בדיעבד כמבואר לעיל[42] מותר לחתוך אותו כשהוא רותח בסכין שחתכו בו בשר וכן כחל חי אע״פ שהיא מלאה חלב כיון שהוא צונן[43] וכן מותר לחתוך בשר בסכין שחתכו בו כחל וכן הדין לאכול זה[44] בכלי שאכל בו זה וה״ה לצלות זה בשפוד שצלו בו זה וה״ה דמותר להניחו בקערה עם בשר צלי אפילו אם שניהם חמים דלאחר צליית הכחל שאנו מתירין בדיעבד דינו כשאר בשר לכל דבר.[יד]

יג. ולפי המנהג ע״פ פסק רמ״א לעיל סימן ו׳ אם עבר וצלה בלא קריעה או קריעה מועטת[45] כל הדברים האלו אסורים לכתחלה[46] ואם נצלה כל צרכו כיון שקרעוהו שו״ע אפילו לא טחו בכותל מותר לחתוך בסכין של בשר אבל קודם שנצלה כל צרכו אסור לכתחלה אא״כ קרעו שו״ע וגם טחו בכותל.

יד אדם

41. This is done so that the odors which emanate from the udder will go out of the oven and not mix with the other meat.

12. Using Meat Utensils with an Udder

42. An udder which was cut and pressed is permitted only after the fact if it has been cooked in a pot by itself (section 7) or if it has been broiled together with other meat (section 6). Nevertheless, even in such situations, we are to regard the udder as ordinary meat and we need not concern ourselves with the milk which had been absorbed inside it. (If this udder which had been cut and pressed were to be broiled by itself, it would be permitted even to begin with.)

43. Since cold food or utensils do not absorb taste from each other, the meat knife will not become forbidden.

44. The udder or the ordinary meat, even when hot.

יג. *Ibid.*
יד. *Ibid.*, paragraph 3.

And [regarding baking] with meat foods, we are stringent not to bake them together, but to place the pudding by the opening of the oven.[41] And it is proper to be careful [to observe this practice] to begin with, even though it is only a mere stringency.יג

12. Any udder which was cut in the length and width and pressed on a wall which is permitted after the fact as explained above[42]—it is permitted to cut it when it is hot with the knife which they use to cut meat. And similarly, [one may use a meat knife to cut] a raw udder, even though it is full of milk, since it is cold.[43] And similarly, it is permitted to cut meat with the knife that they used to cut an udder; and the ruling is similar [in that it is permitted] to eat either one[44] in the plate that he ate the other one. The ruling is similar regarding broiling either one on the spit that he broiled the other one. [Furthermore,] the rule is similar that it is permitted to place [the udder] on a plate with [other] broiled meat, even if both of them are hot, for after broiling the udder which we permit after the fact, it is regarded as other meat for all matters.יד

13. And according to the custom which is in conformity with the decision of the *Rama* above in section 6, if one transgressed and broiled without cutting or with a small cut,[45] all of these things are forbidden to begin with.[46] But if it is fully broiled, since he cut it in the length and width, even if he did not press it on a wall, it is permitted to cut it with a meat knife, but before it is fully broiled it is forbidden [to do so] to begin with, unless he cut it in the length and width and also pressed it on a wall.

Yad Adam

13. Using Meat Utensils with an Insufficiently Prepared Udder

45. In this case, where the udder was not properly cut, it is permitted after the fact according to the *Rama* as long as it was broiled by itself. (An udder which has not been properly cut might be forbidden altogether if broiled with other meat. See section 6.)

46. The actions mentioned above in section 12 are forbidden to begin with, but after the fact, even if any of those actions were performed, everything is permissible (*Rama* 90:3).

טו. ש״ך ס״ק כ״ז.

יד. לכתחלה אסור למלוח כחל עם בשר[47] ובדיעבד אפילו לא קרעו כלל מותר ואפי׳ עלוי׳ בשראט״ו ועיין לעיל כלל ל״ד סימן ט״ו.[48]

כלל מב

דין בשר וגבינה או איסור והיתר הנוגעין זה בזה צוננין

(סי׳ צ״א)

א. סימן צ״א סעיף א׳.

א. בשר וגבינה צוננין[1] שנגעו זה בזה וכן איסור שנגע בהיתר אם הם יבשים לגמרי א״צ אפי׳ הדחה[2]א ואם אחד מהם לח או שניהם לחים קצת ולא מחמת מליחה[3] צריך להדיח מקום נגיעתן[4] ואם הוא דבר שמן כחמאה וחלב[5] לא סגי בהדחה רק צריך שפשוף היטיב ג״כ.[6]

ואין חילוק בין בשר וחלב לשאר איסורין בין שנפל בשר צונן לחלב צונן או היתר גוש לאיסור צלול או להיפך[7] הגוש צריך

יד אדם

14. Salting an Udder With Meat

47. Since it is as if they are being cooked together.

48. It is explained there that a similar rule applies to salting a liver on top of other meat.

1. Forbidden Mixtures of Cold Food

1. If the foods are hot, then the rules are more stringent than those mentioned here, since heat will cause the flavor of each food to spread into the other. The laws regarding hot solid foods (such as meat and cheese) which come into contact with each other are discussed in topic 60.

2. The meat and cheese (or the "permissible food") remain permitted as before. (This ruling applies in a case where particles of the foods will not cling to one another.)

3. If the food is moist because salt drew out moisture from inside the food, the more stringent rules of salted food will, under certain circumstances, have to be followed. This

טו. *Shach*, [chapter 90] paragraph 27.

14. To begin with, it is forbidden to salt an udder with meat.[47] But after the fact, even if he did not cut it at all, it is permissible, even [if placed] on top of [other] meat.[טו] And see above, topic 34, section 15.[48]

Topic 42
Laws Concerning Meat and Cheese, or Forbidden Food and Permissible Food, Which Come into Contact with Each Other While Cold
(based on *Shulchan Aruch-Yoreh Deah* chapter 91)

א. *Shulchan Aruch* chapter 91, paragraph 1.

1. If cold meat and cold cheese[1] have come into contact with each other—or similarly, if a forbidden food has come into contact with a permissible food—if they are completely dry they do not even require washing.[2א] But if one of them is moist or both of them are a bit moist, and it is not because of salting,[3] it is necessary to wash the place of their contact.[4] And if [one of them] is something fatty like butter or forbidden fat,[5] [then] washing is not enough, but it requires thorough rubbing also.[6]

And there is no difference [in the ruling] between [mixtures of] meat and milk or [mixtures involving] other foods prohibited by the Torah [under the following circumstances]: Whether cold meat has fallen into cold milk, or a permitted solid food has fallen into a forbidden liquid, or the other way around[7]—[in all cases] the solid food requires

Yad Adam

is because foods that are salted are regarded as if it they were cooked together. See topic 43, section 9.

4. Due to the moisture, small bits of each of the foods will cling to one other. Therefore, washing is required. (*Aruch Hashulchan* 91:1)

5. Fat from the hind portion of an animal which is forbidden by Torah law (*Vayikra* [Leviticus] 7:23).

6. To remove fatty material that may cling to the other food.

7. For example, cheese falls into a cold meat soup.

ב. שם בש"ך ס"ק י'.
ג. שם סעיף ב'.
ד. שם סעיף ח'.

הדחה[8]ב ולכן צריך ליזהר שלא להניחם יחד בענין שיגעו זה בזה דכיון דעכ"פ צריכין הדחה חיישינן שמא ישכח ולא ידיח.

ב. וכן הדין בכל דבר שצריך הדחה ואפי' להניח יחד[9] על סמך שידיח אסור דחיישינן שמא ישכח. ודוקא דבר שאין דרכו בהדחה אבל דבר שדרכו בהדחה כגון בשר חי שהמנהג קודם שמבשלין אותו מדיחין אותו מותר להניח בכלי איסור[10] וכיוצא בו אע"פ שהוא לח קצת[11]ג ובדיעבד שבישל בלא הדחה או שא"א להדיח[12] מותר.[13] (ל"ט)

דין תשמיש היתר בכלי איסור מבואר הכל בכלל נ"ו.

ג. מותר לצור בשר וגבינה או איסור והיתר במטפחת אחת זה בצד זה וזה בצד זה ולא חיישינן שמא יגעו זה בזהד וכן מותר ליתן בתוך תיבה אחת כד של בשר אצל כד של חלב דמזהר זהירי שלא יפול מזה לזה ומ"מ אם הם מגולים טוב ליזהר לכתחילה

יד אדם

8. This is in accordance with the above, that if moisture is present in one of the foods, then washing is necessary. What is the status of the milk in such cases? The milk into which meat or a forbidden food has fallen (or meat soup into which cheese has fallen) will remain permissible, as noted below in section 6.

The ruling that the meat is permissible after being rinsed applies only to raw meat which does not contain cracks and which has not been spiced. Otherwise, the more stringent rulings mentioned below in section 6 will apply.

All of the regulations mentioned here apply when both the meat and the milk are cold. If one of them is hot, refer to sections 7, 8, and 9 for the relevant rulings.

2. Leaving Foods Together Which Will Have to be Washed; Placing Raw Meat in a Forbidden Vessel

9. For example, leaving cooked meat (which is a bit moist) in contact with cheese or with a forbidden food, or in a forbidden vessel. (Just as a moist kosher food must be washed when coming into contact with forbidden food, it must also be washed when coming into contact with a forbidden vessel.)

10. Since the meat will be washed, he may, for example, place it in a pot which had been used to cook unkosher meat. See topic 56, section 1 for further discussion.

11. Since it is customary to wash it in any

ב. There in the *Shach*, paragraph 10.
ג. *[Shulchan Aruch]* there, paragraph 2.
ד. *[Shulchan Aruch]* there, paragraph 1.

washing.[8ב] Therefore, it is necessary to be careful not to place [such items] together in a way that they will be in contact with each other, for since they at least require washing, we are concerned that one will forget and not wash [the food].

2. And this is the rule for anything requiring washing—that even leaving it together[9] with the idea that he will wash [it later on] is forbidden, for we are concerned that he will forget. But this is only with regard to something which is not customarily washed. On the other hand, something that is customarily washed such as raw meat, where the custom is that before we cook it we wash it, it is permitted to place it in a forbidden vessel,[10] and [so is the case] with similar [food] even though it is a bit moist.[11ג] And after the fact, if he cooked [the food] without washing, or if it is impossible to wash,[12] it is permissible.[13] (See *Binas Adam*, section 39.)

The rules regarding use of a permitted food in a forbidden vessel are fully explained in topic 56.

3. It is permissible to tie meat and cheese, or forbidden food and permissible food, in one cloth with each one beside the other one, and we are not concerned that they will come into contact with each other.[ד] And similarly, it is permissible to place a vessel of meat next to a vessel of milk into one box, as one will be very careful that one should not fall into the other. Nevertheless, if they are uncovered, it is

Yad Adam

case, we are not concerned that he will forget.

Is it also permissible to place raw kosher meat on top of forbidden food? It is possible that there is no direct prohibition against doing so (since it is customary to wash the meat before cooking it), but it would be distasteful to do such a thing. (*Aruch Hashulchan* 91:3)

12. Such as milk which has come into contact with raw meat. (It is impossible to "wash" the milk.)

13. Since they were cold and were not salted, they will not have absorbed taste from one another.

In the case where one cooked the food without washing—if intact particles of forbidden substance were clinging to the food, then it will be necessary that the permissible ingredients be at least sixty times the size of these particles. This will serve to nullify the taste of the forbidden substance. (In general, we can assume that the required sixty was present. See topic 56, section 1.)

ה. סימן ל"ב סעיף ו'.
ו. שם.
ז. ל"ח סעיף ג'.

במקום שאינה צורך כיון שאין דבר המפסיק ביניהם^ה משא"כ לצור במטפחת דאפי' לכתחלה מותר.[14]

ד. וכן מותר להניח כלי שיש בו חלב אצל כלי שיש בו חומץ או שאר משקין אפי' שניהם מגולים דאפי' את"ל שיפול לתוכו חלב יהיה ניכר[15] ואם יפול בתוכו מעט[16] יתבטל בששים[17] אבל אין מניחין כלי שיש בו חלב אצל כלי שיש בו מלח אם שניהם מגולים שמא יפול לתוכו עד שאם היה משים אל לב להשגיח יהיה ניכר החלב בעין במלח וכיון שניכר לא שייך לומר שהוא בטל[18] אך לא ישים לבו ע"ז כי יחשוב מהיכא תיתי שנפל לתוכו וימלח ממנו בשר ומ"מ בדיעבד מותר ולא חיישינן שמא נפל אל המלח.[19]^ו

ה. צריך ליזהר שלא יגע בשר או גבינה בלחם אם א' מהם לח קצת שאם יגעו זה בזה אסור לאכול בו גבינה או בשר ומ"מ אם מדיח קצת המקום שנגע בו מותר.[20]^ז

יד אדם

3. Storing Meat and Dairy Foods (or Permissible and Forbidden Foods) Near Each Other

14. It is permissible because one can use the cloth to form separations between the foods and thereby prevent them from coming into contact with each other.

The rule that meat and dairy foods may be placed near each other do not apply to the table where one is eating. See topic 40, section 11 for the rules that will apply.

4. Placing Certain Pareve Substances Next to Milk

15. One will recognize (by the discoloration of the vinegar) that milk has fallen into it and he will avoid using it with meat.

16. Such that the milk will not be recognizable.

17. The volume of the other liquid would be at least sixty times the milk. In such a case, the taste of the milk will not be detectable and the liquid will remain pareve.

18. A recognizable layer of milk will remain on the salt that will not be absorbed into it. (*Badei Hashulchan* 95:90) As a rule, a substance which is recognizable cannot become nullified (topic 51, section 1). It would then be necessary to find and remove the layer of milk and discard it before placing the salt on meat.

19. And if salt was left next to milk (or any other dairy product which has the same color as salt), although it was not proper to have done so, it is permissible to add this salt to meat. (*Badei Hashulchan* 95:96)

ה. *[Shulchan Aruch]* chapter 95, paragraph 6.
ו. *Ibid. (Shulchan Aruch)* chapter 95, paragraph 5.
ז. *[Shulchan Aruch* chapter 91] paragraph 3.

best to avoid doing so, to begin with, in a situation where there is no need, since there is nothing separating them.ה This is not the rule with regard to tying in one cloth, where even to begin with it is permissible.[14]

4. Similarly, it is permissible to place a vessel containing milk next to a vessel containing vinegar or another liquid even if both of them are uncovered, for even if you will say that milk will fall into it, it will be recognizable;[15] and if [only] a little bit will fall into it,[16] it will become nullified with "sixty."[17] However, one should not place a vessel which contains milk next to a vessel which contains salt if both of them are uncovered, lest [milk] will fall into it such that if he would carefully look [at the salt], the milk would be recognizable as being intact in the salt; and since it is recognizable, it is not appropriate to say that it is nullified.[18] However, [in practice] one would not pay attention to this [possibility] because he will think: "How could it come about that [milk] would fall into it," and he will salt meat with it. Nevertheless, after the fact [salt left near milk] is permissible, as we are not concerned that perhaps [milk] has fallen into the salt.[19]ו

5. It is necessary to be careful that meat or cheese should not come into contact with bread if one of them is a bit moist, for if they will come into contact with each other, it would be forbidden to eat cheese or meat [respectively] with [that bread]. Nevertheless, if he washes the place of contact a little bit, it is permissible.[20]ז

Yad Adam

5. Bread Which Comes Into Contact With Meat or Milk

20. Some authorities disagree and rule that since there is a great tendency for food to adhere to bread, washing the bread cannot help and it will be forbidden to eat it with cheese (or meat) unless a thin layer of bread is cut away at the place of contact. This stringency will apply only if the bread or other food is moist. If both are dry, then there is no concern. (See *Aruch Hashulchan* 91:5)

ח. ואפילו בכפ״מ ל״ע להקל עיין ש״ך סימן ל״א ס״ק כ״א דרוב הפוסקים אוסרין כולו.
ט. בל״י בשם דמש״א.
י. ש״ך שם.
יא. סעי׳ ז׳.

ו. בד״א[21] בצונן חי כגון בשר חי שלא נמלח אבל צלי[22] צונן שנפל לחלב צונן אפילו שניהם אינם מלוחים צריך קליפה[23] ואם יש בו בקעים או שהוא מתובל בתבלין[24] והוא צלי אף על גב שהכל צונן אסור כולו וה״ה אפוי ומבושל צוננים דכיון דנצלה או נאפה או נתבשל אע״ג דהוא צונן רכיך[25] ובולע[26] וכן יש לנהוג במקום שאין הפ״מ[27] ומ״מ החלב מותר דדוקא הגוש בולע מן הצלול אבל אינו מפליט[28] כיון שאינו מלוח ושניהם צוננין.ח

ואם הוא חי[29] אלא שיש בו בקעים או שהוא מתובל בתבלין עד שאינו נאכל מחמת זהט הרבה פוסקים אוסרין כולוי ובש״ע מתיר מ״מ ראוי להחמיר לעצמו אף בחי וגם לאחרים צ״ע שהרי הפ״ח אוסר באמת ביש בקעים אפי׳ בפה״מ.[30]יא

ואם הי׳ אחד מהן מלוח עיין כלל מ״ג.

יד אדם

6. Mixtures of Cold Broiled Meat With Milk; Mixtures Involving Raw Meat Which Contains Cracks or Is Spiced

21. I.e., when do we say that cold meat which has fallen into cold milk remains permissible, and the meat only requires washing (as in section 1 above)?

22. Broiling the meat softens it somewhat and allows the milk to penetrate slightly.

23. The term *k'lipah* (translated: peeling) denotes removing a thin layer from the outside of the food. (See section 11 below.) In this case, a thin layer must be cut off from the entire piece of meat and discarded. The rest of the meat is presumed not to have absorbed any milk and will remain permissible.

24. The meat has been treated with a spice that will tenderize and soften it. The addition of such "spices" or the presence of cracks will allow the milk to penetrate deep into the piece of meat. The amount of "spice" which must be added such that the food is considered "spiced" is noted below.

The *Aruch Hashulchan* (91:37) notes that in most cases, broiled meat will have developed cracks in it.

25. The meat has become softened by one of these cooking processes.

26. As such, if cold baked or cooked meat falls into milk, its outer layer will have to be discarded. If, however, the meat also has cracks or is spiced, the entire piece will be forbidden.

27. It is implied from this statement that in cases of great loss, then we can be lenient and permit the meat in any of these cases after it has been washed. However, the *Chochmas Adam*, in note ח mentions that we

ח. And even in a case of great loss, it requires careful study in order to be lenient. See the Shach 91:21 [who explains] that most authorities forbid the entire thing.
ט. *Bais Lechem Yehudah* in the name of *Damesek Eliezer.*
י. *Shach, Ibid.* paragraph 25.
יא. Chapter 91, paragraph 7.

6. When is this the case?[21] [It is] with cold raw [meat] such as raw meat which is not salted. However, if broiled[22] cold [meat] has fallen into cold milk, even if both of them are not salted, it requires peeling.[23] But if there are cracks in it or it is spiced with spices[24] and it has been broiled, even though everything is cold [when the meat fell into the milk], all of it is forbidden. And so is the ruling for baked or cooked cold food, for since it has been broiled [on a spit] or baked [in an oven] or cooked [in a pot], even though it is cold, it has become soft[25] and it absorbs.[26] And so is the proper practice in a case where there is no great loss.[27] Nevertheless, [in all cases] the milk is permitted, for only the solid food absorbs from the liquid but it does not emit,[28] since it is not salted and both of them are cold.[ח]

And if it is raw[29] but it has cracks in it, or it is spiced with spices so much so that it could not be eaten because of it,[ט] many authorities forbid all of it,[י] but the *Shulchan Aruch* permits it. Nevertheless, it is proper to be strict with oneself even with raw meat, and even [when rendering a decision] for others it requires careful study, since the *Pri Chadash* truly forbids it when there are cracks, even where there is a great loss.[30][יא]

And [with regard to a case] where one of them was salted, see topic 43 [section 10].

Yad Adam

should be strict and follow these rulings (to require peeling, and to forbid the entire piece when it has cracks or is spiced) even when there is a great loss.

Regarding the term "great loss," see the additional note on topic 40, section 5.

28. The meat will not emit its taste into the milk.

29. We have learned that broiled meat is to be treated more stringently than raw meat—that raw meat need only be washed if it falls into milk whereas broiled meat requires peeling. Furthermore, if the broiled meat has cracks or is spiced, it is entirely forbidden. Now we will go on to learn that raw meat should also be treated more stringently if it has cracks or is spiced (according to some authorities).

30. Nevertheless, the *Aruch Hashulchan* (91:37) notes that this is not the majority view. Rather, most authorities rule that when raw meat is involved we do not say that the whole piece of meat becomes forbidden in any case; washing the meat would then be sufficient.

יב. סס בס"ך ס"ק כ"ג.
יג. ס"ך סס ס"ק ז'.

ז. אבל אם אין בו בקעים ולא מתובל בתבלין[31] אפי' צלי רותח ונפל לחלב צונן אפי' נמלח קצת[32] קולף הבשר ושאר הבשר מותר[33] דקיי"ל תתאה גבר ר"ל שהתחתון לעולם גובר[34] וכיון שהתחתון צונן מקרר את העליון[35] ומ"מ אדמיקר לי' בלע פורתא ולכן צריך קליפה[36] ואפי' הצלי שוקע בתוך החלב והחלב צף עליו אינו כצונן לתוך חם דכל שהוא במקומו גובר והחלב כיון שהוא במקומו והצלי נפל בתוכו גובר עליו ומקררו[יב] וה"ה חלב רותח שנפל על בשר צונן בין בעירוי שנפסק הקילוח או לא נפסק הקילוח לעולם צריך קליפה ודי בזה.[37][יג]

ח. אבל בשר וחלב רותחין שנתערבו יחד או אפילו בשר צונן לחלב רותח או חלב צונן לתוך בשר רותח הכל אסור משום

יד אדם

7. תתאי גבר (The Lower Substance Is Dominant)—Applying This Rule When the Lower Food is Cold

31. If one of these conditions were present, the stringencies mentioned in the previous section would apply and the meat might be completely forbidden.

32. Salting a little bit will not affect the status of the meat at all. If however, it were salted a lot, then the meat and the milk would become forbidden, in accordance with topic 43, section 10.

33. Ordinarily, when hot foods are mixed together they transfer their taste to each other. As such, one might suspect that when the hot meat falls into the milk, then a forbidden mixture of meat and milk will result. The *Chochmas Adam* now goes on to explain that this is not the case here, and that the meat remains permissible.

34. I.e., the lower food is the more important in determining the status of the mixture. As such, if the lower food is cold and the upper one is hot, we say that the lower food cools off the upper and we regard the mixture as containing two cold foods. If, on the other hand, the lower food was hot and the upper one was cold, then we say that the lower food heats up the upper one and the mixture is to be regarded as containing two hot foods. (See also topic 60, section 10.)

35. We do not prohibit the meat in this case, for since the cold milk dominates, it will cool off the meat before the taste of the milk can spread through it.

36. Thus, the meat will not absorb the taste of the milk throughout its entire substance. Rather, only the outer layer will absorb the taste of the milk and it therefore must be removed. In addition, the "peel" of the milk (a thin layer of milk surrounding the meat) also becomes forbidden. This "peel", of course, is impossible to remove. We will

יב. *Shach Ibid.*, paragraph 23.
יג. *Shach Ibid.*, paragraph 7.

7. Furthermore, if there are no cracks [in a piece of meat which has fallen into milk] and it is not spiced with spices,[31] even if it is hot broiled [meat] and it has fallen into cold milk, even if salted a little,[32] he is to peel the meat and the rest of the meat is permissible.[33] [This is] because it is established for us that the lower [substance] is dominant, that is to say, the lower one always dominates [the mixture][34] and since the lower one is cold, it cools off the upper one.[35] Nevertheless, while [the milk] is cooling it off it will absorb a little bit, and it therefore requires peeling.[36] And even if the broiled meat is submerged in the milk and the milk floats above it, it does not become like cold food [which has fallen] into hot [food], because whatever is in its [original] location dominates. And since the milk is in its [original] place and the broiled meat fell into it, it dominates over it and cools it off.יב And the same rule applies if hot milk has fallen onto cold meat, whether the stream [of milk] was interrupted while pouring, or [even] if the stream was not interrupted—in all cases [the meat] requires peeling and it is enough with this.[37]יג

8. However, if meat and milk which are hot have become mixed together, or if cold meat [has fallen] into hot milk, or if cold milk [has fallen] onto hot meat, everything is forbidden because the lower

Yad Adam

learn in section 10 that the milk will be permissible as long as its volume is at least sixty times the size of this forbidden "peel." If the milk is less than sixty times its peel, all of it will be forbidden (except in cases involving a great loss).

37. Nevertheless, when other factors are present which favor a lenient ruling, we can be lenient in cases where the stream has been interrupted and permit the food completely. See topic 46, section 5, and topic 59, section 2.

Additional note: The *Aruch Hashulchan* (91:11) raises the following question: How is it possible to establish a rule that in all cases, the lower food dominates? For example, if a lot of boiling milk falls onto a small piece of cold meat, how can one say that the meat will cool off the milk? One who observes the mixture will note that the milk is still hot. Furthermore, how can one say that if a large amount of cold milk falls onto a small piece of hot meat that the meat will heat up the milk, and all of the milk will become forbidden? When one observes such a mixture he sees that the milk remains cold.

Based on this argument, the *Aruch Hashulchan* concludes that the rule that the lower food dominates applies only when the upper and lower foods are present in equal quantity, and we will not necessarily apply the rule when one food is present in much greater quantity than the other.

דתתאה גבר ומחמם העליון והוי כשניהם רותחין[38] וצריך ס׳ לבטל.[39] [יד]

ט. כל מקום שנכתוב רותח ר״ל רותח כ״כ שהיד סולדת בו[40] ואף לאחר שהעבירו מן האש כל זמן שלא נתן אותו בכלי שני נקרא רותח[41] [טו] ואם הוא דבר גוש והיס״ב י״א דאפילו הניחו בכלי שני נקרא רותח ויש לו דין כאלו היה בכ״ר.[42] [טז]

י. כל מקום שצריך קליפה* אם לא קלפוהו ובשלו כך[43] כגון בשר שנאסר כ״ק וחתכוהו לחתיכות דקות בענין שא״א לקלפו עוד וכ״ש חלב או שאר דבר לח שנפל איסור או בשר לתוכו שהחלב היה

יד. ועיין כ״ז עוד בכלל ס׳.
טו. סימן ק״ה סעיף ג׳.
טז. ועי׳ בכלל ס׳ סימן י״ג.

יד אדם

8. תתאי גבר (The Lower Substance Is Dominant)—Applying This Rule When the Lower Food is Hot

38. Therefore, the taste of the two foods will completely spread throughout each other.

39. If either one is sixty times the size of the other, the taste of the latter will be nullified and the mixture will be not become forbidden. Thus, if meat falls into hot milk and the milk is sixty times the meat, the milk is permissible. The meat, however, is forbidden since is has absorbed the taste of milk. If milk falls onto hot meat and the meat is sixty times the milk, then the meat is permissible, but one should discard a thick layer of meat [*netilah*] from the place where the milk fell upon it (*Pri Megadim, Sifsei Daas* 105:16). The milk, however, will be forbidden since it contains the taste of meat.

9. Food Is Considered to Be Hot When It Is יד סולדת בו

40. I.e., one who touches it will pull his hand away from it. When a pot of food is placed on a fire and reaches this temperature it is called "hot," and as a result, the food will absorb the taste from a food or vessel which comes into contact with it. In addition, this hot food will emit its own taste into the other food or vessel.

According to Horav Moshe Feinstein, (*Igros Moshe, Orach Chayim*, volume 4, page 134) it is best to be strict when a Torah prohibition is involved and use 110 degrees Fahrenheit (43 degrees Centigrade) as the temperature from which one would withdraw his hand.

41. Thus, when a pot of hot food is removed from the fire, the contents of the pot are still considered to be "hot." This status is maintained until the food's temperature drops such that the hand will not withdraw from it. (See also topic 46, section 11, where the liquid poured from a "first vessel" is discussed.)

If, however, the contents of the pot were placed into a cold second vessel (*k'li sheini*), then the walls of the vessel would cool them down such that they will no longer absorb or emit taste. This rule applies even if the

י. And see all of this further on in topic 60 [section 10].
טו. [*Shulchan Aruch*], chapter 105 paragraph 3.
טז. See topic 60, section 12. [It is stated there that if a great loss is involved, one can rely on those authorities who rule that solid food in a second vessel has the same status as a liquid.]

food dominates and warms up the upper, and it is as if both of them are hot,[38] and it requires sixty times to nullify.[39]יד

9. Where ever we write [the word] *ro'sei'ach* (hot), it means so hot that the hand withdraws from it.[40] And even after one has removed [the substance] from the fire, as long as he has not placed it into a second vessel, it is called "hot."[41]טו But if it is something solid and [it is hot enough so that] the hand would withdraw from it, some say that even if one placed it in a second vessel it is [still] called "hot" and it has the status as if it were in the first vessel [which had been on the fire].[42]טז

10. In any situation which requires peeling,* if one does not peel [the food] and he cooked it like this,[43] such as where meat became forbidden by the width of its "peel" and he cut it into small pieces in such a way so that it is impossible to peel it any more; and certainly, milk or other liquid into which [hot] forbidden food or meat

Yad Adam

contents of the vessel are still hot enough to make one withdraw his hand from them. Accordingly, if milk was heated in a pot and poured into a bowl, and then a piece of raw meat fell into this bowl of milk while the milk was still hot, the meat will be permitted after it is washed off. Nevertheless, some authorities rule that cooking can take place in a second vessel to the extent of the outer layer of the food. As such, it is proper to follow this opinion and "peel" (remove the outer layer of) the food before it is used. If, however, a loss would be involved, then the food is permitted even without "peeling" it. (*Chochmas Adam* topic 59, section 6. Refer there for further discussion. It is mentioned there that some authorities, including the *Pri Chadash*, are more stringent and rule that the entire food becomes forbidden when falling into hot liquid which is in a second vessel.)

42. This is because the walls of the second vessel will not effectively cool down solid food. (*Aruch Hashulchan* 105:20. See note טז.)

10. Food Which Requires "Peeling" But Was Used Without Being Peeled (Or Which Is Impossible to Be Peeled)

*For example, a piece of hot meat falls into cold milk, causing the peel of the meat to become forbidden. (See section 7.)

43. **Note:** The *Chochmas Adam* will first explain the rules that apply when a forbidden peel is impossible to remove. He will then return to discuss the status of a food with a forbidden peel which was cooked without removing the peel. (Cooking will cause the forbidden taste to spread from the peel throughout the entire piece and might make the entire piece forbidden.)

יז. סעיף ד׳ ובט״ז.
יח. סי׳ ק״כ ש״ך ס״ק ל״ב.
יט. ש״ך סי׳ ס״ט ס״ק ס״ד ובסי׳ ל״ח ס״ד.

ג״כ צריך קליפה[44] אלא שא״א לקלפו בהפ״מ מותר אבל בלא״ה אין להתיר אפי׳ בדיעבד ואפי׳ החלב אסור אם אין בה ס׳ נגד שיעור קליפה[45] ואם הוא בענין שאפשר לקלפו אע״פ שכבר בישל הבשר צריך לקלוף[46][יז] ואם א״י איזו חתיכה שצריך קליפה[47] בטלה ברוב.[48][יח]

וכן אם בישל בקדירה שנאסר מתחלה רק כ״ק[49][50] כגון שמלחו בו בשר להוציא דם[51] או דבר איסור וכיוצא בו[52] וא״כ[53] צריך ס׳ נגד קליפת הכלי וכיון שקליפת הכלי עומד בעין ולכן אם אין ס׳ בתבשיל נגד הקליפה אסור אע״פ שא״א לקלוף התבשיל[54][יט] והכל

יד אדם

44. It is required to remove the "peel" of the milk (a thin layer of milk which surrounds the meat which has fallen into it) as well as the peel of the meat. This has been mentioned in note 36.

45. Since the milk was in contact with the meat or forbidden food until it cooled off, the taste of the meat would have spread into the "peel" of the milk, and this quantity of milk becomes forbidden. (For practical purposes, the size of this peel is equal to the size of the peel of the meat.) As such, there must be present sixty time this peel in the milk to nullify this forbidden portion. Otherwise, all of the milk will be forbidden unless there is a great loss. The same rule holds true with regard to meat whose peel is forbidden and which has been cut into small pieces—if there is not in the meat sixty times its peel, it will be forbidden unless there is a great loss. (In cases involving a great loss, we rely on the opinion of *Rabbenu Tam* who—when peeling is impossible—permits the food and the milk even though sixty times the peel is not present. Otherwise, we follow the *Riva* and other authorities who require sixty times the peel in any case. See also topic 57, section 4.) See the additional note on topic 40, section 5 for the criteria which are used to determine whether a great loss is present.

(One may wonder as to why the *Chochmas Adam* uses the word "certainly" in the phrase: "and certainly milk or other liquid..." Perhaps the meaning is as follows: If we are to be lenient to permit chopped up meat whose peel had become forbidden but this peel is no longer intact and can no longer be removed, then we should certainly be lenient where a liquid is involved. This is because there never was a recognizable peel which could be removed from the liquid, since the taste of the meat became dispersed into it as soon as it had fallen in. [*Matamei Hashulchan* 91:12.])

46. If a piece of meat with a forbidden peel was cooked in a pot without being peeled, he is to discard the peel and the remainder of the piece will be permissible if there is sixty times the forbidden peel. However, without sixty the entire piece will be forbidden. (*Matamei Hashulchan* 91:12)

יז. *Shulchan Aruch* paragraph 4 and the *Taz*.
יח. *Shulchan Aruch* chapter 105, *Shach* paragraph 35.
יט. *Shach* 69:64, and *Shulchan Aruch* 98:4.

has fallen, in which case the milk also requires peeling[44] but it is impossible to peel it—in cases of great loss it is permissible, but without this one may not permit [the food] even after the fact, and even the milk is forbidden, unless there is in it sixty times the size of the "peel."[45] But if it is a situation where it is possible to peel, even if he has already cooked the meat, he should peel it.[46][יז] And if he does not know which piece requires peeling,[47] it is nullified in the majority (בטל ברוב).[48][יח]

In addition, if one had cooked in a pot in which only its peel[49] had previously become forbidden[50]—such as where meat was salted in it to bring out the blood,[51] or a forbidden substance [was salted in it] or something similar to it,[52]—if this is the case,[53] [the contents of the pot] must be sixty times the peel of the pot, for since the peel of the pot stands intact, as such, if there is not sixty times the peel in the cooked food, [the cooked food becomes] forbidden, even though it is impossible to peel the cooked food.[54][יט] And everything [in the pot] combines to

Yad Adam

47. The piece which requires peeling fell into a pot which contains other pieces of meat and it can no longer be identified.

48. In topic 51, section 1, it is explained that if pieces of permissible food are mixed together with pieces of forbidden food and it is impossible to determine which pieces are the forbidden ones—then if the majority of the pieces are permissible, the forbidden pieces will be nullified and all of the pieces may be eaten. (It is, however, customary to discard one of the pieces.)

49. The "peel" of the pot in this case is a thin layer along the inner surface of the pot, where the pot was in contact with the salty food mentioned below.

50. When one cooks forbidden food in a pot, the entire substance of the pot becomes forbidden. Here we are dealing with a different situation, in which only a thin inner layer of the pot had become forbidden.

51. The blood, which is forbidden to be eaten, will be absorbed into the inner layer of the walls (and bottom surface) of the pot as a result of the salt, since salt causes absorption to a limited extent (as explained in topic 57, sections 12 and 13). (If, on the other hand, the blood were cooked in the pot, the blood would be absorbed throughout the entire thickness of the wall of the pot.)

52. For example, a piece of unkosher meat is salted in a pot.

53. That he later cooked in a pot in which such a food had been salted.

54. In this case, the food in the pot cannot be made permissible by peeling, since the taste which had been absorbed into the pot

כ. ש״ך סי׳ צ״א ס״ק ח׳.
כא. בסי׳ תמ״ז ס״ק ל״ג.
כב. סי׳ צ״ו בש״ך ס״ק כ״א.

מצטרף לבטל הקליפה הבשר והרוטב[55] ול״א דחנ״נ[56] כדלקמן כלל מ״ד.[57] כ

והמ״א[58] כתב כא דבכל מקום דצריך קליפה צריך ס׳ נגד הקליפה[59] רק בדין תתאה גבר דאינו אלא מצד החומרא[60] שם מותר אם א״א לקלוף.[61]

יא. שיעור קליפה שנכתוב בכל מקום הוא כדי שתוכל להנטל כולו כאחד לאחר שקלפוהו. כב

יד אדם

has now spread completely through all of the ingredients in the pot. As such, if the ingredients in the pot do not equal sixty times the forbidden "peel" of the pot (thereby nullifying the taste), everything in the pot will be forbidden (even if a great loss is involved).

In the previous case, where a food or liquid requires peeling and it is impossible to do so, it was mentioned that the food is permitted in a situation involving a great loss. Why is the case here different? The *Chochmas Adam* has answered as follows: The previous case involves a situation where the peel is mixed into the rest of the food and no intact peel remains which can be removed. In such a case, there are grounds to permit the food where there is a great loss. Here, however, an intact "peel" remains which is forbidden (in such a case, the inner lining of the pot), and such a peel remains forbidden in any case. (*Aruch Hashulchan* 91:18 in accordance with the *Shach* and *Pri Chadash*) Consequently, if the taste from this peel will be absorbed into other foods, they will become forbidden.

55. Thus, if the total volume of the contents of the pot equals sixty times the peel of the pot, then the mixture will be permitted. See the end of topic 45, where it is stated that a pot generally contains sixty times its peel.

56. The "piece" here refers to the peel of the pot. If a small piece of meat had been salted in the pot, even though its taste spreads throughout the peel of the pot, we will not say that the peel becomes like a piece of *nevelah* (unkosher meat) and thereby require sixty times the entire peel of the pot. Rather, only sixty times the piece of meat is required, since the amount of absorbed forbidden taste cannot be larger than this piece of meat.

57. Refer to the end of section 16 there.

58. According to the *Magen Avraham*, the presence or absence of an intact "peel" which is forbidden will not matter. Why then in the first case are there grounds to permit the food where there is a great loss, but not in the case of the forbidden pot? The *Chochmas Adam* goes on to answer this.

59. In accordance with the case where one cooked in a pot whose "peel" is forbidden.

60. Since, according to the letter of the law, the lower food dominates, then if hot meat falls into cold milk, the meat and milk

כ. *Shach* 91:8.
כא. *Orach Chayim* 447:33.
כב. *Shach* 96:21.

nullify the peel [of the pot]—[both] the meat and the liquid.[55] And we do not say that "the [entire] piece is made inherently forbidden (*nevelah*),"[56] as [explained] further on in topic 44.[57כ]

And the *Magen Avraham*[58] has written[כא] that wherever peeling is required, sixty times the peel us required.[59] It is only with regard to the rule that the lower [food] is dominant, where it is only due to a stringency,[60] there it is permitted if it is impossible to peel.[61]

11. The [required] size of the "peel" which is written everywhere is [enough thickness] such that all of it can be removed in one [solid] piece after peeling it.[כב]

Yad Adam

should be completely permissible. In this instance, it is only as a mere stringency that the peel is to be regarded as forbidden. Accordingly, in cases where food requires peeling as a result of applying the rule that the lower substance dominates, and it cannot be peeled (such as in the cases of the milk or chopped meat mentioned above) the *Magen Avraham* would be lenient and, even if sixty times the peel were not present, he would permit these even without a great loss. (*Matamei Hashulchan* 91:12)

61. As such, we can be lenient in a case where hot meat falls into cold milk if peeling has not been done. However, we cannot be lenient in cases such as where salting causes the peel to be forbidden, nor in other cases where the peel is forbidden according to the letter of the law. (Examples are given in the *Taz* in 91:7.)

11. Definition of "Peeling" (k'lipah)

כלל מג

דין איסור והיתר או בשר וגבינה שנמלחו יחד

(סימן צ״א)

א. קיי״ל דמליח הרי זה כרותח ומדינא דוקא כשנמלח כעין שמולחין לקדירה[1] ושהה כדי מליחה לקדירה[2] דזה נקרא שאינו נאכל מחמת מלחו[3] אפי׳ לא מלחו אלא מצד אחד מיחשב כרותח ואנו אין בקיאין[4] ולכן טוב להחמיר במקום שאין הפ״מ אפילו אם נמלח רק כמליחת צלי.[5] ומיחשב כרותח עד שידיחנו. ומליח כעין מליח דבעי לה לאורחא[6][א] לעולם אפי׳ לאחר שהדיחו כל זמן שלא שראו במים דינו כרותח.[7][ב]

ב. תיכף כשנמלח ומתחיל ציר לצאת[8] נחשב הציר היוצא ממנו כרותח ולכן בין שמלחו בשר כשר ונבלה או בשר וגבינה יחד

א. נראה לי דזה מה שקורין בל״א פעקל פליים שהוא מלוח הרבה.
ב. סעיף ה׳.

יד אדם

1. A Salted Food Is Considered to Be Hot

1. Meat must be salted to draw out its blood before it can be cooked in a pot. During this salting, the surface of the meat must contain so much salt such that the meat is too salty to be eaten. A salted food is to be regarded as hot only when this quantity of salt is present.

2. In order that all the blood be drawn out from meat, it is necessary that salt remain on it for 18 minutes (24 minutes according to some authorities). We are being taught here that salted food remains "boiling hot" even though the salt has already been present on the food for this amount of time. (This explanation is based on the *Aruch Hashulchan* 91:30 and fits well throughout the text of the *Chochmas Adam*. See also the textual note in the left margin.*)

3. The established rule in the *gemara* is that salty food is not regarded as hot unless it is heavily salted such that it is "impossible to be eaten because of its saltiness." The *Chochmas Adam* is saying that this status is reached when the amount of salt present is equivalent to what is needed to draw out the blood from meat to allow cooking the meat in a pot; (and the ruling is not in accordance with those authorities who rule that even more salt is required—enough to preserve the food for a long time). In addition, the status of being "hot" lasts longer than 18 (or 24) minutes.

In sections 3 and 4 below, it is explained that some authorities are more lenient and rule that salted meat is no longer considered to be hot once this period of time has elapsed. (See *Rama* 91:5. This leniency

Topic 43
Laws Concerning Forbidden Food and Permissible Food, or Meat and Cheese, Which Are Salted Together

(based on *Shulchan Aruch–Yoreh Deah* chapter 91)

א. It is my opinion that this is what we call in the Ashkenaz language "pickled meat," which is very salty.

ב. *Shulchan Aruch* [chapter 91] paragraph 5.

*[Textual note: It is noteworthy that the phrase ושהה כדי מליחה לקדירה was not present in the first edition of the *Chochmas Adam*. The translation was composed such that the addition of this phrase does not change the meaning of the original text.]

1. It is established for us that salted food is [considered to be] boiling hot, and according to the law, [this is so] only if [the food] is salted the way we salt for a pot[1]–[even if the food already] has remained [salted] the time [required] for salting for a pot[2]–for [even] then it is called "impossible to be eaten because of its saltiness."[3] Even if one salted it only on one side, it is considered hot. And since we are not expert,[4] it is therefore best to be strict in a situation where there is not a great loss, [and regard food as hot] even if the salting is only sufficient for broiling.[5] And the food should be considered hot until one washes it off. And if the salting is sufficient for the salting required for a long trip,[6][א] in any case, even after washing it–unless he has soaked it in water–it is to be considered as if it were hot.[7][ב]

2. Immediately when [meat] is salted and salty liquid begins to come out,[8] the salty liquid coming out from it is considered hot. Therefore, whether one salts kosher meat with unkosher meat, or meat

Yad Adam

applies only to meat which has been salted to remove its blood.)

4. As to how much salt is actually needed to make the food "hot."

5. When broiling meat, only a small amount of salt need be applied to the meat to assist the heat in drawing out the blood. (*Chochmas Adam* 35:4) Even if only this quantity of salt has been added to a food (which is slightly more than the amount one would add to his food while eating it), it should be regarded as hot unless a great loss will be suffered. (See the additional note on topic 40, section 5 regarding the criteria to determine whether a great loss is present.)

6. This involves a greater quantity of salt (such that the meat has been completely immersed in the salt). This is sufficient to preserve the meat for a long period of time.

7. When food is salted to this degree, washing is not sufficient and the food must be soaked in water to remove its status of being hot.

2. The Liquid Flowing from Salted Food (ציר)

8. Salt has the power to draw out blood and

בתוך שיעור מליחה[9] אוסר אפי' במקום הפ"מ וסעודת מצוה[10]ג ולכן הציר הנוטף ממנו בתוך שיעור מליחה אפי' לא נמלח רק לצלי ואפי' שהה כמה ימים לעולם הוא רותח[11]ד דבציר אין חילוק אם נמלח לקדירה או לצלי דאע"ג דלא נמלח כמליחת קדירה ולא נחשב הבשר כרותח מ"מ הציר נחשב כרותח.ה

ג. אבל אחר ששהה שיעור מליחה המתבאר כלל ל' סימן ט'[12] בזה יש חילוק[13] דאם מלח בשר נבילה להוציא דם ושהה שיעור מליחה וקודם הדחה מלחו עמו או שהניחו עליו בשר כשר או גבינה בזה נחלקו הפוסקים כמו שביארנו לעיל כלל ל"ב סימן י"ח י"ט[14] ולכן במקום הפ"מ וסעודת מצוה ג"כ סמכינן על הפוסקים דלא נחשב כרותח והכל מותר בהדחה.ו

ג. סי' ל"א בש"ך סס"ק י"א.
ד. כו"פ שם.
ה. ואם נפל על גבינה או על כלי אוסר כדלעיל כלל ל"ב סימן י"ט ע"ש רמ"א ססעי' ה'.
ו. ש"ך ס"ק י"א.

יד אדם

other fluids which are present inside the meat. When fluids are being emitted from the meat and mix with the salt, they are called **ציר** (salty liquid).

9. The salted meat was mixed together with the other food within 18 (or 24) minutes after the salt was applied to the meat.

10. In such a case, it is as if the unkosher meat or cheese has been cooked together with the salted meat, resulting in a forbidden mixture. (Furthermore, if the case involves meat whose blood is being removed by this salting, then the salty fluid flowing from the meat will contain forbidden blood, and contact with this salty blood can make other food forbidden. However, if the mixture occurs more than 18 (or 24) minutes after the salt was applied, there are grounds to be lenient as noted in sections 3 and 4.)

11. We have learned that according to the letter of the law, meat is regarded as hot only if it is heavily salted, and there are grounds to be lenient after the meat has been salted 18 (or 24) minutes. This, however, is not the case with the salty liquid which drips from salted meat during the first 18 (or 24) minutes after the salt is applied. This liquid is to be considered as hot even if the meat had not been heavily salted, and it remains hot permanently. See note ה.

What is the status of salty liquid which drips out after 18 (or 24) minutes? There is a difference of opinion in this matter, as explained below in the notes on section 3.

3. Meat Which is Salted More Than 18 (or 24) Minutes

12. Meat had been salted to remove its blood, and the salt has already been on the meat for the required time of 18 (or 24) minutes.

13. Some say the salted meat is no longer regarded to be hot, whereas others rule that it remains hot until it is rinsed. (See note 14 for further details.)

14. Some authorities rule that the salted

ג. *Shach* 91:11 (end).
ד. *Kreisi u'pleisi* there.
ה. And if [the salty liquid] fell onto cheese or into a vessel, it makes [the food or vessel] forbidden, as noted previously—topic 32, section 19; refer there. *Rama* [chapter 91], end of paragraph 5.
ו. *Shach*, paragraph 11.

with cheese, together–[if they are together] during the time [required] for salting[9] [the foods] become forbidden even in a case where there is a great loss and [the food is needed] for a meal involving performance of a precept (*mitzvah*).[10ג] Furthermore, the salty liquid which drips from [meat] during the time [required] for salting–even if [the meat] was salted only for broiling and even if [the salty liquid] remained many days– is hot constantly.[11ד] For with regard to the salty liquid, there is no difference if it was salted enough for a pot or for broiling. For even though the [food] was not salted [the required amount] for salting to [cook in] a pot and the meat is [thus] not regarded as hot, nevertheless, the salty liquid [which drips from the meat] is regarded to be hot.[ה]

3. However, after remaining the amount of time [required] for salting which is explained in topic 30, section 9[12]–in this matter there is a difference [of opinion].[13] [For example,] if one salted unkosher meat to draw out [its] blood and [the meat] remained [salted] for the time [required] for salting, and before washing [it off] he salted with it, or placed upon it, kosher meat or cheese–in this matter the authorities differ, as we have explained previously in topic 32, sections 18 and 19.[14] Therefore, in a situation where there is a great loss and also [the food is needed] for a meal that involves performance of a precept, we can rely on the authorities who do not regard [such meat] as hot, and everything is permissible by washing off [the foods].[ו]

Yad Adam

meat does not remain hot after 18 (or 24) minutes and explain as follows: The juices which flow out of the meat after 18 (or 24) minutes are not regarded to be hot because the salt has lost its strength while it was drawing out the blood. In addition, any "hot" salty material remaining on the meat becomes nullified by these juices which continue to flow out of the meat after all of the blood has flowed out. As a result, the meat is no longer regarded to be hot, and other foods which come into contact with this meat will not become forbidden.

Others disagree and rule that even the juices which continue to flow out of the meat after the time required for salting has elapsed are also to be regarded as hot, and therefore, the meat with the salty material on it remains hot. As such, any food coming into contact with the salted unkosher meat will become forbidden unless the salt had been rinsed off from the meat. The *Chochmas*

ז. עיין שס בש"ך ובכו"פ.
ח. ר"ל מבלי מלח.

ד. בד"א דאמרינן דלאחר ששהה שיעור מליחה לא נחשב רותח[15] שמלחוהו להוציא דם דכיון דהמלח מוציא הדם אמרינן דתש כחו אבל בשר שמלחוהו שנית לאחר שהדיחו אותו ממליחה להוציא דמו ונגע בגבינה וכן בשר נבילה ובשר כשר שנמלחו או נגעו יחד לאחר שנמלח פעם ב' כיון שהמלח הזה לא עשה שום פעולה ולא תש כח המלח כלל לעולם הוא רותח אפילו שהה כך כמה ימים כ"ז שלא ידיחוהו ואוסר ההיתר שנגע בו ולא מהני אפילו הפ"מ וסעודת מצוה.[ז]

ה. הא דנאסר ע"י מליחה דוקא כשטמא מליח דנחשב כרותח ואז אע"פ שהטהור תפל[ח] הטמא שהוא רותח מבליע להיתר[16] וכ"ש בשניהם מלוחים שאפילו אין נוגעים זה בזה ממש אלא שמונחים בענין זה שהפליטה והציר של זה נוגעת בזה אפ"ה אסור.[17]

ולכן בשר שחוטה שמלחו עם בשר נבלה אפי' מלח הבשר להוציא דם וא"כ הכשרה טריד למיפלט דם ל"א איידי דטריד למיפלט לא בלע דנהי דלא בלע דם טרפה מ"מ בולע ציר טרפה[18]

יד אדם

Adam notes that the prevailing practice is to follow the second opinion, except when a great loss would be involved and the food is needed for a meal involving a precept. (See the additional note on topic 40, section 5 where these criteria are discussed.)

4. Meat Which Is Salted a Second Time

15. This question is asked in accordance with the lenient authorities mentioned in the previous section. The others would rule that the salted meat remains hot in any case.

5. Mixtures of Kosher and Unkosher Food Where One or Both Are Salted

16. This is an important basic principle that relates to salted food: When a salted food comes into contact with an unsalted food, the salted food is regarded as being hot and will therefore transmit its taste into the unsalted food. The unsalted food, on the other hand, will not transmit its taste into the salted food. (This is the opinion of the majority of authorities, as noted below.)

17. They become forbidden according to the *Chochmas Adam* even though only the liquids

ז. See there in the *Shach* and *Kreisi u'pleisi*.

ח. [The word *tafeil*] means unsalted.

4. When is it that we say: After [the meat] has remained for the time [required] for salting, [then] it is no longer regarded as hot?[15] [This is] when one salted it to draw out the blood, for since the salt has drawn out the blood, we say that its strength has become weakened. However, if one salted meat a second time after he had washed it from the salting which was [performed] to draw out the blood, and [the meat] came into contact with cheese—and similarly, if unkosher meat and kosher meat were salted [together] or came into contact with each other after being salted a second time—since this salt does not perform any action and [therefore] the strength of the salt has not weakened at all, [the food] is always hot, even if it stays [salted] like this many days, as long as he does not wash it. And it will prohibit any permissible food that comes into contact with it, and even a great loss and [use for] a meal involving a precept will not help [to permit it].[ז]

5. When we prohibit [mixtures of kosher and unkosher food] because of salting, it is only when the unkosher food is salted and is [therefore] considered hot. Then, even though the kosher food is unsalted,[ח] the unkosher food which is "hot" causes absorption of its taste into the permissible food.[16] And certainly [we prohibit mixtures] when both of them are salted, for [in such a case] even if they do not actually come into contact with each other but they are placed such that the emitted fluid and salty liquid of one is in contact with the other, even so, it is forbidden.[17]

Furthermore, if kosher slaughtered meat was salted with unkosher meat, even if the meat was salted to draw out the blood and therefore the kosher meat was involved in emitting blood, we do not say: "While it is involved in emitting [the blood] it does not absorb," for although [by this principle] it does not absorb the blood [emitted by] the unkosher meat, nevertheless, it absorbs the salty fluid [emitted] from the unkosher meat.[18] Salty fluid from a forbidden animal[19] or

Yad Adam

on their surfaces are in contact with each other. The *Aruch Hashulchan* (end of 91:22) rules that the food does not become forbidden in this case.

18. Thus, although we say that while the kosher food is emitting its own blood it will not absorb the blood from the unkosher meat, this principle does not apply to limit

ט. עיין סימן ע' סעיף ג' ובש"ך ס"ק כ'.

וציר נבלה וטריפה[19] ושרצים[20] אסור מה"ת דילפינן מדכתיב הטמאים[21] לרבות צירן.

אבל אם הטמא תפל והכשר מלוח אפילו נוגעים זה בזה מ"מ אין כח בבשר המלוח לחמם את הטמא שעי"ז יפלוט ויבליע בטהור וא"צ אלא הדחה[22] ומ"מ במקום שאין הפ"מ יש להחמיר גם בזה אם נוגעים זה בזה ממש דס"ל דאין חילוק בין טמא מלוח או טמא תפל[23] אלא כשאינם נוגעים רק שעומדין בסמוך בכדי שפליטה של זו נוגעת בזו ואז אפילו הדחה לא צריך ונ"ל דעכ"פ בזה[24] במקום הפסד קצת סגי בקליפה[25] כיון דרוב פוסקים מתירים לגמרי.[26] ט

ו. אע"ג דקיי"ל בחם ע"י אור תתאה גבר כמו שנבאר לקמן כלל ס'[27] מ"מ במליחה אין חילוק בין שהטמא המליח למטה והטהור התפל למעלה או להיפך דלעולם המליח מבליע בתפל ואינו בולע ממנו[28] דדוקא ברתיחת אור יש חילוק דמחמת אור שהוא גובר

יד אדם

absorption of other fluids emitted from the unkosher meat. The kosher meat will therefore become forbidden.

19. Whether it is *nevelah* (not slaughtered properly) or *terefah* (unkosher due to a disease or developmental abnormality of one of the internal organs).

20. Such as a mouse.

21. The letter ה in the word **הטמאים** (*Vayikra* [Lev.] 11:31) implies that fluids emitted by creeping animals are included in the prohibition to eat these animals.

22. According to the letter of the law, it is sufficient to wash off the kosher meat, since, as noted above, only salted food can transmit taste to another food, but unsalted food does not do so. (An exception to this rule is where the unkosher unsalted food is a liquid. In such a case, kosher salted food which comes into contact with it becomes forbidden unless it is completely dry. See section 8 below.)

23. These authorities rule that even if the kosher food alone is salted, it can cause the unkosher food to become "heated" and emit its taste into the other food. (*Taz* 70:10)

24. Where they actually are in contact with each other. (It has been mentioned that in this case, it is best to be stringent and forbid the piece of kosher meat.)

25. It is enough to remove a thin layer from the salted kosher meat where it came into

ט. See *Shulchan Aruch* 70:3 and *Shach* paragraph 20.

creeping animal[20] is forbidden by the Torah. We derive from [the expression]: "The unkosher ones,"[21] written [in the Torah] that their salty fluid is included [in the prohibition].

However, if the unkosher [meat] is unsalted and the [kosher] meat is salted, even if they come into contact with each other, nevertheless, there is not power in the salted [kosher] meat to "heat" up the unkosher [meat] such that [the unkosher meat] would thereby emit [its taste] and cause absorption [of this taste] into the kosher [meat]. As such, only washing [is required].[22] Nevertheless, in a situation where there is not a great loss, it is proper to be stringent also in this case if they actually came into contact with each other, for some [authorities] rule that there is no difference whether the unkosher [meat] is salted or the unkosher [meat] is unsalted.[23] However, where they are not in contact but they are only standing next to each other such that the emission of one is in contact with the other one—then even washing is not required. And it is my opinion that at least in such a situation[24] if there is [even] a small loss it is enough with peeling[25] since most authorities permit it completely.[26ט]

6. Even though it is established for us that [when one food has been] heated by a fire [then] the lower [food] dominates, as we will explain later on in topic 60 [section 10],[27] nevertheless, with salting there is no difference whether the unkosher salted food is below and the kosher unsalted food is above, or the other way around, for in all cases, the salty food will cause absorption into the unsalted food and it will not absorb from it.[28] It is only with regard to heat from fire that there is

Yad Adam

contact with the unsalted forbidden piece.

26. As such, in this case, even if we are to be stringent and say that the piece is forbidden, we can at least rely on the lenient authorities mentioned below in section 11 that salting causes emission only into the "peel" of the other food which comes into contact with it.

6. Does the Lower Food Dominate When It Is "Hot" Due to Salting?

27. This has also been explained in topic 42, section 7.

28. The salted food will not absorb taste from the unsalted food.

מרתיח את חבירו או מצנן אותו כי כן דרך תולדות האור אבל מחמת מליחה אין כח באותו שהוא תפל לבטל כח המליחה כי כן דרך המליחה שאינה יכולה להתבטל כ"א ע"י הדחה וכן אין כח במליחה לעשות התפל כמליח.[י]

ז. מ"מ נ"ל בספק טרפה ויש בו עוד צדדים להקל שנמלח עם טהור והיה טמא מלוח וטהור תפל למטה והטמא למעלה יש לסמוך בהפ"מ וסעודת מצוה ג"כ על הפוסקים[יא] דאף במליחה אמרינן תתאה גבר[29] דאע"ג דרמ"א כתב שם[30] דנוהגין כהפוסקים דאין חילוק[31] י"ל היינו דוקא בודאי טרפה אבל לא בס"ט[יב] ומותר עכ"פ ע"י קליפה אפילו לדידן.[32]

ח. הא דטהור מליח וטמא תפל מותר[33] היינו שהטמא יבש אע"ג שהוא לח קצת דכיון שהוא תפל אין כח במלח שבטהור להפליט[34][יג] אבל כשהטמא התפל צלול והטהור המלוח הוא ג"כ לח קצת אסור דכיון שהוא מלוח בולע מן הצלול אבל אם הטהור יבש לגמרי אע"ג שהוא מלוח אינו בולע מן הצלול התפל

י. סימן ק"ה ש"ך ס"ק מ"א.

יא. וכן סתם הש"ע שם סעיף י"א.

יב. וכעין זה ממש כ' המ"ב בסימן ל"ז לענין חהר"ל בס"ט שנתערב ע"ש.

יג. כ"כ הפ"א בסימן ל"א ומשמע אבל אם היה הטמא מלוח אע"ג שהוא יבש אסור הטהור וכן משמע ג"כ מדברי רמ"א סימן ל"א וצ"ע דבהדיא איתא באו"ה כלל י"ב סימן ז' וז"ל דאפילו שניהם מלוחים ורק האחד לח והשני יבש אותו היבש חשוב לכל דבר כתפל שאם הנבלה יבישה וכשרה לחה מותרת עכ"ל. והפ"א אזיל לשיטתו דס"ל דאם נתלחלח אח"כ אסור כמו שאכתוב בסמוך וצ"ל דר"ל יבש לא יבש לגמרי אלא ר"ל דבר גוש אע"ג שהוא לח קצת לאפוקי צלול.

יד אדם

7. Applying the Rule That "The Lower Substance Is Dominant" to Salted Food When There Are Other Grounds to Be Lenient

29. As such, the kosher food which is on the bottom will remain permissible.

30. Chapter 105, paragraph 11.

31. The salted forbidden food will cause the kosher food to be forbidden, no matter which one is above the other.

32. Even if we are to be stringent and say that the piece is forbidden, we can at least rely on the lenient authorities mentioned in section 11 who rule that salting causes emission only into the "peel" of a food which comes into contact with it. Thus, after removing a thin upper layer from the meat, the rest of it will be permissible.

8. Salted Kosher Meat Mixed with an Unkosher Unsalted Liquid

33. This has been mentioned in section 5 (third paragraph in the English translation).

34. And therefore the salted kosher food will not absorb any forbidden taste.

What is the rule if the unkosher food is salted and dry, and the kosher food is salted? It is probable that here also, the kosher food is permissible, as the *Chochmas Adam* states a difference, since as a result of the fire which predominates, it warms up its neighboring food or [its absence] cools it off, for such is the nature of what is derived from a fire. However, [when there is "heat"] due to salting there is no power in that [food] which is unsalted to nullify the power of the salt, for such is the manner of salting that [its effect] is not able to become nullified except by washing. And similarly, there is no power in salting to make the unsalted food as if it were salted.'

7. Nevertheless, it is my opinion that in a case of questionably unkosher meat where there are other aspects [which allow one] to be lenient–[such as where] it is salted with kosher meat and the [questionably] unkosher meat is [the one which is] salted, and the kosher meat which is unsalted is on the bottom and the [questionably] unkosher meat is on top–in cases of great loss where in addition [the food is needed for] a meal involving a precept, there [are grounds] to rely on the authorities[יא] [who rule] that even regarding salting we say the lower one is dominant.[29] For even though the *Rama* writes there[30] that we conduct ourselves according to the authorities who say there is no difference,[31] it is possible to say that this is so only where there is definitely unkosher meat, but not with doubtfully unkosher meat.[יב] And at least it should be permissible with peeling, even according to us [who follow the *Rama*].[32]

8. The rule that [a mixture of] salted kosher food and unsalted unkosher food is permissible,[33] this is when the unkosher food is dry, [or] even if it is a little moist, for since it is unsalted there is no power in the salt which is on the kosher food to cause [the unkosher food] to emit [its taste].[34][יג] However, if the unkosher unsalted food is liquid and the kosher food also is a little moist, it is forbidden, for since it is salted it absorbs from the liquid. But if the kosher food is completely dry, even though it is salted, it does not absorb from the unsalted liquid, for since it has already become dried out from its salt, it is as if it

י. *Shulchan Aruch* chapter 105 [paragraph 11]; *Shach* [there] paragraph 41.

יא. And so the *Shulchan Aruch* concludes there (chapter 105) in paragraph 11.

יב. And the *Masas Binyamin* writes precisely in accordance with this in chapter 37 regarding a "piece that is fit to honor [a guest]" where doubtfully forbidden meat became mixed. Refer there.

יג. This is what the *Pri Chadash* writes in chapter 91, and he implies that on the other hand, if the unkosher food were salted, even though it is dry, the kosher food would be forbidden. And so it is implied also from the words of the *Rama* in chapter 91 (paragraph 5). But this requires further study, as it is explicitly [written] in the *Issur v'heter* topic 12 section 7, and this is the wording: That even if both of them are salted and only one is wet and the second is dry, the dry one is regarded as unsalted for every matter, such that if the unkosher meat is dry and the kosher meat is wet, [the kosher meat remains] permissible. (end quote)

And the *Pri Chadash*, follows his own opinion [which we do not accept], as he rules that if [salted food] becomes wet after [being dried out] it is forbidden, as I will write shortly. And it is necessary to say that he means [the unkosher food is] "dry" [but] not "completely dry"; that is to say, it is a solid food, even though it is a little moist, excluding [only] a liquid.

דכיון דכבר נתייבש ממלחו ה״ל כאלו לא נמלח כלל[35][יד] ודוקא צלול ממש כחָלב וכיוצא בו אבל חֵלב רך שאינו מהותך לא מקרי צלול.[טו]

ט. בשר וגבינה שניהם מלוחים שנגעו זה בזה אם הם יבשים או לחים ולא מחמת מליחה[36] סגי בהדחה אבל אם הם לחים מחמת המלח[37] שניהם אסורים ול״א איידי דטריד למיפלט לא בלע דזה לא שייך רק בדם[38] דמישרק שריק אבל לא בשאר דברים.

ואם א׳ מהם מלוח וא׳ תפל המלוח מותר בהדחה שאינו מפליט מן התפל[טז] והתפל אסור שהוא בולע מן המלוח.[39][יז]

י. בשר מלוח שנפל לחלב אע״ג שהחלב אינו מלוח שניהם אסורין דהבשר חשוב כטהור מלוח לטמא תפל צלול דאסור[40] והחלב ג״כ אסור דכיון שהבשר מלוח מפליט לתוך החלב.

ואם החלב לבד מלוח י״א דהחלב מותר דדוקא הבשר אסור שבולע מן החלב, אבל החלב מותר דאין כח במלח אלא להבליע ולא להפליט[41] וי״א דהכל אסור דכיון דאחד מהם מלוח וצלול שניהם

יד. והפ״ח בס״ק ט״ו כתב דלפי מה דקיי״ל דלעולם לא פסק כח המלח א״כ אפילו בזה אסור דכיון דנתלחלח חוזר להיות רותח וכדעת הגאונים אבל בחו״ה לא משמע כן שהרי ס״ל דאפילו בנמלח להוציא דם לא פסק כח המלח כמש״כ הש״ך בשמו בסימן ל״א ס״ק י״א ואפ״ה כ׳ בכלל י״ב סימן ד׳ דאם נתייבש פ״א כבר פסק כח המלח ואפילו נתלחלח אח״כ.

טו. ש״ך שם ס״ק י״ד.

טז. וע׳ סי׳ ד׳ ה׳.

יז. שם סעיף ה׳ ובש״ך ס״ק י״ג.

יד אדם

in notes יג and יד. As a general rule, if salted food has dried out completely, the food is to be regarded as if it were unsalted. (*Aruch Hashulchan* 91:23)

35. The food will then be permissible if it is washed off, and the liquid is also permissible. (*Aruch Hashulchan* 91:23) What will be the rule if only the liquid is salted? Refer to section 10 below.

9. Meat and Cheese Coming into Contact with Each Other, Where One or Both Are Salted

36. For example, each of them was salted and the salt dried up on them, and they each became wet again. The salt in this case does not make the food "hot" and the food is to be regarded as unsalted. This is in accordance with the end of note יד on section 8 that once salted food dries out, the power of the salt has dissipated. Even if the food becomes wet again, we can disregard the presence of the salt. (*Kaf Hachayim*)

37. Such as where meat is salted and the meat becomes wet while the salt is drawing out the blood.

38. As such, if salted meat is emitting blood and other blood drips onto it, then this blood will not be absorbed into the salted meat (as mentioned above in note 18.) However, if the meat comes into contact with salted dairy food, it can absorb its flavor.

39. Again, these rules apply only if the salted food remains moist due to the salting.

were not salted at all.[35]יד And [the above stringency] is only for a real liquid like milk and similar things. However, soft fat which has not melted is not called a liquid.טו

9. If meat and cheese, both of which are salted, come into contact with each other—if they are dry, or wet but not [wet] due to salting,[36] it is enough with washing. But if they are wet due to the salt,[37] both of them are forbidden, and we do not say that while [the meat] is involved with emitting [blood] it will not absorb [the flavor of the cheese], for this applies only to blood[38] because it is slippery, but not to other things.

And if one of them is salted and one is unsalted, the salted one is permitted after washing it, since it does not cause [any flavor] to be emitted from the unsalted food,טז but the unsalted food is forbidden because it absorbs from the salty food.[39]יז

10. If salted meat fell into milk, even though the milk is not salted, both of them are forbidden, as the meat is regarded as kosher salted food [falling] into an unkosher unsalted liquid, so that it is forbidden.[40] The milk is also forbidden, for since the meat is salted, it emits [its taste] into the milk.

And if only the milk is salted, some say that the milk is permissible, for only the meat is forbidden because it absorbs from the milk, but the milk is permissible because there is no power in the salt except to cause [taste] to be absorbed [into other food] but not to cause [the other food] to emit [its taste];[41] but some say that the whole [mixture] is forbidden for since one of them is salted and is a liquid, both of them become for-

יד. And the *Pri Chadash* in paragraph 15 has written that according to the established ruling that [even after 18 minutes] the power of the salt never stops, as such, even in this case it should be forbidden, since when it becomes wet it reverts to being "hot," and this is in accordance with the opinion of the *geonim* (the Babylonian scholars who lived after the period of the *gemara*). However, in the *Issur v'heter* it does not appear so, for he holds that even when [meat is] salted to draw out the blood, the power of the salt does not stop, as the *Shach* writes in his name in chapter 91, paragraph 11. And even so, he writes in topic 12 section 4 that if it had been dried out at one time, the power of the salt has already dissipated, even if it becomes wet afterwards.

טו. *Shach* there (chapter 91,) paragraph 14.

טז. See [above,] sections 4 and 5 [for additional regulations that apply].

יז. *Shulchan Aruch* there, [chapter 91,] paragraph 5, and in the *Shach* paragraph 13.

Yad Adam

If the salted food has completely dried out, it is as if it were unsalted.

10. Mixtures of Meat and Milk Where One of Them Is Salted

40. In accordance with section 8 above. However, if the meat is completely dried out then both remain permitted, in accordance with the end of note יח.

41. Therefore, there would be no taste of meat emitted into the milk and it will be permissible.

אסורים דמבליע וגם מפליט מן הבשר וה"ה בשאר איסור.[42][יח]

יא. [יט] הא דאוסר במליחה מחלוקת בין גדולי הראשונים רוב הפוסקים ס"ל דלעולם אין כח במליחה להבליע אלא בכדי קליפה[43] אפילו היה האיסור שמן[כ] וי"א דדוקא באיסור כחוש דינו בקליפה אבל כשאחד מהם שמן לא מיבעי אם האיסור שמן ומלוח דמפעפע הרבה[44] אלא אפי' אם האיסור כחוש ומלוח[45] ובשר שמן נוגע בו אמרינן אזיל ההיתר ומפטם לאיסור[46] ועושה אותו שמן וחוזר האיסור ואוסר.[47][כא] ודוקא שהיה גם ההיתר מלוח דאז יכול לפטם[כב] אבל אם ההיתר תפל אע"ג דהמלוח הטמא אוסר מ"מ אין כח בהיתר לפטם כיון שהוא תפל ואינו אוסר רק כ"ק[48][כג] ובהפ"מ

יח. שם ס"ק ע"ו ובס"ק י"ז כ'* משמע אפילו מלוח הכל שרי** ודבריו אינם מדוקדקים דא"ל כוונתו אפילו מלוח הכל ז"א דאם הטמא לא מלוח אזי נאסר היטב והאו"ה מיירי בחלב מלוח ובשר יבש דהחלב מותר והבשר אסור כ"כ בהדיא בכלל י"ב סי' י"ב. ואם כוונתו הטהור מלוח ויבש א"כ מאי זה שכ' הכל שרי שהרי מיירי בא' טמא וצ"ל דמיירי מבו"ח והבשר יבש לגמרי אע"ג שהוא מלוח.

יט. סימן ק"ה. כ. סעי' ט' בהגהת רמ"א. כא. ש"ע שם. כב. ועיין לקמן כלל ס' סי' ד' ה' וכ"ש לענין מליחה. כג. ש"ך ס"ק כ"ח ומה שהקשה שם הש"ך דלמה לא כ' המחבר דין זה אפי' באיסור כחוש לגמרי י"ל דהמחבר ס"ל כמ"ש הש"ך בס"ק י"ט בשם הד"מ ע"ש.

יד אדם

42. For example, the rule is the same if kosher meat has fallen into a salted soup made from unkosher meat.

11. To What Extent Does Salting Prohibit a Food? The Difference Between Lean and Fatty Food

43. The taste of the salty food penetrates into the other food by only this small amount. As such, it is necessary to remove only a thin layer of food at its place of contact with the salty forbidden food.

44. We have learned above that if a food is salted and moist, its taste will spread into other foods that come into contact with it. Now we are learning (according to some authorities) that the degree of spreading into the other food will be greatest if the salted food is fatty, for then the taste will penetrate throughout the other food. As such, if a forbidden fatty food is salted and it comes into contact with permissible food, the latter will become completely forbidden. See also section 16 below.

45. In a case where the salted forbidden food is lean, only the peel of the food which comes into contact with it will ordinarily become forbidden. The *Chochmas Adam* now goes on to explain that if the permissible food is fatty and it is also salted, then the ruling is more stringent and the entire food will become forbidden.

46. The fatty taste of the permissible food will spread throughout the forbidden food.

47. Since this forbidden food is salted and is now "fatty," it can go on to make the piece of fatty meat completely forbidden.

48. The taste of the forbidden food, since it is not fatty, will penetrate only through the peel of the permissible food at their point of contact.

bidden because [the salt] causes absorption [of milk into the meat] and it causes emission from the meat [into the milk]. And so is the ruling for other forbidden [mixtures].[42]יח

11. יט"When we prohibit a food because of salting, there is a disagreement among the great early authorities. Most authorities rule that in all cases, salt has only enough power to cause absorption by the width of the peel,[43] even if the prohibited food was fatty.כ And others say that only when the prohibited food is lean, then the rule is [that the absorption is the width of] the peel. However, if one of them is fatty [then the rules are as follows]: There is no question that if the forbidden food is fatty and salted that [its taste] will spread a great deal [throughout the other food];[44] furthermore, even if the forbidden food is lean and salted,[45] and fatty meat comes into contact with it, we say that the permissible food comes and "fattens" the forbidden food[46] and makes it fatty, and the forbidden food can then go on and prohibit [the other food].[47]כא But this [applies] only if the permissible food is also salted, for [only] then it is able to fatten.כב However, if the permissible food were unsalted, even though the unkosher salted food prohibits [the permissible fatty food], nevertheless, there is no power in the permissible food to "fatten" [the other food] since it is unsalted, and it makes it forbidden only by the width of the peel.[48]כג And in case of

יח. [*Shach* chapter 91] paragraph 15; and in paragraph 17 he writes:* It is implied that even with salty food everything is permitted.** And his words are not exacting, for if we say that his intent is [to teach]: "Even if everything is salted [it is permitted]"—this cannot be so, because if the unkosher liquid were salted, then the dry food would become forbidden. Furthermore, the *Issur v'heter* (whom the *Shach* mentions as his source) is dealing with salted milk and dry meat, where the milk is permissible and the meat is forbidden. So it is written explicitly [there] in topic 12, section 12.

And if his intent is that [even if] the kosher food is salted and dry, [everything is permitted] if so, why is it written: "Everything is permitted"? [This also cannot be so,] since he is dealing [with a case] where one is unkosher. It is [therefore] necessary to say that he is dealing with meat and milk and the meat is completely dry, [and the meat and milk are permitted] even though [the meat] is salted.

יט. [Based on *Shulchan Aruch—Yoreh Deah*,] chapter 105.

כ. Paragraph 9 [there] in the note of the *Rama*.

כא. *Shulchan Aruch* there.

כב. And see further on, topic 60, sections 4 and 5, and [the limitations mentioned there regarding transmission of taste of broiling food] certainly would apply to salting.

כג. *Shach* [chapter 105,] paragraph 28. And regarding what the *Shach* asks there as to why the author [of the *Shulchan Aruch*] does not record this rule even when the forbidden food is completely lean, we can answer that the author [of the *Shulchan Aruch*] holds as the *Shach* had said in paragraph 19 in the name of the *Darkei Moshe*. Refer there. [This is explained further in topic 60, section 5.]

*The *Rama* (91:5) states that if kosher salted meat is completely dry, it will not absorb taste from an unkosher liquid. (This ruling has been mentioned above in section 8.) The *Shach* quoted here is commenting on this statement.

**The translation is in accordance with the second version mentioned below. The alternate translation, which is rejected by the *Chochmas Adam* in this paragraph, would be: "It is implied that even if everything is salted, it is permitted."

כד. ע״ש בש״ך ס״ק כ״ח וכ״כ הפ״ח בסי׳ ק״ה ס״ק י״ט וס״ק ל״ה.
כה. שם סעיף ט׳.

יש להתיר אפילו בשניהם מלוחים אם האיסור כחוש[49] ולא אמרינן במליחה אזיל היתר ומפטם.[50] כד

יב. ודוקא אם האיסור דבוק בחתיכה[51] או שנוגע ממש באיסור אבל אם אינו נוגע באיסור ממש אלא שנוגע בחתיכה הנוגעת באיסור כגון חֵלב אפי׳ שמן ואפי׳ דבוק בחתיכת בשר וחתיכת בשר נוגעת בבשר זה ולא נוגע בחלב עצמו אותה חתיכה מותרת אפי׳ בלא קליפה דאין כח במליחה לפעפע מחתיכה לחתיכה[52] דדוקא בבישול שיש שם רוטב או בצלייה שהוא רותח הרבה[53] אבל במליחה אע״ג דדינו כרותח דצלי׳[54] מ״מ לענין זה גרע דאינו מפעפע מחתיכה לחתיכה. כה

יג. ולפ״ז[55] אפי׳ יש כאן חתיכות הרבה הנוגעים בחלב[56] עד שיש בכולם ס׳ לבטל החלב אלא שאין בכל אחד ואחד

יד אדם

49. And it is enough to remove the outer peel of the meat, as long as the forbidden food is lean.

50. We may follow those authorities who rule that one food can fatten another only when they are broiled together (topic 60, section 3).

Note: The discussion here, which continues through section 14, represents the opinion of the *Bais Yosef*. See below beginning with section 15 for the customary practice in accordance with the *Rama*.

12. When Will Salting Cause Transmission of Absorbed Taste from One Piece to Another?—the Opinion of the "Bais Yosef"

51. This could happen if forbidden fat is left attached to kosher meat when the meat is salted to remove its blood.

52. It is true that salting causes the taste to go from the forbidden fat to the meat that is attached to it (or that is in contact with it). However, salting cannot transmit the absorbed forbidden taste through one piece of meat to another one. Even if a piece of meat is attached to the fat, this piece is not regarded as being part of the primary forbidden substance, but it is viewed as if it were a separate entity which has absorbed the taste of the forbidden fat. (This represents the opinion of the *Bais Yosef*. See section 15 below for the opinion of the *Rama*.)

53. The liquid in the pot of food, or the intense heat involved in broiling, assist in spreading the taste.

כד. Refer there to the *Shach*, paragraph 25; and the *Pri Chadash* writes similarly in chapter 105, paragraphs 19 and 35.
כה. Paragraph 9 there [in the *Shulchan Aruch* chapter 105].

great loss there are grounds to be lenient even if both of them are salted if the forbidden food is lean,[49] and we will not say with regard to salting that the permissible food goes and fattens.[50][כד]

12. And it is only when the [salted] forbidden food is attached (דבוק) to the [kosher] piece[51] or actually comes into contact with the forbidden food—[only then we say that the salt causes transmission of taste]. However, if it does not actually come into contact with the forbidden food but it comes into contact with a piece of food which is in contact with the forbidden food—for example: forbidden fat [is in contact with a piece of meat], even if [the fat] is very fatty and even if it is attached to the piece of meat, and [another] piece of meat comes into contact with this meat but it does not come into contact with the forbidden fat itself—that [other] piece is permissible even without peeling, as salting does not have the power to spread [absorbed taste] from one piece to [another] piece.[52] For it is only with cooking [that this can occur] where there is liquid, or with broiling where it is very hot,[53] but with salting, even though it is regarded as being hot like broiling,[54] regarding this matter it is more lenient [than broiling], as [salting] cannot spread [absorbed taste] from one piece into [another] piece.[כה]

13. And in accordance with this,[55] even if there are many pieces which are in contact with the forbidden fat[56] such that there is in all of them sixty [times the size of the fat] to nullify the fat, but there is not [sixty times the fat] in any one of them to nullify the fat, every

Yad Adam

54. This is a general principle: The "heat" from salting resembles the heat of broiling food. As the *Chochmas Adam* goes on to explain, the rule that salting cannot transmit taste from one food to another is an exception to the principle that the heat of salting resembles broiling. See also topic 60, end of section 4.

13. Transmission of Absorbed Taste When Many Pieces Are Present

55. The rule that salting will not cause transmission of taste from one piece to another.

56. There are many pieces of meat touching each other, some (or all) of which are in contact with the forbidden fat.

כו. ש"ך שם בסי' ל"ב ס"ק ח' בשם או"ה ויש שם ט"ס וצריך להיות או"ה כלל י"ד דין ח' ועיין לקמן בדין חנ"נ סי' י"ז.

לבטל החלב כל חתיכה שאין בו ס' אסור[57] ולהיפך[58] כל חתיכה שלא נגעה בחלב ממש אלא בזו שנגעה בחלב מותר ולסברא זו הסכים הב"י בש"ע שם.[59]

יד. ואם אינו יודע אם נגעה בכולן כולן אסורות דבכ"א הוא ס' מה"ת[60] ומ"מ אם נתערבה אחת מהם או נפלה לקדירה לא אמרינן חנ"נ[61] אפילו לדעת רמ"א[62] ויצטרך ס' נגד כולה אלא אם יודע כמה היה האיסור כגון שנגע בכזית חלב אין צריך ס' אלא נגד הכזית דכיון שלא הוברר האיסור שמא אין כאן איסור כלל ל"א חנ"נ.[63] [כו]

ואם ידוע שלא נגעה אלא בא' ואינו ידוע איזו היא ויש בכל החתיכ' ס' לבטל החלב כולן מותרות דחד בתרי בטיל[64] אבל אם אין

יד אדם

57. The total bulk of all the pieces of meat will not matter, since the pieces cannot transmit absorbed taste to one another. Rather, each piece which is in contact with the fat is to be evaluated as a separate entity.

58. If the pieces of meat total less than sixty times the fat, we do not say that all of them are forbidden. Rather, every piece...

59. (105:9) See section 15 below for the opinion of the *Rama*.

14. Transmission of Absorbed Taste When Contact Is Doubtful

60. For each and every piece, if it did come into contact with the forbidden fat (and the piece is not sixty times the size of the fat), then the taste of the fat would be recognizable in the meat and it would be forbidden by the Torah. When there is a doubt regarding a Torah prohibition, we must be stringent and avoid eating the doubtfully forbidden food.

61. We do not view the doubtfully forbidden piece as if it were inherently forbidden as an entire piece of unkosher meat (*nevelah*) and thereby require sixty times the size of the entire piece of meat to nullify it. Rather, (as the *Chochmas Adam* goes on to explain), we measure in accordance with how much forbidden taste is in the piece of meat. We say that the maximum amount of forbidden taste in the meat cannot be more than the size of the piece of forbidden fat that was in contact with it. As such, if the piece of fat was smaller than the piece of meat, we require that the contents of the pot be sixty times the size of the fat.

62. Whereas the *Bais Yosef* rules that a piece of food becomes inherently forbidden (*nevelah*) only when the prohibition of meat and milk is involved, the *Rama* rules that it applies to other forbidden foods as well. (See topic 44, section 7.) Nevertheless, the *Rama* is lenient in cases such as this where the food is

נו. *Shach* 92:8 in the name of the *Issur v'heter*. And there is a printer's error there, as it should read: *Issur v'heter* topic 14, rule 8. And see further on regarding the rule that a piece becomes inherently forbidden [topic 44], section 17.

piece which does not have sixty [times the fat] is forbidden.[57] And the other way around[58]—every piece which did not actually come into contact with the fat, even though [it was in contact] with this piece that was in contact with the fat, is permissible. And the *Bais Yosef* has agreed to this reasoning in the *Shulchan Aruch* there.[59]

14. And if one does not know whether [the forbidden fat] came into contact with all of them, all of them are forbidden, because each one [represents] a doubt according to the Torah.[60] Nevertheless, if one of these pieces became mixed [with others] or if it fell into a pot, we do not say that the piece is inherently forbidden (*nevelah*),[61] even according to the opinion of the *Rama*,[62] such that we should require sixty times all of it. Rather, if one knows how large the forbidden substance was, such as where [a piece of meat may have come into contact] with forbidden fat the size of an olive, it is not required to have more that sixty times the size of an olive, for since the forbidden state [of the meat] is not clarified, for perhaps there is no prohibition at all, we do not say that the piece [of meat] has become inherently forbidden.[63][נו]

[However,] if it is known that only one of the pieces came into contact [with the forbidden fat] but it is not known which one, and there is in all of the pieces [together] sixty times to nullify the forbidden fat, all of them are permitted. [We apply the rule] that one [forbidden piece mixed] with two [permissible pieces] is nullified.[64] Nevertheless, if

Yad Adam

only doubtfully forbidden. (If, on the other hand, it were certain that the fat did come into contact with the meat, then the *Rama* would say that the meat has become "inherently forbidden" *[nevelah]* and we would view it as if it were an entire piece of unkosher meat. If this piece of meat were to fall into a pot of food, everything in the pot would become forbidden unless its contents were at least sixty time the size of the piece of meat—even if the piece of fat which was in contact with the meat was smaller than the meat).

63. The principle that meat does not become inherently forbidden in cases of doubt is mentioned below in topic 44 section 17. Compare with topic 44 section 4 below, where similar reasoning applies.

64. It is explained in topic 51 (sections 1 and 9), that if pieces of permissible food are mixed together with pieces of forbidden food and it is impossible to determine which pieces are the forbidden ones—then if the majority of the pieces are permissible, the forbidden pieces will be nullified and all of

כז. ק״ה סעיף ט׳.
כח. שם.

בכולן ס׳ לבטל החלב גם בזה אסור שהרי חלב עם בשר הוי מבשא״מ[65] וא״כ אם יבשלם יתן טעם חלב.[66]כז

טו. אבל רמ״א כ׳ דמנהג מדינותינו לשער כל מליחה בששים[67] ובזה יש קולא וחומרא קולא דאפי׳ חתיכה זו שנגעה בחלב ואין בה לבד ס׳ נגד החלב כיון שיש שם עוד חתיכה שנגעו זה בזה הרי אנו מצרפים הכל ואמרינן דחלב מפעפע מחתיכה לחתיכה כמו בבישול[68] ומכל מקום כל חתיכה שנגעה בחלב צריך קליפה דלא אמרינן ודאי דמפעפע אלא ספק. וא״כ ממ״נ אם מפעפע הרי הכל מצטרף לבטל ואם אינו מפעפע הרי לרוב הפוסקים אינו אוסר רק כ״ק אפי׳ בשמן.

וגם יש לפ״ז חומרא דאם אין בין הכל ס׳ אז כל חתיכה אפי׳ לא נגעה בחלב או בחתיכה שדבוק בה החלב אלא שנגעה בחתיכה אחרת שנגעה בחתיכה זו שהחלב דבוק בה כולן אסורות.[69]כח (מ׳)

יד אדם

the pieces may be eaten. As such, the one forbidden piece of meat (which has absorbed the taste of the fat) will be nullified by the others which are in the majority. (It is, however, customary to discard one of the pieces of meat.)

65. Even though they come from the same animal, they are regarded as two different foods. (This is the case if the meat is lean. Refer to topic 51, section 8.) In a mixture where two different kinds of food are involved, the rule that a forbidden food becomes nullified by a majority of permissible food does not apply. Rather, by rabbinical decree, it is necessary that the permissible pieces should be sixty times the forbidden substance. (topic 51, section 9). Therefore, although the one forbidden piece of meat has been nullified due to the presence of a majority of permissible pieces, the flavor of the forbidden fat absorbed into it has not been nullified. (See the next note.)

66. If one will go on and cook the pieces of meat together in one pot, the taste of the fat will spread to all the pieces and make all of them forbidden (unless the amount of permissible food is sixty times the forbidden food). The rabbis therefore prohibited all of the pieces (unless sixty is present) to prevent the possibility that one will mistakenly cook them together (thereby making all of them forbidden) and then eat them (topic 51, section 9).

15. When Will Salting Cause Transmission of Taste From One Piece to Another?—The Rama's Opinion

67. The *Rama* rules that when there are

כו. *Shulchan Aruch* 105:9.
כח. *Ibid.* (105:9)

there is not sixty times among all of them to nullify the forbidden fat, also in this case it is forbidden, because forbidden fat and meat are regarded as two different types of food,[65] and therefore if one will cook them [together the forbidden piece] will give forth the taste of the forbidden fat.[66]כז

15. However, the *Rama* has written that the custom in our lands is to measure all [cases] of salting with sixty,[67] and in this there is a lenient aspect and a stringent aspect. The lenient aspect is that even if this piece [of meat] which came into contact with forbidden fat does not have sixty times the forbidden fat itself, since there are other pieces there that are in contact with one another, we combine everything and say that the forbidden fat spreads from piece to piece, as it does in cooking.[68] Nevertheless, every piece which came into contact with the forbidden fat requires peeling, as we do not say that [the taste] certainly spreads [through that piece into the others], but it is doubtful. As such, no matter how you look at it, [these rulings are proper,] for if [the taste of the fat] spreads [to all the pieces of meat], all [of the pieces] combine to nullify [the fat], and if it does not spread, behold, according to most authorities, [salting] forbids only the width of the peel, even with fatty food.

And there is also a stringent aspect according to this, for if there is not [all together] sixty [times the forbidden fat], then each piece, even if it did not come into contact with the forbidden fat or with the piece attached to the forbidden fat, but it came into contact with another piece [and this other piece] was in contact with the piece attached to the forbidden fat, all of them are forbidden.[69]כח (See *Binas Adam*, section 40.)

Yad Adam

many pieces of meat touching each other, some of which are touching forbidden fat, we assess the total of all of them when determining if sixty times the forbidden fat is present. This is in contrast to the opinion of the *Bais Yosef* in section 13 above who treats each piece as a separate entity.

68. As such, if all of the pieces together equal sixty times the fat, they will all be permissible.

69. In this case, the *Bais Yosef* would permit all the pieces that did not directly touch the fat, even if sixty times the forbidden fat were not present.

כט. וכי״ד סי׳ ס״ד.
ל. שם ס״ק ל״ח.
לא. וכ״ל דר״ל כדי קליפה דמ״ש מדין שאח״ז.

טז. עוד מנהגינו שאין לחלק בין כחוש לשמן דאפילו אם האיסור כחוש דינו כשמן דאין אנו בקיאין איזה הוא שמן[70] ומ״מ בהפ״מ יש להתיר במליחה ע״י קליפה אם האיסור כחוש לפי ראות עינינו כגון בהמה כחושה וכיוצא בו אע״ג דיש לגזור אטו שמן.[71]

ואם האיסור הוא דבר כחוש בטבעו כגון החוטין והקרומין האסורין[72] וגיד הנשה[73] ושומנו[74] הנזכרים בכלל כ״ח[כט] יש להתיר ע״י קליפה אם יש הפסד קצת דבאלו לא שייך למיגזר אטו שמן[75] ואם האיסור כחוש והוא איסור דרבנן ולא שייך בו שמנונית אפי׳ אין בו הפסד קצת א״צ אלא כ״ק.[ל]

יז. ולענין חמץ בפסח אע״ג שהוא כחוש מחמירינן לאסור אותה חתיכות שנמצאה החטה עליה כולה[76] וחתיכות האחרות הנוגעות בחתיכה זו ולא נגעו בחטה בודאי מותרין ע״י קליפה[77] ואם מסופק שמא נגעה החטה בשאר חתיכה כולן אסורין[78][לא] ואף שידעינן בודאי שלא נגע אלא באחד מהן ולא ידעינן

יד אדם

16. When Do We Differentiate Between Lean and Fatty Food?

70. It is often difficult to decide whether a given piece of meat is fatty or lean. Therefore, even when salted meat is lean, we still apply the more stringent status of salted fatty meat to it. We will thus prohibit the entire piece which comes into contact with a forbidden salted food, and peeling alone will not be sufficient. (See section 11 above.)

71. By being lenient only when there would be a great loss (see additional note on topic 40, section 5), this will prevent one from mistakenly permitting a food which came into contact with a salty forbidden food which is fatty.

72. These are structures in the animal which must be removed together with the forbidden fat.

73. The *gid hanashe* is the sciatic nerve, which originates from the spinal cord and courses into the back of the thigh. It is forbidden to be eaten by Torah law. (*Bereishis* [Gen.] 32:33)

74. The fat which runs along the *gid hanashe* is permitted by Torah law but is forbidden by rabbinical decree.

75. Since these structures are always lean, they could not be confused with fatty food.

כט. And in *Yoreh Deah* chapter 64.
ל. *Shach* 105:38.
לא. It is my opinion that this means [they are forbidden] only by the width of their peel, from what is stated in the ruling after this.

16. It is also our custom not to differentiate between lean and fatty [food], in that even if the forbidden food is lean, it is to be regarded as if it were fatty, as we are not expert as to which [food] is fatty.[70] Nevertheless, in situations involving a great loss, one can permit [the food], where salting is involved, by peeling [it] if the forbidden food is lean according to our assessment, such as [with meat from] a lean animal or similar things. [One may be lenient in such cases], even though it is proper to rule [that the food is prohibited] due to [situations involving forbidden] fatty food.[71]

But if the forbidden food is something lean by its nature, such as "cords" and membranes which are forbidden,[72] or the *gid hanashe*[73] and its fat[74] which are mentioned in topic 28,[כט] one can permit [meat salted together with any of these] by peeling if there is a bit of a loss, for with these it is not appropriate to decree [that they are forbidden] due to [confusion with] fatty food.[75] And if the forbidden food is lean and is prohibited by the rabbis and there is no fattiness related to it [at all], then even without a bit of a loss, [the food] requires only peeling.[ל]

17. And regarding *chometz* on *Pesach*, even though *chometz* is lean, we are stringent to prohibit the entire piece upon which a grain of wheat was found.[76] And if other pieces came into contact with this piece but did not touch the grain of wheat, they are certainly permissible by peeling.[77] But if it is doubtful whether the wheat came into contact with other pieces, all of them are forbidden.[78][לא] And even if we know with certainty that it was in contact with only one of them and

Yad Adam

17. Salted Mixtures of chometz

76. If a piece of meat was salted and a grain of wheat was found on it, the meat will absorb taste from the grain (which is *chometz*) and become forbidden. If, on the other hand, the meat was not salted, it would be sufficient to rinse off the meat. (*Orach Chayim* 467:14.) This stringent ruling applies only if the grain shows signs of having become *chometz* (it has split or has become softened). In addition, the grain must be moist from the salting (*Biur Halacha* there). If these two conditions are not present, the meat becomes permissible after washing it off.

77. Even peeling is not required if it is certain that the grain of wheat itself did not touch the other pieces. See *Mishnah Berurah* 467:75 and *Shar Hatsiyun* 135.

78. Here, however, we will not be strict to forbid the pieces in their entirety. Rather, in such cases of doubt, we permit each piece of meat after "peeling" off its outer layer.

באיזו נגע מדינא כולן אסורין וטעונין קליפה דחמץ בפסח לא בטל ברוב[79] וא״כ אם נתבשלה בלא קליפה אוסרת תערובתן[80][לב] ואם ירצה יכול למכור הכל לנכרי[81] או להשהות החתיכות האחרות המונחות עמה עד אחר הפסח.[82]

ודוקא שמצא החטה בעודה מונחת במלח קודם שהדיחו אבל אם מצאה לאחר שהדיח הבשר ע״כ נפל לאחר המליחה דאל״כ היה נופל ע״י ההדחה[83] ואם מצא בתוך עוף שהוא חלול אפילו לאחר הדחה אסור דאמרינן מה שלא נפל הוא מחמת שמונח בתוכו ומכל מקום אם יש לתלות שעכשיו נפל אפי׳ בעוף מותר.[לג]

וכל זה שנמצא במליחה להוציא דם אבל אם נמצא בחבית שמלחוהו שם[84] כל מה שמונח בציר אסור כולו[85][לד] ועיין בחיבורי ח״א כלל קכ״ב.

לב. עיין בא״ח סי׳ תס״ז במ״א ס״ק ל״ג.
לג. שם במ״א ס״ק ל׳.
לד. שם במ״א.

יד אדם

79. We are more stringent with *chometz* than with other forbidden foods, and we say that it does not become nullified. As such, the leniency mentioned at the end of section 14 (that doubtfully forbidden pieces are nullified by a majority of permissible ones—see note 64) will not apply.

80. If pieces require peeling (because there is doubt whether they may have come into contact with the wheat) but they were not peeled and were cooked in a pot with other food, the entire contents of the pot becomes forbidden. (See *Mishnah Berurah* 467:75.)

81. In the case where many pieces were salted together and a grain was found on one of them, all of them may be sold to a gentile. Even though meat that is cooked together with a grain of wheat on *Pesach* would have to be destroyed (since the taste of *chometz* was absorbed into it), we are nevertheless more lenient when salting is involved. (*Mishnah Berurah* 467:78)

82. The other pieces, (the ones that did not come into contact with the grain) may be kept until after *Pesach*. (According to some authorities, he may also keep the piece that actually came into contact with the grain if he removes the place of contact. See *Mishnah Berurah* 467:77 and *Shar Hatsiyun* 138.)

83. The grain would have fallen off the meat when the salt was washed off. The meat would then be permissible by rinsing it off.

84. Meat was salted to be preserved and placed in a barrel. A collection of salty fluid which had dripped from the meat is present

לב. See *Magen Avraham* 467:33 in *Orach Chayim*.
לג. *Magen Avraham* there, 467:30.
לד. *Magen Avraham, Ibid.*

we do not know which one it touched, according to the law, all of them are forbidden and require peeling, since *chometz* on *Pesach* is not nullified by a majority [of permissible pieces].[79] As such, if it is cooked without having been peeled, it prohibits the mixture.[80]לב [Nevertheless,] if one desires, he may sell the entire thing to a gentile,[81] or he may keep the other pieces that were lying with it until after *Pesach*.[82]

[All of the above applies] only where he found the wheat while still lying in the salt before [the meat] was washed off. However, if one found it after the meat was washed off, then perforce, [the wheat] must have fallen [onto the meat] after the salting, for if this were not the case, if would have fallen off [the meat] during the washing.[83] [However,] if it is found inside poultry which is hollow, even [when found] after washing, it is forbidden because we say that the reason it did not fall off [during washing] is because it was lying inside it. Nevertheless, if we can attribute that it fell [into the poultry] now [after the salt was washed off], even regarding poultry it is permissible.לג

And all of this applies where [the wheat] was found during salting to draw out blood. However, if it was found in a barrel in which they have salted it,[84] whatever is lying in the salty fluid is entirely forbidden.[85]לד And refer to my work *Chayei Adam*, topic 122 [beginning with section 20].

Yad Adam

at the bottom of the barrel and a grain was found in this fluid.

85. Since this fluid is very salty, the grain of wheat is to be regarded as having been cooked together with any meat that is in contact with the fluid.

כלל מד

דין איסור והיתר על ידי בישול ודין חתיכה נעשית נבילה ואפשר לסוחטו

(סימן צ״ב)

א. חתיכת בשר שנפלה ליורה של חלב רותח או להיפך שנפל מעט חלב לקדירה רותח של בשר משערין בששים שאם יש ששים נגד הבשר או החלב מותר[1] ואם לאו הכל אסור.

ואין חילוק לדידן אם היתה החתיכה כולה ברוטב[2] או חציה ברוטב[3] ונפל איסור על מה שחוץ לרוטב (שיטת ר״י)[4] דלעולם אם יש ס׳ בכל מה שבקדירה נגד האיסור מותר ואם לאו הכל אסור שהרוטב מבלבל ומוליך הטעם בשוה בכל הקדירה.[5]

יד אדם

1. Meat and Milk Which Are Cooked Together; A Piece of Meat in a Pot of Liquid Upon Which Milk Has Fallen

1. When sixty is present, the taste of the other substance will not be noticeable and it becomes nullified. (See topic 51, section 8.) For example, assume that milk has fallen into a pot containing hot liquid and pieces of meat. If the milk falls directly into the liquid, then the mixture will be permissible if the pot contains at least sixty times the milk. If the milk lands on one of the pieces of meat, then the rules mentioned below will apply.

2. We are dealing with a pot containing hot liquid and several pieces of meat, and some milk fell onto one of the pieces of meat. If the milk has fallen directly onto a piece of meat which is completely submerged except for a portion of its upper surface which protrudes above the surface of the liquid, then the rule is the same as stated in note 1: If the total contents of the pot are equal to at least sixty times the milk, then the mixture is permitted, and it is not necessary for the piece of meat itself to be sixty times the milk.

It should be noted that when the *Chochmas Adam* states that the piece is completely in the liquid, this does not mean that all surfaces of the piece are completely surrounded by liquid. Rather, the meaning is: It is completely in the liquid except for a portion of its upper surface which protrudes above the surface of the liquid. (This can be the case where the top of the piece is rounded. *Kaf Hachayim*, end of 92:5).

Topic 44
Laws Concerning Forbidden Food and Permissible Food Which Are Cooked [Together]; the Rule That "A Piece Becomes Inherently Forbidden" and Whether It Is Possible to Extract [Forbidden Taste]

(based on *Shulchan Aruch–Yoreh Deah* chapter 92)

1. If a piece of meat fell into a pot of hot milk—or the other way around, if a bit of milk fell into a hot pot of meat—we measure with sixty [as follows]: If there is sixty times the meat or the milk, it is permissible;[1] and if not, everything is forbidden.

According to our practice, there is no difference if the piece is completely in the liquid,[2] or if it is partially [submerged] in the liquid[3] and a forbidden substance fell on [the portion] that was outside of the liquid. (This is the opinion of the *Ri*.)[4] Thus, in all cases, if everything which is in the pot [measures] sixty times the forbidden substance, it is permissible; but if not, everything is forbidden. [This is because] the liquid mixes up and transmits the [forbidden] taste equally throughout everything which is in the pot.[5]

Yad Adam

3. The meaning is: It is partially submerged such that a substantial part of the of the piece protrudes above the surface of the liquid (more than just a portion of its upper surface). Again, the rule is that the piece is to be regarded as if it were completely submerged in the liquid, and it is governed by the same rule mentioned in note 1.

4. The *Ri* is the one who rules that whatever is partially submerged in the liquid in the pot is to be regarded as if it were completely in the liquid. We will soon learn that Rashi rules differently: that the portion of the meat outside of the liquid is to be regarded as if it were outside the pot.

5. As such, we do not say that the piece of meat upon which the milk fell is forbidden and the rest of the contents of the pot will be permissible. Rather, if the pot does not contain sixty times the quantity of the milk, the entire pot becomes forbidden. Of course, we are dealing with a situation in which the contents of the pot have been heated over a fire and are hot (as defined in topic 42, section 9). If the meat upon which the milk falls is cold, then the more lenient rulings men-

א. ל״ב וש״ך שם.

ומ״מ יש חילוק[6] דאם כולה ברוטב אף החתיכה עצמה מותרת שהרי תיכף כשנפלה נתחלק טעם האיסור בכולן[7] אבל במקצתה חוץ לרוטב יש להחמיר במקום שאין הפסד מרובה לאסור אותה החתיכה דיש אומרים דכיון דמקצתה חוץ לרוטב אין האיסור מתפשט בכולה[8] (שיטת רש״י דסבירא ליה דבמקצתה ברוטב אין כל מה שבקדרה מצטרף)[9] דבשלמא כל הקדירה מותר ממה נפשך[10] אם היה מפעפע לתוך הקדירה הרי יש כאן ס׳ לבטל ואם לא פעפע לפנים פשיטא דמותר[11] אבל החתיכה עצמה שמא אינו מפעפע בכל הקדירה וא״כ נ״נ[12] ולכן יש אומרים דאסורה[13] ולפ״ז שאר חתיכות הנוגעות בחתיכה זו צריכין נטילה.[14]א

יד אדם

tioned in topic 42 will apply. (See sections 1 and 6 there.)

6. Although the *Chochmas Adam* has just stated that there is no difference whether the piece of meat on which the milk fell is partially or fully submerged, this is only in accordance with the opinion of the *Ri*. However, there is a practical difference if Rashi's opinion (mentioned in note 4) is taken into account, as the *Chochmas Adam* now goes on to explain.

7. The taste of the forbidden substance (in this case, the milk) will immediately spread equally throughout all of the pieces in the pot. (Nevertheless, although the piece itself is permitted, one should remove and discard a thick layer from the part of the meat upon which the milk has fallen. See topic 60, section 7.)

8. The milk which falls onto the piece of meat does not spread throughout the pot but its taste spreads only through the part of the meat which is above the liquid. (See the additional note on topic 40, section 5 regarding the criteria to determine whether a great loss is present.)

(Rashi is being explained in accordance with the *Bach* and *Shach*, cited by *Matamei Hashulchan* 92:4. The *Taz*, on the other hand, understands Rashi to be saying that the taste spreads through the entire piece of meat. Since the *Chochmas Adam* here bases himself on the *Shach* as stated in note **א**, the notes here will also follow the opinion of the *Shach*.)

9. According to *Rashi*, the milk will remain absorbed in the portion of that piece of meat which is above the level of the liquid, and it will not spread into the rest of the contents of the pot. As such, the portion of the meat which is above the liquid is forbidden. Furthermore, according to Rashi, the remaining contents of the pot will always be permissible since the taste of the milk never reaches it.

10. If the pot contains sixty times the milk, the remaining food in the pot is permissible, whether one follows the opinion of the *Ri* or *Rashi*.

א. *Shulchan Aruch* chapter 92 and *Shach* there, paragraph 4.

Nevertheless, there is a difference,[6] for if the entire [piece] is in the liquid, even the piece itself is permitted, since, immediately when [the forbidden substance] falls on it, the taste of the forbidden substance is spread out into all of them.[7] However, if part of [the piece of meat] is outside of the liquid, it is proper to be stringent in a case where there is not a great loss and prohibit that piece, as some authorities say that since part of it is outside the liquid, the forbidden substance does not spread into all of it.[8] (This is the opinion of *Rashi,* who rules that if part of it is in the liquid, whatever else is in the pot does not combine with it.)[9] Although it is so that in any case, whatever is in the pot is permissible[10]—for if [the taste of the forbidden food] would spread throughout the [contents of the] pot, then there is sixty to nullify; and if it does not spread inside [the pot], then it is obvious that it is permissible[11]—however, regarding the piece itself, perhaps [the milk] does not spread [from it] throughout the rest of the pot, and if so, it becomes inherently forbidden *(nevelah).*[12] As such, some [authorities] rule that [the piece] is forbidden.[13] And according to this [ruling], the other pieces that come into contact with this piece require removal [of their point of contact].[א][14]

Yad Adam

11. The other contents of the pot must be permissible, since the milk never spread into them.

12. Since (according to *Rashi*) the portion of the piece of meat above the liquid absorbs and retains the milk, it will become *nevelah* (it will become as if it were a piece of unkosher meat).

13. Some later authorities rule that we are to follow Rashi's opinion, and it is therefore proper to remove the piece from the pot and discard the portion which was above the liquid. (Nevertheless, if the portion of the piece above the liquid is sixty times the amount of milk which has fallen onto it, the piece will remain permissible according to everyone.)

14. *Netilah* (removing) involves removing a layer of the food equal in thickness to the width of the thumb, and involves a much thicker layer than *k'lipah* (peeling).

When food is present in a pot of hot liquid, the taste of all of its contents spreads completely throughout each other. This is not the case with hot broiled foods which come into contact with each other (where the foods being cooked are not immersed in liquid), for in such a case the taste of one penetrates only into the outer layers of the other. When a piece of meat lies above the level of the liquid in a pot, then it has the status of meat which is being broiled.

According to *Rashi,* when milk falls onto the portion of a piece of meat which lies

ב. ע׳ ש״ך ס״ק ו׳ וס״ק י״ג.

ב. ואם ניער אח״כ[15] הקדרה או כיסה אותה[16] יש להחמיר ג״כ להצריך ס׳ נגד כל החתיכה שהרי לסברא זו[17] נעשית החתיכה נבילה[18] אך במקום הפסד אין לחוש לכל זה דהעיקר כדעת הפוסקים[19] כיון דמקצתה ברוטב הרוטב מבלבל תיכף הטעם ומוליך הטיפה בכל הקדירה בשוה ואפילו בבשר בחלב[20] וכל שכן בשאר איסורין.[ב]

ג. והוא הדין אפילו כולו חוץ לרוטב[21] ותיכף[22] כשנפל האיסור ניער או כיסה הקדרה מצטרף הכל לבטל האיסור דעל ידי הניעור או הכיסוי נתחלק הטעם בכל הקדרה ודוקא שניער וכיסה כל כך עד שהרוטב היה עולה למעלה מעל החתיכה אבל אם לא ניער

יד אדם

2. A Partially Submerged Piece with Absorbed Forbidden Taste Which Becomes Mixed into the Pot

15. We are dealing with a case where milk fell on a partially submerged piece of meat. The pot was then stirred, mixing this piece together with the other contents of the pot.

16. Covering the pot causes the heat and steam of the pot to rise, so that even those parts of the food which are outside the liquid will be regarded as if they were in the liquid.

17. According to *Rashi*, who rules that if a piece is partially submerged in the liquid, the portion which is not in the liquid is to be regarded as completely outside of it.

18. The reasoning is as follows: When milk falls on to the piece of meat, the entire portion of the piece which is above the liquid immediately becomes forbidden as a mixture of meat and milk. As such, when the forbidden piece becomes mixed into the liquid (by stirring or covering the pot), it will

above the liquid, then we are to regard the portion above the liquid as a piece of unkosher meat. As such, if other pieces of meat come into contact with the part that is above the liquid, it is as if they are touching a piece of unkosher meat which is being broiled. These other pieces do not become completely forbidden, but they will be permitted once their points of contact are removed. According to the *Ri*, on the other hand, the partially submerged piece of meat and any others which are in contact with it remain permissible as long as the pot contains sixty times the amount of milk that fell onto the piece.

Actually, there are some authorities who rule that even according to *Rashi*, the pieces remain permissible without removing their points of contact with the forbidden piece. The *Chochmas Adam* rules in accordance with this more lenient opinion. See section 6 below.

ב. *Shach* there [chapter 92] paragraphs 6 and 13.

2. And if one stirred the pot afterwards[15] or covered it,[16] it is proper to be stringent also to require [the pot to contain] sixty times the entire [upper portion of the] piece, since according to this opinion,[17] the piece had become inherently forbidden.[18] However, in case of a loss, one need not be concerned about all this as the fundamental ruling is in accordance with those authorities[19] [who rule that] since part of [the piece of meat] is in the liquid, the liquid mixes the taste immediately and transmits the drop [of liquid] throughout the entire pot equally. [This is the rule] even regarding [mixtures of] meat and milk,[20] and certainly with other prohibitions.[ב]

3. And the rule is the same even if [the piece of meat] is entirely outside of the liquid[21] if immediately,[22] when the forbidden substance had fallen [onto the meat], he has stirred or covered the pot [as then] everything combines together to nullify the forbidden food, since by the stirring or covering the taste becomes spread throughout the entire pot. But this is only if he stirred or covered such that the liquid would rise upward above the piece. However, if he did not stir so

Yad Adam

be necessary for the pot to contain sixty times that part of the piece of meat to nullify it (and it will not be sufficient to have sixty times the amount of milk that fell onto the piece). The *Ri*, on the other hand, would rule that the piece of meat never became forbidden and it certainly could not go on to prohibit the other contents of the pot.

If the meat has not absorbed milk but has absorbed a forbidden substance (such as melted forbidden fat), we can be more lenient in accordance with section 7 below.

19. Including the *Ri*.

20. Which is more stringent than other mixtures. (See section 7 below.)

3. A Piece Outside the Liquid Which Has Absorbed Forbidden Taste

21. For example, a piece of meat is partially submerged in the liquid, and there is a piece of meat on top of it which is not in contact with the liquid at all. Some milk then spills onto this piece of meat which is outside of the liquid. If the following action is performed, then the meat will have the same status as if it had been immersed in the liquid.

22. What is the time interval meant by the word "immediately"? Perhaps it denotes the amount of time it would take for the liquid to be fully absorbed into the piece of meat.

כל כך רק שמקצתה היתה בקדירה לא מהני (דהיינו לרש"י)[23] ואם לא ניער תיכף ומיד כשנפל לא מהני מה שמנער אח"כ דכיון שכבר קיבלה טעם מן האיסור נ"נ[24] וקיי"ל אפשר לסוחטו אסור[25] כדבסמוך.[26]

ד. ואם נפלה על חתיכה אחת אע"פ שהוא חוץ לרוטב אם אינו יודע על איזו חתיכה נפלה[27] אע"פ שלא ניער תיכף מותר לנער או לכסות הקדרה בכדי שתתפשט הטעם בכולו[28] ולא אמרינן דמבטל איסור לכתחלה[29] כיון שאין כאן איסור ודאי דשמא אין כאן איסור כלל דשמא לא נפלה על חתיכה זו[30] וכן לא אמרינן דחתיכה נעשה נבילה[31] דכיון שאינו יודע איזו חתיכה היא לא אמרינן דחתיכה נ"נ כדלקמן סימן י"ז וזהו לדעת הב"י.

אבל דעת רמ"א דגם בזה אסור לנער דכיון דהיה אפשר לברר

יד אדם

This could be visually observed. (See *Aruch Hashulchan* 92:10.)

23. According to the *Ri*, the meat need not be completely submerged, since he rules that the taste will spread from it throughout the pot even if it only partially submerged.

24. During the delay, the meat has become a piece of forbidden food according to both the *Ri* and *Rashi*. When this piece is then mixed into the pot, it will be necessary that the contents of the pot be sixty times the piece of meat. On the other hand, if the pot is stirred without delay, it is required that the contents be only sixty times the amount of milk that had fallen onto the piece of meat.

25. The Hebrew phrase is **אפשר לסוחטו אסור**. This phrase is best understood as a question and answer, as follows: "Is it possible to extract [all of the forbidden taste? No! Therefore, the food remains] forbidden."

With regard to the case in question here, the moment the piece of meat becomes forbidden because it absorbs milk or a forbidden substance, the piece remains permanently forbidden. This is the case even if the piece will be placed in a pot of hot liquid which will cause forbidden taste to be extracted from it. The reason is that we say: **אפשר לסוחטו אסור**—Although IT IS POSSIBLE TO EXTRACT some of the absorbed taste, nevertheless, all of the absorbed taste can never be removed; the piece therefore remains FORBIDDEN. As such, this forbidden piece will have to be removed from the pot and be discarded, and the rest of the contents of the pot will be permitted (if the pot contains sixty times the forbidden piece). See also the second paragraph of section 5 below.

26. See section 8.

much, such that only part of it was [submerged in the liquid] in the pot, it does not help. (This is according to Rashi.[23]) And if he did not stir immediately when [the forbidden food] had fallen [onto the meat], it does not help if he stirs later on, for since [the meat] has already received taste from the forbidden food it has become inherently forbidden *(nevelah)*.[24] And it is established for us that it is not possible to extract [the forbidden taste,][25] as noted [below] shortly.[26]

4. And if [the milk] has fallen on one piece, even though [the piece] is outside of the liquid—if he does not know upon which piece it has fallen,[27] even though he did not stir [or cover the pot] immediately, it is permitted to stir or cover the pot in order that the taste should spread throughout all of it.[28] And we do not say that "he is nullifying a forbidden food to begin with,"[29] since there is no definite forbidden food here, for perhaps there is no prohibition at all for perhaps it did not fall on this piece.[30] And furthermore, we do not say that the piece has become inherently forbidden *(nevelah)*,[31] for since it is not known which piece it is, we do not say that the piece becomes inherently forbidden, in accordance with section 17 further on, and this is the opinion of the *Bais Yosef*.

However, the opinion of the *Rama* is that also in this case it is forbidden to stir [the food], since it is possible to clarify [which piece] is

Yad Adam

4. A Piece Which Has Absorbed Forbidden Taste and Cannot Be Identified

27. Many pieces of meat are present and milk has fallen onto one of them, but we cannot identify this piece.

28. Once the pot is stirred or covered, then its contents will be permissible as long as the pot contains at least sixty times the milk which fell onto the piece.

29. In general, we rule that one may not, to begin with, intentionally nullify a forbidden food. (For example, if one ounce of milk falls into thirty ounces of a meat soup, it is forbidden to add thirty ounces of water into the mixture so that the milk will be nullified.) However, in the case being discussed here, we do not prohibit stirring the pot, even though a forbidden food is being nullified.

30. One cannot point to any specific piece and say that it is definitely forbidden.

31. We do not say that the piece of meat upon which the drop has fallen is to be regarded as a piece of forbidden food *(nevelah)*. (If we did so, the pot would have to contain sixty times the piece of meat.)

ג. סס בס״ך ס״ק ח׳.

האיסור על ידי טעימת נכרי כל חתיכה וחתיכה בפני עצמו[32] אע״ג דאין אנו סומכין להתיר ע״י טעימה היינו לחומרא[33] אבל לא לקולא[34] ולכן אם לא ניער בתחלה לא יועיל הניעור אח״כ שכבר נעשית נבלה.ג

ה. טיפת חלב שנפלה לתוך בשר רותח ולא היה בבשר ששים לבטל את החלב ונאסרה החתיכה מחמת החלב נעשית כל החתיכה איסור כאלו היתה כולה נבילה ולכן אם בשלה עם אחרות[35] צריך ששים לבטל כולה ולא אמרינן כיון שידוע שאין בחתיכה זו רק מעט חלב שיהיה די שיהיה בכולם ששים לבטל החלב[36] זה לא אמרינן כדבסמוך סימן ז׳.

ולכן אם יש ששים נגד החתיכה[37] ומכירה משליכה דקיי״ל אפשר לסוחטו אסור[38] כדלקמן[39] ואחרות מותרות ואם אינה מכירה כיון שיש ששים נגד החתיכה אז הרוטב מותר והחתיכות אם חתיכה זו שנאסרה אינה ראויה להתכבד[40] כולם מותרים כדין יבש ביבש דבטל ברוב[41] ואם ראויה להתכבד כולן אסורות[42] דאע״ג דאם בלעה

יד אדם

32. The gentile will then tell us which piece has the taste of the milk absorbed into it.

33. If there are grounds to say that food has absorbed a forbidden flavor, then even if a gentile tastes the food and tells us that there is no trace of the flavor of the forbidden substance, we nevertheless are stringent and prohibit the food. (Topic 51, section 6.)

34. We cannot be lenient and permit a mixture containing a piece of forbidden food if a gentile can clarify which of the pieces are forbidden by tasting them.

5. The rule: חתיכה נעשית נבילה—The Piece Becomes Inherently Forbidden

35. One took this forbidden piece of meat and placed it into a pot with other pieces.

36. One might think that the mixture should be permitted as long as the entire contents of the pot is equal to sixty times the amount of milk that was absorbed into the piece.

37. The pot contains enough liquid, meat, and other food such that they are at least sixty times the size of the forbidden piece that was placed in it. Therefore, the contents of the pot remain permissible.

38. Even though the absorbed milk is being extracted from the forbidden piece of meat while the piece is cooking, nevertheless, it remains forbidden. This is because it is not possible for all the milk to be extracted. See note 25 regarding the term אפשר לסוחטו and its translation.

ג. *Shach* there, paragraph 8.

forbidden by having a gentile taste each and every piece by itself.[32] And even though [nowadays] we do not rely [on a gentile] to permit [a food] by tasting, this is [only] for being stringent,[33] but not for being lenient.[34] And therefore, if he did not stir [the pot] at the outset [soon after the milk had fallen on the piece], stirring afterwards will not help, for [that piece] has already become inherently forbidden.[ג]

5. If a drop of milk has fallen onto [a piece of] hot meat and there was not sixty [times as much] in the meat to nullify the milk and the piece [of meat therefore] became forbidden because of the milk—[then] the whole piece becomes forbidden as if it were entirely forbidden meat. Therefore, if one cooked it with others[35] there must be in the pot sixty [times the forbidden piece] to nullify all of it. And we do not say: since it is known that there is only a little bit of milk in this piece, it should be enough if all together there is sixty to nullify the milk.[36] We do not say this, as [noted] shortly in section 7.

Nevertheless, if there is sixty times the [forbidden] piece[37] and we recognize [the piece], we [must] throw it out, as it is established for us that it is not possible to extract [the forbidden taste][38] as [noted] later on.[39] And the other [pieces] are permissible. And if we cannot distinguish it [from the other pieces], since there is sixty times the piece, then the liquid is permissible; and [regarding] the pieces [of meat in the pot]—if this piece which became forbidden is not fit to honor [guests with it],[40] all of them are permissible in accordance with the law of [a mixture of] dry food with dry food which is nullified by a majority.[41] But if it is fit to honor [guests], all of them are forbidden.[42] Although [a

Yad Adam

39. In section 8.

40. I.e., it is not a piece of meat of proper quality and size which one would serve to a guest.

41. In topic 51 (sections 1 and 9), it is explained that if dry pieces of permissible food are mixed together with pieces of forbidden food and it is impossible to determine which pieces are the forbidden ones—if the majority of the pieces are permissible, then the forbidden pieces are nullified and all of the pieces may be eaten. (See also section 21 there where it is explained that in a case such as this the individual pieces of meat have the status of "dry food.")

42. All of the pieces become forbidden due to the rabbinical ruling that a piece which is fit to serve to a guest cannot become nullified. As such, even if the pot contains much

שאר איסורין אע״ג דראויה להתכבד בטלה כיון שאין איסורו מחמת עצמו[43] מ״מ בשר וחלב הוי איסור מחמת עצמו[44] כמבואר לקמן כלל נ״א וכלל נ״ג.[ד]

ו. ואע״ג דלענין זה אמרינן דחשיב כנבילה[45] וכאיסור מחמת עצמו ולא כבלוע[46] מ״מ אם נגעה חתיכה זו בחתיכה אחרת[47] חם בחם בלא רוטב לא חשיב לענין זה רק כבלוע[48] כמו שנתבאר כלל ס׳ סי׳ ט׳[ה] דקים להו לחז״ל שאין שום טעם יוצא מהחלב אלא ע״י רוטב.[49][ו]

ז. מה״ת לא אמרינן חתיכה נ״נ אלא דוקא בבו״ח דכל חד באנפי נפשיה שרי וכי איתנהו בהדדי אסור הלכך הבשר נעשה

ד. סעיף ג׳.
ה. ש״ך בסי׳ ק״ה ס״ק י״ז וע״ש הטעם לחלק.
ו. שם.

יד אדם

more than sixty times the piece, all of the pieces will be forbidden.

43. For example, melted forbidden fat was absorbed into a piece of kosher meat which is fit for guests, thereby making the piece forbidden. In such a case, the piece will indeed be nullified if it falls into a pot whose contents are sixty times its size, because the rabbinical decree declaring that a piece fit for guests cannot be nullified will not apply. Why are we lenient in this case? This is because the piece of meat is not forbidden by its own intrinsic nature, but due to the fat which it absorbed.

If, on the other hand, a piece of unkosher meat (derived from an improperly slaughtered animal) which is fit to honor guests falls into a pot with other pieces of meat and it cannot be identified, then the rabbinical decree will apply: The forbidden piece will not be nullified and all the pieces of meat in the pot will be forbidden. The decree will apply because the meat is forbidden by its own intrinsic nature.

The *Chochmas Adam* now goes on to explain that a piece of kosher meat which has absorbed milk falls into the second category, i.e., it is regarded as a food which is prohibited due to its own nature.

44. Therefore, if it is fit to honor guests, then it will not become nullified. A piece of meat which contains absorbed milk is considered to be forbidden by its own nature because each of the components by itself is permitted, and only when they become mixed together are they forbidden. Nevertheless, we will learn in the next section that with regard to certain matters, a piece of meat which has absorbed milk is not to be treated with the stringencies of a food which is forbidden by its own nature.

6. When Is Meat and Milk Regarded to Be an איסור מחמת עצמו—Forbidden Due to Its Own Nature?

45. And as such, when a piece of meat becomes forbidden because it has absorbed milk, the size of the forbidden substance is

ד. [*Shulchan Aruch*, chapter 92] paragraph 3.
ה. *Shach* chapter 105, paragraph 17. Refer there for the reason to differentiate.
ו. *Ibid.*

piece of food] which absorbed [taste from] other forbidden foods becomes nullified even though it is fit to honor [guests], this is because its prohibition is not due to own nature.[43] However, [a mixture of] meat and milk is a prohibition due to its own nature.[44] [These rulings are] explained later on in topic 51 [section 10] and topic 53 [section 7].ד

6. Even though in this matter [mentioned above] we say that [a piece of meat which has absorbed milk] is regarded as inherently forbidden,[45] and it is like a forbidden food which is forbidden due to its own nature and not as if [the forbidden component] were [merely] absorbed,[46] nevertheless, if this piece came into contact with another piece,[47] each one being hot but without [the presence of] liquid, the [milk] is regarded only as absorbed regarding this matter[48] as explained in topic 60, section 9,ה for it is established by our sages (of blessed memory) that no taste at all is emitted from the [absorbed] milk except by way of liquid.[49]ו

7. According to the Torah, we do not say that a piece becomes inherently forbidden except with [mixtures of] meat and milk, where each one by itself is permitted, but when they are together [the mixture] is forbidden. As a result, the meat [which has absorbed milk]

Yad Adam

regarded to be the size of the entire piece of meat (and not just the size of the milk which was absorbed into it).

46. It is not to be treated as meat which has merely absorbed a forbidden substance, but with the more stringent status of meat which is forbidden by its own intrinsic nature. (See the end of section 5 above.)

47. This piece of meat which has milk absorbed into it came into contact with an ordinary kosher piece of meat.

48. If the piece which absorbed milk were to be treated as forbidden by its own nature, we would be stringent and rule that other pieces which come into contact with it would become forbidden. (In some cases, the pieces would become entirely forbidden. In others, it would be necessary to remove a thick layer at the point of contact. See topic 60.) This, however, is not the case here. Rather with regard to this matter, we treat the meat with the more lenient status of a permissible food which has absorbed a forbidden substance; in such a situation, there is no transfer of taste unless liquid is present.

49. The taste of the absorbed milk in a piece of meat is not transferred into another piece unless liquid is present. Since no liquid is present, the kosher piece of meat will remain completely permissible.

איסור ואם אכל חצי זית מבשר וחצי זית מחלב לוקה.[50][ז] ובשאר איסורין נחלקו הפוסקים יש אומרים דלא אמרינן כלל חנ״נ אפי׳ מדרבנן ולכן אם נפלה כזית נבילה בקדירה ולא היה בו ששים לבטלו ונאסרו כל החתיכות שבקדירה אם חזרה אחת מן חתיכות ההיתר הזה שנאסר[51] ונפלה לקדירה אחרת א״צ ס׳ אלא נגד כזית הנבילה[52] וכן פסק בש״ע בסי׳ צ״ב וסימן ק״ו אבל אנו נוהגין על פי הכרעת רמ״א כאותן הפוסקים דבכל איסורין אמרינן חנ״נ עכ״פ מדרבנן וא״כ צריך ס׳ נגד החתיכה שנפלה.[53][ח]

ומ״מ לענין חתיכה שחציה ברוטב קיל מבשר וחלב לעיל סי׳ א׳ ב׳ דבזה לא חיישינן כלל לשיטת רש״י ואמרינן דמפעפע בכל

ז. כמבואר בט״ז סי׳ צ״ב ס״ק ט׳ כוונתם.* ולי נראה דכוונתם דס״ל דאע״ג דעכ״ע דאורייתא מ״מ אין לוקין כשיטת ר״ת מביאו הפ״ח בא״ח סי׳ תמ״ב והיינו דוקא בשאר איסורין דההיתר עכ״פ לא נעשה נבלה משא״כ בבשר וחלב דלוקין עליו.

ח. סעיף ד׳.

יד אדם

7. Does the Principle חתיכה נעשית נבילה (A Piece Becomes Inherently Forbidden) Apply to Forbidden Mixtures Other Than Meat and Milk?

50. In general, in order to incur the Torah penalty of lashes for eating a forbidden food, one must eat a piece which is at least the size of an olive. If half an olive-size of milk and half an olive-size of meat were cooked together, then one will incur the penalty of lashes when eating them, since it is the mixture that the Torah prohibits. On the other hand, if half an olive-size of forbidden fat was cooked together with half an olive-size of meat, one will not receive lashes for eating the mixture.

51. We are dealing with a piece which is larger than the size of an olive (i.e., larger than the piece of forbidden meat which had fallen into the pot).

52. The reason is that this is the maximum amount of forbidden taste that any piece could have absorbed. Thus, even if the piece falling into the second pot was twice the size of an olive, it is necessary for the pot to contain only sixty times the size of an olive to nullify it. (If the piece which fell into the second pot was less than the size of an olive, then it would certainly be sufficient for the second pot to contain sixty times the size of this piece.)

53. We will need sixty times the entire piece in the second pot, even though the piece of forbidden meat which caused the prohibition was much smaller. As such, if the piece falling into the second pot was twice the size of an olive, it will be necessary that the

becomes [inherently] forbidden, and if one ate [a mixture] where there is half an olive-size of meat and half an olive-size of milk he is to receive lashes.[50][ז]

[However,] with regard to other prohibitions, the *halachic* authorities disagree: Some rule that we do not say at all that a piece becomes inherently forbidden, and there is not even a rabbinical decree [to this effect]. Therefore, if an olive-size of forbidden meat fell into a pot and there was not sixty [times as much] in [the pot] to nullify it and [as a result] all of the pieces in the pot became forbidden–[then] if one of these permissible pieces which became forbidden[51] will have gone on and fallen into another pot, we will need only sixty times the olive-size of forbidden meat.[52] And this is how the *Shulchan Aruch* has ruled in chapter 92 and chapter 106. However, we conduct ourselves according to the decision of the *Rama* in accordance with those authorities [who rule] that with regard to all forbidden foods we say that a piece does become inherently forbidden, at least by rabbinical decree. As such, we would require sixty times the size of the piece that fell [into the second pot].[53][ח]

Nevertheless, regarding a piece that is partially [submerged] in liquid, [other prohibitions will be treated] more leniently than meat and milk [explained] above in sections 1 and 2, for in this matter we are not concerned at all with regard to the opinion of *Rashi* and we say that [the taste of the absorbed forbidden substance] spreads throughout

ז. It is explained by the *Taz* 92:9 that this is the intent [of *Tosafot*].* It is my opinion that the intent [of *Tosafot*] is that they feel that even though according to the Torah the taste [of a food] is regarded like the food itself, nevertheless, one will not receive lashes [when eating an olive- size portion of food which contains absorbed forbidden taste]. This is in accordance with the opinion of *Rabbenu Tam* quoted by the *Pri Chadash* in *[Shulchan Aruch]—Orach Chayim* chapter 442. But this is only regarding other prohibitions where the [originally] permissible food at least does not become inherently forbidden [according to the Torah]. This is not the case with meat and milk, where one will receive lashes for [eating an olive-size of meat which has absorbed the taste of milk or vice versa].

ח. *Rama* 92:4.

**Chullin* 100a, beginning with the word בשקדם. Regarding the concept of טעם כעיקר, see notes on topic 46 section 1, and topic 51 section 8.

Yad Adam

second pot contain 120 times the size of an olive to nullify it.

The *Chochmas Adam* has noted that we have accepted the ruling of the *Rama* that "a piece becomes inherently forbidden" even when prohibitions other than meat and milk are involved. Nevertheless, we are often more lenient when dealing with these other prohibitions since in any case, this ruling applies to other prohibitions only by rabbinical decree. One such leniency is about to be mentioned.

ט. ע"ש בש"ך ס"ק י"ג.
י. סימן ק"ו.

הקדירה[54] ומ"מ לענין אותה חתיכה[55] במקום שאין הפסד יש לאסור.ט

ח. ואף לדעת הש"ע[56] מ"מ החתיכה עצמה שנאסרה תחלה[57] נשארה באיסורה אע"פ שיש עכשיו ס' נגד הכזית נבילה שנבלע בו תחלה דקיימא לן אפשר לסוחטו אסור[58] ר"ל דלא אמרינן שאפשר לסחוט האיסור עכשיו שיצא כולו ממנו ולהתפשט בקדירה שנית[59] ואף שיש מקילין גם בזה וס"ל דאפשר לסוחטו מותר[60] בשאר איסורין[61] מ"מ לא קיי"ל כן.י

יד אדם

54. In section 1 above it is explained that according to *Rashi,* if milk falls onto a partially submerged piece of meat, the milk will remain in the portion of the piece which is above the liquid and will make it inherently forbidden (unless the piece is sixty times the milk). It was then explained in section 2 that if this piece were to be mixed into the other ingredients of the pot, then the entire pot will become forbidden (unless the pot contains sixty times the forbidden portion of the piece). The *Chochmas Adam* has mentioned there that it is proper to be strict and follow Rashi's opinion in cases where a significant loss is not involved.

We are now learning here that in cases where prohibitions other than meat and milk are involved, (for example, a piece of meat in a pot became forbidden because melted forbidden fat has fallen onto it), we need not be concerned about *Rashi's* opinion and prohibit the contents of the pot. Rather, we will rule in accordance with the *Ri* that when the forbidden substance falls onto the meat, the taste immediately spreads throughout the entire pot and therefore all of the contents of the pot will combine to nullify the forbidden fat. Only in cases involving meat and milk (where there is no question that the piece of meat can become inherently forbidden) do we consider being stringent to prohibit the entire contents of the pot.

55. I.e., the piece partially in the liquid upon which the forbidden substance has fallen. (Compare with note 13 above.)

8. אפשר לסוחטו—Is It Possible to Extract Forbidden Taste?

56. I.e., the *Bais Yosef,* who rules that a piece of meat which absorbed taste from a forbidden food (other than milk) does not become inherently forbidden.

57. The "piece" here denotes the piece mentioned in the second paragraph of section 7—the one which became forbidden in the first pot and then fell into the second pot (see below). Even though the absorbed taste in the piece becomes nullified in the second pot, the piece itself remains in its forbidden state.

In summary: An olive-size of forbidden meat fell into a pot containing pieces of kosher meat, and they all became forbidden because the pot did not contain sixty times

ט. See the *Shach* there, paragraph 13.
י. *Shulchan Aruch*, chapter 106.

the entire pot.[54] In any case, regarding that piece,[55] in a situation where there is no loss it is proper to forbid it.[ט]

8. [Nevertheless,] even according to the *Shulchan Aruch*,[56] the piece itself which became forbidden in the beginning[57] remains in its forbidden state, even if there is now [in the second pot] sixty times the olive-size of forbidden meat which was absorbed into [this piece] at the beginning; for it is established for us, that it is not possible to extract [the forbidden taste].[58] This means: We do not say that it is now possible to extract the forbidden taste, such that all [the forbidden taste] will be emitted from [the piece] and spread throughout a second pot.[59] And even though there are [authorities] who are lenient even in this matter and rule that it is possible to extract [the forbidden taste][60] with regard to other prohibitions,[61] this is not the established ruling for us.[י]

Yad Adam

the forbidden piece. Then one of these newly forbidden pieces fell into a second pot of food, and this pot contains more than sixty times the olive- size piece which had caused the first pot to become forbidden. The contents of the second pot remain permissible according to the opinion of the *Bais Yosef* in the *Shulchan Aruch*. Nevertheless, (even though the *Bais Yosef* rules that the piece did not become inherently forbidden,) the piece still continues to remain in its forbidden state even after its absorbed taste is nullified in the second pot.

58. See note 25 regarding this phrase.

59. When a piece has become forbidden in one pot and is placed into a second pot of hot liquid, some, but not all, of the forbidden taste will be emitted from the piece into the contents of the second pot. Therefore, the piece remains forbidden. As such, if sixty times the original forbidden substance is present in the second pot, then the contents of the pot remain permissible. However, the piece which had absorbed the forbidden taste must be removed and discarded.

60. These authorities will rule that whenever we do not apply the rule that a piece becomes inherently forbidden, then we will also be lenient and rule that it is possible for all the forbidden taste to be extracted from the piece. They will rule that if sixty times the forbidden substance is present in the second pot, then even the piece which had absorbed the forbidden taste will become permissible.

The phrase: אפשר לסוחטו מותר is best understood as a question and answer: "Is is possible to extract [all of the forbidden taste? Yes! Therefore, the piece will be] permissible." Compare note 25.

61. With prohibitions other than meat and milk.

יא. שם וע"ש בט"ז ס"ק ט"ו.
יב. ש"ך. וכפ"ח מסייס.
יג. ביש"ש סימן ס' כביאו הט"ז שם.

והכו"פ כתב דדעת המחבר בסי' צ"ב סעיף ד' להתיר באיסור דרבנן גם אפשר לסוחטו.[62]

ט. וי"א דאע"ג דבכל איסורין קיי"ל חנ"נ[63] היינו דוקא לח ביבש[64] אבל לח בלח כגון יין נסך[65] ליין כשר או חלב נימוח לשומן נימוח ואח"כ נפל ממנו להיתר אחר לא אמרינן[66] חנ"נ[67] ואין צריך ס' אלא נגד האיסור לבד[68]יא ואין חילוק אם ההיתר האחר לח או יבשיב וטעמא דמילתא דבדבר לח וצלול לא שייך ביה בליעה[69] אלא שנבלל ומתערב האיסור עם ההיתר יפה ומשום הכי[70] לא אמרינן חנ"נ. ובהפסד גדול יש לסמוך על זה בשאר איסורין אבל לא בבשר וחלב.[71]

ואם בשלו חתיכה נבלה בקדירה ולא היה בקדירה לבטל[72] ונטלו מהרוטב ונתנו לקדירה אחרת דעת רש"ליג דצריך ס' נגד כל

יד אדם

62. I.e., in a case where the absorbed forbidden taste is only rabbinically prohibited (such as chicken which has been cooked in milk), the *Bais Yosef* is lenient such that in addition to ruling that the piece does not become inherently forbidden, he also rules that it is possible to extract all of the forbidden taste. If, however, a Torah prohibition is involved, even though the piece does not become inherently forbidden, we still say that it is not possible to extract all the taste. See also topic 51, section 24.

9. Does חתיכה נעשית נבילה (The Piece Becomes Inherently Forbidden) Apply to Mixtures of Liquids?

63. In accordance with the *Rama* as explained in section 7.

64. I.e., where a liquid is absorbed into a solid food. (For example, melted forbidden fat falls onto a piece of kosher meat and is absorbed into it.)

65. Literally, poured wine. The term refers to wine which is forbidden because it is suspected that a gentile poured it for idolatrous purposes.

66. The word "piece" here denotes the first mixture of the two liquids. We do not say that this first mixture becomes inherently forbidden.

67. And therefore, if some of this mixture falls into a pot of food, it is not necessary to have sixty times the entire volume of the mixture that has fallen in.

68. For example, if one ounce of forbidden wine falls into five ounces of kosher wine, and the mixture falls into a pot of food, the pot will not be required to contain sixty times the mixture (which would be 360 ounces). Rather, it will be sufficient if the pot

יא. *Ibid.* [*Shulchan Aruch* 92:4], and see the *Taz* there, paragraph 15.
יב. *Shach* [paragraph 14]. And the *Pri Chadash* concludes [similarly].
יג. In the *Yam shel Shlomo* chapter 60. The *Taz* quotes it there.

And the *Kreisi u'pleisi* has written that the opinion of the author [of the *Shulchan Aruch*] in chapter 92, paragraph 4 is to be lenient when dealing with [food] forbidden by a rabbinical prohibition also with regard to [the rule of whether or not] "it is possible to extract [forbidden taste]."[62]

9. There are some who say that even though it is established for us that for all forbidden foods [we apply the principle that] a piece becomes inherently forbidden,[63] this applies only [to a mixture of] liquid with solid.[64] However, [a mixture of] liquid with liquid, such as forbidden wine[65] with kosher wine, or melted forbidden fat with melted permissible fat, where afterwards [a portion] from it fell into another permissible food—we do not say that the "piece"[66] becomes inherently forbidden,[67] and we [therefore] require sixty times the forbidden [liquid] alone,[68][יא] and there is no difference if the other permissible food [into which the mixture falls] is liquid or dry.[יב] And the reason for this [leniency] is that with something fluid and liquid, "absorbing" is not relevant.[69] Rather, [the liquids] are mingled together and the forbidden one becomes mixed up well with the permissible one, and because of this[70] we do not say that the "piece" becomes inherently forbidden. And in a situation involving a great loss we can rely on this [opinion in cases regarding] other forbidden foods but not for [mixtures] of meat and milk.[71]

If one cooked a piece of forbidden meat in a pot and there was not enough in the pot to nullify [it][72] and he took some of the cooked liquid and placed it into another pot, the opinion of the Maharshal[יג] is that

Yad Adam

contains 60 ounces to nullify the one ounce of forbidden wine in the mixture.

69. A solid food (acting like a sponge) can absorb a liquid into it (for example, a piece of meat can absorb milk), but a liquid cannot "absorb" another liquid.

70. One is not absorbed throughout the other but is merely mixed with it.

71. This is the ruling of the *Rama* in 92:4. The *Chochmas Adam* will next mention the opinion of the *Maharshal* who rules that this leniency cannot be applied in a case where the mixture of the two liquids is cooked. (See the additional note on topic 40, section 5 regarding the criteria to determine whether a great loss is present.)

Note: If solid matter becomes dispersed into a liquid, or if absorbed taste in a vessel is emitted into a liquid, the mixture has the same status as a mixture of two liquids.

72. As such, the liquid in the pot as well as the pieces of kosher meat which are in it all become forbidden.

יד. הגיאו יש״ש שם.
טו. ש״ך שם.

הרוטב אע״ג דהוי לח בלח[73] כיון דהחתיכות אסורות לא חלקו חכמים בדבר וגם הרוטב אסור כולו ולא אמרינן שלא יצטרך בקדירה ב׳ ס׳ רק לפי חשבון האיסור שיש ברוטב כגון שהיה בקדירה ראשונה ארבעים נגד האיסור[74] וא״כ לא היה ברוטב רק חלק אחד מארבעים של האיסור כדאמרינן אין המדומע מדמע אלא לפי חשבון[75] זה לא אמרינן.[76]

אבל דעת המרדכי בשם הראב״ן[יד] אפילו ברוטב אינו צריך לשער רק לפי חשבון חוץ מבשר וחלב דאין חילוק אם נאסר החלב מבשר ונפל לחלב נעשה הכל נבילה.[77][טו] ונ״ל לפ״ז[78] דה״ה אם נפל מעט חלב למים ונפל מן המים לבשר אין צריך לשער רק לפי ערך החלב שנפל למים כגון שנפל רביעית[79] חלב לכ׳ רביעיות מים ונפל מזה רביעית לבשר אין צריך ששים רק לחלק עשרים מרביעית

יד אדם

73. Actually, the first mixture is not a mixture of liquid with liquid. Rather, the taste of a solid food (the forbidden meat) has become dispersed throughout the liquid in the first pot. Nevertheless, such a mixture has the same status as a mixture of two liquids as noted above.

74. The permissible ingredients (liquid plus meat) were equal to forty times the amount of forbidden liquid which fell into the pot.

75. This is a rule that refers to *terumah* (a portion set aside from agricultural produce that must to given to a *kohen*). In accordance with this rule, if a certain mixture containing *terumah* falls into other food, we do not view the first mixture as being entirely *terumah*. Rather we determine the status of the first mixture by calculating the percentage of *terumah* in it.

Accordingly, in the case at hand, one might conclude that the second pot need not contain sixty times the volume of the liquid which fell in but only sixty times one-fortieth of the mixture.

76. Thus, when dealing with mixtures of cooked liquids, we do not determine the percentage of forbidden matter in the first mixture, but we will need sixty times the entire amount which fell into the second pot. As such, we could not permit the second pot according to the *Maharshal* even in cases of great loss unless it contains sixty times the entire amount of liquid which fell into it.

77. When cooked mixtures of milk and meat are involved, then even according to the *Mordechai*, we cannot be lenient with taste dispersed into a liquid, and we must treat it with the same stringency as taste absorbed by a solid food. As such, if a small piece of meat was cooked in milk, the taste of the meat becomes dispersed in the milk

יד. The *Yam shel Shlomo* quotes it there.
טו. *Shach* there.

we require [the second pot to contain] sixty times the [entire] liquid [which fell into it]. Even though it is [a mixture of] liquid with liquid,[73] since the pieces [of kosher meat which were in the liquid became] forbidden, the sages did not differentiate [between the meat and the liquid] in this matter, and [therefore] also the cooked liquid [in the first pot becomes] entirely forbidden. And we do not say that it is necessary to have in the second pot only sixty times the proportion of the forbidden portion which is in the cooked liquid. For example, if [the permissible substance] was forty times the forbidden substance in the first pot,[74] and as such, the cooked liquid consisted only of one-fortieth forbidden substance, one [might conclude] in accordance with what we say: The mixture does not mix [with other foods] except according to proportion[75]—[but] we do not say this [here].[76]

However, the opinion of the *Mordechai* in the name of the *Ravan*[יד] is that even with regard to cooked liquid we are required only to measure according to the proportion [of forbidden substance], with the exception [of mixtures] of meat and milk where there is no difference [between mingled tastes in solids and liquids], for if milk had become forbidden from [being cooked with] meat and [this milk then] falls into other milk, the entire [milk] had become inherently forbidden.[77][טו] And it is my opinion that in accordance with this,[78] the same rule would apply if a little milk falls into [hot] water and a little of that water [falls] into meat, that one need not measure except according to the proportion of the milk that fell into the water. For example, if a *revi'is*[79] of milk fell into twenty *revi'os* of water, and from this [mixture] a *revi'is* fell into meat, we require only sixty times one-twentieth of a *revi'is*, as

Yad Adam

and the milk becomes inherently forbidden. Then, when this forbidden milk falls into other milk, the latter must contain sixty times the forbidden milk, and it will not be enough for it to contain sixty times the piece of meat.

78. That when forbidden substance is dispersed into a liquid, even by means of cooking, we measure by the proportion of the forbidden substance in the liquid (with the exception of milk which was cooked with meat). The *Chochmas Adam* now goes on to give an example in which milk and water are cooked together and states that in this case also, it is proper to measure according to the proportion of milk in the water.

79. A measure of liquid approximately equal to half a cup.

שהרי אין ברביעית זה שנפל אלא לפי שיעור.[טז] ועיין לקמן כלל מ"ו סימן ז' דאין לסמוך על זה[80] כי אם במקום הפסד וצורך גדול.[81] ויבש ביבש לעולם לא אמרינן חנ"נ אף בבשר וחלב אלא לעולם כל שניתוסף אחר כך היתר הוי נתערב לכתחלה.[82]

י. אפילו במקום דאמרינן חנ"נ אם קודם שנודע לו התערובת הוסיף עליו היתר עד ס' נגד האיסור[83] במקום הפסד מרובה

טז. ועיין בפמ"ג סימן צ"ב ס"ק כ"ד בט"ז. ועיין סי' צ"ט סעי' ו' בהגהת רמ"א כזית חלב כו' דמשמע דוקא כשהיה במים ס' נ"ל דאו"ה אזיל לשיטתו דכתב להדיא בכלל כ"ד סימן ז' דלא אמרינן לשער לפי חשבון המדומע אלא דחשבינן הכל כרוטב של נבילה.* ולפי"ז גם מש"כ בש"ע בצלים הבלועים מבשר** אינו ר"ל לפי חשבון אלא כנגד כל הבשר ואם היה רוטב נגד כל הרוטב*** אבל לפ"ד המרדכי בשם ראב"ן שכתבתי לעיל לעולם משערינן לפי חשבון.

יד אדם

80. To rely on the *Mordechai* who rules that a mixture of cooked liquids is governed by the same rule as uncooked liquids.

81. The *Maharshal* will rule that if milk and water are cooked together, the mixture is to be judged as if it were completely milk. If this mixture will then fall into a pot of meat, then sixty times the mixture will be required. (See topic 46, section 7.) The *Chochmas Adam* now rules that there must be a great need for the food in addition to a great loss in order to be lenient in accordance with the *Mordechai* (who requires only sixty times the milk) and overrule the opinion of the *Maharshal* (who will require sixty times the mixture).

See also note 95 below where it is mentioned that most authorities (including the *Aruch Hashulchan*) rule that even without a great loss, when milk is cooked with water one may measure with respect to the milk alone. The reason for this leniency is that when milk and water are cooked together, the resulting mixture is permissible, and when a permissible mixture is involved we do not say that the entire mixture becomes inherently like one its components. Thus, according to these authorities, when a mixture of milk and water falls into a pot of meat, it is necessary for the pot to contain only sixty times the milk (and it need not contain sixty times the mixture).

82. We judge it as if the first mixture never existed. Therefore, if such a mixture falls into a pot of food, only sixty times the forbidden substance will be required (and not sixty times the mixture). The definition of a dry food is discussed in topic 51, sections 21-24.

10. Laws Concerning Nullifying a Piece Which Became Inherently Forbidden (nevelah)

83. We are dealing with a case such as where a piece of kosher meat absorbed forbidden fat and became inherently forbidden *(nevelah)* and this piece of meat fell into a pot of food which contained less than sixty times the piece. Then someone added additional ingredients to the pot before the existence of the mixture became known, such that it now contains sixty times the forbidden piece. The question is as follows: Do we say that in all such cases that the entire contents of the pot became inherently forbidden when the piece fell in, and therefore the addition of the extra ingredients will not help? Or, are there grounds to be lenient and rule that if the final mixture contains sixty times the forbid-

there is not in the *revi'is* which fell [into the meat] except its [actual] amount [of milk].טו And refer further on to topic 46, section 7 [where it is stated] that we are not to rely on this [leniency][80] except in a situation where there is a loss and a great need.[81]

And [in mixtures involving] dry food with dry food, we never say that a piece becomes inherently forbidden even with meat and milk, but always, wherever permissible food is added afterwards [to a mixture], it is like an initial mixture.[82]

10. Even in a situation where we say that a piece becomes inherently forbidden—if, before [the existence of] the mixture became known to him, he added permissible food to it so that there is sixty times the forbidden food,[83] in a case of a great loss and a meal [involv-

טו. And see the *Pri Megadim* [paragraph 15] regarding chapter 92, paragraph 24 in the *Taz*. And see chapter 99, paragraph 6 in the note of the *Rama*: "If milk the size of an olive [fell into water and was nullified in sixty times as much, and then the water fell into a pot of meat, (the mixture) is permissible, even if the meat is not sixty times the milk."] This implies that [the mixture is permissible] only if there was sixty times [the milk] in the water, [but if there was less than sixty times, the water would become inherently forbidden, as if it were entirely milk.] It is my opinion that the *Issur v'heter* [who is the *Rama's* source for this ruling] is going according to his opinion in topic 24, section 7 where he wrote explicitly that we do not say to measure according to the proportion of the mixture. Rather, we regard the entire liquid as inherently forbidden.*

And according to this, also what is written in the *Shulchan Aruch* regarding onions which have absorbed [taste] from meat,** [the *Shulchan Aruch*] does not mean to measure according to the proportion [of meat] but according to all of the meat, and if [they had absorbed] cooked liquid [they are measured] according to all of this cooked liquid.*** However, according to the opinion of the *Mordechai* in the name of the *Ravan* which I have written above, we always measure according to the proportion.

*See, however, the *Aruch Hashulchan* (end of 92:34), who questions this deduction of the *Chochmas Adam* as follows: The reason the *Rama* mentions sixty is not to imply that if the water contains less than sixty times the milk, then the mixture will be inherently forbidden (i.e., as if it were entirely milk). Rather, the *Rama* means that sixty is required in order to nullify the milk altogether. (See topic 51, section 32.) If less than sixty were present, then the milk would not be nullified and one would then measure by the proportion of milk in the mixture (and not regard the water as if were entirely milk).

The opinion of the *Issur v'heter* is discussed further in note י on topic 46.

**(*Shulchan Aruch* 94:6) It is stated that if onions had absorbed the taste of meat (for example, a few onions had been cooked in a pot together with a small piece of meat) and they are cooked in a pot of dairy food, the pot need not contain sixty times the onions, but only sixty times the meat from which the taste was absorbed.

***For example, onions were cooked in ten ounces of soup consisting of one-tenth meat fat. If the onions are then cooked in a pot of milk, it is not enough for the pot to contain sixty times the one ounce of fat. Rather it must contain sixty times the entire ten ounces of soup. (We are dealing with a case where the entire volume of soup was less than that of the onions. If the onions were smaller, then it will not be necessary to have more than sixty times the size of the onions.) The *Chochmas Adam* now goes on to explain that the *Mordechai*, on the other hand, will require the milk to contain only sixty times the one ounce of meat fat. In topic 46 (at the end of section 7) it is mentioned that one should not rely on this leniency except when there is a great need and a significant loss would result.

In cases where there is enough milk to nullify the meat taste in the onion, then according to the *Chochmas Adam*, it is not even necessary to discard the onion, as explained below in section 12. (See note 102 where it is mentioned that some authorities require that the onion be discarded.)

(Refer also to note 100, where it is mentioned that according to Rabbi Akiva Eiger, when the taste of meat permeates an entire food [such as where an onion was thinly sliced with a meat knife] and it then falls into a pot of hot milk, it is not enough to have sixty times the taste of the meat. Rather, it will be necessary in all such cases for the volume of the milk to be sixty times the entire onion. Rabbi Akiva Eiger would rule similarly in this case: If onions are cooked with meat, it will not be enough to have sixty times the meat or even sixty times the entire liquid in which they were cooked. Rather, sixty times the onions will be required in all cases.)

יז. דהיינו או״ה ורמ״א סימן צ״ט וכו״פ שכן דעת תוס׳ בבכורות כ״ב ומתרץ קושיית הש״ך ס״ק ט״ו.
יח. שכן מוכח שם בתוס׳.
יט. עיין סי׳ צ״ט בט״ז שם והפ״ח והמנ״י מפקפקים בזה.

וסעודת מצוה יש לסמוך על המתירין[יז] דכיון דלא נודע וכבר נתבטל[84] ולא יטעום טעם איסורא[85] ובלאו הכי הרבה פוסקים ס״ל דלא אמרינן חנ״נ בשאר איסורין[86] ומ״מ אותה חתיכה אסורה[87][יח] וכל שכן באיסור דרבנן דיש להקל אבל בבשר וחלב דלכ״ע מה״ת חנ״נ אין להקל.

יא. במקום דלא אמרינן חנ״נ[88] אם ריבה עליו[89] בשוגג[90] או באונס[91] ואפילו לאחר שנודע לו התערובת מותר ואם טעה בדין זה שסבור שמותר להרבות[92] במקום הפסד מרובה יש לסמוך ולהתיר ודיינינן ליה כשוגג.[יט]

יב. לא אמרינן חנ״נ אלא באיסור שנפל להיתר ומכל שכן בבשר וחלב[93] שנתבשלו יחד[94] אבל קדירה שבשלו בה ירקות או מים ונפל לתוכה חלב ואח״כ נפל הכל לבשר לא אמרינן

יד אדם

den piece, then the mixture will be permissible?

(When there is a mixture of kosher and unkosher food and the permitted food is less than sixty times the forbidden food, the mixture, of course, is forbidden. Furthermore, it is forbidden to add additional permissible ingredients to the pot in order that the permissible food should become more than sixty times the forbidden food and thereby nullify it. In the case here, however, when the additional food was added there was no intention to nullify the forbidden food. As such, we can be lenient and permit the mixture under certain circumstances. See also topic 52 beginning with section 6.)

84. And by tradition, the rule that a piece becomes inherently forbidden does not take effect until the existence of the mixture becomes known. (See *Aruch Hashulchan* 99:33.)

85. Since the mixture now consists of less than one-sixtieth forbidden food its taste will no longer be recognizable. There are therefore grounds to be lenient. (Regarding "a case of great loss and a meal which involves performance of a precept," see the additional note on topic 40, section 5.)

86. Other than meat and milk. This can serve as additional grounds to be lenient.

87. The piece which had absorbed the forbidden substance (and had become inherently forbidden) remains forbidden, since it is not possible to extract all of the forbidden taste from it (in accordance with section 8 above).

11. Nullifying a Component of a Mixture When the Mixture Does Not Become Inherently Forbidden (nevelah)

88. Such as a mixture of solid foods. (See end of section 9.)

[יז]. I.e., the *Issur v'heter* and the *Rama* chapter 99 [paragraph 5] and the *Kreisi u'pleisi*, as this is the opinion of *Tosafot* in *Bechorot* 52, and the question of the *Shach* in paragraph 15 is answered.

[יח]. This is demonstrated in *Tosafot* there.

[יט]. See chapter 99 in the *Taz* there [paragraph 9]; the *Pri Chadash* and the *Minchas Yaakov* contest this.

ing] a precept, one can rely on those who permit [the mixture].[יז] This is because [the forbidden piece] was not known [to be present] and it was already nullified [before the mixture became known to him][84] and he will not be able to taste the forbidden flavor.[85] And even without this [lenient ruling], many authorities rule that we do not say that a piece becomes inherently forbidden regarding other forbidden foods.[86] Nevertheless, that piece is still forbidden.[87][יח] And certainly with [a food which is] rabbinically forbidden one can be lenient. However, with meat and milk, where according to everyone a piece becomes inherently forbidden according to the Torah, one may not be lenient.

11. In a situation where we do not say that a piece becomes inherently forbidden,[88] if one added to [the mixture][89] unknowingly[90] or due to extenuating circumstances[91] even after [the existence of] the mixture became known to him, [the mixture will be] permissible. Also, if one erred in this law and he thought that it is permissible to add [permissible food to the pot],[92] in a situation where there is a great loss, there are grounds to permit [the food] and we judge it the same as [a case of adding] unknowingly.[יט]

12. We do not say that a piece becomes inherently forbidden except where a forbidden food fell into a permitted food, or of course with [mixtures of] meat and milk,[93] and they were cooked together.[94] However, if there is a pot in which one cooked green vegetables or water and milk fell into it, and afterwards the entire [mixture] fell into

Yad Adam

89. Such that the permissible food is now sixty or more times the forbidden food.

90. He added permissible food to the pot, not knowing that the forbidden food was present.

91. The permissible food accidentally fell into the pot.

92. He knew of the presence of the forbidden food, and he thought that he was permitted to add permissible food to the pot until the forbidden food would become nullified.

12. Can Permissible Ingredients Become Inherently Forbidden (nevelah)?

93. Such as melted forbidden fat falling onto cheese, or milk falling onto a piece of meat.

94. The cooking will cause the flavor of the liquid to spread through the solid food and make it forbidden.

כ. סימן ל״ד סעיף ו׳ וע״ש בש״ך.

שנחשוב כל מה שיש בקדירה כאלו הוא חלב אלא אי ידעינן כמה חלב נפל לתוכו א״צ לשער רק נגד החלב[95]כ ולכן בצלים שחתכן בסכין של בשר[96] ונתנן לקדירה של חלב א״צ ס׳ אלא נגד הבלוע שבו אם ידוע כמה בשר בלוע בו[97] או ס׳ נגד כדי נטילה[98] מהבצלים שהרי הבצלים אינו בולע יותר מכדי נטילה כדלקמן כלל מ״ט[99] או אם ידוע כמה נגע מסכין ישער ששים נגד מקום הסכין אפילו נחתכו דק דק.[100] אך מן הסתם הדרך לחתוך בכל הסכין ואם יש ס׳[101] הכל מותר וא״צ להסיר הבצל שכיון שהיה היתר לא שייך לומר אפשר

יד אדם

95. We do not say that the mixture of milk, water, and vegetables becomes *nevelah* (inherently forbidden) and is to be regarded as if it were completely milk. Rather, if this mixture falls into meat, we measure according to the milk alone. For example, assume one is cooking 45 ounces of water, and 5 ounces of milk fall in. Such a mixture is one-tenth milk. If ten ounces of this mixture fall into a pot of meat, then it is not necessary for the pot to contain sixty times the ten ounces. Rather only sixty times the one ounce of milk in the mixture is required.

In the end of section 7 in topic 46, the *Chochmas Adam* rules that this leniency (to measure with respect to the milk alone) can be relied upon only in cases of loss and great need. Many authorities, however, rule that this is not so, and one may measure with respect to the permissible ingredient alone in any case. (See *Aruch Hashulchan* 92:34.) Refer also to note 81.

96. The "meat knife" here is one which absorbed meat taste because it was used to cut hot meat. Even though the onion is cold, the pressure from the cutting plus the sharpness of the onion causes the knife to emit its absorbed taste into the onion (topic 49, section 1).

97. For example, a new knife had been used to cut a small piece of hot meat, and the same knife was used to cut an onion. The onion then fell into a pot of hot milk. In such a case, the meat taste in the onion will be transferred into the contents of the pot, and the taste of milk in the pot will be transferred to the onion. Nevertheless, it will not be necessary for the pot to contain sixty times the onion, since the onion did not become inherently forbidden. Rather, since the amount of meat taste in the onion cannot be more than the size of the piece of meat, it will be enough for the pot of milk to contain sixty times the meat.

98. I.e., the pot of milk must contain sixty times the outer thickness of the onion along its cut surfaces. This is much thicker than its *k'lipa* [outer peel]. According to the *Mishnah Berurah* 461:24, it is equivalent to the width of the thumb.

99. See sections 2 and 3 there. As such, even if a large amount of meat had been sliced with the knife, the pot of milk need not con-

כ. *Shulchan Aruch* 94:6, and see the *Shach* there.

meat, we do not say that we should consider everything which is in the pot as if it were milk. Rather, if we know how much milk has fallen into it, we can measure with respect to the milk alone.[95] כ Furthermore, if onions were cut with a meat knife[96] and were placed into a [hot] pot of milk, it is required only to have sixty times the amount [of meat] absorbed into it, if it is known how much meat was absorbed into it;[97] or [the pot must contain] sixty times the outer thickness[98] of the onions, since the onions [when being cut] do not absorb into more than their outer thickness, as [explained] later on in topic 49;[99] or if it is known how much of the knife came into contact [with the onion], he should measure sixty corresponding to the place of the knife [used for cutting them], even though they were very thinly sliced,[100] although normally, the usual way is to cut with the entire knife. And if there is sixty,[101] everything is permissible and it is not [even] necessary to remove the onion, for since [the absorbed taste] was permissible, it is not applicable to say [that it is not] possible to extract [the forbidden

Yad Adam

tain more than sixty times the outer thickness along the cut surfaces of the onion. This is because the absorbed meat taste in the knife will not penetrate any deeper than this. The *Chochmas Adam* goes on to explain that if the volume of the portion of the knife blade which came into contact with the onion is smaller than this, then it is sufficient to have sixty times that part of the knife blade. (See the next note.)

100. In a case where many cuts were made with the knife in order to slice the onions very thin (and the cut surface of the onions is therefore very large), it is still enough to have sixty times the part of the knife blade used to cut the onions. It will not be necessary for the pot of milk to contain sixty times the entire onion, since the onion is not inherently forbidden. Rather, it is sufficient to have sixty times the portion of the knife blade which came into contact with the onions, since the amount of meat taste in the onions cannot be greater than this. (For example, if one knows that he used only the middle third of the knife blade while cutting the onion [and the tip of the blade and the portion near the handle did not come into contact with the onion], then it will be sufficient to have sixty times the volume of the middle third of the blade.)

(Rabbi Akiva Eiger [on *Shulchan Aruch* 94:6] disagrees. Since in this case the taste of meat permeates the entire onion, it will not be sufficient to have sixty times the knife blade. Rather, the milk will have to contain sixty times the entire onion when it is thinly sliced. Compare with the second paragraph of note טו and footnotes thereon.)

101. If the contents of the pot are at least sixty times the absorbed taste of meat in the onions.

לסוחטו.[102] [כא] ודוקא שנתבשלו[103] אבל אם נכבשו הבצלים עם שאר דברים הבצלים נשארו באיסור דע״י כבישה אינו פולט הטעם כולו.[כב]

אבל אם חתכו בסכין של איסור[104] לדעת הב״י בש״ע דלא אמרינן בשאר איסורין[105] חנ״נ גם בזה סגי בס׳ נגד הנטילה ואם חתכו דק דק[106] סגי בס׳ נגד מקום הסכין ומ״מ צריך להסיר הבצלים מהאוכל ע״י סינון או בענין אחר דאע״פ דלא אמרינן חנ״נ מ״מ אפשר לסוחטו אסור כדלעיל סימן ח׳ ולדעת רמ״א[107] בחתך בסכין של איסור אם ידוע הנטילה סגי בדיעבד ששים נגד הנטילה שנעשה נבילה ואם חתכן דק דק צריך ס׳ נגד כל הבצל אפילו הוא גדול יותר מן הסכין שהרי כל חתיכה וחתיכה נ״נ.[108] [כג]

ואם חתך בסכין של חמץ קודם הפסח אפילו יש בו ס׳ מותר להשהותו ואסור לאכלו בפסח דמ״מ משהו איכא.[109] [כד]

כא. ע״ז סימן ל״ו ס״ק כ׳ וש״ך סימן צ״ד סס״ק כ״ג.

כב. מ״א סימן תמ״ז ס״ק ל״ח.

כג. סימן ל״ו סעיף ח׳ וסימן ל״ד סעיף ו׳.

כד. סימן תמ״ז מ״א ס״ק ל״ח.

יד אדם

102. In this case, we do not apply the principle which states that it is not possible to extract absorbed forbidden taste from food. (See section 8, and note 25 above.) This is because an onion which has absorbed the taste of meat is not a forbidden food, and nearly all of the meat flavor will be extracted during the cooking. As such, we allow this onion to be eaten. (Some authorities disagree with this and rule that the onion, when thinly sliced, must be removed and discarded. See *Aruch Hashulchan* 94:27 and 96:9.)

(In the cases involving an onion cut with a meat knife, if a great loss were to be incurred, there are grounds to be lenient even if sixty times the knife blade were not present. The basis for this leniency is that the taste is not being transmitted directly by the meat but only in a secondary way, such that by the time the taste reaches the onion it has become somewhat weakened. See topic 49, section 7.)

103. The onion which absorbed the taste of meat becomes permissible only if it was cooked with the milk, but not if it was mixed with milk in the following way.

104. For example, it contains forbidden taste because it had been used to cut hot unkosher meat. The forbidden taste will be transferred from the knife into the onion while it is being cut. The pieces of this onion then fall into a hot pot of permissible food, and as a result, the forbidden taste in the onion will be transmitted into the entire pot of food. The *Chochmas Adam* will now discuss the criteria for nullifying the absorbed forbidden taste in the onion.

105. A forbidden mixture which does not involve meat and milk.

106. And therefore, the total outer thickness is very large.

107. Who rules that we say a piece becomes

כא. *Taz* 96:5, *Shach* 94:23 (end).
כב. *Magen Avraham* 447:38
כג. *Shulchan Aruch* 96:1 and 94:6.
כד. *Magen Avraham* 447:38.

taste].[102]כא But this is only if they were cooked.[103] However, if the onions were soaked [for 24 hours] with other things, the onions remain in their forbidden state since by soaking they do not emit all of the [absorbed] taste.כב

However, if one cut [an onion] with a knife which is forbidden[104] according to the opinion of the *Bais Yosef* in the *Shulchan Aruch*, that we do not say regarding other forbidden foods[105] that the piece can become inherently forbidden, also in this case it is enough to have sixty times the outer thickness [of the onion]. And if one sliced it very thin[106] it is enough to have sixty times the portion of the knife [used for the cutting]. Nevertheless, it is necessary to remove the onion from the food by straining or in another manner, for even though we do not say that the piece becomes inherently forbidden, nevertheless, "it is not possible to extract [the forbidden taste]," as noted previously in section 8. And according to the opinion of the *Rama*,[107] if one cut with a forbidden knife—if the outer thickness [which became forbidden due to contact with the knife] is known, then it is enough after the fact to have sixty times the outer thickness, as this was [the portion] which became inherently forbidden. But if he had sliced them very thin, he requires sixty times the entire onion, even if it is very much bigger than the knife, because each and every piece has become inherently forbidden.[108]כג

And if one cut [an onion] with a *chometz* knife before *Pesach*, even though there is sixty in it, it is permissible to keep [the cut food during *Pesach*] but it is forbidden to eat it on *Pesach*, for still in all, there is a small amount [of *chometz*].[109]כד

Yad Adam

inherently forbidden, even regarding forbidden mixtures that do not involve meat and milk.

108. And it is not sufficient to have sixty times the knife blade in this case.

(See the end of section 3 in topic 49 that there might be grounds to be lenient in cases of necessity, as follows: Since the taste entered the onion without being cooked, we can say that the onion does not become inherently forbidden, in accordance with section 13 below. As such, even if the onion were very thinly sliced with a forbidden knife, it would be sufficient for the pot to contain sixty times the blade.)

109. Even though it was cut before *Pesach* (when *chometz* is still permissible and nullification can still take place), one still may not eat it on *Pesach*. The reason is that actual particles of *chometz* may have gotten into the

יג. יש אומרים דאפילו בבשר וחלב לא אמרינן חנ״נ אלא דוקא אם הוא דרך בישול או צלי או צונן לחם דגם זה הוא דרך בישול.[110] ושאר איסורי תורה כיון שאין אומרים בהם חנ״נ אלא משום לתא דבשר בחלב[111] משום הכי לא אסרינן גם כן אלא דומיא דבשר וחלב דהיינו דרך בישול אבל ע״י מליחה וכבישה בשאר איסורין אע״ג שאסור מן התורה[112] ומכ״ש בבשר וחלב דאינו אלא מדרבנן[113] וכן בשאר איסורין שהם מדרבנן אפילו ע״י בישול[114] לא אמרינן חנ״נ.[כה]

וי״א דאפי׳ באיסורי דרבנן אמרינן חנ״נ[כו] ומכל מקום במליחה יש להתיר לצורך הפסד מרובה אפילו בשמן[115] ולא אמרינן חנ״נ כיון דלהרבה פוסקים אפילו בשמן די בקליפה[116][כז] ולהסוברין

כה. פ״ח סימן ל״ג ס״ק י״ז בשם הר״ן וכ״כ הש״ך בשמו בסי׳ קל״ד ס״ק ע״ז.
כו. ט״ז בסי׳ ל׳ ס״ק ד׳ יש״ש פג״ה סוף סי׳ ל״ה וכו״פ שם בשם תוס׳ וכן מצאתי בהו״ה כלל כ״ד סי׳ ה׳ שכ״כ בהדיא וכ״מ עוד שם סי׳ ו׳.
כז. ש״ך בסי׳ ל״ג ס״ק ע״ז ובסי׳ כ״ג ס״ק י׳ משמע דטעמו כמש״כ הר״ן כיון דמליחה אינו אסור בבשר וחלב מה״ת וא״כ משמע שמסתפק בזה.

יד אדם

onion while it was being cut. However, one who keeps it in his possession will not transgress the prohibition against having *chometz* in his possession on *Pesach*. (See *Chayei Adam* 121:29 that there are sometimes grounds to be lenient in cases of great urgency.)

13. Can Mixtures Forbidden By Rabbinical Decree Become Inherently Forbidden (nevelah)?

110. (This is in accordance with topic 42, section 7 that the lower food dominates.) As we learned previously, the Torah prohibits milk and meat only when they are actually cooked together, but not when they are soaked together for 24 hours or salted together. Nevertheless, these last two methods are considered cooking with respect to other foods which are forbidden by the Torah. (topic 40, section 1)

111. I.e., the basic Torah rule that a piece becomes inherently forbidden applies to meat and milk, and the rabbis extended this rule to other forbidden foods. It is therefore reasonable to assume that the rabbis did not extend this rule to situations which do not apply to meat and milk.

112. For example, forbidden fat is salted together, or soaked together in a liquid for 24 hours, with permissible meat. The meat is regarded as being cooked with the fat and is forbidden.

113. Where the meat and milk are salted together, or soaked together for 24 hours. Alternatively, where chicken is cooked with milk. (See *Aruch Hashulchan* 92:25.)

114. For example, meat which had been cooked together with rabbinically forbidden fat (such as the fat that surrounds the *gid*

13. Some authorities say that even regarding meat and milk we do not say that a piece becomes inherently forbidden unless it specifically [becomes mixed] in the usual manner of cooking or broiling, or with cold [falling] into hot as this is also a manner of cooking.[110] And with respect to other foods forbidden by the Torah, since we do not say that a piece becomes inherently forbidden regarding them except due to their relationship to meat and milk,[111] therefore we also do not forbid them except [when the mixture] is similar to [a forbidden mixture of] meat and milk, which [becomes forbidden by the Torah only] in the normal manner of cooking. However, regarding salting or soaking in the case of other forbidden foods, even though [the food] is forbidden according to the Torah;[112] and certainly regarding [mixtures of] meat and milk which are forbidden [only] by the rabbis;[113] and also other forbidden foods which are [only] rabbinically forbidden, even [if actually] cooked[114]—[in all of these situations] we do not say that a piece becomes inherently forbidden.[כה]

And some authorities [disagree with the above and] say that even with [regard to foods] that are forbidden by the rabbis we say that a piece becomes inherently forbidden.[כו] Nevertheless, regarding salting, it is proper to permit if there is a great loss even with fatty food[115] and we do not say that a piece becomes inherently forbidden, since according to many authorities even with fatty food it is enough with peeling.[116][כז] And those who feel with regard to a rabbinically forbidden

כה. *Pri Chadash* 92:17 in the name of the *Ran*, and the *Shach* 134:16 writes similarly in his name.

כו. *Taz* 90:4, *Yam shel Shlomo* chapter *gid hanashe* end of section 35, and *Kreisi u'pleisi* there in the name of *Tosafot*. And so I have found in the *Issur v'heter* topic 24 section 1 that he writes this explicitly, and I have also found it there in section 6.

כז. The *Shach* in 92:16 and 22:10 implies that his reason is like that written by the *Ran*—since salting is not forbidden by the Torah with regard to mixtures of meat and milk. As such, it implies that he would be in doubt about this [leniency].

Yad Adam

hanashe). In all of these cases, if the piece of meat which absorbed forbidden taste will fall into another pot of meat, one would not necessarily require that the pot contain sixty times the piece to permit the mixture. Rather (according to these authorities), it will be sufficient to have sixty times the amount of forbidden food whose taste was absorbed, even if the piece of meat is much larger.

115. Even though salted fatty foods have more of a tendency to spread the taste, as noted in topic 43, section 11.

116. Many authorities rule that after removing a thin outer layer of meat which came into contact with salted forbidden food, the rest of the meat will be permitted (topic 43, section 11). Even though in practice we are strict to prohibit the entire piece of meat, here, where a piece of meat came into contact with forbidden salty fatty food and the meat then fell into a pot of other food, we can be lenient and presume that only the peel of the piece of meat became forbidden. The pot of food will then remain permissible. (See *Shach* 22:10.)

כח. ע"ז סימן נ"ג ס"ק י"ג.

דבאיסור דרבנן לא אמרינן חנ"נ הוא הדין דאפשר לסוחטו מותר[117] כדמוכח להדיא מדברי הרמב"ם שהביא הפ"ח שם.

יד. עוד אנו נוהגין על פי רמ"א שבמקום שהאיסור דבוק כגון חתיכת בשר שדבוק בו חתיכת חלב אע"ג דיש ס' בכל מה שבקדירה נגד החלב אסור הכל עד שיהיה ס' באותו חתיכה נגד החלב[118] או שיהיה ס' נגד כל החתיכה שהחלב דבוק בו[119] דחיישינן שמא פעם אחת נשאר לבדו ברוטב בסוף העירוי[120] או שמא פעם אחת הוציאו רותח חוץ לקדירה ואם כן[121] נעשה נבלה[122] וכשיחזירנה לקדירה אוסר כל הקדירה[123] לדידן דקיי"ל חנ"נ[124] כח והש"ך בסימן ע"ב ס"ק י"ח כתבו הטעם דאותה חתיכה שהאיסור דבוק בה ממהרת לבלוע האיסור תחלה ונעשית תיכף נבלה.

ולכן כשיש בקדירה ס' נגד החלב שדבוק בחתיכה לדעת הב"י דלא אמרינן חנ"נ וא"כ אע"פ שיש ס' בקדירה[125] צריך ליזהר שלא

יד אדם

117. I.e., we will assume that all of the forbidden taste is extracted when the forbidden piece is cooked and it becomes permissible to be eaten. (See also note 60 above regarding the translation.) As such (according to these authorities), if a piece of chicken was cooked in milk and the piece falls into a hot pot of meat which contains more than sixty times the absorbed milk, the entire mixture will be permitted. Even the piece of chicken will be permitted because we are lenient to say that while the piece is cooking in the hot pot, the absorbed milk is extracted from it.

14. איסור דבוק—An Attached Forbidden Substance

118. Otherwise the attached meat will become forbidden when it is heated, since it will absorb taste from the fat.

119. The pot must contain sixty times the piece of meat plus sixty times the fat.

120. When pouring the contents out of the pot, it is possible that the piece will remain behind in a small amount of hot liquid and the liquid will be less than sixty times the amount of fat.

121. If one of these situations were to occur, and there would no longer be enough meat and liquid present to nullify the taste of the forbidden fat.

122. The meat, since it is hot, will absorb the taste of the fat and become inherently forbidden unless the piece of meat is sixty times the size of the attached fat.

123. The entire contents of the pot will be

כח. *Taz* 92:12.

food that we do not say that a piece becomes inherently forbidden, it will also be the case that it is possible to extract [the forbidden taste][117] as it is shown explicitly from the words of the *Rambam* that the *Pri Chadash* quotes there.

14. We are also accustomed to follow the *Rama* that in a situation where the forbidden food is attached, such as a piece of meat which has a piece of forbidden fat attached to it, [if such a piece fell into a hot pot], even though there is sixty times the forbidden fat among everything that is in the pot, everything is forbidden, unless there will be sixty times the fat[118] in that piece [of meat which is attached to the fat], or unless there will be [in the pot] sixty times the entire piece to which the forbidden fat is attached.[119] [The reason for this stringency is] we are concerned that perhaps at one time [the piece with the attached fat] will be left by itself in the liquid at the end of pouring[120] or perhaps at one time it was removed from the pot while hot. If so,[121] [the attached meat] becomes inherently forbidden[122] and when he returns it to the pot it makes the entire pot forbidden[123] according to us who rule that the piece becomes inherently forbidden.[124]כח And the *Shach* in 72:18 has written the reason [for the stringency]—that the piece which has the fat attached to it will absorb the forbidden taste very quickly at the beginning, and it will become inherently forbidden immediately.

Therefore, if the pot contains sixty times the fat that is attached to the piece [of meat]—[if we go] according to opinion of the *Bais Yosef* who rules that we do not say that a piece becomes inherently forbidden—as such, even though there is sixty [times the size of the forbidden fat] in the pot,[125] one must be careful that he should not take out

Yad Adam

forbidden unless it contains sixty times the entire piece (the forbidden fat plus the meat which is attached to it).

124. We follow the *Rama* and rule that the piece becomes inherently forbidden even for prohibitions other than meat and milk. On the other hand, the *Bais Yosef*, who rules that in such cases the piece does not become inherently forbidden, would rule that it is sufficient in this case if the pot contains sixty times the forbidden fat.

125. As a result, the contents of the pot remain permissible according to the *Bais Yosef*. Nevertheless, one must still be careful with the meat attached to the fat to prevent it from becoming forbidden, as follows.

יוציאנה תחילה דאם יוציאנה אז כיון שאין ס׳ בחתיכה גופה נגד החלב יאסור החלב את החתיכה[126] וגם לא יסיר שום דבר מהקדירה בעוד שחתיכת האיסור בתוכו דחיישינן שמא תשאר באחרונה בשעה שאין בקדירה ששים לבטל החלב אלא יניחנה עד שתצטנן הקדירה[127] ואז אף החתיכה מותר אבל לדעת רמ״א יסירנה מיד דלמה יניחנה בחנם בקדירה שהרי החתיכה נשאר באיסורו.[128][כט]

טו. ולאו דוקא דבוק בתולדתו[129] אלא אפילו דג טהור שנמצא במעיה לאחר שנתבשל שרץ או דג טמא. אבל בנמצא שרץ בראשו לא הוי דבוק שהמים יכול לבא לשם.[130][לא] ונ״ל דאם יש ספק אם יש כאן ס׳[131] כגון שנשפך[132] וכיוצא בו יש לסמוך ולהתיר דאף דקיי״ל דבוק י״ל דוקא בודאי איסור ולא בספק[133] ואפשר

כט. סי׳ ק״ו סעיף ב׳ ועיין שם בש״ך.

ל. ט״ז סי׳ צ״ב ס״ק י״ב ושם ס״ק י״א ע״ש וצ״ל בשם מהרי״ל היינו מה שכתב בשמו ס״ק י״ב ועיין בש״ך סי׳ צ״ב ס״ק י״ז.

לא. ואמנם זה לא מהני רק שיערה כל הדגים והרוטב בפעם אחת אבל אם לקח עם כף הראש לבד וא״כ אף שלא נקרא דבוק עכ״פ צריך ס׳ בראש לבד ודינו כדלקמן כלל ס״א.

יד אדם

126. If it is removed from the pot while it is hot, the taste of the forbidden fat will be absorbed into the piece of meat and make it forbidden.

127. When there will no longer be any transfer of taste.

128. The piece is forbidden in any case and we are concerned that it will go on to make the entire contents of the pot forbidden. This piece should therefore be removed immediately, and the remaining contents of the pot will then be permissible if they are at least sixty times the size of the entire piece (the fat plus the attached meat).

15. Definition of דבוק (Attached); Nullification of a Forbidden Substances in Cases of Doubt

129. I.e., it need not be like forbidden fat where the forbidden substance is attached to the meat as a result of the normal development of the animal.

130. The water enters into the head and completely surrounds the creeping thing. (*Taz* 92:12. Compare *Chochmas Adam* topic 34, section 7.) Therefore, if the head of this fish is cooked in a pot with other ingredients, sixty times the entire head will not be required. Rather, it will be sufficient if the pot contains sixty times the creeping thing. See also note **לא**.

131. After cooking a kosher fish, an unkosher fish is found in its stomach. Since the unkosher fish is regarded as being "attached" to it, the other contents of the pot must be equal to sixty times the size of the kosher fish (unless the kosher fish itself is sixty times the size of the unkosher fish). The *Chochmas Adam* is now dealing with a case

כט. *Shulchan Aruch* 106:2, and see the *Shach* there.
ל. *Taz* 92:12; and there in paragraph 11 there is a printer's error, and it should say: "In the name of the *Maharil*"; which refers to what is written in his name in paragraph 12.* And see in the *Shach* 72:17.
לא. However, this [leniency regarding the head of a fish] does not help unless he will pour out all the fish and all the liquid at one time. But, if he will take the head out by itself with a spoon, nevertheless, even though it is not called "attached," at least there must be in the head alone sixty times [the size of the creeping thing], and the ruling is as noted later on in topic 61.

[the piece with the attached fat] first, for if he takes it out, then since there is not sixty times the forbidden fat in the piece itself, the forbidden fat will cause the piece [of meat] to become forbidden.[126] Furthermore, he should not remove anything at all from the pot while the forbidden piece is in it, for we are concerned that perhaps [the forbidden piece] will remain at the end when there is no longer sixty times as much in the pot to nullify the forbidden fat. Rather, he should leave it until the pot will cool down[127] and then even the piece [of meat attached to the fat] will be permissible. However, according to the *Rama*, he should remove it immediately, for why should he leave it in the pot for no reason, as the piece remains in its forbidden state [in any case].[128]כט

15. And [the forbidden substance] need not be attached specifically [as a result of] its development[129] [for the above stringencies to apply]. Rather, even a kosher fish [is regarded as being "attached" to an unkosher] creeping thing or an unkosher fish which is found in its stomach after it is cooked. However, when a creeping thing is found in its head, it is not [regarded as] attached, since the water [in which the fish is cooking] is able to enter there.[130]ללא And it is my opinion that if there is a doubt whether there is sixty here,[131] such as where it was poured out[132] and in similar cases, there are grounds to be lenient, for even though it is established for us that it is "attached," it is possible to say that this is only where there is a definite prohibition but not in case of a doubt.[133] And it is possible that this is the rule regarding an animal

*Our texts have the phrase: "In the name of the *Rashal*."

Yad Adam

where we are unsure if the required sixty is present.

132. The pot cooled down and the liquid in which the fish was cooked has been poured out, so that it can no longer be measured. Can we then be lenient and permit the other food which was cooked together with the fish?

133. As such, we would not forbid the entire kosher fish unless it is definitely known that the permissible contents of the pot were less than sixty times the kosher fish.

לב. וכעין זה כתב המ"ב סי' ל"ז.
לג. סימן ל"ו ש"ך ס"ק ע'.
לד. ש"ך סי' ל"ב ס"ק ח'.

דה"ה בספק טריפה[134]לב וכן לענין חנ"נ בנשפך[135] יש להתיר בשאר איסורין.[136]

טז. לא אמרינן איסור דבוק אלא כשהחתיכה עומד בפני עצמו אבל לא בחצי חתיכה כגון שחתך בצל בסכין של איסור ונאסר ממנו כדי נטילה[137] ונתנוהו בקדירה של היתר לא אמרינן שיהיה איסור דבוק ויצטרך ס' נגד כל הבצל אלא כל הקדירה מצטרף לבטל כדי נטילה ומותר[138] וי"א דבכה"ג לא אמרינן ג"כ חנ"נ.[139]לג

יז. לא אמרינן חנ"נ אלא כשיש כאן איסור מבורר אבל אם אינו מבורר כגון שיש כאן ספק שמא אין כאן איסור כלל אע"ג דאסור מספק מ"מ לא אמרינן חנ"נ כגון חתיכה ספק נגע באיסור או לא אבל ספק טרפה[140] הוא איסור מבורר ועיין כלל מ"ג סי' י"ד.לד

יד אדם

134. A piece of meat from an animal which is questionably *terefah* (it might be forbidden due to an abnormality in one of its internal organs) fell into a pot of food (containing liquid and other meat). The liquid was poured out after the pot cooled off and we are not sure if the required sixty had been present. Will the other pieces of meat in the pot be forbidden? The *Chochmas Adam* is suggesting that we can be lenient in such a case.

135. For example, a piece of meat became forbidden because it absorbed some forbidden fat, and the piece fell into a pot containing meat and liquid. The liquid from the pot was then poured out after it cooled off and we do not know whether or not there had been sixty times the piece that became inherently forbidden.

136. But not with a piece of meat which absorbed milk and thereby became forbidden.

16. The Stringencies of an Attached Forbidden Substance Apply Only to a Separate Entity

137. A knife had been used to cut hot unkosher meat and that same knife was used to cut an onion. The outer thickness of the cut surface of the onion (where it came into contact with the knife) must be removed (see notes 96 to 98), and it is this outer layer which is now the forbidden "piece."

138. The contents of the pot remain permissible as long as sixty times the outer thickness is present.

לב. And the *Masas Binyamin* chapter 37 writes similar to this.
לג. *[Shulchan Aruch]* chapter 96, *Shach* paragraph 9.
לד. *Shach* 92:8.

which is doubtfully *terefah*.[134]לב And similarly regarding a piece that became inherently forbidden from which [the liquid of the pot] was poured out,[135] there are grounds to permit [such mixtures] with other forbidden foods.[136]

16. We do not say that a forbidden substance is "attached" except when the [forbidden] piece stands [as a recognizable entity] by itself, but not when [the forbidden portion is merely] part of a piece. For example, one has cut an onion with a knife used for forbidden food, and its outer thickness [thereby] became forbidden[137]; if one [then] placed it in a pot of permissible food, we do not say that it should be considered as if the forbidden portion were "attached" [to the rest of the onion] and require [the pot to contain] sixty times the entire onion. Rather, all of the pot combines to nullify the "outer thickness" and it is permissible.[138] And some say that in such a case also we do not say that the piece becomes inherently forbidden.[139]לג

17. We do not say that a piece becomes inherently forbidden except when a clear cut prohibition is present, but if it is not clear cut, such as where a doubt is present as to whether or not there is a prohibition at all—even though [the food] is forbidden because of the doubt—nevertheless, we do not say that the piece becomes inherently forbidden. [This applies,] for example, if it is questionable whether or not a piece [of hot food] came into contact with a forbidden food. However, if something is questionably *terefah*,[140] this is [regarded to be] a clear cut prohibition. And see topic 43, section 14 [and topic 44, section 4 for application of this rule].לד

Yad Adam

139. When the forbidden food is not a separate entity but only the outer layer of a piece, we do not say that it becomes inherently forbidden. Therefore, according to these authorities, it will not even be required to have sixty times the outer thickness of the onion, but only sixty times the amount of forbidden taste it absorbed if the latter is smaller. For example, if the knife had been used to cut only one very small piece of forbidden meat, then the maximum absorbed forbidden taste would be the size of that piece of meat, and only sixty times that piece would be required.

17. A Piece Becomes Inherently Forbidden Only When the Prohibition Is Clear Cut

140. Meat is questionably forbidden due to an abnormality of one of the animal's internal organs.

יח. לא אמרינן חנ״נ אלא באוכל אבל בכלי לא אמרינן חנ״נ כגון כלי חדש[141] שבלע כזית איסור או כזית בשר ובתוך מעת לעת בישל בתוכו היתר או חלב לא אמרינן שיצטרך ס׳ נגד כל הכלי[142] דלא שייך לומר שגוף החרס יעשה נבלה ולכן אין צריך ס׳ אלא נגד כזית שבלע[143] וכן אפי׳ קדירה ישנה של היתר או של בשר ולאחר מעת לעת[144] בישל בה כזית איסור או של חלב ובתוך מעת לעת של בישול הכזית הזה חזר לבשל בה היתר או בשר אע״ג די״ל דכאן כיון שיש בקדירה זו בלוע[145] וא״כ נעשה הבלוע נבלה[146] אפ״ה א״צ ס׳ אלא נגד הכזית שבלע בתוך מעת לעת זה[147] שמה שבלע הקדירה קודם מעת לעת היה לפגם ואם כן לא נאסר הבלוע.

אבל אם בישל בקדירה היתר או בשר ובתוך מעת לעת בישל בה כזית איסור או חלב וא״כ נאסר הבלוע ונעשה נבלה[148] ולכן כשחזר ובישל אח״כ בתוך מעת לעת היתר או בשר יש אומרים

יד אדם

18. Can a Vessel Become Inherently Forbidden (nevelah)?

141. I.e., a vessel which has never been used and therefore has no absorbed taste in it. If a vessel had been used previously but was not used during the previous 24 hours, it has the same status as a new vessel, since any absorbed taste in it will have become spoiled. A vessel which has been used during the past 24 hours is called "old."

142. I.e., it is not necessary that the contents of the pot be at least sixty times the material of the pot.

143. Since we do not know exactly how much taste the pot absorbed, we assume that it absorbs all of the taste of the olive-size piece, and sixty times this amount will be required.

144. Such a pot is regarded as new since any taste absorbed into it has spoiled.

145. The taste of the permissible food or meat which had been previously cooked in the pot. Let us assume that the amount of food cooked previously was greater than or equal to the volume of the material of the pot. In such a case, the volume of the absorbed tasted is considered to be equal to the material of the pot.

146. One might say that the absorbed taste in the pot from the previous cookings would combine with the olive-size of forbidden food or milk, and the absorbed taste would thereby become inherently forbidden. If this were the case, then the contents of the pot would have to be at least sixty times the material of the pot.

147. It is indeed necessary to have sixty

18. We do not say that a piece becomes inherently forbidden except regarding food, but regarding a vessel we do not say that a piece becomes inherently forbidden. For example, if a new vessel[141] absorbed [taste from] an olive-size of forbidden food or an olive-size of meat [which was cooked in it], and within 24 hours he cooked in it a permissible food or milk [respectively], we do not say that it is necessary to have sixty times the entire vessel,[142] because it is not applicable to say that the material of the earthenware [vessel] should become inherently forbidden. Therefore, one needs only sixty times the olive-size that it absorbed.[143] And similarly, even [with regard to] an old pot [used previously] for permissible food or for meat in which, after 24 hours [since its last use],[144] one cooked an olive-size of forbidden food or of milk [respectively], and within 24 hours of cooking this olive-size piece he went on to cook in it permissible food or meat [respectively], even though it is possible to say that here, since there is [previously] absorbed taste in this pot,[145] and as such, the [previously] absorbed taste should become inherently forbidden,[146] even so, it is not necessary to have sixty except corresponding to the olive-size that it absorbed within this 24 hours.[147] For what the pot absorbed [previously] before the 24 hours has become spoiled, and consequently, the absorbed taste [from that time] does not become forbidden.

However, if one cooked permissible food or meat in the pot, and within 24 hours he cooked in it an olive-size of forbidden food or milk [respectively], in such a case, the absorbed [taste] becomes prohibited and becomes inherently forbidden.[148] Therefore, if one went on and cooked afterwards permissible food or meat within 24 hours—some say

Yad Adam

times the olive- size of forbidden food or milk, but the taste absorbed into the pot before this time can be ignored since it was already 24 hours old.

It should be noted that when a vessel absorbs forbidden taste, it is certainly forbidden to cook in it again until it is kashered. Here, we are dealing with situations where such a vessel was used for cooking without being kashered, and we wish to determine if the food cooked in it may be eaten or if it must be discarded.

The concept that taste absorbed in a vessel can make food forbidden is discussed further in topic 46, section 1.

148. The *Chochmas Adam* will go on to explain that if permissible food or meat will subsequently be cooked in the pot within 24 hours of this second cooking, it will not be

לה. סי' צ"ח ס"ק כ"ח. לו. ועיין בט"ז סי' צ"ח ס"ק ח' בסופו ועיין בת"ח כלל כ"ח וכלל פ"ה.

דהבלוע[149] נ"נ וצריך ס' נגד כל הקדירה או נגד כל מה שבישל בקדירה בפעם ראשון קודם שנאסר[150] ויש אומרים דבבלוע לעולם לא אמרינן נ"נ[151] ובמקום הפסד מרובה בכלי מתכת או של עץ כיון שיוכל להפריד האיסור ולהוציאו ע"י הגעלה[152] יש להקל ולומר דבבלוע לא אמרינן *חנ"נלה ובכלי חרס[153] נ"ל דבשאר איסורין[154] במקום הפסד מרובה לא אמרינן ג"כ נ"נ כיון דהרבה פוסקים ס"ל דלא אמרינן בשאר איסורין חנ"נ ובבשר וחלב יש להחמיר.[155]לו

ואם לקח מן הקדירה בכף חתיכת דג טמא וכיוצא בו שהיה ס' בקדירה כנגד האיסור והחזיר הכף לקדירה[156] צריך ס' נגד האיסור לבד ולא נגד הכף אם הוא הפסד מרובה דלא אמרינן בבלוע חנ"נ[157] אפילו בישן[158] ואם היה גם כן מעט תבשיל עם האיסור בכף והחזיר

יד אדם

sufficient to have sixty times the olive-size of the forbidden food or milk. Rather, according to some authorities, the pot will have to contain sixty times the meat or permissible food present at the time of the first cooking (if this amount is larger than the size of an olive). The maximum amount that can be required is sixty times the material of the pot.

149. The absorbed taste in the pot from the first cooking of permissible food or meat.

150. The latter applies if the amount of food cooked in the pot the first time is less than the volume of the material of the pot and greater than the size of an olive.

151. And it will be sufficient to have sixty times the olive- size of forbidden food or milk. We thus ignore absorbed taste which was present before the last cooking, even though 24 hours had not elapsed.

152. This would extract all of the forbidden taste and make the vessel permissible to use.

*I.e., the absorbed taste in the vessel.

153. Which cannot be made kosher by means of boiling water. Since the forbidden taste can never be totally removed from such a vessel, it is to be treated more stringently.

154. Where mixtures of meat and milk are not involved.

155. In summary, one should require sixty times the vessel (or the amount cooked during the first cooking if this is smaller than the vessel) but if a great loss is involved, we do not require this (and it is enough to have sixty times the olive-size portion from the second cooking). However, when the case involves an earthenware vessel with the prohibition of meat and milk, it is proper to be strict even when a great loss is involved and require sixty times the vessel.

156. The spoon, which now contains absorbed taste from the forbidden food, is returned into the pot together with the forbidden food. The question now is as follows: Will it be sufficient if the pot contains sixty

לה. Chapter 98, *Shach* paragraph 21.
לו. And refer to the *Taz*, chapter 98, end of paragraph 8. And see the *Toras Chatas* topics 51 and 85.

that the absorbed [taste][149] had become inherently forbidden and he needs sixty times the entire [material of the] pot or [sixty] times everything he cooked in the pot the first time before it became forbidden;[150] but other [authorities] say that regarding absorbed [taste] we never say that it becomes inherently forbidden.[151] And in a situation where there is a great loss–with a metal or wood vessel, since one will be able to separate away the forbidden [taste] and remove it by means of kashering with boiling water,[152] one can be lenient and say that with absorbed [taste] we do not say that a piece* becomes inherently forbidden.[לה] But regarding an earthenware vessel[153]–it is my opinion that with other forbidden foods[154] in a case of a great loss we also do not say that [its absorbed taste] becomes inherently forbidden, since many authorities rule that we do not say that a piece becomes inherently forbidden with regard to other forbidden foods, but with meat and milk it is proper to be strict.[155][לו]

And if one took a piece of unkosher fish or something like it with a spoon from a pot, where [the permissible food] in the pot was sixty times as much as the forbidden food, and he returned the spoon into the pot,[156] he requires sixty times the size of the forbidden food alone and not [sixty] times the spoon if there is a great loss, as we do not say with regard to absorbed [taste] that a piece becomes inherently forbidden,[157] even with an old [spoon].[158] But if there was also a little cooked food with the forbidden food on the spoon and he returned

Yad Adam

times the forbidden food, or will the pot have to contain additional ingredients in order to nullify the absorbed forbidden taste in the spoon.

157. If there would be a great loss, we do not say the "piece," i.e., the permissible absorbed taste in the spoon, becomes inherently forbidden. See the next note regarding a case where there is not a great loss.

158. I.e., even with a spoon which was used with hot permissible food within the previous 24 hours. (The spoon in our situation would usually be an "old spoon." This is because when it was inserted into the pot to remove the forbidden fish, it will have absorbed taste from the other contents of the pot at that time. Nevertheless, it is possible for the spoon to be "new," such as where the forbidden fish was floating on top of the liquid in the pot and a new spoon was used to lift them out. Since the spoon was not immersed into the contents of the pot, it will have no absorbed taste in it other than from the food that it is presently holding.)

In accordance with the guidelines mentioned above, if the spoon is "old" and there is not a great loss, then we should be strict

הכל לקדירה אע״ג שבקדירה יש ס׳ נגד האיסור מ״מ עכשיו כיון שהכניס הכף בכלי ראשון[159] גם הוא נעשה כלי ראשון לחומרא[160] לז וא״כ נעשה התבשיל שהוא עם האיסור בכף נבלה[161] ולכן[162] אם ידע כמה היה התבשיל והאיסור שבכף והם פחות מן כל הכף א״צ ס׳ אלא נגד האיסור והתבשיל[163] ואם אינו יודע כמה היה התבשיל[164] צריך ס׳ נגד כל הכף שהרי אינו יודע כמה בלע הכף.[165] לח

לז. ועיין כלל נ״ט סי׳ ג׳.
לח. סי׳ ק״ז בש״ך ובמנ״י כלל נ״ח ס״ק כ׳.

יד אדם

and say that the absorbed taste in the spoon has become inherently forbidden. It will then be necessary for the pot to contain sixty times the forbidden food plus sixty times the spoon to nullify the absorbed forbidden taste in it. (See topic 46, section 8 for further details.)

159. I.e., a vessel which was heated directly by the fire.

160. We have learned (topic 42, section 9) that as a general rule, "cooking" (which results in transfer of taste from one food to another) does not take place in a "second vessel" (**כלי שני**). (If food is transferred from a vessel which was heated by the fire into another vessel, the latter is called a "second vessel.") We are learning here that the spoon in this case is to be treated as a "first vessel" and not as a "second vessel" the reason being that a spoon which was inserted into a hot "first vessel" is itself to be regarded as a "first vessel" if a stringency will result. (See topic 59, section 3.)

161. Since they are together on the spoon which is a "first vessel" they absorb each other's taste and the cooked food becomes inherently forbidden. It will therefore be necessary to have sixty times the volume of the forbidden food plus the cooked food on the spoon. Unless there is a great loss, sixty times the spoon will also be required. (See *Kaf Hachayim* 107:14.)

162. We have mentioned above that in cases of great loss, even with an "old spoon," we require only sixty times the forbidden food plus the cooked food on the spoon but not sixty times the spoon itself. We will now learn that in such cases, if the volume of the spoon is larger than the foods on it (such as where a thick wooden spoon was being used) then it will be necessary instead for the pot to contain at least sixty times the entire spoon.

163. As noted above, if a great loss would not be incurred, it is necessary to have sixty times the foods plus sixty times the spoon.

לז. And see topic 59, section 3.
לח. Chapter 107 [paragraph 7] in the *Shach* and in *Minchas Yaakov* topic 51, paragraph 20.

everything into the pot, even though in the pot there is sixty times the forbidden food, nevertheless, now, since he inserted the spoon into a "first vessel,"[159] [the spoon] also becomes a "first vessel" regarding stringencies.[160] לז As such, the cooked food which is with the forbidden food on the spoon becomes inherently forbidden.[161] Accordingly,[162] if one knew how much cooked food and forbidden food were on the spoon and they are less than [the volume of] the entire spoon, he needs only sixty times the forbidden food and the cooked food;[163] and if he does not know how much the cooked food was,[164] he will need sixty times the entire spoon, for he does not know how much the spoon absorbed.[165] לח

Yad Adam

164. He is uncertain whether or not the cooked food plus the forbidden food was less than the size of the spoon. In such a case, we must assume that the cooked food plus the forbidden food was at least equal to the size of the spoon.

165. We assume that the spoon was filled with forbidden taste, and sixty times the entire spoon will be required. (If, however, a great loss is not involved, sixty times the spoon plus the foods on it will be required.)

Note: Whenever it is stated that "sixty times the entire spoon" is required, the meaning is "sixty times the entire portion of the spoon which was inserted into the food." See topic 46, section 6.

(Textual note: The word גם found here in other current editions was inserted as a result of a printer's error.)

כלל מה
דין טיפת חלב שנפל על הקדירה ודין אם זב חלב או איסור תחת קדירה

(סימן צ"ב)

א. עיין לקמן סי' ו'.

א. טיפת חלב שנפלה על קדירה שבשל בה בשר וכן טיפת איסור על קדירה של היתר מספקא לן אי מפעפע בכל הקדרה או אינו מפעפע[1] ולכן אם נפלה כנגד התבשיל[2] אין צריך אלא[3] ס' נגד הטיפה והתבשיל מותר ממ"נ דאם מפעפע מסתמא פעפע לפנים[4] ואז יש ס' בתבשיל לבטל ואם אינה מפעפע פשיטא דכשרה ומכל מקום יערה התבשיל מיד מצד השני שלא כנגד נפילת האיסור ולא ימתין עד שיצטנן[5] דחיישינן שמא נשאר עוד מעט שעדיין לא פעפע[6] ואם יערה התבשיל באותו צד אפי' אם הקדירה חדשה[7] ובבו"ח[8] בענין דלא נ"נ[9][א] מ"מ אסור לבטל

יד אדם

1. Regulations Regarding Forbidden Liquid Which Has Splashed onto a Pot

1. There is a doubt whether or not the taste spreads through the walls of the pot into its contents. *Rashi* and *Tosafot* are among those who rule that when the pot is hot, indeed the taste will penetrate into the contents of the pot. (*Aruch Hashulchan* 92:35)

The term "hot" denotes that the item is hot enough such that one would withdraw his hand from it when touching it (topic 42, section 9). If the temperature of the pot was less than this when the liquid splashed onto it, then there would certainly be no transfer of taste of the liquid into the contents of the pot.

2. For example, the pot is half full and the drop fell onto the lower half of the pot.

3. The word "only" is used here because in some of the cases noted below, more than sixty (i.e., sixty times sixty-one) is required.

4. Not only has it spread through the material of the pot, but probably into the contents of the pot as well.

5. The reason for not waiting is stated below: Lest the liquid on the outside surface of the pot continue to spread into the pot's contents. By pouring out the contents immediately, we will minimize the spread of the milk (or forbidden material) into the contents of the pot. (In some of the cases mentioned below, it is advisable to wait for the pot to cool off before emptying it. This is not the case here. See also note 13.) The *Chochmas Adam* now goes on to explain why the contents should not be poured out on the side upon which the drop has fallen.

Topic 45

Laws Concerning a Drop of Milk Which Has Fallen onto a Pot [of Meat], and the Regulations Regarding Milk or Forbidden Liquid Which Has Flowed under a Pot

(based on *Shulchan Aruch—Yoreh Deah* chapter 92)

א. See further on, section 6.

1. If a drop of milk has fallen onto [the outside surface of] a pot in which meat was being cooked—or similarly, if a drop of forbidden [liquid has fallen] onto a pot of permissible food—it is doubtful whether [its taste] spreads throughout the entire pot or if it does not spread [throughout the pot].[1] As such, if [a drop] has fallen alongside the cooked food,[2] then we require only[3] sixty times the drop, and the cooked food would be permissible either way: For if [the drop] does spread, probably it has spread inside[4] and then there is sixty in the cooked food to nullify [the taste of the drop]; and if it does not spread, obviously [the contents of the pot] are permissible. Nevertheless, one should pour out the cooked food immediately from the opposite side, not adjacent to [the place where] the forbidden [liquid] has fallen, and he should not wait until it will cool off[5]—as we are concerned that a little bit has remained that still has not spread,[6] and if he will pour out the cooked food from that side, even if the pot is new[7] such that if meat and milk are involved[8] it is a situation where [the pot] does not become inherently forbidden,[9א] nevertheless, [this should not be done

Yad Adam

6. There is still some taste concentrated in the part of the pot where the drop has fallen.

7. A "new" vessel is one which has never been used. Any vessel which has not been used during the past 24 hours also has the status of a "new" vessel. (Any absorbed taste which is more than 24 hours becomes spoiled and can be disregarded.)

8. When mixtures of meat and milk are involved, we are more lenient with "new" earthenware vessels than with "old" ones. (An "old" vessel is one that was used with hot food during the past 24 hours, and thereby contains absorbed taste which is beneficial.)

Why are old earthenware vessels treated more stringently than new ones? If the pot was an "old" meat vessel, then when a drop of milk falls onto the pot, some of the

לכתחלה[10] וכ"ש בנפל איסור[11] דמבטל איסור[12] וגם לא ימתין עד שיצטנן[13] דשמא מפעפע[14] ולכן[15] הקדרה לעולם אסורה.[16]

ואם אין בתבשיל ס' נגד הטיפה שנפל אף התבשיל אסור.

ב. ואם עבר ובישל בקדירה זו שהיה בו ס' בתוך מעל"ע[17] דינו כמו בתבשיל ראשון וצריך ס' נגד מה שנפל בבישול הראשון אבל אם לא היה בתבשיל ראשון ס' נגד הטיפה וא"כ נאסר התבשיל

יד אדם

absorbed meat taste in its wall will become mixed with the taste of the milk and become *nevelah* ("inherently forbidden," as if it were a piece of forbidden food. This has been explained in the second paragraph of topic 44, section 18.) A new vessel, on the other hand, does not contain any absorbed taste which can become inherently forbidden.

(When a forbidden substance [other than milk and meat] has been absorbed into a vessel of any material, then an "old vessel" can be treated with the same lenient status as a "new vessel" when a great loss is involved. This is because, according to many authorities, forbidden substances other than meat and milk cannot cause food [nor absorbed taste in a vessel] to become inherently forbidden. In addition, even when a dairy vessel absorbs meat taste or vice versa, we can also be lenient with metal or wooden vessels in cases of great loss, and treat an old vessel with the same lenient status as a new one. The reason for treating these vessels leniently is that it is possible to remove the absorbed forbidden taste by kashering them. When a great loss is involved, we are strict to say that absorbed taste in a vessel becomes inherently forbidden only with earthenware vessels, and only when the prohibition of meat and milk is involved. See topic 44, section 18 for further discussion.)

9. Even though the pot does not have the more stringent status of a vessel which has become inherently forbidden, one should still avoid pouring out the food along the side where the drop has splashed.

10. This is to be understood as follows: If absorbed taste from the forbidden drop is present in the wall of the pot and one pours out the pot's contents along that wall, the absorbed taste will indeed be nullified, since there is sixty times as much in the pot. Nevertheless, one should avoid acting in this manner (even with a new pot) because it is not proper to rely on nullification to permit a mixture of meat and milk.

When pouring out the contents of the pot, it should be done all at once. Otherwise, the contents of the pot which are left behind might become forbidden if at any one time they are less than sixty times the amount of splashed milk. (See *Darkei Teshuvah* 92:110.)

11. Until now, the *Chochmas Adam* was dealing with a case where milk has fallen onto a pot of meat. Now, he is mentioning a case where a drop of forbidden liquid has fallen onto a pot which contains permissible food.

12. This is even more undesirable than nullifying milk which has fallen on a meat pot.

13. Once the pot is cold, it would not matter

because] it is forbidden to nullify to begin with.[10] And certainly, [one should not pour out in this manner in a case] where forbidden [liquid] has fallen [onto the pot][11] since he will be nullifying a forbidden substance[12] and he also should not wait until [the pot] will cool off,[13] for perhaps it will spread.[14] And therefore,[15] the pot in all cases will be forbidden.[16]

And if the cooked food does not contain sixty times as much as the drop which has fallen [on the pot], even the cooked food [in the pot] will be forbidden.

2. And if one transgressed and cooked in this pot that had in it sixty [times the drop and it is] within 24 hours,[17] it is to be judged the same as the first cooked food, and [therefore] we require [that there be now in the pot] sixty times what has fallen [onto the pot] during the first cooking. However, if there had not been sixty times the drop [in the contents of the pot] during the first cooking, and as such, the entire cooked food became forbidden and it [in turn] will have made the

Yad Adam

if its contents were poured out on the side where the drop has fallen, since no transmission of taste occurs when everything is cold. Nevertheless, it is still undesirable to do so in these cases.

14. The longer one waits to empty the pot, the greater the absorption into the contents of the pot.

15. Since we are concerned that the taste of the substance which has fallen onto the pot is suspected to remain within its walls. (*Aruch Hashulchan* 92:43)

16. If it is an earthenware pot, it could no longer be used for cooking. On the other hand, if a metal pot were involved it could be kashered. The rules are the same for milk which splashed on a meat pot, or for a forbidden substance which splashed onto a pot of kosher food. See also topic 46, note 22.

2. One Who Cooked with a Pot Which Became Forbidden Due to Splashed Liquid

17. As noted above, if a pot contains sixty times the splashed liquid, even though the contents of the pot are permitted, the pot becomes forbidden. If one were to cook again in this pot and more than 24 hours had elapsed since the liquid had splashed onto the pot, then the food from this second cooking would be permitted after the fact. This is because after 24 hours, any absorbed taste in the pot will have become spoiled, and when it is emitted into the new contents of the pot it will impart a detrimental taste. Although it is forbidden to cook food in a pot which contains absorbed forbidden taste, nevertheless, if the absorbed taste in the pot is detrimental we will permit the food cooked in that pot after the fact (topic 55,

כולו ואוסר כל הקדירה[18] ואם כן צריך בתבשיל השני ס' נגד כל הכלי ואין לך כלי שיהיה ס' בתוכו כנגד כל הכלי[19] ואם כן כל התבשיל אסור.

ג. ואם הוא קדירה שאין דרך להשתמש בו במועט אלא דוקא הרבה[20] באופן שיהי' תמיד ס' נגד מה שנפל[21] כיון די"א דכלי דדרכו להשתמש תמיד הרבה מותר להשתמש בו לכתחלה[22] אף שנפל בו איסור[23][ב] ואע"ג דלא קיי"ל הכי[24][ג] מכל מקום בזה דנפל נגד הרוטב ואינו אלא ספק שמא מפעפע וא"א לבא לידי איסור מה"ת[25] סמכינן על המתירין ומותר לכתחלה לבשל באותה קדירה וכן בקדירה קטנה ונפל מעט עד שלעולם עכ"פ יש בו ס' נגד מה שנפל.[ד]

אבל אם יש ספק אם יש בתבשיל ששים נגד מה שנפל[26] אע"ג די"ל דהוי ס"ס[27] שמא אינו מפעפע ואת"ל דמפעפע שמא הי' ס'[28] דמה שנסתפקו הראשונים אינו נכנס בגדר ס'[29] כמש"כ הפ"ח בכללי

ב. בסי' ל"ט סעי' ז' ובסי' קכ"ב סעי' ה' ובח"ח סי' תנ"ח וב"ח סי' מ"ח.
ג. כמו שכ' הט"ז והש"ך שם.
ד. מנ"י כלל כ"ו ס"ק ה' וכו"פ סי' ל'.

יד אדם

section 6). The *Chochmas Adam* now goes on to explain the rules that apply if less than 24 hours have elapsed since the liquid had splashed onto the pot.

18. The taste of the first cooked food which became forbidden will have been absorbed throughout the material of the pot. It will therefore be necessary to have sixty times the material of the entire pot.

19. See topic 46, section 1.

3. Leniencies Which May Apply to a Pot Which Always Contains a Large Quantity of Liquid When It Is Heated

20. The pot upon which the forbidden drop has fallen is always filled with a large amount of food and/or liquid when it is heated.

21. Thus, if the pot were made of earthenware (which cannot be kashered), it would still be permissible to use it for cooking.

22. The reason these authorities are lenient is that since the pot is used only with a large amount of liquid, the taste of the forbidden substance will certainly be nullified.

23. These authorities rule that this leniency applies not only to milk which splashes onto a meat pot, but even to forbidden liquid which splashes onto a pot.

24. And if, for example, a forbidden drop falls into a large earthenware pot, we rule that the pot will become forbidden and can no longer be used for cooking. (See topic 52, section 10.) If the pot were made of metal, it could not be used again until it is kashered.

25. Firstly, it is doubtful whether the

ב. [Shulchan Aruch] Yoreh Deah 99:7, 122:5, and Orach Chayim chapter 451 and Binas Adam section 41.
ג. As the Shach and the Taz write there.
ד. Minchas Yaakov topic 56, section 5, and Kreisi u'pleisi chapter 90.

entire pot forbidden,[18] in such a case we require in the second cooked food sixty times the entire vessel. Since there is no vessel whose contents will be sixty times the entire vessel,[19] as such, all of the [second] cooked food is forbidden.

3. And if it is a pot which one does not normally use with a small amount but only with a large amount[20] in such a way that there would always be sixty times what had fallen [on it, we can be lenient].[21] [This is] because there are some authorities who say that a vessel whose normal use is always with a large amount is permissible to be used [even] to begin with,[22] even though forbidden [liquid] had fallen upon it.[23]ב Although we [generally] do not accept this ruling,[24]ג nevertheless, in this case where [the drop] fell alongside the liquid and there is only a doubt whether or not [the taste] spread [into the contents of the pot] and it is impossible to lead to a Torah prohibition,[25] we rely on those who are lenient and [rule that] it is permissible, [even] to begin with, to cook in that pot. And similarly, [it is permissible to use even] a small pot if a little bit has fallen on it if at all times, there will be [in the pot] at least sixty times what has fallen [on it].ד

However, if there is a doubt whether there is in the cooked food sixty times what has fallen,[26] even though it is possible to say that there is a double doubt[27] [as follows:] Perhaps [the taste] does not spread [through the pot], and even if you say it does spread perhaps there is sixty[28]—[nevertheless,] with regard to what the early authorities are unsure is not classified as a "doubt"[29] as the *Pri Chadash* has written in

Yad Adam

splashed material enters into the contents of a pot (see section 1). Furthermore, since the pot is only used for large amounts, the taste of the forbidden drop will be nullified in any case.

26. Milk falls onto a pot of meat and it is uncertain whether the contents of the pot are sixty times the size of the drop which had fallen upon the pot.

27. And in many cases where such a double doubt exists, we are lenient.

28. Maybe the pot does contain sixty times the drop. This reasoning should then serve as a basis to be lenient and permit further use of the pot even if it cannot be kashered.

29. The early authorities disagree as to whether on not the taste can go through the walls of the pot, as noted above in section 1. According to the *Pri Chadash*, such a doubt cannot be used as one of the components of a double doubt to serve as a basis for a lenient decision.

ה. כדאיתא כלל מ״ד.
ו. ט״ז סימן צ״ב ס״ק כ״ד בשם תו״ה כלל ל״ח סי׳ ג׳.

ס״ס[30] ובהפ״מ צ״ע עיין בב״י סי׳ נ״ט ובב״א סי׳ מ״א אך בסי׳ צ״ז בש״ך סק״ב כ׳ ג״כ ספק שמא אינו מפעפע ולכן יש להקל.[31]

ד. ודוקא שבישל בו עכשיו בשר[32] או בטיפה של איסור[33] אבל אם בשל מים בקדירה של בשר[34] ונפל טיפת חלב על הקדירה כנגד המים ובתוך מעל״ע בישל בו בשר[35] אפי׳ לא היה במים ס׳ נגד הטיפה מותר הבשר[36] דאי לא עברה הטיפה בבישול ראשון גם עתה לא תעבור ואם עברה מ״מ אין בקדירה מן החלב אלא לפי שיעור החלב שנתערב במים[37] דהא בהיתר לא חשבינן כל החתיכה כבליעה עצמה[38]ה ונגד דבר המועט ההוא[39] מסתמא יש ס׳ בתבשיל שלאחר כך.ו ונ״ל דמ״מ אסור לבשל באותן מים בשר[40] כיון שאין בו ס׳ ושמא מפעפע לפנים ופשיטא דאסורא עם חלב (כדלקמן כלל מח) אבל מותר לשתותה כך ומזה תדין לטיפת רוטב של בשר שנפל לכלי

יד אדם

30. Therefore we cannot be lenient in the case at hand since only one valid "doubt" is present. (A doubt regarding the circumstances is a true doubt, but not a doubt regarding a halachic decision.)

31. According to the *Shach*, there is a true "double doubt" here and we can rely on his opinion in cases involving a great loss. (Regarding the term "great loss," see the additional note on topic 40, section 5.)

4. Milk Falling on a Meat Pot Which Contains Pareve Ingredients

32. Only if meat was present in the pot when milk falls on it will the stringencies in section 2 apply (such that if there is less than sixty times the drop during the first cooking, then any food subsequently cooked in the pot will be forbidden.)

33. When forbidden liquid splashes onto a pot, no matter what type of food is in the pot, we say that the pot becomes completely forbidden if it does not contain sixty times the drop, and any food subsequently cooked in the pot will be forbidden.

34. A pot that had contained hot meat during the previous 24 hours.

35. After the pot was emptied out, the pot was not kashered, and meat and water were added to this pot and cooked in it.

36. This lenient ruling represents the opinion of the *Issur v'heter*. We will learn below that others rule that the meat cooked later on will be forbidden if the pot contained hot meat during the previous 24 hours.

37. For example, if two drops of milk have fallen onto a pot containing eighty drops of water, we regard the pot as containing two drops of milk and no more than this. When

ה. As in topic 44 [section 12. In topic 46, section 7, the *Chochmas Adam* rules that one should not rely on this leniency (to measure with respect to the milk alone) except in cases of great loss. Nevertheless, it appears that one can be lenient in cases such as this where only absorbed taste in a vessel is involved, as noted in the end of topic 48, section 18.]

ו. *Taz* 92:24 in the name of the *Issur v'heter* 31:3.

[Textual note: The following statements in the text (up to the word "coffee") are found in early editions of the *Chochmas Adam* but are omitted in the other current printed editions.]

the rules of double doubts.[30] But in a case involving a great loss this requires investigation—see in the *Bais Yosef* chapter 59 and in the *Binas Adam* section 41. Nevertheless, in chapter 97 in the *Shach*, paragraph 2, he has written [that indeed we can accept as] a "doubt" also [the consideration] that perhaps [the taste of the drop] does not spread. And therefore, there are grounds to be lenient.[31]

4. It is only where one has cooked meat in it now,[32] or [if it is a case] where a drop of forbidden liquid [has fallen on a pot].[33] However, if one was cooking water in a meat pot[34] and a drop of milk has fallen onto the pot alongside the water and [afterwards] within 24 hours he cooked meat in it,[35] even if the water was not sixty times the drop, the meat is permissible.[36] [We reason as follows:] If the drop had not passed through [the pot into its contents] during the first cooking, also now it would not pass through. And if [the drop] had passed through, nevertheless, there is milk [absorbed] in the pot only in accordance with the amount of the milk that was mixed with the water,[37] for with permissible substances, we do not consider the entire "piece" to be like the absorption itself.[38][ה] And corresponding to that small amount[39] probably there is sixty in the cooked food that is cooked afterwards.[ו] And it is my opinion that in any case, it is prohibited to cook meat in this water,[40] since it does not contain sixty [times the milk], for perhaps [the milk] does spread inside. And it is obvious that it is forbidden [to mix the water] with milk (as noted later on in topic 48 [section 2]), but it is permissible to drink [the water] as is. And from this we may rule regarding a drop of meat soup which has fallen onto a vessel in

Yad Adam

meat is later cooked in the pot, we will not need sixty times the eighty drops of water but only sixty times the two drops of milk.

38. The word "piece" here denotes the water in the pot, and the "absorption" is the milk that has fallen onto the pot and might be absorbed into its contents. We do not say that all of the water in the pot becomes like milk, with the result that the meat which is later cooked in this pot would become forbidden unless it were sixty times the amount of water. Rather, sixty times the milk is sufficient to nullify it. Refer to note ה.

39. The few drops of milk that have fallen onto the pot.

40. The *Chochmas Adam* is now dealing with the status of the water which was present in the meat pot when the milk splashed onto it. Even though (according to the *Issur v'heter*) it is permissible to drink this water, it should not be used with meat or dairy food.

ז. כ״כ בחו״ד שם בהדיא.

שבשלו בו קאווע.[41] (מא) ומסיים באו״ה שם[42] אבל אם נפל במקום הריקן[43] אע״פ שלא בישל אלא מים[44] ובתוך מעל״ע בישל בו בשר נאסר הבשר[45]ז

ולפי דעת המרדכי שכתבנו כלל מ״ד סי׳ ט׳ אפשר דיש להקל בהפ״מ גדול אף בנפל טיפת איסור כנגד המים ובתוך מעל״ע בישל בו היתר.[46]

אך צ״ע[47] דאו״ה אזיל לשיטתו שכ׳ בכלל כ״ד סימן ט׳ דבבלוע בכלי ל״א חנ״נ[48] אבל לפי מאי דקי״ל לעיל כלל מ״ד סי׳ י״ח דאף בבלוע אמרינן חנ״נ בכ״ח[49] וא״כ אין חילוק בין אם בישל

יד אדם

41. Milk may not be added to that coffee unless sixty times the drop was present. This is in accordance with topic 48, section 2 that if one has boiled water in a meat pot which was used that day for meat, then he may not brew coffee with that water if he desires to add milk to it.

The following question is raised in the *Binas Adam* (section 41): What is the status of a coffee pot (a pot which is used only to brew coffee, and milk is never placed in it) if a drop of meat soup has fallen onto its outside surface and the contents of the coffee pot is less than sixty times the drop of soup? Can one continue to brew coffee in such a pot if he will add milk to the coffee after it is poured into a cup? The *Chochmas Adam* there rules that although it will be forbidden to cook milk in such a pot, it is permitted to brew coffee in the pot even if milk will later be added to the coffee. This is because we are unsure whether or not the taste of the drop spreads into the pot's contents; furthermore, since a large amount of water is always used in such a pot, the drop will be nullified even if its taste does penetrate into the contents of the pot. Nevertheless, one should wait 24 hours before brewing coffee (or cooking water) in this pot if milk will be added to it. (Compare topic 52, section 10.)

42. Topic 31, section 2.

43. I.e., on the outside of the pot above the level of the pot's contents. Such a drop is to be treated more stringently because there is no food or liquid alongside it to nullify it, and the taste of the drop remains within the walls of the vessel. As such, any meat substances which will come into contact with this portion of the vessel within 24 hours can become forbidden.

44. When the drop fell on it he was not cooking meat, but only water.

45. According to the *Chochmas Adam* in section 5, the meat will remain permissible if the pot will contain sixty times sixty-one the size of the drop.

46. The *Mordechai* quoted there rules that when a taste becomes dispersed throughout a liquid, even if the liquid is cooked, we do not say that a piece (in this case, the water) becomes inherently forbidden. For example, if two drops of forbidden liquid splash on a pot containing eighty drops water, the water becomes forbidden because sixty is not pre-

ז. The *Issur v'heter* writes so there explicitly.

[Textual note: In the other current printed editions of the *Chochmas Adam* the next two paragraphs are transposed. Also note that the entire paragraph in the braces is not present in early editions of the *Chochmas Adam* and was apparently added at a later time.]

which one brews coffee.[41] (See *Binas Adam*, section 41.) And the *Issur v'heter* there[42] concludes: But if it fell on the empty portion,[43] even though he was cooking only water in it,[44] and within 24 hours he cooked meat in it, the meat becomes forbidden.[45ז]

And according to the opinion of the *Mordechai* [in the name of the *Ravan*] which we have written in topic 44 section 9, it is possible that there are grounds to be lenient in case of a very great loss, even if a forbidden drop has fallen alongside the water and within 24 hours he had cooked in it permissible food.[46]

{However, this requires investigation,[47] as the *Issur v'heter* is going according to his opinion which he has written in topic 24, section 9, that we do not say "a piece becomes inherently forbidden" regarding what is absorbed in a vessel;[48] but according to what is established for us previously in topic 44, section 18 that even regarding what is absorbed we say that "a piece becomes inherently forbidden" with earthenware vessels[49]—as such, there is no difference whether one was

Yad Adam

sent. Nevertheless, we will not view this water as consisting of eighty forbidden drops, but as containing only a volume of two forbidden drops. As such, just as there are grounds to be lenient with respect to a meat pot containing water upon which milk has splashed (and we will not prohibit meat that is later cooked in the pot), so we can also be lenient when drops of forbidden liquid have splashed on a pot containing water (and permit what is later cooked in the pot, as long as the pot then contains sixty times the forbidden drops).

As the *Chochmas Adam* mentions, we should rely on the *Mordechai* only in cases involving a very great loss. Otherwise, we should be strict in accordance with the *Maharshal* (topic 44, section 9) that the cooked water in the pot becomes inherently forbidden. As such, the meat later cooked in the pot will become forbidden unless its volume is sixty times the water.

47. We must investigate the lenient ruling of the *Issur v'heter* mentioned above that if milk has fallen on a meat pot which contains water and the drop is alongside the water, then the meat subsequently cooked in the pot will be permissible.

48. The "piece" mentioned here is the absorbed meat taste in the material of the pot. This discussion involves a pot which was used to cook meat within the past 24 hours and contains absorbed taste of meat. If milk now splashes on this pot, do we say that the milk combines with this absorbed meat taste to make the pot entirely forbidden? The *Issur v'heter* rules that the pot does not become inherently forbidden, and therefore, the water which is cooking in this pot while the milk splashes on it will not become forbidden. Furthermore, if one cooks meat in this pot, only sixty times the drops of milk is needed, as noted above.

49. This applies to "old" earthenware ves-

מים או בשר דאם הקדירה ב"י מבישול הבשר א"כ נ"נ[50] וצריך ס' נגד הקדירה[51] וצ"ל דהט"ז[52] מיירי בקדירה חדשה או אינו ב"י[53] לכן לא הביא הט"ז דין אם נפל במקום הריקן דבחדשה או אינו ב"י אין חילוק.[54]

ה. ואם נפלה הטיפה כנגד מקום הריקן[55] ובאותו צד שאינו אצל האש[56] חיישינן שמא מפעפע בדופן הקדירה עד סמוך לרוטב[57] כ"כ שאין ס' נגד הטיפה[58] הרי נאסר מהקדירה שבלעה בשר[59] או איסור[60] ס' פעמים נגד הטיפה סך הכל ס"א פעמים[61]

יד אדם

sels even in cases where a great loss is involved. (We also apply the rule to vessels made of other material, but only in cases that do not involve a great loss. See note 8.)

50. The absorbed taste of the meat which is present throughout the material of the pot becomes inherently forbidden when milk falls onto it.

51. It will be necessary for the contents of the pot to be sixty times the pot. As such, the ruling mentioned at the end of section 2 will apply: Since there is no vessel whose contents will be sixty times the entire vessel, the entire contents of the pot (the water cooking in it when the milk fell on it, as well as the meat later cooked in the pot) will become forbidden.

52. When he quotes the above lenient ruling of the *Issur v'heter*.

53. Such a pot also would have no absorbed taste in it which could become inherently forbidden and it is regarded as a new pot.

54. As explained in the *Chochmas Adam* below in section 6. In such a case we are lenient even when a drop falls above the pot's contents, since there is no absorbed taste in the pot which becomes inherently forbidden.

5. Stringencies Which Apply to Liquid That Splashes on a Pot Above The Level of Its Contents

55. We are continuing the discussion of milk which falls onto the outside surface of a pot of meat, or forbidden liquid which falls onto a pot of permissible food. In this case, the drops fall onto the pot above the level of its contents. It is mentioned below that we are dealing with a situation in which the pot had been used for meat in the past 24 hours and it therefore contains absorbed taste of meat which is beneficial. The concern here is the forbidden mixture created when the drops of milk combine with the absorbed meat taste in the material of the pot.

56. Pots would be cooked by placing them on the floor of an oven next to a pile of burning wood. We are dealing with a situation where the drops did not fall on the portion which faces the fire. If the drops do fall on the part of the pot which faces the fire, then we are more lenient as explained in section 8 below.

cooking water or meat [when the milk fell on the pot], for if the pot had been used [earlier] on that day for cooking meat, then it becomes inherently forbidden[50] and we need sixty times the pot.[51] And it is necessary to say that the *Taz*[52] is dealing with a new pot or one that has not been used within the last 24 hours,[53] and for this reason the *Taz* does not quote the rule regarding [a drop] which has fallen onto the empty portion, since for a new vessel or one that has not been used for 24 hours there is no difference [where the drop falls].[54]]

5. And if the drop has fallen alongside the empty portion[55]—if it is on the side which is not next to the fire,[56] we are concerned that perhaps [the taste] will spread into the wall of the pot up until the liquid[57] such that there will not be sixty times the drop,[58] [and therefore the part] of the pot which had absorbed meat[59] or forbidden substance[60] becomes forbidden in the amount of sixty times the drop, altogether, sixty-one times [the drop].[61] As such, if there will not be in the cooked

Yad Adam

57. It will spread down toward the liquid, but it will not reach it. If the absorbed taste would extend downward so that it would be adjacent to the contents of the pot, it would become nullified if the pot were to contain at least sixty times the drop. However, we must consider the possibility that the absorbed taste will not reach down to the level of the food and therefore it cannot be directly nullified by it.

58. I.e., the taste will spread very little through the wall of the pot, and therefore, any absorbed taste in the pot adjacent to the drop will not be enough to nullify it.

If the taste of the drop would spread through a section of the wall of the pot greater than (or equal to) sixty times its size, it would become nullified by the other absorbed tastes in the walls of the pot. However, we must be concerned that it spread to a lesser extent (such that the absorbed taste in the area of spread will be less than sixty times the drop), in which case the taste has not been nullified. In such a case, the absorbed taste present in the area into which the drop spreads will become inherently forbidden. The maximum volume of absorbed taste which can become forbidden from the drop will be slightly less than sixty times the drop. (For if the drop will spread into absorbed taste sixty or more times its size, the taste of the drop will be nullified and the result will be no forbidden taste at all.)

59. In a case where meat had already been cooked in this pot earlier in the day and now a drop of milk has fallen onto it.

60. Such as where permissible food had been cooked in this pot earlier in the day and now a drop of forbidden substance has fallen on it.

61. As noted above, the maximum amount of absorbed taste that can become forbidden

ח. עיין במנ״י כלל נ״ו ס״ק ז׳.

וא״כ אם לא יהיה בתבשיל ס׳ פעמים ס״א ויערה התבשיל דרך אותו צד שנפלה הטיפה יאסור התבשיל ולכן יניחנו ולא יגע בה עד שיצטנן[62] אבל לא יערה דרך צד השני כדלעיל סי׳ א׳ דהכא חיישינן שמא ינענע הקדירה ויגע הרוטב בצד שנפל הטיפה ויאסר התבשיל. ומ״מ אפי׳ לא היה בתבשיל ס׳ פעמים ס״א ועירה התבשיל באותו צד ונאסר התבשיל[63] מ״מ אם חזר ובישל תבשיל אחר בתוך מעל״ע ויש בו ס׳ פעמים ס״א מותר התבשיל ול״א בזה דכל הקדירה נ״נ.[64]ח

ו. ודוקא אם הקדירה ישנה והיא בת יומא* ואם כן הבלוע בקדירה נ״נ ולכן צריך ס׳ פעמים ס״א אבל אם הקדירה חדשה[65] אע״ג שעכשיו מבשל בה וחשוב כישנה[66] מכל מקום ל״צ ס׳ פעמים ס״א

יד אדם

will be slightly less than sixty times the size of the drop. All together, (when we add this amount to the drop itself), the total amount of forbidden substance will be slightly less than sixty-one times the drop. (For practical purposes we can assume that this amount is simply sixty-one times the drop.) As such, in order to nullify this forbidden substance, it will now be necessary to have sixty times this amount, that is, sixty times sixty-one (3660) times the drop.

Since, according to this formulation, all of the forbidden taste in the pot lies above the level of the food, the food will remain permissible. A problem will arise, however, when one will pour out the contents of the pot, as the *Chochmas Adam* goes on to explain.

62. After the pot cools off, the forbidden taste in the pot can no longer be transmitted to the food. Subsequently, the food can then be poured out from the pot and it will remain permissible (as long as the food is at least sixty times the drop). See, however, the additional note below.

63. In such a case, since the food became forbidden, one might suspect that the taste of this food which will be absorbed into the pot will go on to make it forbidden (similar to section 2 above).

64. I.e., we do not require sixty times the entire material of the pot, but only sixty times sixty-one times the size of the drop. Since the food which had been cooked in the pot is not forbidden according to many authorities (as long as sixty times the drop was present—see section 7 below), we will not be strict to say that the taste of this food goes on to make all of the absorbed taste in the entire pot inherently forbidden. (*P'eir Hashulchan* 92:357)

Additional note: The *Chochmas Adam* has concluded that if the liquid falls on the empty portion, the food remains permissible

ה. See *Minchas Yaakov* 56:7.

food sixty times sixty-one [times the drop] and he will pour the cooked food along that side on which the drop has fallen, he will make the cooked food forbidden. Therefore, he should leave [the pot] and not touch it until it will cool off.[62] He should not, however, pour [it out] along the other side as above in section 1, because here we are concerned that perhaps he will shake the pot and the liquid will come into contact with the side upon which the drop has fallen and the cooked food will become forbidden. Nevertheless, even if there was not sixty times sixty-one in the cooked food and he poured the cooked food on that side and the food became forbidden,[63] still in all, if he went on and cooked another food [in the same pot] within 24 hours and there is sixty times sixty-one [times the size of the drop in the pot], the food is permitted, and we do not say regarding this that all of the pot is made inherently forbidden.[64ה]

6. It is only when the pot is "old" and was used on that day,* and as such, what was absorbed into the pot has become inherently forbidden—only then sixty times sixty-one [of the size of the drop] is required. However, if the pot is "new,"[65] even though he is cooking in it now and it is [therefore to be] considered as if it were "old,"[66] nevertheless, it is not necessary to have sixty times sixty-one either

Yad Adam

and one should leave the pot to cool off before removing the food. This is the rule according to the letter of the law. Nevertheless, the *Shulchan Aruch* (92:6) rules that the customary practice is to be strict and prohibit the food in such a pot unless it contains sixty times sixty-one of the volume of liquid which has fallen onto it. One reason for this custom is that we are concerned that during the cooking, the contents of the pot may rise and come into contact with the forbidden portion of the wall. (*Issur v'heter* 31:2) It appears that the *Chochmas Adam* rules that one should be strict and act in accordance with this custom, with the exception of certain difficult situations where one may be lenient. In such cases, one may permit the contents of the pot as long as they are at least sixty times the splashed liquid. See section 7 below for examples of such situations.

6. Leniencies Which Apply to a "New Pot" or a Covered Pot

*The pot upon which the drop splashes had been used during the past 24 hours.

65. Or it is not a new pot but it was not used during the last 24 hours.

66. Since the pot is absorbing the taste of the food presently inside it, one might consider it to have the rule of an "old" pot.

ט. כדלעיל כלל מ״ד סי׳ י״ח.
י. פ״ח ס״ק כ״ג.

ממ״נ אם בישול מפעפע למעלה אם כן נתבטל הטיפה בס׳[67] ואם אינה מפעפע למעלה למקום הריקן אם כן לא היה שם בלוע מבשר ל״ש לומר דהבלוע נ״נ[68] וכן ישנה והיא אינה בת יומא דהבלוע שבה לפגם אם כן אין כאן בלוע[69] וגוף החרס[70] ל״א נ״נ לכולי עלמא[71] ט ולכן אפילו בנפל על מקום הריקן סגי כשיש בתבשיל ס׳ פעמים נגד הטיפה ומ״מ לא יערה באותו צד וכדלעיל סימן א׳ ב׳ ג׳.

וכן אם הקדירה מכוסה והקדירה רותחת דאז כשנופל תיכף ההבל מבלבל הכל ואם כן אין חילוק* דאפי׳ נפל במקום ריקן סגי בס׳ נגד הטיפה.י

ז. ובשעת הדחק כגון בע״ש או לצורך אורחים או הפ״מ או לעני יש להקל ולהתיר אפילו בנפל במקום הריקן כשיהיה בתבשיל ס׳ נגד מה שנפל דסמכינן על הפוסקים דבלוע לא נ״נ אפילו בכ״ח[72] ויניח עד שיצטנן ואם קשה לו להמתין עד שיצטנן אז יערה מיד מצד השני והקדירה אסורה.

ח. ואם נפל באותו צד שכנגד האש ונפל שם דבר מועט הכל מותר אפילו בלא ס׳ ואפילו הקדירה מותר שהאש שורף

יד אדם

67. Since the contents of the pot is greater than sixty times the size of the drop, if the taste of the contents spreads upward it will nullify the drop.

68. Thus, the area above the contents of the pot will have the same status as that of a new pot.

69. Therefore, such a pot has the same status as a new pot.

70. The same certainly applies to vessels made of other materials.

71. Rather, only what has been absorbed into the material in the past 24 hours can become inherently forbidden.

*Due to the motion of the boiling, the entire pot is considered to be alongside the food.

7. Leniencies Which Apply Under Difficult Circumstances

72. We can be lenient here with earthenware, even though it is generally to be treated more stringently than other materials. (Refer to topic 44, section 18.)

The background material regarding this leniency (that sixty is sufficient in cases of urgency, and sixty times sixty-one will not be required) has been explained in the additional note to section 5. The *Chochmas Adam* goes on to explain that it is preferable to allow the pot to cool off, and the reason for this has already been explained in section 5: He may shake the pot and then the liquid in

ט. As noted above, topic 44, section 18.
י. *Pri Chadash* paragraph 23.

way you look at it—for if the [present] cooking spreads [the taste of the cooked food] above [to the level of the drop], then the drop becomes nullified in sixty;[67] and if it does not spread above to the empty portion, then there will not be any absorbed taste there from meat, and it will not be relevant to say that the absorbed taste became inherently forbidden.[68] And similarly with an old [pot] which has not been used on that day, where the absorbed taste in it is detrimental, then there is no [significant] absorbed taste.[69] And regarding the material of earthenware [vessels][70] we do not say that it becomes inherently forbidden according to all authorities.[71][ט] Therefore, even if it has fallen on the empty portion it is enough if there is sixty times the drop in the cooked food. Nevertheless, one should not pour it out on that side and [other rules apply] as above in sections 1, 2, and 3.

Furthermore, if the pot is covered and the pot is boiling, so that when [the drop] falls, immediately the heat mixes up everything, then there is no difference [where the drop has fallen],* for even if it has fallen on the empty portion it is enough if there is sixty times the drop [in the contents of the pot].[י]

7. And under difficult circumstances, such as on the eve of the Sabbath or for the needs of guests or where a large loss is involved or for a poor person—there are grounds to be lenient and permit [the food] even where [the drop] has fallen on the empty portion if there will be in the cooked food [only] sixty times what has fallen, for we can rely on those authorities who rule that what is absorbed [in the pot] does not become inherently forbidden, even regarding earthenware.[72] And [in such cases] one should leave it until it cools off, but if it is difficult for him to wait until it cools off, then he may pour it out immediately from the second side. The pot [in any case] will be forbidden [as noted above in section 1].

8. If [the drop of milk] has fallen on that side [of the pot] which is facing the fire, and [only] a little bit has fallen there, everything is permissible, even without sixty [times the drop being in the pot], and even the pot is permissible [and need not be kashered], as the fire

Yad Adam

the pot will come into contact with the side upon which the drop has fallen. The entire contents of the pot will then become forbidden (unless sixty times sixty-one is present).

יא. פ״ח בשם או״ה וכ״כ המנ״י כלל כ״ה ס״ק י״ב דלא כט״ז.
יב. שם סעיף ז׳.
יג. פ״ח שם.

ומייבשו תיכף בנפילתו אבל כשנפל הרבה אזי דינו כדלעיל בשלא כנגד האש.

ט. טיפה הנופלת על גבי כיסוי קדירה אם הקדירה מרתיח דהזיעה עולה תמיד ומגיע אל הכיסוי דינו כאלו נפלה על הקדירה כנגד הרוטב[73] שהרי מבלבל הטעם תיכף ולא חיישינן שמא באותה פעם לא עלתה הרתיחה. ומותר ממ״נ אם עלתה הרי מתפשט למטה[74] ואם לא עלתה הרי גם כן לא יתפשט למטה[יא] ואם לא התחיל להרתיח עדיין לא נאסר כלל מה שבקדירה אפילו אין בו ס׳ שהרי אינו מפעפע כלל למה שבקדירה דעדיין הוי צונן[יב] והכיסוי אם היס״ב נאסר ואם לאו סגי בהדחה[יג] ועיין לקמן כלל מ״ו מדין כיסוי.

י. מחבת שמבשלים בה חלב על האש ולמעלה ממנה קדירה של בשר אם המחבת מגולה והזיעה עולה מן החלב לקדירה שעליה והוא קרוב כ״כ שהי״ס בזיעה במקום שנוגע בקדירה[75] צריך שיהיה בתבשיל של בשר ס׳ נגד כל החלב[76] אבל אם אין הי״ס בזיעה הכל מותר וכן אם המחבת שעם החלב מכוסה ואם כן אין

יד אדם

8. Leniencies Which Apply if Liquid Splashes on the Part of the Pot Which Is Near the Fire

9. Laws Concerning a Forbidden Drop Which Falls on a Pot Cover

73. It is sufficient if the contents of the pot are equal to sixty times the size of the drop. This rule is analogous to the second paragraph of section 6.

74. And it is nullified if the contents of the pot are at least sixty times the size of the drop, since the heat mixes up everything immediately.

10. Transmission of Taste Via Steam

75. I.e., the pot of milk is so close to the meat that if one would place his hand next to the pot of meat, the heat from the steam would be so intense that he would withdraw his hand. (See topic 42, section 9.)

(The steam must have attained this temperature only if the pot of meat is cold. If the pot of meat is hot, then the pot will be forbidden even if the steam is not so hot that one's hand would withdraw from it. See also *Darkei Teshuvah* 92:173.)

76. This is because the steam is absorbed into the pot. As such, the food as well as the pot becomes forbidden unless the pot of

יא. *Pri Chadash* in the name of the *Issur v'heter*, and the *Minchas Yaakov* 55:12 has written similarly, not in accordance with the *Taz*.
יב. [*Rama*] 92:7.
יג. *Pri Chadash* there.

burns and dries out [the drop] immediately when it falls. However, if a large amount has fallen, then the rule is the same as above regarding [the side of the pot] which is not facing the fire.

9. If a drop falls on the cover of a pot—if [the contents of] the pot are boiling such that steam is always rising and reaching the cover, the rule is the same as [a drop] falling on the pot alongside the liquid,[73] since the taste is mixed up immediately. And we are not concerned that perhaps at that moment [when the drop fell] it was not boiling up well, for it is permissible either way you look at it—if it was boiling up well [the taste of the drop] spreads downward,[74] and if it was not boiling up well [the taste of the drop] also will not spread downward [to reach the contents of the pot].[יא] But if [the pot] still did not begin to boil, what is in the pot is not forbidden at all even if there is not sixty, as [what is on the cover] does not spread at all to what is in the pot for it is still as if it were cold.[יב] And regarding the cover—if [it is so hot that] one would withdraw his hand from it, it becomes forbidden; and if not, [it is regarded as cold and] it is sufficient to wash it.[יג] And see further on in topic 46 [sections 3,4, and 5] regarding [additional] rules [which apply] to a cover.

10. If there is a pot in which one is cooking milk over a fire and above it there is a pot of meat—if the pot [of milk] is uncovered and steam is rising from the milk to the pot that is above it, and it is so near that the hand would withdraw from the steam at the location where it comes into contact with the pot [of meat],[75] [then] it is necessary that there be sixty times the entire milk in the cooked dish of meat.[76] However, if the hand would not withdraw [due to the heat] of the steam, everything is permissible. And similarly, if the pot that contains the milk is covered, then the steam is not [directly] from the milk

Yad Adam

meat contains sixty times the pot of milk. (*Aruch Hashulchan* 92:54) If sixty is present, then only the pot will become forbidden (*Madanei Hashulchan*, 92:154).

יד. פס סי' נ"ב.

הזיעה מחלב עצמו ומותר[77] דהוי כשתי קדרות שנגעו זו בזו דמותר.[78]

יא. קדירה של בשר צוננת או אפילו חמה קצת רק שאין היס"ב שעומדת על הכירה[79] וכיוצא בו במקום צונן והיתה עומדת אצלה קדירה של חלב רותחת ומחמת הרתיחה היה זב החלב מן הקדירה למטה אל הקדירה אם נפסק הקילוח מן הקדירה הרותחת קודם שהגיע אל הצונן דינו ככלי שני[80] ומותר הכל[81] אבל אם לא נפסק הקילוח אפילו נזחל תחלה על הכירה ומן הכירה על הקדירה מכל מקום הוי כעירה מכלי איסור[82] ואוסר כ"ק והכא הקדירה עולה במקום קליפה ואסורה והבשר מותר אפי' בלא קליפה.יד

יב. בד"א[83] שהקדירה והמקום שעומד עליו צונן אבל אם הקדירה של בשר חמה והוא כלי ראשון[84] וכ"ש עומד אצל האש אפילו נשפך עליה צונן ממש הכל אסור הקדירה והתבשיל עד

יד אדם

77. Even if the upper pot is resting on the lower pot (as long as they are dry). (*Madanei Hashulchan* 92:159)

78. If a pot of milk comes into contact with a pot of meat in an oven, the pots and their contents remain permissible, as long as the surfaces which come into contact with each other remain dry (topic 57, section 7).

See topic 62 with regard to the circumstances when it is permitted to cook permissible food and forbidden food (or meat and milk) in the same oven.

Additional note: The statement in the *Chochmas Adam* that "the steam is not from the milk itself" is difficult to understand. Presumably, the *Chochmas Adam* means that because the pot of milk is covered, there is no steam from the milk at all.

11. Hot Milk Flowing Onto a Cold Pot of Meat

79. It is standing on the floor of an oven. The practice was to kindle wood which was inside the oven, and the pot of food to be cooked would be placed next to the fire. In this case, since the pot is not hot enough such that one would withdraw his had from it, it is to be regarded as cold.

80. Once the hot liquid has left the pot in which it was cooked (which is known as the *kli rishon*—"first vessel") and it has flowed onto a "second vessel" (*kli sheini*), it loses a good deal of its heat. Such liquid is no longer regarded to be hot enough to transfer its taste into other vessels or foods. In this case, the liquid lying on the floor of the oven will be

ד. Chapter 92 there [in the *Rama*, paragraph 7.]

itself and it is permissible,[77] as it is like two pots which touch each other, where [the rule is that] they are permissible.[78]

11. If a pot of cold meat—or even [a pot which is] a little warm but not so hot that one's hand would withdraw from it—is standing on a stove[79] or in a similar location in a cold place, and a boiling pot of milk was standing next to it, and because of the boiling, milk overflowed from the pot [and flowed] down to the pot [of meat]—if the stream [of milk] from the boiling pot was interrupted before it reached the [cold] pot, it is judged as a "second vessel,"[80] and everything is permissible.[81] However, if the stream is not interrupted, even if it flowed first onto the stove and from the stove onto the pot, nevertheless, it is as if he poured [directly] from a forbidden vessel[82] and it prohibits by the thickness of the peel. And in this case, the pot counts in place of the peel [of the food] and it is forbidden, and the meat [inside the cold pot] is permissible even without [discarding its] peel.ד

12. When does this apply?[83] When the pot and the place on which it is standing is cold. However, if the pot of meat is hot and it is a first vessel[84]—and certainly if [the pot is now] standing next to the fire—even if something actually cold is spilled on it, everything is forbidden, [both] the pot and the cooked food, unless there will be [in the

Yad Adam

regarded as being in a "second vessel" and will not render the pot forbidden.

81. If, however, the pot was hot, then the pot itself becomes forbidden (and must be kashered) and the status of the food is questionable if sixty times the milk is not present in the pot. See section 19 below.

82. We have learned that a "first vessel" transfers taste throughout its entire contents, whereas a "second vessel" generally does not transmit its taste at all. Liquid which is being poured directly from a "first vessel" has an intermediate status: Its taste will spread into foods and vessels, but only by "the thickness of the peel," i.e., the taste will spread only into the thin outer layer of the food or vessel. See topic 46, section 11, and topic 59, section 2.

12. Cold Milk Flowing Onto a Hot Pot of Meat

83. When do we say that if the stream is interrupted the pot with its contents are permissible; and if it is not interrupted, although the pot itself becomes forbidden, the contents remain permissible?

84. I.e., the contents of the pot were heated over the fire in this vessel.

שיהיה ס' נגד מה שנפל[85] דהקדירה כיון דעומדת במקומה הוי כתתאה[86] וגובר[87] ודינו כצונן לתוך חם דכולו אסור ודינו כדלעיל סימן א' ב' ג'.[88] טו

יג. בד"א דאפילו קילוח צונן אוסר כולו דוקא כשנפל על הקדירה דחשבינן לקילוח עילאה ולקדירה תתאה אבל אם זב תחת הקדירה ממש לא אמרינן כיון שהקדירה עומד במקומו יש לו דין תתאה אלא הזב תחת הקדירה הוא התחתון ולכן אם זה שזב תחת הקדירה הוא צונן דינו כחם לצונן[89] והקדירה אסורה משום קליפה[90] והתבשיל מותר.[91] טז

יד. בד"א[92] שנשפך במקום צונן אבל אם נשפך אצל האש שאותו מקום הוא מרותח ועדיף מכ"ר[93] ולכן אפילו העמיד עליו קדירה צוננת הכל אסור אפי' התבשיל עד שיהיה בו ס' נגד

טו. שם.
טז. פ"ח סי' צ"ב ס"ק ל"ב וכ' דל"ד למש"כ כלל מ"ב סי' ז' בצלי רותח שנפל לחלב צונן דאפי' בשוקע בתוכו החלב הוא הצונן כיון שעומד במקומו שא"כ דעכ"פ גם תחת הצלי יש חלב משא"כ כאן.*

יד אדם

85. I.e., unless the pot contains sixty times the amount of liquid that flows onto it. If sixty is present, although the pot becomes forbidden, its contents remain permissible. The *Aruch Hashulchan* (92:48) states that if the floor of the oven is level and smooth and therefore the liquid will not form puddles, then the spilled liquid will only come into contact with the outer circumference of the pot, and the pot would certainly contain at least sixty times this amount.

86. I.e., even though the forbidden liquid makes contact with the lower portion of the wall of the pot and they are both on the same level, nevertheless, the pot is regarded as the lowermost item, since it remains standing in its place.

87. The pot will heat up the liquid that has reached it such that both the pot and the milk will now be hot. This is in accordance with the rule that "the lower one dominates" which is explained in topic 42, sections 7-8. (If, however, the liquid comes into contact with the bottom surface of the pot we can be more lenient, as explained in the next section.)

88. For example, if the pot contains more than sixty times the liquid that came into contact with it, it should be emptied immediately and one must not pour it out along the side that is in contact with the liquid. The contents of the pot will then be permissible.

pot] sixty times what has fallen.[85] [This is so because] the pot, since it is standing in its place, is like the "lower one"[86] and it dominates,[87] and the rule is that of cold falling into hot where all of it is forbidden, and [it is governed] by the rules noted above in sections 1, 2, and 3.[88טו]

13. When is it so that even if the stream is cold that it makes all of it forbidden? This is only when it has fallen on the [wall of the] pot, since we regard the stream to be above and the pot below. However, if it actually flowed under the pot, we do not say that since the pot stands in its place that it has the status of being the lower item; rather, what flowed under the pot is the lower one. Therefore, if what flowed under the pot is cold, it has the rule of hot [falling] into cold,[89] and the pot is forbidden because [it constitutes] the "width of the peel"[90] and the cooked food is permissible.[91טז]

14. When is this so?[92] Where [the liquid] was spilled out in a cold place. However, if it was spilled out next to the fire where the location is boiling hot, it [even] surpasses a "first vessel"[93] and therefore even if one placed a cold pot on it everything is forbidden, even the cooked food [in the pot], unless there will be sixty times what was

טו. *Ibid.*

טז. *Pri Chadash* 92:32, and he writes that it is not similar to what is written in topic 42, section 7 regarding hot broiled food which has fallen into cold milk, where even if it is immersed in it, the milk is the cold item [and is regarded as the lower one] since it stands in its place. It is different there for at least under the broiled meat also there is [cold] milk, which is not the case here.*

[Textual note: Section 19 printed below is out of place, and it should follow this section as section 14. This is how it is printed in the early editions of the *Chochmas Adam*.]

*In the case where milk flows under the pot, there is no portion of the pot which is under the milk. Therefore, even though the pot stands in its original place, the milk is the lower item.

Yad Adam

13. Cold Milk Which Flowed Under a Hot Pot of Meat

89. The liquid under the pot will dominate and cool off the pot.

90. See topic 42, section 7 where it is explained that even though the lower cold item dominates and cools off the upper one, the peel of the upper item becomes forbidden.

91. This is only if the hot pot is not near the fire. If the hot pot is standing next to the fire, then the more stringent rules of section 15 will apply.

14. A Pot of Meat Placed on Hot Milk Which Is Next to the Fire

92. I.e, when are we lenient to say that if a cold pot is placed on spilled hot milk, everything is permissible? This ruling is mentioned by the *Chochmas Adam* in section 19. (In the early editions of the *Chochmas Adam* the text of section 19 precedes this section.)

93. The intense heat from the burning wood causes the spilled liquid to be on even a higher level than a "first vessel" and more transmission of taste will occur. (As noted above, pots of food were cooked by placing

הנשפך[94]יז (מ״ב) מ״מ נ״ל דאם יש ספק אם יש ס׳ בקדרה נגד מה שזב דמותר מס״ס שמא היה ס׳ וספק שמא אינו מפעפע לפנים.[95]יח

טו. וכן אם הנשפך הוא צונן ובמקום צונן אלא שהקדירה שנשפך תחתיו הוא עומד אצל האשיט מחמת רתיחת האש שאצלה א״א לומר תתאה גבר[96] כי חום העליון שבקדירה מרתיח התחתון ואינו מניחו להתקרר ובולע שפיר ואוסר כולו[97] וצריך ס׳ ולא אמרינן תתאה גבר אלא כשהעליון אינו עומד אצל האש.[98]כ

טז. וכ״ש אם ב׳ הקדירות של בשר ושל חלב עומדים אצל האש וזב מאחד לתחת השני דצריך ס׳.[99]

יז. וכל זה שהמקום שזב החלב או האיסור היה נקי בלא אפר[100] אבל אם היה זב תחת האפר המונח שם וא״כ נעשה הדבר הזב לפגם ואינו אוסרכא ומ״מ נ״ל שאם זב הרבה והיה שם מעט אפר אין להקל[101] והכל לפי הענין בשגם דגוף הדין אם אפר פוגם אינו מוסכם אליבא דכולי עלמא לכן אין להקל כ״א לצורך גדול

יז. ש״ך ס״ק ל״ג ויש״ש ופ״ח ומנ״י וכו״פ.
יח. ועיין בנ״א.*
יט. כן הוא ביש״ש ואו״ה.
כ. הש״ך בס״ק ל״ג ל״ג וכ״כ רש״ל בפג״ה סי׳ ל״ח בהדיא.
כא. מ״י כלל י״ז ס״ק כ׳.

יד אדם

them in an oven. The pot to be cooked was place on the oven floor next to a pile of burning wood.)

94. If, on the other hand, a HOT POT is placed on hot milk, then some authorities rule that sixty is required even if the hot milk is not next to the fire. See section 19 below.

95. In cases when there is a doubt as to whether sixty is present, we can rely on the more lenient opinion of the *Chavos Daas* mentioned in the footnote on note יח.

15. Cold Milk Which Flowed Under a Hot Pot of Meat Next to the Fire

96. We cannot say that the cold liquid dominates here and cools down the pot.

97. All of the contents of the pot will become forbidden from the absorbed taste of the liquid that flowed under the pot.

98. Since when the upper one (the pot) is next to the fire, the liquid underneath the pot cannot cool it off.

16. Pots of Meat and Milk Next to the Fire, Where Liquid Flows from One of Them

99. The food in the second pot is forbidden unless it contains sixty times as much as the liquid flowing under it. (The pot itself is forbidden in any case.)

17. Leniencies Which Apply if Ashes Are Present

100. Ashes would be produced when the

יז. *Shach* [chapter 92], paragraph 32, and *Yam shel Shlomo* and *Pri Chadash* and *Minchas Yaakov* and *Kreisi u'pleisi*.
יח. And see the *Binas Adam*.*
יט. So it is in the *Yam shel Shlomo* and the *Issur v'heter*.
כ. The *Shach* in [chapter 92] paragraphs 32 and 33, and the *Rashal* in the chapter *gid hanashe*, section 38 write this explicitly.
כא. *Minchas Yaakov* 17:20.

spilled.[94][יז] (See *Binas Adam*, section 42.) Nevertheless, it is my opinion that if there is a doubt whether there was in the pot sixty times what flowed [under it], then it is permissible due to a double doubt–perhaps there was sixty, [and even if there was not sixty] perhaps it does not spread inside [the pot].[95][יח]

15. And so if the spilled [milk] is cold and the location is cold, but the pot under which it spilled is standing next to the fire,[יט] due to the heat of the fire that is next to [the pot] it is impossible to say that the lower one dominates,[96] since the heat of the pot, which is the upper one, will heat up the lower one and will not allow [the pot] to cool off, and it will absorb [the taste of the milk] well and make all of it forbidden[97] unless there is sixty [times as much in the pot]. [Thus] we do not say that the lower one dominates unless the upper one is not standing next to the fire.[98][כ]

16. And certainly, if two pots of meat and milk are standing next to the fire and [liquid] from one flows under the second, sixty is required.[99]

17. And all of this [applies] if the place where the milk or forbidden substance flowed was clean without ashes,[100] but if it flowed under ashes that are lying there, as such, the [taste of the flowing] substance is spoiled and it will not make [the pot] forbidden.[כא] Nevertheless, it is my opinion that if a large amount flowed and there was a little bit of ashes there, one should not be lenient,[101] and it is all according to the situation, especially since the actual rule whether or not ashes spoil [taste] is not agreed upon unanimously. Therefore, one should not be lenient unless there is a great need. And it is also my

Yad Adam

*The *Chochmas Adam* (in the *Binas Adam*, section 42) mentions that the *Chavos Daas* is lenient and permits the contents of a cold pot of food place on hot milk. The reasoning is as follows: Because the pot of food is cold, the taste of the milk which enters into the material of the pot does not enter into the pot's contents. He concludes that unless there is a great loss or there are other grounds to be lenient, the accepted practice is to be strict and prohibit the food, in accordance with the *Shach* cited here.

wood in the oven would burn. Only if the area were free of ashes can a pot and its contents become forbidden as described in the previous sections.

101. One should not assume that a small amount of ashes would spoil the taste of the liquid.

כב. ואפשר דבזה גם הצ״י אוסר ואינו דומה לסעי' ל״ה* ששם בשלו האפר עם מים.

ועוד נ״ל דל״ד למש״כ הצ״צ בענין הזייף[102] ששם מבשלין האפר עם המים[103] משא״כ בזה שרק שזב תחת האפר.[כב]

יח. ואם לא ראה בשעה שזב אלא שמצא שקרקע הכירה הוא לח מקדירה זו לזו[104] אבל אינו יודע אם נגע בקדירה אחרת או לא וגם אינו יודע כמה זב נ״ל דאפי' שניהם עומדים אצל האש מותר[105] דהוי ס״ס ס' שמא לא הגיע עד הקדירה הב' ואת״ל שנגע שמא היה ס' ופשיטא דלא מחזיקינן איסור אם לא ראה כלל שזב.

יט. ואם נשפך חלב או איסור רותח על קרקע וכיוצא בו במקום שאין מרותח מחמת אש[106] והעמיד עליו קדירה צוננת הכל מותר דכיון דנשפך כבר ונפסק הקילוח[107] הרי אנו דנין המקום שנשפך עליו ככלי שני והכל מותר רק שידיח הקדירה ואם היתה הקדירה רותחת הרי זה כחם לתוך צונן דבעי קליפה[108] וא״כ הקדירה אסורה והתבשיל מותר והמנ״י בכלל נ״ו ס״ק כ״א כ' כיון דעכ״פ עדיין הנשפך רותח שהיס״ב רק דהוי ככ״ש ולכן כיון שהעמידו עליו קדירה מרותחת בקל מתבשל אף ע״י כ״ש[109] ולכן צריך ס' נגד הנשפך.

יד אדם

102. Ordinary soap is produced by mixing animal fat (generally from an unkosher animal) and boiling it together with wood ash.

103. The case there involves soap which fell into a pot of hot liquid. We can permit the liquid because the ash is actually inside the liquid in the pot and gives it a bad taste.

18. If a Pot Overflowed and the Circumstances Are in Doubt

104. For example, a pot of milk boiled over and one finds a stream of milk extending towards a pot of meat. If the stream of milk definitely reached the pot of meat and was not interrupted, then the pot, and possibly its contents, would become forbidden in accordance with sections 11 and 12 above.

105. The contents of the pot are permissible due to the "double doubt" about to be mentioned. However, since only one of the doubts applies to the pot (whether the stream touched it), the pot should be kashered. (If it cannot be kashered, there are grounds to be lenient in accordance with the end of section 3. See *Madanei Hashulchan* 92:144.)

19. A Pot of Meat Placed on Hot Milk Which Is Not Next to the Fire

106. If the milk was in a location which is heated by the fire, then the very stringent ruling of section 14 applies (and even the food will be forbidden).

כב. And it is possible that in this case, the *Bais Yosef* also would forbid it, and it is not similar to the end of chapter 95 [paragraph 4],* because there they cooked the ashes with the water.

opinion that this is not similar to what the *Tzemach Tzedek* writes regarding soap[102] because there [where the mixture is permitted] he is cooking the ashes with the water,[103] whereas in this case it only flows under the ashes [outside of the pot].כב

18. If no-one was watching at the time that [a pot] overflowed, but one noticed that the floor of the oven was wet [extending] from this [pot] toward another [pot][104] and he does not know if [the stream actually] touched the other pot or not, and he also does not know how much flowed, it is my opinion that even if both of them are standing next to the fire, it is permissible,[105] for there is a double doubt–it is doubtful whether or not [the stream] reached the second pot, and if you say that [the stream] did come into contact with it, perhaps there was sixty [times as much in the pot]. And it is obvious that if no-one saw that [any liquid] has flowed, [then] we do not presume that anything has become forbidden.

19. And if [hot] milk or a forbidden liquid spilled out onto the floor [of an oven] or a similar location, in a place which is not hot due to the fire,[106] and one placed a cold pot on it–everything is permissible, for since it was spilled out already and the stream was interrupted,[107] we judge the place upon which it spilled as a "second vessel" and everything is permissible and one need only wash the pot. But if the pot was hot, it is like hot falling into cold which requires "peeling,"[108] and as such, the pot is forbidden and the cooked food is permissible. But the *Minchas Yaakov* in topic 56, paragraph 21 writes that if at least what was spilled out is still hot enough such that the hand would withdraw from it, although it is like a "second vessel," nevertheless, when one places a hot pot on it [the pot] readily becomes cooked even by a "second vessel,"[109] and therefore it is required to have [in the pot] sixty times what was spilled out.

Yad Adam

*The *Bais Yosef* there mentions that ashes inside a pot of water will effectively spoil the taste of any fat that clings to the walls of the pot.

---

107. If the stream had not been interrupted but it reached the pot directly, the more stringent ruling of section 11 will apply. (The pot will be forbidden but the food remains permissible.)

108. It is similar to the case described at the end of section 13.

109. Even though we usually say that liquid

ואם כבר נבלע הכל בקרקע ואינו נשאר ממש אע״פ שהעמיד עליו קדירה רותחת מותר דכיון דנבלע בתוכו ה״ז כקדירה שבלוע מן התבשיל ושתי קדרות הנוגעות זו בזו מותרין.[110]

כ. נר של חלב העשוי כנר של שעוה שנטף ממנו טיפה על כלי אין צריך אלא גרידה[111] דפסק כח רתיחתו אבל אם נפל טיפה מחלב מהותך שדולק בנר שקורין לאמפ[112] כל הכלי אסור אע״פ שנפסק הקילוח[113] כיון שרתיחתו ע״י אור הוא מרותח הרבה עד שאפילו כשנפסק עדיין יש לו דין כ״ר אבל אם נטף מצד אחר מן הכלי שהפתילה בתוכו[כג] או שנפל טיפה מחלב שנרתח בקדירה אצל האש כיון דפסק הקילוח לא חשיב ככ״ר.[114][כד]

וכן אם נפל הנר הדולק על כלי או אפי׳ אם הסיר הפחם וזרק על כלי ל״א שכבר נשרף החלב כי עדיין יש בו לחלוחית[כה] וכולו אסור[כו] ומ״מ בנרות העשוין מחלב שעומד ימים רבים ומוסרח למאוד טרם שנעשה נרות הוי נטל״פ ומותר.[כז]

כא. כל מקום שכתבנו דצריך ס׳ נגד קליפת הכלי[115] עיין בש״ך סי׳ ס״ט ס״ק ס״ה דמהפוסקים משמע דלעולם יש

כג. ש״ך שם ס״ק ל׳.
כד. תה״ד סי׳ קע״ו.
כה. עיין פ״ח כי׳ ק״ח ס״ק כ״ג.
כו. וכ׳ בפמ״ג דלריך ליבון ולא מהני הגעלה.*
כז. כו״פ שם.

יד אדם

transferred to a second vessel does not cook, according to the *Minchas Yaakov* we do not say this here, since the pot being placed on the liquid is boiling hot.

110. As noted above in the end of section 10.

20. Forbidden Fat from Candles Which Falls onto a Vessel

111. It is necessary only to scrape off the fat that clings to the vessel.

112. A lamp consists of a vessel which holds a flammable liquid, and a flame is present on one side of the vessel which slowly burns the liquid. The ruling is more stringent here since the heat is more intense when the flame is in contact with a liquid. In the first case, where a solid candle is involved, the droplets are not heated to the same extent.

113. The stream of melted fat from the lamp was not continuous. In such a case the liquid should not have the status of a "first vessel" but it should be treated more leniently. This, however, is not the case here.

114. And it will not prohibit the vessel upon which it falls. In these cases, the fat itself was not in direct contact with the flame and is therefore to be treated more leniently. As such, when the stream is interrupted, only scraping is necessary. If, however, the stream

כב. *Taz* there, [chapter 92] paragraph 30.
כד. *Terumas Hadeshen* chapter 176.
כה. See the *Pri Chadash* 108:23.
כו. And the *Pri Megadim* writes that it requires kashering by fire, and kashering with boiling water will not help.*
כז. *Kreisi u'pleisi* there.

And if everything had already been absorbed into the floor [of the oven] and none of it actually remained, even though one placed a hot pot on it, it is permissible, for since it was absorbed inside it, [the oven floor] is like a pot which had absorbed from the cooked food [which was inside it], and two pots which come into contact with each other are permissible.[110]

20. If a candle made out of forbidden fat is formed like a wax candle, and a drop from it drips on a vessel, [the vessel] requires only scraping,[111] since the strength of its heat had dissipated. But if a drop of the melted forbidden fat— which was burning in a light called a "lamp"[112]—has fallen [onto a vessel] the entire vessel is forbidden; for even though the stream was interrupted,[113] since its heat is [directly] from a flame it is very hot. As such, even though [the stream] is interrupted, it still has the rule of a "first vessel." However, if it dripped from the opposite side of the vessel from where the wick is located,[כג] or if a drop of forbidden fat which was boiled in a pot next to the fire has fallen [on a vessel], since the stream was interrupted, it is not considered to be a "first vessel."[114][כד]

And similarly, if the burning candle [of forbidden fat] has fallen onto a vessel, or even if one removed the charcoal [left from the wick] and threw it onto a vessel, we do not say that the forbidden fat has already burned up because there is still fluid in it,[כה] and all of [the vessel] is forbidden.[כו] Nevertheless, candles which are made of forbidden fat that stand for many days and are very foul smelling before being made into candles—they impart a detrimental taste and [therefore the vessel on which they fall] is permissible.[כז]

21. [Regarding] every place where we have written that it is necessary to have sixty times the "peel" of the vessel,[115] refer to the *Shach* chapter 69 paragraph 65, that from the *halachic* authorities it is

Yad Adam

*It is similar to a gentile's knife which had been used with unkosher meat broiling over a fire. In such cases, kashering by fire is required.

21. Rules Concerning the "Peel" of a Vessel Which Became Forbidden

is not interrupted, then the peel of the vessel will become forbidden (topic 59, section 2).

115. Such as in topic 42, section 10 and topic 57, section 1.

ס' במה שבתוך הכלי נגד הקליפה זולת בקערה רחבה ואינה גבוהה ובאמת קערות כאלו היו בימיהם ועדיין הם נמצאים בגליל פוזנא אבל בקערות שלנו המקיל וסומך על סתימת לשון הפוסקים כח דהתירא עדיף.[116] (מ"ג)

כלל מו

דין חלב שנתבשל בקדירה של בשר ודין קדירה וכף של בשר וחלב שתחבן זה בזה

(סימן צ"ג צ"ד)

א. קדירה שבישל בו בשר הרי נבלע בו טעם בשר ולכן אסור לבשל בו חלב מן התורה בתוך מעת לעת[1] דקיימא לן טכ"ע דאורייתא[2] וכן אם בישל בו איסור[3] אסור לבשל בו היתר ואם בישל

יד אדם

116. In order to make a lenient ruling, it must be thought out very carefully to be certain that a transgression is not being performed. The meticulous care which must be taken to make a lenient ruling makes it especially authoritative.

We have learned in section 2 above (and in topic 46, section 1) that there is no vessel whose contents are equal to sixty times the vessel. In this section, we learn that when only the peel of the vessel is forbidden, the pot generally does contain sixty times its peel.

The *Chochmas Adam* has mentioned that low flat vessels might not contain sixty times their peel, but such vessels were not in use in his time. However, the plates we use nowadays, which are low and flat, most likely do not contain sixty times their contents. *(P'eir Hashulchan* 91:193)

1. Milk Cooked in a Meat Pot (or Vice Versa); Kosher Food Cooked in a Forbidden Pot

1. When meat is cooking in a pot, the heat from the cooking causes the taste of the meat to be transferred into the material of the pot, and this taste remains beneficial for 24 hours. If one will cook dairy in this pot within 24 hours of cooking the meat, the heat of the cooking will cause the absorbed meat taste in the pot to be emitted into the dairy

implied that in all cases whatever is inside the vessel is [at least] sixty times the peel, except for a wide pot which is not tall. Actually, pots like this were common in their days, and they are still found in the area around Posen [in Poland], but [regarding] our pots, one who is lenient and relies on the unqualified language of the *halachic* authorities [is acting properly], as the strength of a lenient ruling is very great.[116] (See *Binas Adam*, section 43.)

Topic 46

Laws Concerning Milk Cooked in a Meat Pot; Regulations Regarding a Pot and Spoon Which Are Meat and Dairy and One Was Inserted Into The Other

(based on *Shulchan Aruch—Yoreh Deah* chapters 93, 94)

1. If meat has been cooked in a pot, the taste of the meat becomes absorbed into it. Therefore, it is forbidden to cook milk in it according to Torah law if it is within 24 hours [of cooking the meat],[1] for it is established for us that [the principle:] "when there is taste [and no substance] it is like the essence [of the food]" is mandated by the Torah.[2] And similarly, if one cooked forbidden food in [a pot][3] it is for-

Yad Adam

food, thereby creating a forbidden mixture. (This applies even if the pot was thoroughly cleaned before cooking the dairy food in it.) If, however, the dairy food is cooked in the pot after 24 hours has elapsed, then the dairy food remains permissible. The reason is that according to Torah law, we can disregard any absorbed taste which is more than 24 hours old, since it has become spoiled. See also note 19.

2. According to the principle of טעם כעיקר (literally, "the taste is like the essence"), when a food or vessel has absorbed the taste of another food, even though no substance of this other food is now present, we regard the absorbed taste as if it were the "essence" of the food, that is, we consider it to be like the food itself. For example, if one has cooked forbidden food in a pot, the taste of the food will have been transmitted into the pot. Even after cleaning out the pot, the taste of the forbidden food will still remain inside the material of the pot. We view the presence of this taste as if the forbidden food itself were present, and it is therefore forbidden to cook in this pot again (unless it is kashered).

There is a controversy among our early

בו חלב[4] או בקדירה של איסור דבר היתר בתוך מעל"ע[5] קיימא לן דאין לך כלי שיהיה בתוכו ס' נגד כל הכלי[6][א] ואם כן נאסר התבשיל ובבו"ח[7] אסור הכל בהנאה וישליך לבהכ"ס[8] ובשאר איסורין מותר בהנאה[9] ואין חילוק בין שהיה הכלי של מתכת או עץ או חרס דלעולם משערינן נגד כולו.[10][ב]

ב. בד"א דצריך ס' נגד כולו[11] אם לא ידעינן כמה בלע הקדירה מן החלב או האיסור בתוך מעל"ע זה[12] אבל אם היתה חדשה

א. אם לא שיהיה רוחב הקדירה גדול ונחושתו דק וכ"ל שהוא כעין יורה גדולה עיין ש"ך סי' צ"ג ס"ק א'.*

ב. סי' צ"ג לאפוקי מדעת ראב"ד דס"ל דבמתכת ועץ אין צריך לשער נגד כולו כיון שאפשר להפריד האיסור אלא משער באומד יפה כמה יצא מן הכלי דלא קיי"ל הכי ש"ך סי' צ"ח ס"ק י"ב.

יד אדם

authorities whether this principle is mandated by the Torah, or if it is a result of a rabbinical enactment. (This is important to clarify since we can sometimes be more lenient in cases of doubt when a prohibition is rabbinical in origin.) *Rashi* and the *Rambam* rule that this principle is rabbinical in origin. However, *Tosafot*, the *Tur*, and others rule that it is mandated by the Torah, and this is the accepted ruling. These authorities derive support from the Torah's command to kasher the unkosher vessels which were captured from the country of Midian before they could be used. (Numbers 31:23) From this we see that the Torah requires removal of any forbidden taste which remains absorbed inside a vessel, as we are to regard the taste as the food itself. (*Aruch Hashulchan* 98:1-11) Refer to topic 51, section 8 for further discussion of this principle.

3. Such as a pot that had been used to cook forbidden fat.

4. He cooked milk in a pot which had been used to cook meat.

5. It is less than 24 hours since he had cooked the meat (or forbidden food) in that pot, and the absorbed taste is therefore beneficial.

In these cases, the taste of the meat (or forbidden food) will be permeating all of the material of the pot. Therefore, we assume that the amount of meat taste (or forbidden taste) is equal to the volume of the material of the pot. If one goes on and cooks milk (or permissible food) in that pot, the contents of the pot will be permissible only if they are at least equal to sixty times the volume of the material of the pot. (In such a case, the meat taste [or forbidden taste] would no longer be detectable and would become nullified.) However, SINCE IT IS ESTABLISHED...

6. The contents of a vessel will always be less than sixty times the volume of the material of that vessel. Therefore, the taste absorbed in the walls of the pot will not be nullified.

7. If the case involved cooking meat in a milk pot, or vice versa.

8. The food must be discarded since it is forbidden to derive benefit from it (topic 40, section 2). Furthermore, the pot is also forbidden and may no longer be used for cooking (unless it is kashered), since it now contains absorbed tastes of both meat and milk. (See also the end of section 8 below.)

bidden to cook permissible food in it. And if one [now] cooked milk in it,[4] or if he [now] cooked a permissible food in a forbidden pot, [and it is] within 24 hours[5]—since it is established for us that there is no vessel which contains sixty times the entire vessel[6א]—as such, the cooked food [in the pot] is forbidden, and with meat and milk,[7] it is forbidden to derive benefit from anything and it is to be thrown out in the bathroom;[8] and regarding other forbidden foods, it is permissible to derive benefit.[9] And there is no difference whether the vessel is made out of metal or wood or earthenware—we always measure with respect to all of it.[10ב]

2. When is it so that it is necessary to have sixty times all of it?[11] It is when we do not know how much [meat or] milk or forbidden food the pot absorbed in the past 24 hours.[12] However, if [the pot] was

א. Unless the diameter of the pot is large and it is made out of thin material, and it is my opinion that [such a vessel would be] like a very large kettle—see *Shach* 93:1.*

ב. *Shulchan Aruch* chapter 93. This [statement] excludes the opinion of the *Raavad* who holds that with metal and wood it is not necessary to measure with respect to all of it since it is possible to separate the forbidden taste [by kashering] but one measures with a reasonable estimate as to how much [absorbed taste] came out from the vessel. We do not rule according to this [opinion]. *Shach* 98:12.

*One can use rules of geometry to determine when a pot will contain sixty times its contents. If, for example, a standard 6 quart (5.7 liter) pot is 2/3 full, then the contents of the pot will be sixty times the material of the pot only if the thickness of its metal is less than .45 millimeter. (A standard 6 quart pot is approximately 25 centimeters in diameter and 12 centimeters high. If its diameter was increased to 50 centimeters, then the contents [when 2/3 full] would be sixty times the pot's material if the metal were up to .6 millimeter thick.) The calculations can be found in *Basar B'chalav* (illustrated) by Ehud Rosenberg, pages 167-168.

Yad Adam

9. One may derive benefit from permissible food that has absorbed their taste, just as one may derive benefit from the forbidden food itself. As such, one can feed the food to his animals or sell it to a gentile.

10. It is always necessary to have sixty times the material of the pot. There are, however, exceptions to this rule which are explained in the next section.

2. Leniencies Which May Apply When the Amount of Absorbed Taste is Known

11. When do we require that the contents of the pot be sixty times the material of the pot?

12. For example, milk was cooked in a pot, and later in that day a meat food was cooked in the same pot. If we knew how much milk had been cooked in the pot and it was smaller than the volume of the material of the pot, then it would be necessary for the pot to contain only sixty times the milk. Sixty times the material of the pot will not be required, since the amount of absorption in the pot cannot be more than the volume of milk which was actually present.

However, if we are unsure how much milk was cooked in the pot (or if it is known how much milk was cooked in the pot and the amount was equal to or greater than the volume of the material of the pot), then, as the *Chochmas Adam* goes on to explain, sixty times the pot will be required.

ג. ש״ך סי׳ צ״ג ס״ק ח׳.

וידעינן כמה בלע[13] או אפי׳ ישנה אלא דידעינן כמה בלע בתוך מעל״ע זה מהבשר או החלב אין צריך לשער רק נגד מה שבלע מהחלב[14] ואם יש ס׳ כנגדו מותר התבשיל והקדירה אסורה[15] כדלקמן[16] אבל מה שבלע הקדירה קודם מעל״ע[17] א״צ לשער כנגדו אפי׳ אינו יודע כמה בלע דכל מה שבלע קודם מעל״ע כבר נפגם[18] ונטל״פ מותר[19] כדלקמן כלל נ״ד וכן אם בישל בקדירה שאינה בת יומא מבישול כ״ר[20] [21] המאכל מותר דנטל״פ ומ״מ הקדירה אסורה כדלקמן שם וכלל נ״ה.[22]

ג. כיסוי הקדירה מדינא דינו כקדירה וכל הכלים דאם אינו בן יומא אינו אוסר אלא שהמנהג להחמיר בכיסויים שיש להם כעין חלל למעלה והוא קצר בענין שאין יכולים לנקות שם וא״כ יש

יד אדם

13. If the pot (described in the previous note) had never been used previously, and we know exactly how much milk was cooked in the pot, then the volume of milk which was cooked at that time would be the maximum amount of taste that the pot could have absorbed.

14. As such, if the total amount of milk cooked in the pot within the past 24 hours was less than the material of the pot, it is enough to have sixty times what was cooked in the pot. Any milk which had been cooked in the pot more than 24 hours previously can be ignored, as the *Chochmas Adam* mentions below.

This leniency (to measure sixty times what had been cooked in the pot, instead of sixty times the material of the pot) will apply if the pot had not been used at all in the 24 hour period before the milk (or meat, or forbidden food) was cooked in it. If the pot had been used to cook something (even green vegetables) during this period, then it might be necessary to have sixty times the entire pot in any case. The details regarding this have already been explained in topic 44 section 18, in the second paragraph of that section.

15. There is now absorbed taste of meat and milk (or forbidden food) in the pot. As such, if one will later cook food in this pot (without kashering it first), the forbidden taste will be emitted from the pot into this food and cause the food to become forbidden.

16. See section 10.

17. For example, meat was cooked in a new pot, and milk was cooked in it more than 24 hours later.

18. Any absorbed taste in the pot which is more than 24 hours old will impart only an unfavorable taste to other foods. (See topic 55.)

19. It is certainly prohibited to cook with a vessel which has a detrimental forbidden

ג. *Shach* 93:1.

new and we know how much it absorbed,[13] or even if it was old but we know how much it absorbed during this past 24 hours from the meat or milk [or forbidden food], it is necessary to measure only what it absorbed from the milk [or meat or forbidden food].[14] And if there is sixty times with respect to it, the cooked food [now in the pot] is permissible but the pot is forbidden [to be used again][15] in accordance with what [is stated] further on.[16] But [with regard to] what was absorbed into the pot before 24 hours,[17] it is not necessary to measure with respect to it, even if one does not know how much it absorbed, for whatever it absorbed before the [past] 24 hours is already spoiled,[18] and whatever imparts a detrimental taste is permissible,[19] as [noted] later on in topic 54.[ג] And therefore, if one cooked in a pot that had not been used in the past day as a "first vessel"[20] for cooking,[21] the food is permissible as it imparts only a detrimental taste. Nevertheless, the pot is forbidden as [noted] there further on and in topic 55 [section 6].[22]

3. According to the *halacha*, the cover of a pot is judged like the pot or any other vessel, such that if it had not been used in the past day it cannot make something forbidden. However, the custom is to be strict with covers which have something like a narrow tube on top such that one cannot clean out what is there. For in such a case, there

Yad Adam

taste absorbed in it (topic 55, section 6). However, any food cooked in such a vessel remains permissible. Similarly, one may not cook meat in a pot which has a detrimental dairy taste absorbed in it, but if he does so, the meat remains permissible.

20. This term denotes a vessel which was heated up directly by a fire, whether or not it is still on the fire. Only such a vessel will absorb the taste of food which is cooked in it. (If water is boiled in a pot and the water is emptied into another vessel, the latter has the status of a "second vessel." If meat is then added to the hot water in this vessel, the vessel will not absorb the taste of the meat. This is because the water had already been cooled down when it was transferred from the first to the second vessel.)

21. He had not cooked the meat, milk, or forbidden matter in the pot during the past 24 hours, but only previous to this time.

22. As such, if the pot is metal it cannot be used again for cooking unless it is kashered. If it is earthenware it cannot be kashered and can no longer be used for cooking. See topic 55, section 7 that in cases involving a great loss, earthenware vessels sometimes can be used for cooking after waiting 24 hours.

ד. סי׳ ל״ג.
ה. שם.

שם בעין מחמת הזיעה והרתיחה שעלה שם ובבעין לא מהני מעת לעת[23] ולכן אוסרין אפילו אם הכיסוי אינו בן יומא ואע״ג שמה שהוא בעין הוא דבר מועט מ״מ חיישינן שהזיעה של בשר[24] עולה למעלה עד שאין ס׳ נגד הבעין וא״כ אותו הבעין נ״נ וצריך ס׳ פעמים ס״א נגד אותו מקום של כיסוי כדלעיל בכלל הקודם סי׳ ה׳[25] ומ״מ במקום שיש עוד צד להקל וכן לצורך שבת או הפסד יש להתיר בכל הכיסוים דאם אינו בן יומא מותר.[ד]

ד. אם לקחו כיסוי רותח מקדירה שמבשלין בה בשר ונתנו אותו על קדירה שמבשלין בה חלב אם שניהם חמין שהיס״ב שניהם אסורים דסתם כיסוי רותח יש בו לחלוחית ונבלע בקדירה וכן מן הקדירה עולה הבל לכיסוי[26] ולא גרע מכף חולבת שתחב בקדירה של בשר דצריך ס׳ נגד הכף ה״נ צריך שיהיה בתבשיל ס׳ נגד הכיסוי[27] וה״ה אפילו אם הכיסוי צונן ויבש רק שהיא בת יומא אם היתה מונחת על הקדירה החמה עד שהתחילה להזיע עד שהיס״ב בזיעה הכל אסור דתתאה גבר[28][ה]

יד אדם

3. Stringencies Which Apply to a Pot Cover

23. A period of 24 hours helps with absorbed taste since it becomes detrimental after that time, but a 24 hour wait does not affect the status of intact food particles.

24. We are dealing with a pot of meat which is covered by a dairy cover.

25. We are concerned that the taste of the intact food material (which is now forbidden as a mixture of meat and milk) will spread through the cover and make the absorbed taste in that part of the cover inherently forbidden. The maximum part of the cover that can become forbidden in this way is sixty times the size of the food material. (See note 58 on topic 45.) Consequently, the maximum amount of forbidden substance will then be the food material itself plus a portion of the cover which is sixty times its size, a total of sixty-one times the food material. We will thus need sixty times this amount (sixty times sixty-one the size of the intact food-material) to nullify the forbidden taste and permit the contents of the pot. (Refer to note 61 there.)

4. Placing a Cover from a Meat Pot onto a Hot Dairy Pot

26. Thus, both the pot and the cover will absorb taste from each other and become forbidden. (If no moisture is present, then no absorption of taste will occur, in accordance with the end of the next section.)

ד. *Shulchan Aruch* chapter 93.
ה. *Shulchan Aruch* there.

would be intact [food] material [remaining] there caused by the steam and the boiling up that occurs there. And with intact material, 24 hours does not help.[23] Therefore, we prohibit [the contents of such a pot] even if the [forbidden] cover was not used in the past 24 hours. And even if what is intact is a small amount, nevertheless, we are concerned that the steam from the meat[24] rises upward such that there is not [in the steam] sixty times what is intact, and if this is so, that intact [food material] will become inherently forbidden [and its taste will spread into the cover], and we will require sixty times sixty-one with respect to that place in the cover, as [explained] above in the previous topic, section 5.[25] Nevertheless, in a situation where there is another reason to be lenient, and similarly, for the Sabbath or where there is a loss involved, there are grounds to permit [the contents of the pot] with all covers, such that if it has not been used on that day [the contents of the pot are] permissible.[ד]

4. If one took a hot cover from a pot in which one is cooking meat, and he placed it on a pot in which he is cooking milk, if both of them are hot such that the hand would withdraw from them, both of them are forbidden, as in general, a hot cover will have moisture [on it] which will be absorbed into the pot, and similarly, steam will go up from the pot to the cover.[26] And it is no worse than a dairy spoon which one inserted into a pot of meat, where we require sixty times the spoon. [Therefore,] here also, we require that there will be sixty times the cover in the cooked food.[27] And the rule is similar even if the cover is cold and dry but it had been used [for meat] during the past day: If it was lying on the hot pot [of milk] until it began to produce steam [hot enough] such that the hand would withdraw from the steam, everything is forbidden since the lower item dominates.[28][ה]

Yad Adam

27. We have already learned (at the beginning of this section) that the pot and cover are forbidden and cannot be used again (unless they are kashered). Now we are learning that the contents of the pot will also be forbidden unless the contents equals sixty times the size of the cover.

28. The hot steam from the bottom heats up the cold material (the pot cover) above it and therefore makes it forbidden. (This is the case if the steam is so hot that the hand would withdraw from it, as noted in topic 45, section 10.) This in turn will make the pot and its contents (if it is less than sixty times the cover) forbidden.

ו. שם בש"ך ס"ק ו'.

ה. ואם לקח כיסוי חם שהיס"ב מקדירה שמבשל בה בשר והניחו על קדירה של חלב צוננת אם הכיסוי יבש שאין בו לחלוחית הכל מותר אבל מסתמא יש בו לחלוחית ומכ"ש אם ידע שהיה בו לחלוחית שהיס"ב המאכל צריך קליפה ואם אינו יכול לקלוף[29] דינו מבואר כלל מ"ב סימן י'.[30]

והקדירה אם אינו הפסד כל כך[31] יש לאסור אותה ובמקום הפסד אף הקדירה מותרת דטיפה אחת כח חמימותה פוסק[32] וגרע מעירוי[33] שנפסק הקילוחי ואם אין מאכל בקדירה ושניהם יבשים הרי זה כשני קדירות שנגעו זה בזה[34] דמותרים ואם אחד יש בו לחלוחית דינו שוה לדין הנזכר דיש להחמיר לאסור הקדירה וכן הסומך או מניח כף של חלב בקדירה של בשר דינו כנזכר.

ו. התוחב כף חולבת שהוא בתוך מעת לעת מתשמיש כלי ראשון[35] אף ע"פ שעכשיו צונן ונקי בקדירה של בשר רותחת שהוא כלי ראשון שהיס"ב ואפילו לאחר שהעבירו מן האש[36] או

יד אדם

5. Placing a Cover from a Hot Meat Pot onto a Cold Dairy Pot

29. Such as where the contents are chopped into small pieces, or are liquid.

30. It is stated there that the contents of the pot are permitted if a great loss is involved. Why do the contents require peeling? This is because the taste of the forbidden hot droplets which fall from the cover onto the food will penetrate into the "peel" of the cold food. (See topic 42, end of section 7.) Nevertheless, here there are grounds to permit food which cannot be peeled, even when a great loss is not involved, because of the reasons mentioned below (the heat of single drops dissipates rapidly, and there is not a continuous stream from the cover to the food). One must first ascertain, however, that the pot's contents are at least sixty times the size of the droplets which fell into it. (*Madanei Hashulchan* 93:29)

31. Such as where the pot is metal and can be kashered.

32. The drop will not be very hot when it makes contact with the pot or its contents.

33. I.e., the rule will not be the same as the usual case when liquid is "poured" (or is spilled) from a "first vessel" onto a cold item in which case the outer layer becomes forbidden. This is because "pouring" causes the outer layer to become forbidden when the stream is continuous, whereas in the case where a drop falls from a pot cover, the stream is interrupted. These factors (single drops which lose heat rapidly, and an interrupted stream) allow us to be lenient in this case.

א. *Shach* there (chapter 93) in paragraph 6.

5. If one took a cover, which is hot enough that his hand would withdraw from it, from a pot in which he is cooking meat and placed it on a pot of cold milk, if the cover is dry such that it has no moisture, everything is permissible. However, [since] most likely there is moisture on it—and certainly, if he knew that [the cover] had moisture—[if it is hot enough such] that his hand would withdraw from it, the food will require peeling. And if he is unable to peel [the contents of the pot][29] the rule is as explained in topic 42 section 10.[30]

And [regarding the status of] the pot—if there is not so much of a loss,[31] it is proper to forbid it. And in a situation [involving] a loss, even the pot is permissible because the strength of the heat of a single drop [falling from the cover] dissipates[32] and [its strength] is less than that of "pouring"[33] since the stream is interrupted.[א] And if there is no food in the pot and both of them are dry, it is like two pots which touch one another [when they are dry],[34] in which case they are permissible. And if one has moisture, its rule is like the rule we have mentioned that it is proper to be stringent and forbid the pot. Similarly, if one leans or places a dairy spoon in [an empty] meat pot, the rule is as we have mentioned.

6. If one inserts a dairy spoon which had been used during the past 24 hours in a "first vessel" [of dairy food][35]—even if now [the spoon] is cold and clean—into a pot of hot meat which is a "first vessel" [which is hot enough] such that one's hand would withdraw from it, even after it has been removed from the fire;[36] or the reverse situation;

Yad Adam

34. This rule has been mentioned in note 78 in topic 45.

6. Inserting a Dairy Spoon into a Pot of Meat (or Vice Versa); Inserting a Forbidden Spoon into a Pot of Kosher Food

35. During the past 24 hours, the spoon had been used in a pot of dairy food which had been heated directly by a fire, and the food was hot enough so that one's hand would withdraw from it if he would touch it. Such a spoon will contain absorbed dairy taste which is beneficial. (If the spoon had not been used in hot dairy food during the past 24 hours but only prior to that time, the more lenient rulings in section 10 will apply.)

36. I.e., the spoon was inserted after the pot was removed from the fire, but the pot was still hot enough such that one's hand would withdraw from it. The contents of such a pot is still hot enough to cause the absorbed dairy taste in the spoon to be transferred into the meat contents of the pot, and to transfer

איפכא וכן כף איסור בקדירה של היתר צריך ס׳ נגד כל מה שתחב מהכף בתוך התבשיל[37] אם אינו יודע כמה בלע ואם יודע כמה בלע צריך ס׳ נגד כל מה שבלע[38] ומבואר לעיל כלל מ״ד סי׳ י״ח אבל מה שלא תחב בתבשיל אפילו מה שהוא בתוך חלל הקדירה א״צ לשער נגדו. ואפי׳ בכלי מתכת[39] אע״ג דחם מקצתו חם כולו ואע״ג דקיימא לן בחתיכה שמקצתה ברוטב שמפעפע ומפליט מכולו כדלעיל כלל מ״ד[40] זהו דוקא במאכל אבל בכלי אפילו כלי מתכת קיי״ל דאינו מפליט מכולו[41] ז ואם אינו ברור עד כמה תחב משערינן בסתם מה שדרך לתחוב דהיינו ראש הכף[42] ח ואם תחב צד השני מן הכף[43] צריך ג״כ ששים נגד מה שתחב דאע״ג דאינו מפליט מכולו[44] מ״מ מוליך בליעתו בכולו.[45] (מ״ה)

ז. כדעת המ״א בסי׳ תנ״א ודעת הש״ך בסימן קכ״א ודלא כפו״פ שמחמיר בזה ומדייק מדכתב בש״ע כל מה שנכנס בקדירה ועיין באחרונים ובב״א סי׳ מ״ד וראיה מאו״ה כלל ל״ז סעיף ב׳ שכתב בהדיא לתוך התבשיל והוא בעצמו כתב שם דאינו מפליט מכולו אלא שמסתפק בזה משום שנעלם ממנו שהם דברי המ״א וכתב זה מסברתו* ע״ש.

ח. סי׳ ל״ד ובש״ך סק״א.

יד אדם

the taste of the meat into the dairy spoon. (See topic 42, section 9. If the spoon comes into contact with the pot's contents outside of the pot while the contents are being poured from it, see section 11 below.)

37. If the contents of the pot are at least sixty times the size of the spoon, then any taste emitted by the dairy spoon into the contents of the pot will be nullified. As such, the contents of the pot remain permissible. However, (in the cases where a dairy spoon was inserted into a meat pot, or vice versa,) the spoon has become forbidden, since it now contains absorbed taste of both meat and milk. It therefore should not be used again until it is kashered. (See section 8 below.) It goes without saying that a forbidden spoon (such as one that was used with hot unkosher meat) may not be used again until it is kashered.

These rulings involve a spoon inserted into a pot containing liquid and other ingredients. If no liquid is present, refer to topic 57, section 6 and notes thereon.

38. If he knows how much was absorbed and the amount absorbed is less than the size of the spoon, such as where he had placed the spoon in only a few drops of hot milk, he will need only sixty times those few drops when inserting that spoon into a pot of meat.

[This leniency (to measure sixty times the amount of milk instead of sixty times the material of the spoon) will apply if the spoon had not been used for hot meat in the 24 hour period before the milk was absorbed in it. If the spoon had been used for hot meat during this period, then it might be necessary to have sixty times the entire spoon in any case. The details regarding this have already been explained in topic 44 section 18, in the second and third paragraphs of that section.]

39. The spoon is metal, which conducts heat very well.

40. This is mentioned in section 1 there, in accordance with the *Ri*.

41. But taste is emitted only from the part that is submerged in the contents of the pot.

or similarly, if a forbidden spoon [was inserted] into a pot of permissible food—[in all of these cases] we require [that the pot contain] sixty times the entire portion of the spoon which was inserted into the cooked food.[37] [This applies] if he does not know how much [the spoon] had absorbed, but if he knows how much the spoon had absorbed, he requires sixty times what it absorbed[38] as explained above in topic 44, section 18. However, we are not required [in any case] to measure sixty times the portion which was not inserted into the cooked food, even though it had been inside the space of the pot, and even if the utensil is metal[39] such that when part of it is hot all of it [then] becomes hot. And even though it is established for us that if a piece [of food] is partially [submerged] in liquid that [the absorbed taste] spreads [throughout the piece] and is emitted from all of it as [explained] above in topic 44,[40] this [applies] only to food, but regarding a utensil, even a metal utensil, it is established for us that it does not [emit taste] from all of it.[41][ז] And if it is not clear how much [of the spoon] he inserted, we generally measure by how much one is accustomed to insert it, which is the "head" of the spoon.[42][ח] And if he inserted the second side of the spoon,[43] he requires also sixty times what he inserted, for even though [the spoon] does not emit from all of itself,[44] nevertheless, its absorbed taste is conducted through all of it.[45] (See *Binas Adam*, paragraph 45.)

ז. This is in accordance with the opinion of the *Magen Avraham* in [*Orach Chayim*] chapter 451, and the opinion of the *Shach* in chapter 121. It is not in accordance with the *Kreisi u'pleisi* who is stringent regarding this, and derives from [the words] "Whatever enters into the pot" written in the *Shulchan Aruch* [that we must measure by the amount of the spoon which entered inside the space of the pot]. And refer to the later authorities and the *Binas Adam*, section 44. And there is a proof from the *Issur v'heter* topic 37, paragraph 2 where he writes explicitly [that we measure only by what was inserted] into the cooked food. And he him self (the *Kreisi u'pleisi*) writes there that [the spoon] does not cause emission [of taste] from all of it, but he is in doubt about this because it was hidden from him that this is the opinion of the *Magen Avraham*, and he wrote this from his own reasoning.* Refer there.

ח. *Shulchan Aruch* chapter 94, and in the *Shach* paragraph 1.

*The *Kreisi u'pleisi* drew a lenient conclusion from his own reasoning, but was not willing to rely on it in this matter without support from another authority. Nevertheless, the *Aruch Hashulchan* (94:1) rules that it is necessary to have sixty times the entire portion of the spoon which is in the pot.

Yad Adam

42. The rounded end of the spoon, and not the handle.

43. For example, he had used a spoon in the normal way to stir hot milk, and then he inserted the opposite end (the handle) of the spoon into a pot of meat.

44. Rather, it emits only from the portion that is currently submerged.

45. The taste of milk which had been absorbed through the rounded end of the spoon is transmitted throughout the spoon. If the spoon is then placed upside down in a meat soup, the portion of the spoon in the

ט. ודלא כש״ך.

ז. אם תחב הכף בקדירה ב׳ פעמים אם נודע בנתיים[46] כבר נתבטל[47] ונעשה היתר ולכן אע״ג שתחבו עוד הפעם הרי חוזר להתבטל באותו ס׳ גופה[48] אבל אם לא נודע בינתיים לדעת הב״י בש״ע צריך ב׳ פעמים ס׳[49] דמתחלה[50] צריך ס׳ נגד החלב וחיישינן שמא נשאר בו מעט חלב וכשהוציא מן הקדירה נעשה כל הכף נבילה מבשר וחלב וצריך לבטל הכף פעם שנית ודעת הפ״ח וכו״פ דלאו דוקא ב׳ פעמים[51] אלא על כל תחיבה צריך ס׳ לדעת הב״י.[ט]

אבל מנהגינו על פי הכרעת רמ״א דסגי בפעם א׳ ששים ואפילו לא נודע בינתיים דהרבה פוסקים ס״ל דבדבר בלוע לא אמרינן חנ״נ ואע״ג דלא קיי״ל הכי כדלעיל סוף כלל מ״ד[52] מ״מ בכה״ג אין להחמיר שהרי אפי׳ איסור עצמו שנפל לקדירה כמה פעמים קיי״ל דא״צ אלא פעם אחת ס׳ כמבואר כלל נ״א סימן ז׳ אבל אם תחב בו כף אחר[53] או שחזר ותחב אותו כף לקדירה של בשר וחזר ותחבו

יד אדם

soup will emit the absorbed taste into the soup.

7. Inserting a Spoon with Absorbed Taste Twice Into the Same Pot; Measuring Absorbed Taste in a Spoon

46. If, before the second insertion, it became known that the first insertion was improper, and the pot contained sixty times the part of the spoon which was inserted.

47. Any forbidden taste emitted by the spoon into the contents of the pot has become nullified.

48. The same contents of the pot will again nullify any further forbidden taste emitted by the spoon.

49. The contents of the pot must be 120 times the part of the spoon which was inserted. This is because nullification does not take place until the circumstances (mentioned in note 46) become known. As such, each insertion of the spoon into the pot adds additional taste which must be nullified. One may now ask: The amount of meat or dairy taste in a spoon cannot be larger than the spoon itself. How then can it be possible that more than the size of the spoon is required in any case? The *Chochmas Adam* now goes on to answer this question.

50. I.e., at the time of the first improper insertion. The case now under discussion is one where a spoon had been inserted into hot milk and within 24 hours it is inserted into a pot of meat. While this dairy spoon is present in the pot of meat, some (but not necessarily all) of the dairy taste in the spoon will be transferred into the meat contents of the pot. In addition, some of the taste of the meat in the pot will be transferred into the spoon.

ט. This is not in accordance with the *Shach* [(94:4) who mentions that two times sixty is the maximum required.]

7. If one inserted the spoon into the pot twice, if it became known in the meantime[46] it has already been nullified[47] and has become permissible. Therefore, even if he inserted it again, it goes on to be nullified by the same sixty itself.[48] However, if it did not become known in the meantime, according to the opinion of the *Bais Yosef* in the *Shulchan Aruch* we require two times sixty;[49] for at first[50] we need sixty times the milk, and we are concerned that perhaps a little [absorbed] milk [still] remains in [the spoon] and when he takes it out of the pot all of the [absorbed taste in the] spoon has become inherently forbidden from meat and milk, and it is necessary to nullify the spoon a second time [when it is reinserted]. And it is the opinion of the *Pri Chadash* and the *Kreisi u'pleisi* that not specifically two times [sixty is required][51] but for each insertion [of the spoon] sixty is required according to the opinion of the *Bais Yosef.*[ט]

However, our custom is in accordance with the decision of the *Rama* that it is enough to have one times sixty [in the pot], even if it did not become known in the meantime, since many authorities rule that with regard to an absorbed substance [in a vessel] we do not say that a "piece becomes inherently forbidden." And even though this is not the accepted ruling as [noted] above at the end of topic 44,[52] nevertheless, in this case we need not be stringent, for even if a forbidden food itself fell into a pot many times, it is established for us that we require [the pot to contain] only one times sixty as explained in topic 51, section 7. However, if one inserted another spoon,[53] or he went on and inserted

Yad Adam

51. This requirement of two times sixty applies only to a case such as this where there were two insertions, and it is not a maximum. Thus, if the spoon were inserted three times, then three times sixty will be required.

52. It is mentioned there (in section 18) that we rely on this lenient opinion only in certain situations, and only where a great loss is involved. Therefore, it seems that we should indeed say that the absorbed taste in the spoon becomes inherently forbidden after the first insertion, and we should require another sixty times the spoon for each additional insertion (unless there is a great loss).

53. A meat spoon (which was used for hot meat in a "first vessel" in the past 24 hours) had been inserted into a pot of hot milk, and a second meat spoon (with the same criteria) was then inserted into the milk.

בחלב[54] לכ"ע צריך כ"כ ס' כפי הפעמים שתחב בו שהרי בכל פעם הוא תחיבה חדשה.[55]

ובכף שתחבו בקדירה שמבשלין בה נבילה ותחבו לקדירה של בשר כשר במקום צורך והפסד גדול יש לסמוך על המרדכי שכתבתי לעיל כלל מ"ד סימן ט' דאפילו ע"י בישול לא אמרינן לח בלח נ"נ[56] וא"כ א"צ ס' אלא כפי שיעור הבשר נבילה שנבלע בכף[57] וכן אם בשלו בקדירה ירקות וכיוצא בו ונתנו לתוכו חלב מעט וניער וכיסה היטיב עד שבודאי נתפשט החלב בכל הקדירה ותחב הכף שניער בו הקדירה של ירקות לקדירה של בשר נ"ל דא"צ לשער רק לפי שיעור החלב כדין בצלים הבלועים מבשר בסימן צ"ד[58] לדעת ראב"ן שם.י

י. באמת באו"ה כלל כ"ד סי' ז' כתב וז"ל איסור שנפל להיתר בין באיסור לח כו' וכ"כ שם בסי' ח' וז"ל ומיהו ברוטב של בשר שנפל לחלב צריך ס' נגד כולה דהוי שם בשר על כל המים כמ"ש המרדכי* פ' כ"ה דקיי"ל כמ"ד דמשערינן כאלו המים כולו בשר ולא כמ"ד במה דבלעי מיא ובכלל ל"א סי' ט"ו כתב דרוטב נבילה שנפל לקדירה לא סגי לבטל לפי המדומע אפשר דנוסח אחר היה לו במרדכי שהרי משמע דאף בבשר וחלב** לא ס"ל כן*** אלא צריך ס' נגד כל החלב וכן משמע מאו"ה הביאו רמ"א סי' צ"ט ססי' ו'**** אך לפי מה שפסק רמ"א בלח בלח דלא אמרינן חנ"נ וא"כ ה"ה בנבילה.

יד אדם

54. The same meat spoon which had been inserted into milk was placed into a hot pot of meat and again into the same pot of milk.

55. See the *Aruch Hashulchan* (94:11) who is lenient to require only one times sixty even in this case.

The following question is raised in the *Binas Adam*, section 47: In a case where a pot of meat food is boiling over and a dairy spoon (used that day for hot dairy food) was repeatedly inserted into the pot to remove some of its contents, can one permit the remaining contents of the pot in a case where it is needed for a *yom tov* meal if the pot contains only sixty times the spoon? The *Chochmas Adam* answers that there are grounds to be lenient and require the pot to contain only sixty times the spoon. If, however, the spoon was sometimes reinserted while it was filled with the meat food (and the meat food in the spoon will have become inherently forbidden when absorbing the dairy taste from the spoon), then it will be necessary for the pot to contain sixty times the meat food held by the spoon if the volume of the food is larger than the spoon. This applies when a great loss is involved. It has been explained at the end of topic 44, section 18 that if a great loss is not involved, then we should require the pot to contain sixty times the spoon plus sixty times the meat food on the spoon.

56. I.e., we do not say that a forbidden liquid (or any other forbidden substance or absorbed taste) which has become dispersed throughout a liquid makes the latter inherently forbidden.

57. We are dealing with a case where a spoon was inserted into two pots of hot liquid. The second pot contains kosher liquid, whereas the first pot contains liquid in which unkosher meat had been cooked. The question here is whether the "piece,"

that same spoon into a pot of meat and he reinserted it into the milk,[54] according to all authorities it is necessary to have as many times sixty [in the milk] in accordance with the number of times that he inserted [the spoon(s)] into it, since each time it is a new insertion.[55]

And regarding a spoon which one inserted into a pot in which unkosher meat is being cooked and [which was then] inserted into a pot of kosher meat, [then] in a situation of necessity and great loss, one can rely on the *Mordechai* [in the name of the *Raavan*] which I have written above in topic 44, section 9 that even through cooking we do not say that a piece becomes inherently forbidden when a liquid [is mixed] with a liquid.[56] As such, we require only sixty times the amount of the unkosher meat which was absorbed into the spoon.[57] And similarly, if one cooked green vegetables in a pot or something similar and placed a little milk in it and stirred and covered it well until the milk has certainly spread throughout the entire pot, and he inserted the spoon with which he stirred the pot of green vegetables into a pot of meat, it is my opinion that he has to measure only according to the amount of milk, similar to the rule of onions which have absorbed [the taste of] meat [which is mentioned] in chapter 94,[58] according to the *Raavan* there.'

'. Actually, the *Issur v'heter*, 24:7, writes [contrary to this ruling]: "If forbidden food falls into permissible food, whether the forbidden food is liquid" [or whether it is solid, the same rule will apply]. And he writes similarly in section 8 there, and this is his wording: "However, regarding meat soup which has fallen into milk, we require sixty times all of [the meat soup], as the name 'meat' applies to all of the water, as the *Mordechai** has written in chapter *kal habasar*, where the law is established for us according to the one who says that we measure as if the water is entirely meat, and not according to the one who says that [we measure only] by what the water has absorbed." And in topic 31, section 15 he has written: "If soup from unkosher meat fell into a pot it is not enough to nullify in accordance with [the proportion of unkosher meat in] the mixture." And it is possible that he had a different version of the *Mordechai*, as [the *Issur v'heter*] implies that even with regard to meat and milk,** [the *Mordechai*] does not hold to this rule*** but requires sixty times all of the milk. And so it seems from the *Issur v'heter* that the *Rama* quotes in chapter 99 at the end of paragrapn 6.**** However, according to what the *Rama* [in chapter 92, paragraph 4] has ruled that [regarding mixtures of] liquid with liquid we do not say that the piece becomes inherently forbidden [but we measure by proportion], this should be the rule also with a forbidden substance [whose taste is dispersed throughout a liquid].

*The *Mordechai* here is dealing with a case where meat had fallen into hot water, such that the hot water becomes a meat soup. Some of this meat soup then falls into milk.

**According to the version of the *Mordechai* quoted by the *Issur v'heter* the above statement is dealing even with meat and milk, such that if milk is cooked in water, all of it must be considered as if it were milk. (This differs from other versions of the *Mordechai* where the case which requires measuring by the entire liquid is not where water was cooked with milk, but where a piece of meat was cooked in the milk. This has been explained in note 77 on topic 44.)

***To measure by proportion.

****It appears from there also that it is not sufficient to measure by proportion. This statement of the *Rama* has been discussed by the *Chochmas Adam* in note טז on topic 44. See also the footnotes thereon.

Yad Adam

i.e., the liquid in the pot of unkosher meat, has become inherently forbidden.

If the liquid does become inherently forbidden, then the contents of the first pot must be treated as consisting entirely of forbidden material. If a spoon is inserted into this pot and then into a pot of kosher liquid, we will require the second pot to contain sixty times the entire amount of liquid in the first pot. If, on the other hand, we are lenient

ודעת רש"ל הביאו הט"ז סימן צ"ב ס"ק ט"ו דבדרך בישול צריך ס' כנגד כולו וכן משמעות כל האחרונים[59] ולכן אין לסמוך ע"ז אלא בהפסד וצורך גדול כי מי יוכל לחלוק עליהם בלא ראיה מוכרחת וכ"ש שכן כ' בהדיא באו"ה גם לענין חלב שנפל למים.[60]

ח. אם יש ששים לבטל[61] אז הקדירה והתבשיל מותרין אבל הכף אסור לבשל בו אפילו עם ירקות ושאר דברים שהרי נ"נ שהיא בלועה מבשר וחלב ואפילו בדיעבד אוסרת אם חזר ותחבה בין בבשר ובין בחלב ובין בשאר דברים אם היא בתוך מעת לעת של תחיבה זו שנאסרת על ידה אע"פ שכבר עבר מעת לעת מבישול ראשון.[62] וה"ה אם לקח עתה עם הכף מאכל מקדירה זו והחזיר המאכל לקדירה צריך ס' נגד כל המאכל שהרי הכף יש לו דין כלי ראשון[63] כדלקמן כלל נ"ט סי' ג' וא"כ המאכל נעשה נבילה

יד אדם

to say that the liquid does not become inherently forbidden, then the maximum amount of forbidden matter which the spoon can absorb would be limited to the size of the piece of unkosher meat. As such, when the spoon is inserted into the pot of kosher liquid, this pot would have to contain only sixty times the piece of meat. (In these cases, we are dealing with a situation where the forbidden substance in the first pot is smaller than the size of the spoon. If it is larger than the spoon, then it will be sufficient to have sixty times the spoon in any case.)

58. *Shulchan Aruch* 94:6—If onions absorbed the taste of meat (for example, onions had been cooked in a pot containing melted meat fat and other liquid) and they were then cooked in a pot of milk, then it is enough for the pot of milk to contain sixty times the meat fat which was present in the first pot, since this is the maximum amount of meat taste which the onions could have absorbed. We do not require that the pot of milk contain sixty times the entire amount of liquid which was in the first pot, but sixty times the melted meat fat will be sufficient. This ruling has been discussed in topic 44, note טז.

59. As such, according to the *Maharshal*, if the milk and greens are cooked together and one inserted a spoon into this mixture and then into a meat pot, it is not enough to have sixty times the milk, but one will need sixty times the entire mixture (or at most, sixty times the size of the spoon). Similarly, in the case described in note 57, it would not be enough for the second pot to contain sixty times the piece of unkosher meat; rather, sixty time the entire liquid would be required (or at most, sixty times the spoon). Regarding onions which absorbed the taste of meat (described in note 58), it will be necessary for the pot of milk to contain sixty times the entire liquid (the melted meat fat plus the other liquid, or at most, sixty times the onions).

[However,] the opinion of the *Maharshal*, quoted by the *Taz* in chapter 92, paragraph 15, is that when cooking we need sixty times all of it, and so is implied from all of the later authorities.[59] Therefore, one should not rely on this [leniency] except in case of necessity and great loss, for who can argue with them without a compelling proof? And certainly [one should avoid being lenient] since this is also written explicitly in the *Issur v'heter* regarding milk that fell into water.[60]

8. If there is sixty [in the pot] to nullify [the taste in the spoon],[61] then the pot and the cooked food are permissible, but it is forbidden to cook with the spoon, even [to use it] with green vegetables and other things, since [the spoon] became inherently forbidden as it has absorbed [both] meat and milk. And even after the fact, it makes [food] forbidden if he went on and inserted [the spoon] into meat or milk or other things, if it is within 24 hours of the insertion [into the pot] by which it became forbidden, even though 24 hours had elapsed from the first cooking.[62] And the rule is similar if one now took food from this pot with the [forbidden] spoon and returned the food to the pot, that we require sixty times all of the food, for the spoon has the law of a "first vessel"[63] as [explained] later on in topic 59, section 3, and as

Yad Adam

60. That the mixture is regarded completely as milk and we do not measure by proportion. (*Issur v'heter* 24:8) However, refer to note 95 on topic 44 where it is mentioned that many authorities (such as the *Aruch Hashulchan*) are lenient to measure by proportion when the first mixture involves permissible substances, even when the components of the mixture are cooked together.

8. The Status of a Dairy Spoon Which Had Been Inserted into a Pot of Meat (and Vice Versa)

61. We are returning to the example mentioned at the beginning of section 6: One inserted a dairy spoon into a pot of meat, or a meat spoon into a pot of dairy food. In the case under discussion here, the pot contains sixty times the portion of the spoon which was inserted.

62. For example, a spoon used in hot milk was placed into a pot of hot meat 12 hours later. The spoon thus becomes forbidden since it has absorbed meat and milk, and if this spoon is inserted into another pot of food, its contents will become forbidden (unless they are greater than sixty times the spoon). The spoon can make this other pot forbidden for up to 24 hours after being inserted into the meat pot, which is up to 36 hours after the insertion into the milk.

63. It has been explained previously (note 160 on topic 44) that according to some

יא. ש"ך סק"י וכ"כ כל האחרונים.*
יב. עיין ש"ך ס"ק ד'.

בתוך הכף שהרי ע"י תחיבה זו נ"נ.[64][יא]

ולאחר מעת לעת מתחיבה זו אסור לכתחלה להשתמש בה כדין כל נטל"פ[65] ובדיעבד[66] מותר בין שתחבה בבשר או בחלב כיון שכבר עברה מעת לעת ואם עברה עליו לינת לילה ואח"כ תחב אותו במין שבישל בו באחרונה בתוך אותו מעת לעת כגון שתחב כף חולבת בקדירה של בשר קודם ערבית[67] ולמחר חזר ותחב אותו בשל בשר[68] צ"ע די"ל כיון דאינו נ"נ בודאי שהרי אפשר שפלט כל החלב שבתוכו וא"כ אין בו בלוע רק בשר[יב] וא"כ אפשר דהוי ס"ס שמא פלט הכל ואת"ל דלא פלט שמא קיי"ל כמ"ד לינת לילה פוגם[69] ועיין לקמן כלל נ"ה סימן ה'.

ואם אין ס' נגד הכף הכל אסור בהנאה והמאכל ישליך לבית הכסא והקדירה אסור להחם בו המים הראוים למאכל ומשתה ואפילו לאחר מעת לעת אבל מותר לבשל בו חמין עם אפר לחוף הראש

יד אדם

authorities, if a spoon is immersed in a hot first vessel, then the spoon itself will become a "first vessel." As such, the food on this spoon will absorb forbidden taste from it.

64. I.e., the cooked food on the spoon as well as the spoon itself are now inherently forbidden. For example, a dairy spoon was inserted into a pot of food to remove a piece of meat, and the pot contained sixty times the size of the spoon. The pot and its contents remain permissible, but the spoon and the meat in the spoon now become inherently forbidden. If the spoon with the meat is now re-inserted into the pot, the entire contents of the pot will be forbidden unless the pot contains sixty times the spoon plus sixty times the piece of meat.

It has been mentioned in note 55 that in cases of great loss, it is sufficient to have sixty times the piece of meat or sixty times the spoon, whichever is larger.

65. In accordance with note 19 above.

66. If one did use the forbidden spoon in hot food without kashering it first.

67. There was sixty times the spoon in the contents of the pot, so that the contents of the pot are permitted, but the spoon has become forbidden. (If sixty was not present, it would not be possible to make the next statement: that perhaps the spoon became kashered by emitting all of its absorbed taste. Rather, if there was not sixty times the spoon in the contents of the pot, then the food as well as the spoon would all be completely forbidden as noted below.)

68. And the pot did not contain sixty times the spoon. Normally, the pot and its contents

יא. *Shach* [chapter 94] paragraph 10, and all the later authorities write similarly.*

יב. See *Shach* paragraph 4.

such, the food in the spoon becomes inherently forbidden because from this insertion [the spoon] has become inherently forbidden.[64]יא

And [even] following 24 hours after this insertion it is forbidden to use [the spoon] to begin with, in accordance with the rule of anything that imparts a detrimental taste;[65] but after the fact[66] [the food] is permissible, whether he inserted it into meat or milk, since 24 hours has already passed. And if [the spoon] remained overnight [after becoming forbidden] and afterwards one inserted it into the kind of food which he cooked with it last [but it was still] during that 24 hours–such as where one inserted a dairy spoon into a pot of meat before the evening,[67] and the next day he went on and inserted it into [a pot of] meat[68]–[the matter] requires investigation, for it is possible to say that since it is not certain that [the spoon] becomes inherently forbidden, for it is possible that [the spoon] emitted all of the milk that was inside it [into the first meat pot], and as such, there might be only meat absorbed in itיב and therefore it is possible that [we can be lenient because] there is a double doubt [as follows]: Perhaps it had emitted all [of the dairy taste into the first meat pot], and if you say that it had not emitted [all of the dairy taste] perhaps the accepted ruling is in accordance with the one who says that staying overnight spoils [absorbed taste].[69] And see further on topic 55, section 5.

And if there is not sixty times the spoon [in the pot], everything is forbidden to have benefit [derived from it] and the food is to be thrown out into the bathroom, and it is forbidden to use the pot to warm water in it which is fit for food or drink, even after 24 hours, but it is permissible to cook hot water in it with ashes to groom the hair. And if one

Yad Adam

*The *Chavos Da'as*, however, rules differently (in accordance with the *Bach*): We do not prohibit a food based on meat or dairy taste which was absorbed in a vessel more than 24 hours previously. As such, in the example given in note 62, the spoon will not make a pot of meat forbidden unless it is within 24 hours of cooking the milk.

should be forbidden, but there are grounds to permit them in this case as noted below.

69. Some authorities, such as *Rashi* and *Rabbenu Tam*, rule that absorbed taste becomes detrimental in even less than 24 hours if the absorbed taste remains overnight in the vessel. Even though we generally are strict and require 24 hours to elapse before regarding an absorbed taste as detrimental, we can rely on this more lenient ruling if there are other grounds to be lenient.

יג. ודברי הש"ך בסי' צ"ד ס"ק ח' שכ' אפי' הכף אסור צ"ע שהרי להדיא כתב רמ"א שם סעיף ה' דאם יש במאכל ס' הכל שרי וכ"כ האו"ה בהדיא בכלל ל"ז סי' ג' וסי' ט' וכ"כ בד"מ ובאמת דברי או"ה סותרין דבכלל ל"ד סי' ט"ו גבי הדחה כ' דהכף אסור וצ"ע.

ואם בישל בה לאחר מעת לעת אע"ג שהמאכל מותר כיון שהיא כבר נטל"פ ישליך דמי הקדירה לנהר[70] וי"א דא"צ ולענין להשתמש בו פירות וצונן מבואר כלל נ"ו.

ט. במה דברים אמורים דאפילו יש ס'[71] מ"מ הכף אסור[72] כשבישל עכשיו בשר בקדירה דאז קיבל הכף טעם מבשר עצמו אבל אם בישל ירקות או מים בקדירה של בשר ב"י[73] ותחב בו כף חולבת ב"י[74] ויש ס' בירקות נגד הכף אז גם הכף מותר שהכף לא קיבלה טעם בשר אלא מנ"ט בר נ"ט[75][יג] (מ"ו) ואפשר מצד המנהג יש לאסור הכף ועיין כלל מ"ח.

י. אם אין הכף בן יומא מבליעת כלי ראשון[76] הקדירה והתבשיל מותרין והכף אסור לכתחלה[77] בין עם בשר בין עם חלב כיון שבלוע מבו"ח אע"פ שא' מהן[78] הי' נטל"פ ואם תחבה למין התבשיל שבקדירה מותר[79] אבל אם תחבו אותו למין התבשיל שהיה

יד אדם

70. Since it is forbidden to derive benefit from the pot (because it absorbed meat and milk), one should take money equal in value to the pot and discard it, and thereby compensate for the benefit he receives by cooking with it.

9. Inserting a Dairy Spoon into Pareve Ingredients Which Are Being Cooked in a Meat Pot

71. I.e., even though the pot contained sixty times the inserted portion of the spoon.

72. Although the contents of the pot remain permissible, the spoon becomes forbidden as noted at the beginning of section 8.

73. The pot had been used on that day to cook meat in it, and now it is being used to cook vegetables.

74. It had been used in hot dairy food during that day.

75. (Literally, an emitted taste from an emitted taste.) Here, the dairy spoon did not absorb taste from meat directly. Rather, the taste of the meat was emitted from the meat into the material of the pot, and from there it was emitted into the present contents of the pot. When the dairy spoon is now inserted into the pot, it absorbs only this weakened meat taste, and according to the letter of the law, such secondary absorbed tastes cannot make a food or vessel forbidden (topic 48, section 1).

The *Chochmas Adam* is dealing with a case where the contents of the pot are at least sixty times the spoon. If they are less than this, then the spoon as well as the food will still be permitted according to the *Bais*

יג. And the words of the *Shach* in chapter 94, paragraph 8 where he writes that even the spoon is forbidden require explanation, for explicitly, the *Rama* wrote there in paragraph 5 that if there is sixty times as much in the food, everything is permissible—[not only the food but the spoon also]. And the *Issur v'heter* writes similarly explicitly in topic 37, section 3 and section 9. And the *Darkei Moshe* writes similarly. Actually the words of the *Issur v'heter* are contradictory, as in topic 34, section 15 regarding washing, he writes that the spoon is forbidden, and it requires explanation [as to why this is so].

cooked in it after 24 hours, even though the food is permissible since [the pot] already imparts a detrimental taste, he should throw away the value of the pot into the river,[70] but some [authorities] say that he need not do so. And [the rules] regarding using it for fruits and cold items are explained in topic 56.

9. When is it said that even if there is sixty[71] the spoon is nevertheless forbidden?[72] This is when one cooks meat now in the pot so that the spoon has absorbed the taste of meat itself. However, if one cooked green vegetables or water in a meat pot which was used that day[73] and he inserted a dairy spoon into it which was used that day[74] and the vegetables are sixty times the spoon, then the spoon will also be permissible, as the spoon did not absorb the taste of meat except in a secondary way.[75]יג (See *Binas Adam*, paragraph 46.) And perhaps based on custom it is proper to prohibit the spoon—refer to topic 48 [marginal note כה].

10. If the spoon was not used on the same day in which it absorbed from a "first vessel",[76] the pot and the cooked food are permissible, and the spoon is forbidden to begin with,[77] whether [to use it] with meat or with milk, since [the spoon] has absorbed [both] meat and milk, even though one of them[78] will be imparting a detrimental taste. And if he inserted it into the type of cooked food that is in the pot, it is permissible,[79] but if he inserted it into the type of cooked food which

Yad Adam

Yosef (topic 48, section 6) but will be forbidden according to the *Rama* (section 10 there).

10. A Vessel Which Contains Tastes of Meat and Milk Where One of Them is Detrimental

76. This statement is made with reference to section 6, where a dairy spoon is being inserted into a pot containing hot meat. Here, however, the spoon had not been used with hot dairy food during the past 24 hours, but only prior to this time. Therefore, any absorbed dairy taste which is present in the spoon has become spoiled. As such, if the spoon is inserted into a pot containing hot meat, the food will not become forbidden.

77. The food and the pot will be permissible (even though the contents of the pot are less than sixty times the spoon), but the spoon should not be used until it is kashered.

78. The one into which the spoon was inserted more than 24 hours ago.

79. If he acted improperly and placed the spoon (described in note 76) into another pot of hot meat on that same day, the food will remain permissible.

יד. וע' בחו"ב כלל ל"ז סי' ח'.

בלוע בכף[80] אם הוא בתוך מעל"ע מתחיבה זו שתחבה בקדירה[81] אפי' בדיעבד אסור שכיון שהכף אינו ב"י[82] א"כ מן הדין נעשה כמין המאכל שהי' בקדירה ונבלע בו וא"כ אוסר[83] וכן אם בשלו בשר בקדירה חולבת אינו ב"י וחזרו ובשלו בו בשר בתוך מעל"ע מותר אבל אם בשלו בו חלב בתוך מעל"ע שבשלו בו הבשר אסור הכל שהרי טעם הבשר שנבלע בקדירה הוא לשבח[84] וכן כל כיוצא בזה[85] ועיין כלל נ"ד.

יא. הא דכתבנו[86] שאם נשתמש א' מן הכלים בכ"ר דצריך ס' נגד כולו[87] דוקא ששימש בו דרך בישול כגון קדרה שבישל בה וכף שתחבו בקדירה שעומדת על האש או אפי' לאחר שהעבירה מעל האש ועדיין היא רותחת שהיס"ב[88] אבל המערה רוטב של בשר מקדירה רותחת לקערה חולבת שנשתמש בו ביום[89] כיון שלא בלעה רק ע"י עירוי[90] וא"כ א"צ ס' אלא כנגד קליפת הקערה[91] דעירוי אינו מבשל ואינו מבליע יותר מכ"קי וכבר כתבנו לעיל בדין טיפת

יד אדם

80. He now inserts the spoon into a pot of hot milk.

81. The spoon had been used in the hot pot of meat during the previous 24 hours.

82. The dairy spoon had not been used during that day in hot milk.

83. As such, the dairy spoon which had not been used for 24 hours took on the status of a meat spoon when inserted into the pot of meat, and the spoon can then go on to make dairy food forbidden.

84. Since it is less than 24 hours old. Thus, even though it was a dairy pot, it took on the status of a meat pot when meat was cooked in it. Such a pot can go on to make dairy food forbidden.

85. Another example: A spoon is forbidden because it has absorbed both meat and milk during that day. If this spoon was inserted into any permissible food (such as vegetables), the food becomes forbidden unless the pot contains sixty times the spoon. (See *Aruch Hashulchan* 94:15.)

11. The Difference Between Liquid in a Hot כלי ראשון ("First Vessel") and Liquid Which Is Poured from It.

86. In section 6 above. The language there is: If one inserts a dairy spoon which had been used during the past 24 hours IN A FIRST VESSEL... we require the pot to contain sixty times the entire portion of the spoon which was inserted into the cooked food.

ד. And refer to the *Issur v'heter* 37:1.

had been absorbed into the spoon,[80] if it was within 24 hours from this [last] insertion when he had put [the spoon] into the pot,[81] then even after the fact [everything] is forbidden. [The reasoning behind these rulings is that] since the spoon had not been used on that day,[82] as such, *halachically* it became similar to the food which was in the pot and from which it has absorbed. Therefore, it can make [the other type food] forbidden.[83] And similarly, if one cooked meat in a dairy pot not used [for dairy] on that day and he went on and [again] cooked meat in it during that day, [after the fact the meat] is permissible; but if he cooked milk in it within 24 hours of his cooking the meat in it, everything is forbidden, for the taste of the meat that was absorbed into the pot is beneficial.[84] And [the same applies] to any similar case.[85] And refer to topic 54 [section 12].

11. Regarding what we have written[86] that if one of the utensils was used in a "first vessel" we require sixty times all of it,[87] this is only where one used it by way of "cooking." For example, one was cooking in a pot and a spoon was inserted into the pot while it is standing on the fire, or even after [the pot] was removed from the fire as long as it is still hot enough so that the hand would withdraw from it.[88] However, if one pours meat soup from a hot pot onto a dairy plate which had been used on that day[89], since [the plate] has absorbed [meat taste] only from pouring,[90] as such, we need only sixty times the peel of the plate[91] since pouring does not cook or cause absorption more than the thickness of the peel.[ד] And we have already written

Yad Adam

87. Since the spoon had been placed in a "first vessel" of dairy food, it had become filled with absorbed taste of milk. Therefore, if this spoon is inserted into a pot of meat, the pot must contain sixty times the entire inserted portion of the spoon.

88. As long as the pot remains at or above this temperature (see topic 42, section 9), it still retains the status of a hot "first vessel." See also topic 59, section 1.

89. The plate had been used during that day for hot dairy food.

90. The plate does not come into contact with the meat soup inside the pot. Rather, the contact is made outside the pot while it is being poured.

91. The soup will be permitted as long as its contents are at least sixty times the "peel" of the plate. (This "peel" consists of a thin layer of the material of the plate at the places where it came into contact with the stream of hot soup.)

טו. ועיין לקמן כלל כ"ז* וכלל כ"ט.**

חלב שזב על קדירה כלל מ"ה סי' כ"א דלעולם יש ס' בכלי נגד קליפתה (מ"ג) וא"כ המאכל מותר והקערה אסורה שבלועה מבו"ח בכדי קליפתה עכ"פ.[92]טו

כלל מז
דין סכין של היתר שחתך בו איסור או מבשר לחלב
(סימן צ"ד)

א. בשר רותח מחום כ"ר[1] שחתך בסכין חולבת שהוא ב"י מתשמיש חלב מכ"ר[2] כגון שחתך בו פיינקוכין וכיוצא בו רותח אע"פ שקנחו יפה אפי' הסכין למטה ל"א תתאה גבר כדלקמן כלל נ"ז סי' א' כיון דיש כאן דוחקא דסכינא אין חילוק[3] דלעולם הבשר הרותח מפליט מן הסכין ובולע ואסור כולו אם אין בו ס' נגד מקום הסכין דהיינו שאם יודע בבירור עד כמה חתך מן הסכין א"צ לשער נגד כולו דאינו מפליט אלא במקום שחותך אבל מן הסתם הדרך לחתוך בכל הסכין וצריך ס' נגד כל הסכין חוץ מן הקתא ואע"ג שיש ס' צריך לקלוף גם המקום שחתך בו[4] כדין כל איסור

יד אדם

92. See, however, the last note on topic 45.

1. Hot Meat in a כלי ראשון ("First Vessel") Which Was Cut with a Dairy Knife

1. I.e., the meat is presently in the vessel in which it was heated over the fire. (See section 3 regarding food which was cut after being removed from this vessel.)

2. If the knife was used to cut hot dairy food while this food was in a "first vessel" (the vessel in which it was heated), then the knife will have absorbed the taste of the dairy food. Then, when the knife is used to cut hot meat, it will go on and emit this dairy taste into the meat. Since the knife had been used for the hot dairy food during that same day, the dairy taste emitted into the meat will be beneficial and make it forbidden.

3. The pressure of the knife cutting through the food increases the absorption of taste into the food. As such, the leniencies resulting from the rule that the lower one dominates (topic 42, section 7) do not apply here.

טו. And refer further on, topics 57* and 59.**

previously regarding the rule of a drop of milk which flows onto a pot [in] topic 45 section 21, that a vessel always has sixty times its peel. (See *Binas Adam*, paragraph 43.) As such, the food is permissible and the plate is forbidden as it has absorbed from meat and milk at least by the width of its peel.[92]טו

*The rules regarding food placed on a forbidden vessel are discussed there.

**The rules pertaining to first and second vessels, and pouring from a "first vessel," are discussed there.

Topic 47

Laws Concerning a Permissible Knife [Used] for Cutting Forbidden Food, or a Meat [Knife Used] for Dairy

(based on *Shulchan Aruch–Yoreh Deah* chapter 94)

1. If meat [which became hot] by the heat of a "first vessel"[1] was cut with a dairy knife which had been used that day with [hot] dairy food in a "first vessel,"[2] such as where one cut pancakes, or something similar, while hot, even though he had wiped [the knife] off well—and even if the knife was underneath we do not say that the lower one dominates as [explained] later on in topic 57, section 1, for since here there is pressure from the knife there is no difference [which one is above the other][3]—for in all cases the hot meat will cause the knife to emit [its absorbed dairy taste] and [the meat] will absorb [the taste] and everything becomes forbidden unless there is [in the meat] sixty times the portion of the knife [used for cutting it]. That is, if one clearly knows how much of the knife he cut with, he is not required to measure with respect to all of [the blade], since it does not emit taste except in the portion that does the cutting. However, in general the usual way is to cut with the entire knife and [it will therefore] be necessary to have sixty times the entire knife except for the handle. And even if there is sixty [times the knife], it is also necessary to peel the place that was cut with it.[4] This is in accordance with the rules of all forbidden

Yad Adam

Therefore, if the knife is cold and it is beneath the hot food when cutting it we will not say that the food becomes cooled off by the knife. Rather, the hot food dominates and will heat up the knife and cause transfer of taste from the knife into the food.

4. The reason for the peeling is that forbidden material from the knife might cling to

כמבואר בכלל ס׳[א] וגרע טפי מחם בחם בלא רוטב דלדעת הש״ע סגי בנטילה[5] כדלקמן כלל ס׳ סי׳ ז׳ דאגב דוחקא מתפשט בכולו ועוד דמסתמא בלע הסכין ג״כ שמנונית כחמאה ובדבר שמן אפי׳ בבלוע מתפשט בכולו כמבואר שם.[ב]

ב. ואם אין הסכין בן יומו או שאינו יודע דאז אמרינן מסתמא אב״י כדלקמן כלל נ״ה וא״כ א״צ ס׳ נגד הבלוע בסכין שהרי הוא לפגם.[6]

מ״מ לא אמרינן סתם סכין נקי[7] כמו דקיי״ל סתם כלים נקיים אלא אדרבה אמרינן סתם סכין שמנונית טוח על פניו לכן צריך קליפה דעל כל פנים אין בשמנונית הרבה רק דבר מועט ואינו מתפשט יותר מכ״ק ובין כך וכך הסכין צריך להגעיל שהרי יש בו בלוע מבו״ח.[ג]

ג. ואם הבשר בכלי שני[8] ועדיין היס״ב י״א כיון שהוא דבר גוש דינו ככ״ר כמבואר כלל ס׳ סימן י״ב[9] ולהאומרים דאין חילוק בין גוש (מ״ח) וצלול[10] אפילו אין הסכין ב״י צריך לקלוף הבשר

א. עיין ט״ז ופ״ח סי׳ צ״ד סעיף ז׳.
ב. ועיין סי׳ צ״ד בש״ך ס״ק כ״ז ובסי׳ ק״כ ס״ק כ״ג שמסתפק בכלי שבלע שומן.
ג. שם סי׳ צ״ד.

יד אדם

the cut surface of the food. In addition, the absorbed taste emitted by the knife may be concentrated in the peel of the food.

5. As such, when two such hot foods come into contact each other (for example, kosher meat comes into contact with unkosher meat when they are hot), we do not say that the entire permissible food becomes forbidden if there is less than sixty times the forbidden food. (See topic 60, section 1.) When cutting with a knife, on the other hand, we say that the entire cut food becomes forbidden as noted above.

2. Leniencies Which Apply if the Knife Had Not Been Used on That Day

6. The cut food will therefore be permissible but this will only be the case if it is known that the knife was clean.

7. I.e., a knife whose status is not known to us is not presumed to be clean of food matter. It is to be treated more stringently than other utensils in this respect.

3. Hot Meat in a כלי שני ("Second Vessel") or Cold Meat Which Was Cut with a Dairy Knife

8. When the meat was cut, it was not in the vessel in which it was heated but it had been transferred into a second (cold) vessel. (See topic 42, section 9.)

9. This is because the walls of the second

א. See the *Taz* and *Pri Chadash* on 94:7.
ב. [See topic 57, section 1.] And see the *Shach* 94:27 and 105:23 where he is in doubt about a vessel which absorbed fatty food.
ג. *Ibid.* chapter 94 [paragraph 7].

food as explained in topic [57 and] 60.[א] And [cutting hot food with a knife] is worse than hot food touching hot food without liquid, as [in the latter case], according to the *Shulchan Aruch*, it is sufficient with removal [of a thick layer of the foods][5] as [explained] later on in topic 60, section [1 and] 7, [but here] as a result of pressure [of the knife, the taste] spreads through all of it. Furthermore, it is probable that the knife has also absorbed fatty food such as butter, and with something fatty, even what is absorbed [into a utensil] spreads through all of [the food] as explained there.[ב]

2. And if the knife had not been used on that day [for hot dairy food], or it is not known [if it was used] in which case we say that it probably was not used on that day—in accordance with what is [explained] later on in topic 55 [section 8]—in such a case, it is not necessary to have sixty times what had been absorbed into the knife, since [the absorbed taste] is spoiled.[6]

However, we do not presume that an ordinary knife is clean,[7] although the law is established that ordinary vessels are [presumed to be] clean. Rather the opposite [is true regarding a knife] since we say that an ordinary knife has grease smeared on its surface. Therefore, peeling [of the cut surfaces of the meat] is required, for at least there would not be a large quantity of grease but only a small amount, and it does not spread through more than the width of the peel [of the cut surface]. And in any of these cases, the knife must be kashered with boiling water since there is absorption in it from milk and meat.[ג]

3. And if the meat is in a "second vessel"[8] and it is still [hot enough such that] the hand would withdraw from it—some [authorities] say that since it is a solid food, it has the rule of a "first vessel" as explained in topic 60, section 12.[9] And according to those who say that there is no difference between solid and liquid[10] (see *Binas Adam*, paragraph 48), even if the knife was not used that day, it is necessary to peel

Yad Adam

vessel will not cool off the food since no liquid is present. According to these authorities, everything will be forbidden (unless the meat is sixty times the knife) as explained above in section 1.

10. These other authorities rule that a solid has the same rule as a liquid in that it does not absorb or emit taste in a "second vessel."

כיון שעכ״פ יש בו חימום דכ״ש ודוחקא[11] וכן אפי׳ היה הבשר צונן נכון לקלוף הבשר ואין חילוק בין שהסכין ב״י או לא כיון שסתם סכין שמנונית קרוש עליו ויש כאן דוחקא דסכינא[12] אבל מדינא בבשר צונן א״צ אלא הדחה ושפשוף היטיב[13][ד] והסכין צריך נעיצה.[14][ה]

ד. וה״ה אם חתך היתר בכלי איסור נמי דינא הכי.

וזה הכלל (א) אם חתך בו רותח שהיס״ב ועדיין הוא בכ״ר צריך הגעלהי (ב) ואם חותך דבר שהיס״ב ומונח בכ״ש יש להגעיל הסכין ובמקום צורך יש לסמוך להקל דאפי׳ בדבר גוש כיון שמונח בכ״ש סגי בנעיצה (ג) ואם חתך בו צונן סגי בהדחה היטיב (ד) ואם חתך בו דבר קשה כגבינה קשה אע״פ שהגבינה צונן צריך נעיצה.[15]

ד. ואע״ג דבסימן ק״ה סעיף ג׳ כ׳ דאינו אוסר כלל וכ״כ בסי׳ ס״ח דכ״ש אינו מפליט ומבליע וא״כ קשה למה צריך קליפה ואפשר דחושש לדעת או״ה מטעם גוש כיון שהיס״ב ועושה כמו פשר להצריך קליפה או מטעם דוחקא כמש״כ הט״ז. ובאמת באו״ה כלל ל״ו לא חילק כלל בין כ״ר לכ״ש דלשיטתו כל גוש דינו ככ״ר וכתב אפי׳ בצונן נכון לקלוף אבל מדינא מותר בצונן בשפשוף כמ״ש הש״ך בסי׳ י׳ בס״ק כ׳ ובסי׳ ס״ד בש״ע סעיף י״ז.

ה. שם.

ו. שם ל״ד וע״ש בש״ך.

יד אדם

11. Since the knife was not used during that day, even peeling would ordinarily not be required (since any absorbed taste will be detrimental). Furthermore, absorption does not occur from the heat of a second vessel (according to these authorities) and again no peeling should be necessary. Nevertheless, when both pressure from the knife and the heat of a second vessel are present, the meat should be peeled.

12. The pressure from the knife while slicing the food will cause the grease on it to be absorbed into the food.

13. If it is known that the knife was clean, then (according to those who rule that no absorption generally takes place in a "second vessel") even meat which was cut while hot in a "second vessel" will only require washing and need not be peeled. (This is the opinion of the *Aruch Hashulchan*, 94:31- 32. Rabbi Akiva Eiger in the name of the *Toras Chatas* rules similarly.)

14. This statement apparently refers to a knife which was used to cut hot meat while it is in a "second vessel," for since there is also pressure while cutting with it, it is not enough to wash off the knife. Rather, insertion into the ground to kasher it is also required. (*Aruch Hashulchan* 94:31. See section 8 below where the procedure for "insertion" into the ground is discussed.)

This ruling is in accordance with those who rule that no absorption generally takes place in a "second vessel." Those who rule that absorption does occur when hot food is present in a "second vessel" will require kashering with boiling water. It is best to act in accordance with this more stringent the meat since at least [the meat] had heat of a "second vessel" and [there was also] pressure [from the knife].[11] And similarly, even if the meat was cold it is proper to peel the meat, and there is no difference whether or not the knife was used on that day, since an ordinary knife has solidified grease on it and there is pressure from the knife.[12] Nevertheless, according to the letter of the law, with cold meat one needs only washing and rubbing well.[13ד] And the knife requires insertion [into the ground].[14ה]

4. And the same rules apply if one cut permissible food with a forbidden knife—the rules are also the same [as a dairy knife used to cut meat].

And these are the rules [regarding kashering the knife]: (a) If one cut [food] with it which is hot enough so that his hand would withdraw from it and it is still in a "first vessel" [the knife] will require kashering with boiling water.[ו] (b) If one cuts something hot enough so that the hand would withdraw from it and it is lying in a "second vessel," one should kasher the knife with boiling water, but in a case of necessity, one may rely on the leniency [mentioned in section 3] that even with something solid, since it is lying in a "second vessel," it is enough to insert [it into the ground—see section 8]. (c) If he cut [soft] cold food with it, it is sufficient to wash it well. (d) If he cut something hard with it, such as hard cheese, even though the cheese is cold, it requires insertion [into the ground].[15]

ד. And even though in chapter 105, paragraph 3 [the *Rama*] has written that [a "second vessel"] does not make forbidden at all, and it is written similarly in chapter 68 [paragraph 11] that certainly it does not emit [taste] or cause absorption [of taste], and as such it is difficult as to why [the *Rama* here in 94:7 states that] peeling is necessary*it is possible that [the *Rama*] is concerned about the opinion of the *Issur v'heter* regarding solid food that since the hand would withdraw from it [it is to be regarded as still in a "first vessel"] and [the *Rama*] made a kind of compromise to require peeling; or it is because of pressure [of the knife] as written by the *Taz*. Actually, in the *Issur v'heter* topic 36 he does not differentiate at all between a "first vessel" and a "second vessel" because according to his opinion all [hot] solid food is to be judged like a "first vessel." And he wrote that even with cold food it is proper to peel, but according to the letter of the law cold food is permissible with rubbing, as the *Shach* has written in 10:20, and in the *Shulchan Aruch* 64:17.

ה. *Ibid. (Shulchan Aruch* 94:7)

ו. Chapter 94 there, and see the *Shach*.

Yad Adam

opinion, as explained in part (b) of the next section.

4. Guidelines for Kashering a Knife

15. Even though everything is cold, the pressure from the cutting action causes food material to stick to the knife when cutting hard food. Insertion (as described in section 8) is therefore required, and it will serve to clean off any remaining food material, as well as to remove absorbed taste which is present in the outer surface of the knife.

See section 8 below for additional regulations that apply to kashering a knife. (The basic rules for kashering vessels and utensils are discussed in topic 74.)

ואם מללו גבינה בריב אייזין נקי של בשר או של איסור[16] מותר הגבינה אם אינה מלוחה כמליחת בשר[17] כיון שהיה נקי ואם לא היה נקי צריך ס׳ נגד מה שהיה בעין.[18] וכ״ז אם אב״י ואם היה ב״י ונקי וחתך גבינה קשה כיון שהסכין צריך נעיצה יש להחמיר ולהצריך קליפה ובמקום הפסד יש להקל.[ז]

ז. ע״ש בפ״ח.
ח. סי׳ ס״ד סעיף י״ז.
ט. סי׳ י׳ בש״ך ס״ק כ׳.

ה. ולכן צריך למחות במנקרי בשר[19] בסכין של היתר שלא יחתכו בסכין חלב שאסור מה״ת אלא יגררו אותו בענין שלא יהיה בו דוחקא דסכינא ובדיעבד ידיחו וישפשפו אותו המקום היטיב[ח] ולא סגי בהדחה לבד דדוקא בדם מהני הדחה דנוח להעבירו משא״כ בחלב.[ט]

ו. בשר שמלחו להוציא דמו בין שהוא עדיין תוך שיעור מליחה[20] או כבר שהה שיעור וחתך ממנו בסכין אם לא נתייבש עדיין הציר עליו סגי בהדחה[21] ואם כבר נתייבש הציר צריך נעיצה וכן נוהגין לכתחלה שלא לחתוך בסכין צלי שצולין בלא מליחה על

יד אדם

16. The grater had been used with unkosher food.

17. This is explained in topic 43, section 1. If the cheese were heavily salted, then due to its sharpness, it would absorb from the grater and become forbidden. (See topic 55, section 2, and topic 49, sections 10 and 11.)

18. I.e., the grated cheese must be sixty times as much as the recognizable food particles which were on the grater.

The rules which apply to fruits which are cut with a knife are discussed in topic 49, sections 7, 8, and 9.

5. Using a Knife to Remove Forbidden Structures from Meat

19. Such as removing forbidden fat from an animal. We are concerned that when a knife is used to cut away the forbidden fat while it is still attached to permissible meat, then the pressure of the cutting will cause some of the forbidden fatty material to cling to the permissible meat. (*Perisha* 64:27–28)

6. Laws Concerning a Knife Which Was Used to Cut Meat Before Its Blood Has Been Removed

20. I.e., it was during the time when the salt was actively drawing out the blood, which is the first 18 (or 24) minutes after the meat was salted. We will not be more stringent here if the meat was cut during this time.

21. If the meat was cut with a knife before the blood and salty material remaining on its

ז. See the *Pri Chadash* there.
ח. *Shulchan Aruch* 64:17.
ט. *Shach* 10:20.

And if one grates cheese with a clean meat grater or one that is forbidden,[16] the cheese is permissible as long as it is not so salty as [is required for] the salting of meat,[17] since [the grater] is clean. But if it was not clean, it is necessary to have sixty times what was recognizable.[18] And all of this [applies where the grater or knife] was not used on that day. And if [a knife] was used on that day and was clean and he cut hard cheese [with that knife], since the knife requires insertion [as noted above], one should be stringent and require peeling [of the cheese], but in a situation involving loss, one can be lenient.[ז]

5. Therefore, it is necessary to protest against those who remove forbidden structures from meat[19] with a knife which is used for permissible food—that they should not cut fat which is forbidden by Torah law with that knife, but they should scrape away [the forbidden fat] in such a way that there should not be pressure from the knife [into the fat and then into the meat]. But after the fact that place [where the knife cut into the meat] should be washed and rubbed well.[ח] And it is not enough with washing [the meat] alone, as it is only with blood that washing [alone] helps because it is easy to remove it, but this is not the case with forbidden fat.[ט]

6. If meat was salted to draw out its blood, whether it was during the required time for salting[20] or if that time had already elapsed, and one cut [a piece] from it with a knife, if the salty liquid [on the knife] still had not dried up, it is enough to wash [the knife].[21] But if the salty liquid has already dried up, it requires insertion [into the ground]. And we are accustomed, to begin with, not to cut broiling meat with a knife if [the meat] is broiling on a spit without being salted

Yad Adam

surface were washed off, the knife remains permissible. Because blood is slippery (as noted in the next section) there will not be significant absorption of blood into the knife, even though "heat" from salting, or even heat from a fire, is present. Therefore, washing the knife is sufficient to remove any blood that is now on it.

השפוד[22] כל זמן שלא נצלה כ״צ מפני דם שנבלע בסכין והמחמיר בין במליחה ובין בצלי להגעיל תע״ב ובדיעבד מותר.[י]

ז. אבל בשר טרפה שנמלח וחתכו בסכין היתר בתוך שיעור מליחה הסכין צריך הגעלה דדוקא ממליחת איסור דם לא נאסרה דדם מישרק שריק אבל בשר טריפה שיש שם שמנונית איסור נבלע בסכין עכ״פ כ״ק[23] וכ״ש צלי אסור שעל האש שחתכו בסכין שנאסר הסכין כדלעיל סי׳ ד׳.[יא]

ח. סכין של איסור[24] אסור להשתמש בקביעות אפילו בצונן ואפילו לחתוך בו רק פת בקביעות[25] ואם רוצה להשתמש בו בדרך ארעי צריך נעיצה י״פ בקרקע קשה וכל פעם ופעם ינעץ במקום אחר כדי שתהיה בכל פעם קרקע קשה שע״י הנעיצה כבר נתרחב הגומא קצת ואינו מנקה השמנונית ואז מותר לחתוך בו אפילו דבר חריף[26] כצנון ובצל ומליח דע״י הנעיצה מעביר ומפליט מה שבקליפת הסכין ואם יש בו גומות צריך הגעלה וצריך לנקות מקודם הגומות ואז יגעילנה ואם יש לחוש שמא נשתמש בצלי על האש דאז הגעלה לא מהני כדלקמן[27] ילבין אותו[28] ואם א״א ללבן

י. סי׳ ס״ע בש״ך ס״ק פ״ז.

יא. וכן אם חתכו בסכין בשר חזיר שמייבשין אותו אסור הסכין כי ידוע שמולחין אותו הרבה ולעולם דינו כרותח כדלעיל כלל מ״ג סימן א׳.

יד אדם

22. In this instance we rely on the broiling alone to draw out the blood, and blood will not be completely drained out from unsalted meat until it is fully broiled.

7. A Knife Used to Cut Salted Unkosher Meat

23. As a general rule, the heat of salting causes the taste of a salted food to be absorbed into the peel of a vessel which comes into contact with it. See topic 57, section 13.

In this section the *Chochmas Adam* mentions that the salty meat is cut during the time required for salting. If this time period had elapsed, there are grounds to be lenient in accordance with topic 43, section 3.

8. Using a Forbidden Knife After Insertion into the Ground or Sharpening It

24. For example, it was used to cut hot forbidden fat, or a dairy knife was used to cut hot meat.

25. The knife may, however, be used on a temporary basis in cases of necessity without kashering it with boiling water, but only if the following procedure is carried out.

26. Such foods absorb taste from a knife more readily than others, as explained in topic 49. (Rubbing the knife with steel wool will also help to the same extent as inserting in the ground.)

י. *Shach* 69:87.
יא. And similarly, if one cut pig's meat which they had dried out with a knife, the knife is forbidden, because it is known that they salt it very much and in all cases it is judged as being hot, as [explained] previously in topic 43, section 1.

[first],[22] [and this should be avoided] as long as it not fully broiled. [This is] due to blood which will be absorbed into the knife [while cutting the meat]. And one who is stringent, both with salted meat and with broiling meat to kasher [the knife] with boiling water is praiseworthy, but after the fact [if the knife was not kashered, even hot food cut with it] is permissible.'

7. However, if unkosher meat was salted and cut with a knife [normally used] for permissible food during the required time for salting, the knife requires kashering in boiling water, for it is only when the salted forbidden substance is blood that [the knife] does not becomes forbidden, because blood is slippery. However, [with regard to] unkosher meat where forbidden grease will be absorbed into the knife at least by the width of its peel,[23] and certainly with forbidden meat which is broiling over a fire which one cut with a knife—the knife becomes forbidden as noted above in section 4 [and below in section 8].יא

8. A knife which is forbidden[24] may not be used on a regular basis even for cold food, and even to cut only bread with it regularly [is forbidden].[25] And if one desires to use it on a temporary basis [for cold food], it requires insertion into hard ground ten times, and each and every time he should insert it into a different place in order that each time it will be [inserted] into hard ground, for by inserting it the hole has been widened a little and it will not clean off the grease [in subsequent insertions]. And then it is permissible to cut even a sharp food[26] with it such as radish or onion or salty food, since insertion [into the ground] cleans off and causes emission of whatever is in the outer layer of the knife. But if there are indentations in it, it requires kashering in boiling water, and one must clean out the indentations first and then kasher it. And if there is concern that perhaps [the knife] was used with broiled meat over the fire, then kashering with boiling water will not help as [explained] later on,[27] and he is to kasher it with fire.[28] And

Yad Adam

27. The rules concerning kashering with boiling water and with fire are explained in topic 74. See also *Chayei Adam*, topic 125.

28. He is to burn it on a fire until it is red hot.

יב. סי׳ קכ״ח.

היטיב משום הקתא[29] ילבין ואח״כ יגעיל[30] או שישחיזנה במשחזת של נפחים היטב ואח״כ יגעילנה דמהני כליבון אם יכול לנקות הגומות.[31]

עוד יש תקנה לחתוך בו צונן אם אי אפשר בנעיצה כגון שהארץ נקרש מחמת הקור שישחיזנה במשחזת של נפחים היטב וזה מועיל כמו נעיצה אם אין בו גומות. ובדיעבד אם השחיז היטב במשחזת של נפחים ונשתמש בו רותח[32] מותר.[יב]

ט. דין סכין של בשר לאכול בו גבינה ולחם מבואר בכלל מ׳ סימן י״ד. ודין סכין ששחט בו מבואר בכלל ג׳.

כלל מח

דין נ״ט בר נ״ט

ודין הדחת כלים של בשר וחלב או איסור והיתר יחד

(סימן צ״ה)

א. קיי״ל נ״ט בר נ״ט[1] מותר[2] כגון דגים או ביצים אפילו קלופים וכיוצא בו שנתבשלו או נצלו בקדירה של בשר ב״י[3]

יד אדם

29. The handle would be damaged if kashered directly by fire.

30. In order to kasher the handle.

31. Of course, once the knife is appropriately kashered with boiling water, [or, when required, with fire (or sharpening) plus boiling water], it may used on a regular basis, even for cutting hot food. Insertion into the ground, on the other hand, is good only for cutting cold food on a temporary basis. As noted below, sharpening the knife without placing it in boiling water helps only to the same extent as insertion into the ground.

32. And it was not kashered with fire or boiling water.

9. Miscellaneous Rules Regarding a Forbidden Knife

1. Secondary Transmitted Taste of Meat or Milk in a Pareve Food

1. The Hebrew term is **נותן טעם בר נותן טעם**, more literally, an emitted taste from an emitted taste. This phrase is used to denote a taste which has undergone two transfers. For

יב. *Shulchan Aruch* chapter 121 [paragraph 7].

if it is impossible to kasher it well with fire because of the handle,[29] he should kasher it with fire and afterwards place it in boiling water;[30] or he should sharpen it well on a blacksmith's sharpening stone and afterwards place it in boiling water, since this helps like kashering with fire if he is able to clean out the indentations.[31]

There is another way of rectifying [the status of the knife to allow] cutting cold food with it if insertion [into the ground] is not possible such as if the earth is frozen due to the cold, [namely,] he should sharpen it well on a blacksmith's sharpening stone, and this helps just like insertion if there are no indentations. And after the fact, if he sharpened it well on a blacksmith's sharpening stone and used it for hot food,[32] [the food] will nevertheless be permissible.יב

9. The rules regarding eating cheese and bread with a meat knife are explained in topic 40, section 14. And the rules regarding a knife with which one slaughtered are explained in topic 3.

Topic 48

Laws Concerning Secondary Transmitted Taste; the Regulations Regarding Washing Vessels of Meat and Milk, or Permissible And Forbidden Ones, Together

(based on *Shulchan Aruch–Yoreh Deah* chapter 95)

1. It is established for us that a secondary transmitted taste[1] is permissible.[2] For example, if fish or eggs, even if shelled, or a similar [pareve] food is cooked or broiled in a meat pot which had been used

Yad Adam

example, if one cooks meat in a new pot, the taste of the meat is transmitted into the pot. If (after cleaning out the pot) one later cooks eggs in this pot, the taste is then transmitted from the pot to the eggs. In such a case, we say that the eggs contain SECONDARY TRANSMITTED TASTE from the meat.

It has been explained previously that vessels and foods transmit taste to each other only when they are hot. See topic 42, section 9 for the criteria used to determine when an item is hot.

2. The meaning is: If food containing secondary transmitted taste of meat or milk is mixed with the other type of food (for example, if the egg described in the previous note is mixed with milk), the mixture will be permissible.

We will learn later on (section 17) that a

מקונח יפה או אפילו אינו מקונח אלא שיש ס׳ נגד הממשות[4] מותר לאכלן בחלב שהרי אין כאן אלא נ״ט בר נ״ט ר״ל שהבשר נתן טעם בקדירה והקדירה בדגים וכיון שהטעם קלוש כ״כ[5] אינו ראוי שיחול עליו אחר שנתנו בחלב שם חדש מבו״ה[א] כן סתם בש״ע[ב] אבל אנו נמשכים אחר רמ״א קיי״ל דלכתחלה אסור לאכלן בחלב דכיון שנתבשל בתוכו ה״ז כאלו הבשר היה בעין בתוכו[6] ומ״מ בדיעבד שכבר נתן לתוך החלב מותר דבדיעבד סמכינן על פסק הש״ע בין בנתבשלו בין בנצלו.[7][ג]

ואם לא נתבשל בתוכו[8] אלא שבישל דגים בכלי שאינו לא בשר ולא חלב והניח מרותחין לכלי בשר והכלי היה צונן[ד] מותר לאכלו בחלב אפילו לכתחלה כיון שלא נתבשל בתוכו[9] לא חשבינן להבלוע כאלו היה הבשר בעין וכן אפילו נתבשל בכלי של בשר מותר לכתחלה ליתנם בכלי של חלב[10] כיון שאין אוכלן בחלב ממש ומ״מ

א. אבל אם בישל ביצה אפי׳ אינה קלופה עם בשר אסור לאכלה בחלב.
ב. סי׳ ל״ה.
ג. אחרונים דלא כש״ך ס״ק ד׳.
ד. דאם שניהם חמין הוי כבללה ש״ך סק״ו.

יד אדם

"secondary transmitted taste is permitted" only in cases where the taste is permissible while it is being transferred. If, on the other hand, a forbidden taste is being transferred (such as the taste of unkosher meat), then even secondary transmission will result in a prohibition.

3. Even though the pot had been used on that day to cook meat and the absorbed taste is therefore beneficial, we will nevertheless still regard the fish or eggs which are later cooked in it to be pareve.

4. The fish or eggs together with the other ingredients in the pot are at least sixty times the remaining traces of meat. (If sixty were not present, everything is forbidden in accordance with section 8 below.)

5. By the two transfers.

6. And it is as if this intact meat is present in the pot when cooking the pareve food. If pareve food has already been prepared in a meat pot, then the prohibition to eat the food with milk applies only if the pot had been used to cook meat during the previous 24 hours. See section 2 for further discussion.

7. Whether the pareve food was cooked with water or broiled in the meat vessel, in either case we can be lenient and the pareve food and the milk remain permissible. (See note ג.)

The word לכתחלה (translated "to begin with"), denotes the preferred practice which **should** be followed in any given case, whereas the expression בדיעבד (translated "after the fact") denotes the situation that on that day[3] and it had been cleaned out well, or even if it had not been cleaned out but there is sixty times the food material,[4] it is permitted to eat them with milk, since there is only secondary transmitted taste here, that is to say, the meat transmits its taste to the pot and the pot into the fish. And since the taste [of the meat] is weakened so much,[5] it is not fitting that a new title of "meat and milk" should come upon [this pareve food] after it is placed into milk.[א] This is the conclusion of [the *Bais Yosef* in] the *Shulchan Aruch*.[ב] However, we follow [the opinion of] the *Rama*—that it is established for us, to begin with, that it is forbidden to eat it with milk, for since [the meat] was cooked inside [the pot], it is as if the meat were intact inside it.[6] Nevertheless, after the fact, if one already placed [such food] into milk, [the mixture] is permissible, because after the fact we rely on the decision of the *Shulchan Aruch*, whether it was cooked or it was broiled.[7][ג]

And if [the food] was not cooked inside it,[8] but one had cooked fish in a pot that was not meat nor dairy, and it was placed while hot onto a meat vessel and the vessel was cold,[ד] it is permissible to eat it with milk, even to begin with, for since it was not cooked inside it,[9] we do not regard what was absorbed [into the fish] as if it were intact meat. And similarly, even if [the fish] were cooked in a meat vessel it is permissible, [even] to begin with, to place it in a dairy vessel,[10] since he is not eating it with actual milk. Nevertheless, one must be careful not to

א. However, if one cooked an egg, even if it is not shelled (i.e., the shell is not removed), with meat, it is forbidden to eat it with milk.

ב. [*Shulchan Aruch*] chapter 95 [paragraphs 1 and 2].

ג. Later authorities, not in accordance with the *Shach*, paragraph 4 [who rules that when broiling (with no liquid present), the taste transmitted to the food from the vessel must be treated more stringently, as if it were directly transferred from the first food. The *Chazon Ish* rules in accordance with the *Shach*, but almost all other later authorities rule in accordance with the *Chochmas Adam*.]

ד. If both of them were hot, it would be as if [the food] was broiled [and there might be some transfer of taste. See the] *Shach* paragraph 6. [See also the *Aruch Hashulchan* 95:12 who is lenient even if the plate is hot.]

Yad Adam

exists if the proper practice was not followed. In many situations where the preferred practice was not observed, the food involved might still be permissible.

Sometimes the word לכתחלה has a different connotation: It denotes a practice that **could** be followed without any reservation. It is used in this way in the following statement of the *Chochmas Adam*.

8. The pareve food, although it was present in the meat vessel, was not cooked inside it.

9. The fish was not cooked in the meat vessel, but was only placed inside it while the fish was hot.

10. Although such pareve food should not be mixed with milk as noted above, it can be placed in a clean dairy vessel while the food

ה. עיין פ״ח שם ס״ק ז׳.
ו. שם בש״ע ובחו״ד כלל ל״ד.

צריך ליזהר שלא יתנם בדרך עירוי[11] דהיינו לערות מכלי של חלב לבשר כדלקמן סי׳ י״ג ומ״מ לכבוד שבת וכיוצא בו אם אין לו כלי אחר יש לסמוך על המתירין דמותר לערות ומ״מ ימתין עד שיצטנן קצת מרתיחתו דאז לכ״ע מותר לערות ובשעת הדחק כגון על הדרך מותר לבשל לכתחלה בכלי של בשר וליתנו לכלי של חלב* רק שלא יאכל בחלב.[ה]

ב. אם היה הכלי שנתבשל בו אינו ב״י מותר לאכלו בחלב אפילו לדידן[12] אבל אסור לכתחלה לבשל בכלי שאב״י כדי לאכלו בחלב דנטל״פ אסור לכתחלה[13][ו] וכשחממו מים בכלי של חלב ב״י ולש בהם לחם אסור לאכול הלחם עם בשר אבל אם חממו בכלי שאב״י מותר.[14] ונ״ל דאם אין לו כלי אחר לחמם בו יש לסמוך ולהתיר ללוש בהם אפילו לכתחלה כיון דאיכא תרתי נטל״פ ונ״ט

יד אדם

is hot. (This is permitted even if the meat and dairy vessels had both been used that day for meat and milk respectively. *Madanei Hashulchan* 95:23)

11. When one is transferring hot food from a meat pot to the dairy plate (or a dairy pot to a meat plate), he should not pour it in such a way that there is a continuous stream of liquid between the two vessels.

*Even though one may not normally cook pareve food in a meat pot if he plans to place the food on a dairy vessel, in cases of urgency one may do so.

2. Secondary Transmitted Taste Which is Detrimental

12. If one plans to eat a pareve food with milk, he should not heat up this food in a meat pot. Nevertheless, if the pareve food was already heated in a meat pot and one desires to eat it with milk, it is permitted to do so, even for us who follow the more stringent opinion of the *Rama*. However, this is the case only if the pot had not been used for meat during the 24 hour period before cooking the pareve food. If meat had been cooked in the pot within the past 24 hours, then it is forbidden to eat this food with milk. After the fact, if one did mix this pareve food with milk, we will not require him to discard the mixture. Rather, as explained in section 1, we can be lenient and rely on the opinion of the *Bais Yosef* to permit the mixture.

13. An absorbed taste in a vessel which is more than 24 hours old cannot cause a food to become forbidden according to Torah law, since it has already become spoiled. Nevertheless, the sages have decreed that to begin with, the transmission of such a spoiled taste is forbidden, that is, one should treat it with the same stringencies as if the

ח. See *Pri Chadash* there, paragraph 7.
ו. *Shulchan Aruch* there (95:2), and in the *Issur v'heter* topic 34.

place [the food] "by way of a stream,"[11] that is, [not] to pour from a dairy vessel onto a meat vessel as [explained] later on in section 13. However, in honor of the Sabbath or under similar circumstances, if one has no other vessel he can rely on those authorities who are lenient [and rule] that it is permitted to pour [from a dairy vessel onto a meat vessel]. Nevertheless, he should wait until [the liquid] cools off a little from its boiling heat, for then according to all authorities it is permitted to pour. And [similarly], in cases of urgency, such as on a trip, it is permissible to cook in a meat vessel, [even] to begin with, and [then] put [its contents] into a dairy vessel,* provided that he does not eat it with milk.ח

2. If the [meat] vessel in which [the pareve food] was cooked was not used on that day [for meat], it is permissible to eat [the food] with milk, even according to us.[12] However, to begin with, it is prohibited to cook [a pareve food] in a [meat] vessel which was not used on that day in order to eat it with milk, since transmission of a spoiled taste is forbidden to begin with.[13]ו And if one heated water in a dairy vessel which was used on that day [for dairy] and kneaded bread with it, it is forbidden to eat that bread with meat, but if it was heated in a vessel that had not been used on that day it is permitted.[14] And it is my opinion that if one has no other vessel in which to heat [water] he may rely [on the lenient authorities] to permit kneading with [such water] even to begin with, since there are two [grounds for leniency]: [The pot] emits a detrimental taste, and [the taste emitted into the water] is

Yad Adam

taste were beneficial (less than 24 hours old). As such, if one desires to eat a pareve food with milk—just as he should not heat up this pareve food in a meat vessel which was used that day for meat, so also, he should not heat it up in a meat vessel which was not used that day.

14. After the fact, if he already heated water in a dairy pot for the purpose of kneading (and the pot had not been used that day for dairy), he is not required to discard it and heat up additional water. Rather he may use it to knead the dough and then eat the bread with meat.

בר נ״ט.[15]ז ואף דבאו״ה כתב דוקא דיעבד שכבר הוחם נ״ל דאם אין לו כלי אחר וא״א להשאיל הוי כדיעבד.[16]ח

מים שנתבשל בכלי בשר שאב״י נ״ל דמותר לבשל בו קאווע ולשתותו עם חלב[17] אבל אם חימם בכלי איסור[18] אפי׳ אב״י אסור ללוש בהם או לבשל דזה מיקרי לכתחלה[19] ואפילו אם חממו לצורך שתייה[20] דכל זמן שהמים בעין[21] הוי כלכתחלה דבאיסור ל״ש נ״ט בר נ״ט כדלקמן סי׳ י״ז.ט

ג. קדרה חדשה שבישל בה מים ותחבו בה כף חולבת ואח״כ אפילו באותו יום חזרו ובשלו בה מים פעם אחרת ותחבו כף בשר ושתי הכפות היו ב״י ובשום א׳ מהפעמים לא היו במים ס׳ הקדרה לא נאסר לדעת הב״י בש״ע שהרי לשיטתו אפי׳ תחב שניהם בבת א׳ במים הכל מותר כדלקמן סי׳ ו׳ ומן הדין יכול לבשל בקדרה זו בשר או חלב אך כיון שצריך לקבוע לו תשמיש מסתמא נשאר בו

ז. עיין באו״ה כלל ל״ד דין ו׳ שכתב להדי׳ דאם בדיעבד הוחמו מותר ללוש וכ״כ עוד כלל ל״ג דין י״ג ומש״כ שם בכלל ל״ד בהגה׳ סי׳ ב׳ בשם מהרא״י כיון שלא הוחמו לשתי׳ הוי כלכתחלה ע״ש נ״ל דנרשם בטעות שהרי בהדי׳ אי׳ בש״ד סי׳ ז׳ הגהה זו על כלים של איסור דל״ש בו נ״ט בר נ״ט וכ״כ האו״ה שם דבכלי של איסור אף בזה אסור.

ח. כמ״ש הת״ח כלל י״ז הביאו הט״ז סי׳ ל״א ס״ק ב׳ במתאכסן בבית נכרי.

ט. ועיין בש״ע סימן קכ״ב סעיף ו׳ ובש״ך שם.

יד אדם

15. The taste was first transferred from the dairy food to the pot, and then from the pot to the water, thereby weakening the taste. Thus, because of these two grounds for leniency, the *Chochmas Adam* feels that it is permitted to intentionally warm up the water in a dairy pot to prepare this bread if no other pot is available, as long as the pot had not been used for dairy on that day.

16. If no other pot is available, we may accept the leniencies which normally apply only "after the fact," and we will allow warming the water in a dairy pot to begin with (as long as it has not been used for dairy in the past 24 hours).

17. This applies when one has already heated the water—he need not discard the water, but he may use it to make coffee and add milk to it. However, to begin with, one should not heat water in such a vessel to use it with milk, as noted above.

18. Such as a pot which was used to cook unkosher meat.

19. We are more strict regarding water which one has heated in a forbidden pot and treat it like a case of one who is first beginning the entire process, where the preferred practice must be followed. The reason is state below: The leniency of secondary absorbed taste does not apply to a taste which is forbidden while it is being transferred. (See note 17.) As such, the water should be discarded, and one must heat up water in another pot to brew coffee or knead dough. If however, one mistakenly used

secondary transmitted taste.[15][ז] And even though the *Issur v'heter* has written that [kneading with this water is permitted] only "after the fact," [which means] where [the water] has already been heated—it is my opinion that if one has no other vessel and it is impossible to borrow, then it is like [a case of] "after the fact."[16][ח]

If water has been cooked in a meat vessel which was not used that day [for meat]—it is my opinion that it is permissible to brew coffee in it and drink it with milk.[17] However, if [the water] was heated in a forbidden vessel,[18] even if it was not used that day [for forbidden food], it is forbidden to knead with it or cook [with it] because this is called "to begin with,"[19] even if one had warmed [the water] for drinking needs;[20] for as long as the water is intact[21] it is like a case of "to begin with," for with regard to forbidden food [the leniency] of secondary transmitted taste is not applicable, as [noted] later on in section 17.[ט]

3. If one cooked water in a new pot and inserted a dairy spoon into it and afterwards, even on that day, he went on and cooked water in it another time and inserted a meat spoon [into it], and the two spoons had been used on that day [for hot dairy and meat respectively] and in neither case did the water have sixty times [the portion of the spoon inserted], the pot does not become forbidden according to the *Bais Yosef* in the *Shulchan Aruch*, for according to his opinion, even if he inserted both of them at the same time in water, everything is permissible as [explained] further on in section 6. And according to the letter of the law one is permitted to cook meat or milk in this pot. However, since it is necessary to establish the use [of this pot for the future, and]

ז. Refer to the *Issur v'heter* 34:6 where he writes explicitly that if after the fact [the water] was heated, it is permitted to knead [with it], and he writes similarly in 33:13. And regarding what is written there in topic 34 in note number 2 in the name of Rabbi Isserlein, that since it was not heated for drinking it is like [a case of] "to begin with,"* refer there, it is my opinion that [the note] was recorded in error, as this note is explicitly [stated] in *Shaarei Dura* section 7 regarding forbidden vessels where [the leniency] of secondary transmitted taste is not applicable. And the *Issur v'heter* there writes as such explicitly, that [water heated] in a forbidden vessel, even in such a situation [where there is secondary transmission of taste], is forbidden.

ח. As the *Toras Chatas* writes in topic 17, quoted by the *Taz* in 91:2 regarding one who is a guest in the inn of a gentile.

ט. And refer to the *Shulchan Aruch* 122:6 and the *Shach* there.

---

*It is like a case where one is beginning the entire process, and as such, the preferred practice must be followed. According to this note of Rabbi Isserlein, it would not be permitted to knead with such water and then eat the bread with meat. Rather, it would be necessary to discard the water and heat up water in another pot.

Yad Adam

such water to cook or knead, then the food will be permissible after the fact.

20. Even though, after the fact, one may drink the water if he heated it for this purpose, it is still forbidden for one to knead with this water. See topic 55, section 9.

21. As long as the water has not yet been mixed into dough or other foods.

י. סי׳ ל״ד סעי׳ כ׳ וע״ש בש״ך ופ״ת.
יא. ש״ך שם בסי׳ ל״ד ססק״ ט״ו.
יב. כדלקמן סי׳ י׳.

טעם יותר מהכף האחרון אע״ג דלא חשוב טעם דהוי נ״ט בנ״ט[22] מ״מ טעם קלוש יש בו ולכן יקבע אותו לתשמיש ככף האחרון דהיינו בשר.י

ד. וכ״ש אם נשתמש בשר בקדירה זו שתחבו בה בראשונה כף חולבת ב״י[23] דמותר לבשל אח״כ בה בשר אבל לכתחלה לא היינו מתירים לבשל בה בשר* כיון שצריך עכ״פ לקבוע תשמיש לקדירה כיון שהיא חדשה יש לקבוע לה מחלב שנבלע בה בראשונה.יא

ה. ולמנהגינו ע״פ רמ״א אם תחב ב׳ כפות[24] בפעם א׳ בקדירה אסור הכלייב אבל אם תחבן בזה אחר זה[25] מותר לבשל בקדירה בשר כתחיבת כף האחרון[26] ואע״ג שכבר קבלה הקדירה טעם מכף ב״י חולבת וה״ז כדגים שנתבשלו בקדירה של בשר לעיל סימן א׳ דקיי״ל לשיטתו[27] דאסור לאכלן בכותח דדוקא בדיעבד מותר נ״ט בר נ״ט אבל לכתחלה ע״י בישול אסור[28] שאני התם דהתם הבשר הנבלע בדגים חשוב טעם כי נבלע אוכל באוכל אבל

יד אדם

3. Effects of Secondary Transmitted Tastes on the Future Use of a Vessel

22. The pot did not absorb directly from meat (or milk). Rather, the spoon had absorbed taste directly from the meat (or milk); this taste was then emitted from the spoon when placed into the water and it was then absorbed from the water into the pot.

4. Further Regulations Regarding a Vessel With Absorbed Secondary Tastes

23. We are again dealing with a new pot (i.e., a pot that was not yet used for dairy or for meat), and a dairy spoon was inserted into the pot while its pareve contents are hot. This act should establish the pot as being a dairy pot. However, the pot was used instead for meat, as the *Chochmas Adam* goes on to explain.

*Once a dairy spoon had been inserted into the pot, then meat should not have been cooked in this pot to begin with.

5. Effects of Secondary Transmitted Tastes on a Vessel According to the Rama

24. One is dairy and one is meat and each one had been used on that day. (See section 10.)

25. The meat spoon after the dairy spoon, following the example in section 3.

י. Chapter 94, paragraph 5, and refer there to the *Shach* and the *Pri Chadash*.
יא. *Shach* there in chapter 94, end of paragraph 15.
יב. In accordance with section 10 further on.

it is probable that more taste remains in it from the last spoon [than from the first]—even though it is not regarded as "taste" since it is secondary transmitted taste[22]—nevertheless, there is [at least] a weak taste in it, and therefore, he should set it to be used in accordance with the last spoon, which is meat.י

4. And certainly, if meat was used in this pot in which he first had inserted the dairy spoon which had been used on that day,[23] it is permitted to cook meat in it afterwards. However, to begin with we should not permit cooking meat in it* for since it is necessary at least to establish the use of the pot because it is new, it is proper to set it with respect to the milk which was the first to be absorbed into it.יא

5. Our customary practice is in accordance with the *Rama*, that if one inserted two spoons[24] into a pot at once, everything is forbidden.יב However, if he inserted them one after the other[25] it is permissible to cook meat in the pot in accordance with the insertion of the last spoon.[26] And even though the pot already received taste from a dairy spoon that had been used on that day, and it is like the case of fish which was cooked in a meat pot [described] previously in section 1 where it is established for us in accordance with his opinion[27] that it is forbidden to eat it with dairy food, as only after the fact do we permit secondary transmitted taste, but to begin with when there has been cooking it is forbidden[28]—it is different there because there the [taste of] meat absorbed into the fish is considered as [actual] "taste" because it is [taste of] a food absorbed into a food, but here the taste of the milk

Yad Adam

26. In this instance the *Rama* rules that the pot may be used in the future to cook meat, similar to the ruling of the *Bais Yosef* cited in section 3. There are, however, stringencies which affect the contents of the pot according to the *Rama*. These are mentioned in section 11.

27. The opinion of the *Rama*.

28. We have learned in section 1 that fish cooked in a meat pot should not be mixed with milk (although, after the fact, we will not prohibit the mixture). Why, then, does the *Rama* allow cooking meat in a pot which has absorbed dairy taste from a spoon?

הכא טעם החלב הנפלט מכף חולבת למים וחוזר ונבלע בקדירה אינו חשוב טעם כשיחזור הקדירה ויפלוט אותו לתוך הבשר[29] ועוד דשם אינו אלא ב׳ נ״ט דהיינו הבשר בקדירה והקדירה בדגים ובזה נוהגין להחמיר אבל הכא איכא ג׳ נ״ט החלב בכף והכף אל המים והמים לקדירה ועדיין הוא היתר[30] ובג׳ נ״ט לכולי עלמא מותר.[יג]

ו. קדירה של בשר ב״י שבשלו בו מים או ירקות ותחב בו כף חולבת ב״י אפי׳ אין במים ס׳ נגד הכף מותר הכל לדעת הב״י בש״ע[31][יד] דהוי נ״ט בר נ״ט דהתירא ר״ל הבשר נתן בקדירה והקדירה במים ועדיין היה היתר שהיה מותר לאכול לכתחלה המים והירקות עם חלב[32] ואפילו תחב ב׳ כפות א׳ של חלב וא׳ של בשר ושניהם ב״י בפעם א׳ בקדירה הכל מותר.[טו]

ז. וכן אם הדיח כלי בשר ב״י עם כלי של חלב ביחד במחבת[33] שאינו לא בשר ולא חלב[34] במים רותחין שהיס״ב או אפילו קערות בשר ב״י שהדיח במחבת חולבת ב״י בחמין שהיס״ב אע״ג שבאו ב׳ הפליטות בפעם א׳[35] ל״א דהוי נ״ט בר נ״ט דאיסורא אלא

יג. ונ״ל דיש לדחות טעם זה כמש״כ הש״ך בסי׳ צ״ה ס״ק ה׳ בשם הר״ן בטעם א׳ דמאן לימא לן שלא יתערבו כו׳ ע״ש וא״כ ה״נ שמא בלעה הקדירה מכף החולבת שלא באמצעות המים וא״כ גם הכא אינו אלא ב׳ נ״ט.

יד. סי׳ צ״ה סעיף ג׳.

טו. פ״ח סימן צ״ד ס״ק ט״ו.

יד אדם

29. This is because the taste did not enter the pot directly from food which was cooked in it. Rather, the taste entered the pot only from a vessel (the spoon) which contained the absorbed taste. After absorbed taste is transferred from one vessel to another, then *halachically* it is not considered to be a "taste" which can go on to make other food forbidden.

30. The dairy taste at this point has been considerably weakened since it has been transmitted three times, and the taste is still completely permissible (since it has not yet made contact with the meat).

6. Pareve Food Which Has Secondary Absorbed Tastes from Both Meat and Milk—the Opinion of the Bais Yosef

31. See section 10 below for the opinion of the *Rama*, which is the accepted practice.

32. This is in accordance with the *Bais Yosef* in section 1. The basic principle is that the permissible meat or dairy taste being emitted into the water has become weakened and cannot cause a prohibition.

7. Meat and Dairy Vessels Which Are Washed Together in a כלי ראשון ("First Vessel")

33. The pot here is a "first vessel"—the water

יג. And it is my opinion that this reason can be refuted, as the *Shach* writes in 95:5 in the name of the *Ran* when there is one [transfer] taste: For who says that [emitted taste from meat and from milk] will not be mixed [directly, without water in between], etc.—refer there. As such, here also, perhaps the pot has absorbed [directly] from the dairy spoon without the water in between, and if so, here also there would be only two transmitted tastes.

יד. *Shulchan Aruch* 95:3.

טו. *Pri Chadash* 94:15.

which is emitted from the dairy spoon into the water which [then] goes on and is absorbed into the pot is not considered to be "taste" when the pot will go on and emit it into the meat.[29] Furthermore, over there, there are only two transfers of taste, which is the meat into the pot and the pot into the fish, and in such a case we are accustomed to be stringent; but here there are three transfers of taste–the milk into the spoon, and the spoon into the water and the water into the pot, and it still is permissible.[30] And where there are three transfers of taste, it is permissible according to all authorities.יג

6. [Regarding] a meat pot which had been used on that day [for meat] where one [later that day] cooked water or green vegetables in it and [then] inserted a dairy spoon into it which had been used on that day [for dairy]—even if there is not sixty times the spoon in the water, everything is permissible according to the *Bais Yosef* in the *Shulchan Aruch*.[31]יד This is because there is secondary transmitted taste which is [still] permissible, that is, meat has transmitted [its] taste into the pot and the pot into the water, and still [the taste] was permissible as it was permitted to consume the water and the green vegetables with milk to begin with.[32] And even if he inserted two spoons at the same time into a pot, one dairy and one meat and both of them were used onthat day [for dairy and meat respectively], everything is permissible.טו

7. And similarly if one washed a meat vessel which was used that day together with a dairy vessel in a pot[33] which is neither meat nor dairy[34] [and the pot contains] hot water which [is so hot that] the hand would withdraw from it–or even if meat plates used that day were washed in a dairy pot used that day [where the pot contains] hot water which [is so hot that] the hand would withdraw from it–even though the two emissions come at one time[35] we do not say that there is secondary transmitted taste of forbidden matter, but we regard it as

Yad Adam

was heated while inside the pot. Meat and dairy dishes are placed into this pot of hot water in order to wash them.

34. Rather, the pot is used only to cook pareve food.

35. In these cases, since the water is so hot that one would withdraw his hand from it (see topic 42, section 9), there will be simultaneous transfer of taste from the dairy and the meat vessels into the water (causing the water to become forbidden), and then from

חשבינן ליה לנ"ט בר נ"ט דהתירא שכ"א נבלע בכלי ומן הכלי למים.[36] טז

ח. בד"א[37] אם ברי לו שלא היה שום שומן או חלב דבוק אפילו באחד מהם דאם היה בעין צריך ס' נגד ממשות שהיה על א' מהכלים ואם אין ס' הכל אסור שהרי הממשות הוא נ"ט במים ונעשה המים כמו הממשות וכשנפלט הטעם מן כלי השני אע"פ שהוא נקי הרי המים נ"נ[38] ואסור הכל עד שיהיה ס' נגד השומן[39] יז ואם נסתפק אם היה שומן דבוק בו אמרי' מסתמא היה שומן דבוק בו דאע"ג דקיי"ל סתם כלים הם נקיים[40] היינו לאחר שהודחו אבל אלו שרוצה להדיחם אדרבה מסתמא אינם נקיים. יח

ט. בד"א[41] שהיו שניהם ב"י אבל אם א' מן הכלים אינו ב"י אם השומן דבוק באותו שאינו ב"י הכל אסור שהרי המים נ"נ מהשומן שיש בעין ומפליטת הכלי שהוא ב"י אבל אם השומן דבוק באותו שהוא בן יומו והכלי שאינו ב"י נקי אז אותו שאינו בן יומו אסור מפליטת הכלי שהוא ב"י אבל זה שהוא ב"י מותר שהרי מקבל טעם מכלי שאינו ב"י שהוא לפגם יט וכן אם שניהן אינן ב"י אלא ששומן דבוק בשניהם פשיטא דאסור.

טז. סימן צ"ה סעיף ג'.
יז. שם.
יח. שם בש"ך ס"ק ח'.
יט. שם בש"ך.

יד אדם

the water into the vessels. Since the water is forbidden, one might think that this is not a case of transmitting secondary permissible tastes.

36. See section 10 for the opinion of the *Rama*.

8. Stringencies Which Apply if Fat Was Present on the Vessels

37. When do we say that everything remains permissible when a meat and a dairy vessel are washed together?

38. For example, if meat fat was present on the meat vessel, the entire quantity of water becomes like meat. Then when the dairy vessel emits its taste, the entire quantity of water becomes forbidden as a mixture of meat and milk.

39. The water in the pot must be at least sixty times the amount of fat adhering to the meat dish. Otherwise, the pot and all of the vessels inside it become forbidden.

It should be noted that it makes no difference whether or not the vessel with the fat had been used on that day. Even though absorbed taste in a vessel becomes spoiled after 24 hours, this rule does not apply to intact food material which remains on a vessel. Rather, the taste which is present in intact food material remains beneficial.

40. See topic 55, section 1.

טו. *Shulchan Aruch* 95:3.
טז. *Ibid.*
יז. *Shach* there (chapter 95) paragraph 1.
יח. There in the *Shach* (95:12).

secondary transmitted taste which is [still] permissible, since each one had been absorbed into a vessel and [each was emitted] from the vessel into the water.[36טו]

8. When does the above apply?[37] When one is certain that there was no fat or milk adhering [to the vessel, not] even to one of them. For if there was intact material, it is necessary [that the water] have sixty times the substance that was present on one of the vessels; and if there is not sixty, everything is forbidden, because the intact material transmits taste [directly] into the water and makes the water like the intact material, and when the taste is emitted [into the water] from the other vessel, even though it is clean, the water becomes inherently forbidden[38] and everything becomes prohibited unless there is sixty times the fat.[39טז] And if it is doubtful whether there was fat adhering to it, we say probably there was fat adhering to it, for even though it is established for us that ordinary vessels are [to be regarded as] clean,[40] this is after they were washed, but regarding these which one [now] desires to wash—the opposite [is true], for probably they are not clean.[יז]

9. When is it so?[41] It is when both of them were used on that day. However, if one of the vessels was not used on that day—if the fat is adherent to the one that was not used on that day, then everything is [nevertheless] forbidden, because the water becomes inherently forbidden from the fat that is intact [on one vessel] and from the emission of [taste from] the [other] vessel which was used on that day. However, if the fat was adherent to the one which was used on that day and the vessel which was not used on that day was clean, then the one which was not used on that day becomes forbidden from the emission of the vessel which was used on that day; but the one which was used on that day [remains] permissible, as it receives taste from a vessel which was not used on that day, which is a detrimental [taste].[יח] Moreover, [even] if both of them were not used on that day but fatty material was adherent to both of them, it is obvious that [both] are forbidden.

Yad Adam

9. Leniencies Which Apply If the Meat or Dairy Vessel Had Not Been Used on That Day

41. When do we say that everything is forbidden if fatty material was adhering to one of the vessels, as mentioned in section 8?

כ. שם בהגהת רמ"א.

י. ולמנהגינו ע"פ הכרעת רמ"א כל שנתערב יחד פליטות של שני כלים שהם ב"י חשבינן ליה לנ"ט בר נ"ט דאיסור[42] דדוקא כשעמד טעם ב' בהיתר[43] אמרינן נ"ט בר נ"ט מותר כגון דגים שעלו בקערה של בשר שיש כאן נ"ט בר נ"ט ועדיין אין בו תערובות איסור וכדלעיל סימן א'[44] אבל הכא[45] תיכף נתערבו ב' הפליטות יחד אא"כ יש ס' נגד אחד מן הכלים[46] דכיון דיש ס' נגדו א"כ לא נתן טעם וכדלעיל סימן ט' או שהיה אחד מן הכלים אינו ב"י מבליעת כ"ר[47] דאז ג"כ הכל מותר דאותו שהוא ב"י ודאי מותר שהרי לא קיבל טעם אלא מאינו ב"י שהוא נ"ט לפגם ואותו שאינו ב"י נמי מותר שהרי קיבל טעם מנ"ט בר נ"ט ועדיין הוא היתר כיון שהכלי השני אינו בן יומו[48] וא"כ כל הכלים מותרים.[כ]

יא. ולכן קדרה של בשר שבשלו בה ירקות או מים ותחבו בה כף חולבת ואחד מהם ב"י וא' אינו ב"י הכל מותר מטעם הנזכר בסימן הקודם אלא שנוהגין להחמיר לאסור הכלי שאינו ב"י

יד אדם

10. The Rama's Ruling Concerning Mixtures of Secondary Transmitted Tastes from Meat and Milk

42. We regard the secondary tastes transmitted into the water as constituting forbidden tastes of meat mixed with milk. Such secondary tastes result in a prohibition as noted below in section 17.

43. I.e., only if the taste remains permissible after its second transfer.

44. Two transfers of taste have occurred—from the meat to the plate and then from the plate into the fish, and no dairy taste is present when the taste enters the fish. It is noted in section 1 that if this fish is mixed with milk, the mixture will remain permissible.

45. In the cases mentioned in sections 6 and 7: Where pareve food is being cooked in a meat pot used that day and a dairy spoon used that day is inserted into the pot; or if a dairy spoon and a meat spoon are inserted together into a pot; or if meat and dairy utensils are washed together in a first vessel. In all of these cases, the vessels which are emitting the taste of meat and those emitting the taste of milk are present together in the hot water.

46. The pot contains sixty times the size of the inserted portion of the spoon.

כ. There in the notation of the *Rama* (95:3).

10. But according to our customary practice following the decision of the *Rama*, wherever the emissions of two vessels which were used on that day are mixed together, we regard it as secondary transmitted taste which is forbidden,[42] as only if the second taste stands in a permissible state[43] do we say that a secondary transmitted taste is permissible, such as fish which was placed in a meat plate where there is a secondary taste [of meat in the fish] but still no forbidden mixture, as [noted] previously in section 1.[44] However, here,[45] immediately the two emissions are mixed together, [and everything becomes forbidden] unless: [either] there is sixty times one of the vessels,[46] for since there is sixty times [this vessel], it will not impart any taste, as [noted] previously in [topic 46] section 9; or else, if one of the vessels was not used on that day [in a way] that it absorbed as a "first vessel,"[47] for then also everything will be permissible—the one which was used on that day is certainly permissible, for it has received taste only from what was not used on that day and that emits [only] a detrimental taste; and the one which was not used on that day is also permissible for it has received taste in a secondary way which is still permissible since the other vessel was not used on that day.[48] As such, all of the vessels are permitted.[כ]

11. Therefore, if one cooked green vegetables or water in a meat pot, and inserted a dairy spoon into it and one of them was used on that day and one was not used on that day, everything is permissible due to the reason that was mentioned in the previous section. However, we are accustomed to be stringent to prohibit the vessel which was not used on that day for appearance sake, since the food

Yad Adam

47. If, for example, hot food had been transferred from a pot (the "first vessel") into a bowl (the "second vessel") and a spoon (which was not used that day) was placed into the bowl of food while it was hot, we still regard the spoon as if it were not used on that day. This is because taste is transmitted from food to the spoon only when the more intense heat of a "first vessel" is present. See notes on topic 42, section 9.

48. This other vessel which was not used that day does not contribute a beneficial taste. Therefore, a forbidden mixture of meat and milk is not produced in the water.

משום מראית העין כיון שהמאכל אוכלין במין הכלי שהוא ב״י[49]כא ואינו אלא חומרא בעלמא ולכן אם חזר ותחב כלי זה שאינו ב״י שנאסר בקדרה אחרת אינו אוסר[כב] ומה שנתבשל בתוכו[50] אם הוא מים לבד נוהגין בהן איסור לכתחלה דכיון דאינו מאכל ואין בו הפסד כלל הוי כלכתחלה דאפילו נותן טעם לפגם אסור לכתחלה[51]כג ואם הוא דבר מאכל[52] מותר מדינא לאכלו כמין הכלי שהוא ב״י כגון שהיתה הקדרה של בשר ב״י ותחבו בה כף חלב אב״י מותר לאכול המאכל עם בשר ואם הוא מאכל שאפשר לאכלו בלא שומן או חלב[53] וגם האדם אינו מקפיד בכך הוי לכתחלה[54] ומ״מ יאכלנו במין הכלי שהוא ב״י ר״ל בכלי בשר אם הכלי של בשר היה ב״י ואם אי אפשר לו לאכלו כך[55] הוי כדיעבד[56] ומותר לאכלו בשומן או חלב כמין הכלי שהוא ב״י. כד כה

כא. ע״ז סי׳ ל״ה.
כב. ל״ד סעיף ה׳.
כג. ל״ה סעיף ג׳.
כד. כו״פ סי׳ ל״ד.
כה. ואם הקדירה אב״י ויש ס׳ נגד הכף שהוא ב״י נלע״ד דהכל מותר אפילו לדעת הש״ך שהבאתי בכלל מ״ו סי׳ ע׳ שהרי מן ההכרח בכאן לאכל דוקא המאכל במין הכלי שאב״י היינו הקדירה דנטל״פ לכתחלה אסור ונגד הכף יש ס׳ ואין כאן שום טעם נ״ע בר נ״ע.

יד אדם

11. Pareve Food Which Has Absorbed Secondary Tastes of Meat and Milk and One of Them is Detrimental

49. For example, if the dairy spoon had not been used on that day and the meat pot was used that day, then the contents of the pot become like meat and they cannot be eaten with a dairy utensil. Rather, as mentioned below by the *Chochmas Adam*, they may be eaten only on a meat vessel. (Even though, in general, one may place pareve food which had been cooked in a meat vessel onto a dairy plate [as mentioned in section 1], in this case the rabbis were more stringent. Since a dairy spoon was improperly inserted into this pot, we should take care that no further mix-ups should take place, and the food should be placed only in a meat plate.) Because the food can be used only with meat vessels, we should regard the spoon as if it actually absorbed meat taste and not use it again unless it is kashered. (See *Taz* 95:9.) If, on the other hand, the dairy spoon was used on that day and the pot was the vessel not used on that day, then the food should be eaten only on dairy vessels and the pot should not be used again until it is kashered. (As noted below in the name of the *Pri Megadim*, we do not require the spoon or the pot to be kashered if only water was cooked in the pot, since the water is to be discarded.)

50. We are now discussing the status of the food in the pot mentioned at the beginning of this section, where a dairy spoon was inserted into a meat pot which had not been used on that day. In such a case, we are

may be eaten [only] with the type of vessel which was used on that day.[49] כא And this is but a mere stringency, and therefore, if one went on and inserted this vessel which was not used on that day and which had become forbidden into another pot, it will not make [the contents of this other pot] forbidden. כב And with regard to what was cooking inside it[50]—if it is only water, we are accustomed to forbid [the water] to begin with, for since there is no food [in it] and there is no loss at all it is like case of "to begin with," for even a transmitted detrimental taste is forbidden to begin with.[51] כג And if there is any kind of food [in the pot],[52] it is permissible according to [the letter of] the law to eat it [with food] that is like the type of vessel which was used that day. For example, [the food] was in a meat pot used that day and one inserted a dairy spoon which was not used that day—it is permissible to eat the food with meat. But if it is a food that is possible to eat without [meat] fat—or milk[53]—and the person is also not particular about this, it is a case of "to begin with."[54] Furthermore, he should eat it with the type of vessel which was used that day, that is, with a meat vessel if the meat vessel was the one which was used that day. And if it is impossible to eat it in this way,[55] it is like a case of "after the fact"[56] and it is permissible to eat it with [meat] fat or milk in accordance with the type of vessel which was used that day. כד כה

כא. *Taz* chapter 95 [paragraph 9].
כב. *Shulchan Aruch* 94:5.
כג. *Shulchan Aruch* 95:3.
כד. *Kreisi u'pleisi* chapter 94.
כה. And if the pot was not used that day, and there is sixty times the spoon which was used that day, it is my humble opinion that everything is permissible, even according to the opinion of the *Shach* which I quoted in topic 46, paragraph 9 (note יג), because here, it is necessary to eat the food only with the type of vessel which was *not* used that day, which is the pot, for it emits a detrimental taste [of meat], which to begin with is forbidden [to mix with dairy. And since the food will be eaten on meat vessels, there is no requirement to kasher the meat pot.] And because there is sixty times the spoon, there is no consideration here [to be stringent because of the] secondary transmitted [dairy] taste [from the spoon].

Yad Adam

accustomed to apply the following stringencies.

51. Since this pot of water (described in note 49) absorbed dairy taste from the spoon and it also contains meat taste emitted by the pot, to begin with, we should regard the water as forbidden even though the dairy taste is detrimental.

52. Such as green vegetables cooking in the water. We are more lenient with regard to food in the pot, since a real monetary loss is incurred if it would have to be discarded.

53. If the vessel used that day was the dairy spoon and the food in the pot could be eaten without milk.

54. And in this case one should follow the preferred practice, which is to eat it only with pareve food, and not with meat or milk respectively.

55. If the food could be eaten only when accompanied by meat (or milk).

56. We will not force him to discard the food, since the absorbed taste from the milk or meat is detrimental.

כו. עיין סי' ל"ב בש"ך ופ"ח ס"ק י"ז דמחמיר אף בהפ"מ.

והפמ"ג כתב אם בשלו מים בקדרה שאב"י ותחבו כף חולבת ב"י אפילו אין ס' נגד הכף מותר הקדירה כיון דהמים נשפכין ליכא משום מראית עין.

יב. ואם עירה מים שאינן לא של חלב ולא של בשר על כלים של בשר וחלב יחד בין ששניהם שומן דבוק בהם ובין שא' נקי ואחד שומן דבוק בו ובין ששניהם נקיים במקום הפ"מ יש להתיר ולומר דאע"ג דעירוי מבשל כדי קליפה[57] מ"מ קודם שנמחה השומן ויבליע ויפלוט כבר בטל העירוי ודינו ככלי שני[58] אבל בלא הפ"מ אין להתיר אפילו בשניהם נקיים ולא הוי כנ"ט בר נ"ט כיון דפליטת שניהם מתערבים יחד[59] וקיי"ל עירוי מבשל כדי קליפה.[60] ונ"ל דלעולם יש להורות שימתין מלהשתמש בכלים אלו עד לאחר מעת לעת כדי שלא יהיה בזה חשש איסור דאורייתא.[61]כו

יג. ואם עירה מים מכלי של בשר נקי ב"י על של חלב ב"י מדינא מותר לגמרי לא מבעיא לשיטת הב"י בש"ע[62] אלא

יד אדם

12. Pouring Hot Water onto Meat and Dairy Vessels

57. Hot water which is poured from a "first vessel" causes absorption of taste into the "peel" (outer layer) of a food or vessel. (See topic 46, section 11.) As such, when the hot water is poured on the vessels, the tastes of both meat and milk will be absorbed by the water from the vessels, and then emitted from the water into the outer layers of the vessels. The vessels might thereby become forbidden.

58. And no transmission of taste occurs in a second vessel (see topic 42, section 9 and notes thereon). As such, in case of a great loss (such as an expensive vessel which cannot be kashered) one can be lenient and rule that there is no transmission of the tastes of milk and meat from one vessel to the other by means of the water and they do not become forbidden. (Regarding the term "great loss," see the additional note on topic 40, section 5.)

59. In accordance with the *Rama* in section 10 above.

60. The tastes of milk and meat are thus emitted into the water and then are absorbed into the outer layer of the vessels, thereby making them forbidden.

61. Even when permitting the vessels in cases of loss, it is best to wait 24 hours to use them, since there is a question of a Torah prohibition during this time (according to the *Shach* and *Pri Chadash* mentioned in note כו).

כו. See the *Shach* [paragraph 20] in chapter 95 and the *Pri Chadash* paragraph 17 who are stringent even when there is a great loss.

And the *Pri Megadim* has written that if one cooked water in a [meat] pot which was not used on that day and inserted a dairy spoon which was used on that day, even if there is not sixty times the spoon [in the pot], the pot is permissible, for since the water is to be spilled out, there is no [prohibition] due to appearance sake.

12. If one poured [hot] water, which had not [absorbed taste] of milk nor of meat, onto vessels of meat and milk together, whether both of them had fat adhering to them, or whether one was clean and one had fat adhering to it, or whether both of them were clean—in a situation of great loss one can be lenient and say that even though pouring [hot liquid from a "first vessel"] cooks the width of the peel,[57] nevertheless, before the fat is melted and [the poured water] causes absorption and emission [of the tastes, the heat caused by] the pouring has already dissipated and [everything] has the rule of a second vessel.[58] However, without a great loss, one should not be lenient, even if both of them were clean, as it is not a case of [permissible] secondary transmitted taste because the emissions of both of them are mixed together,[59] and it is established for us that pouring cooks by the width of the peel.[60] And it is my opinion that in all cases, it is proper to rule that one should refrain from using these vessels until after 24 hours, in order that there should be no concern regarding a Torah prohibition [of meat and milk].[61][כו]

13. If one poured [hot] water from a clean meat vessel which was used on that day onto a dairy [vessel] which was used on that day, according to the letter of the law it is completely permitted. There is no question [that it is permitted] according to the opinion of the *Bais Yosef* in the *Shulchan Aruch*,[62] but even according to our custom which

Yad Adam

13. Pouring Water from Meat to Dairy Vessels, or from Forbidden to Permitted Vessels

62. See sections 6 and 7 above, that even if the vessels were present together in a pot of hot water, they would be permissible.

אפי׳ למנהגינו לאסור כששני הפליטות מתערבים יחד זה לא שייך בעירה[63] והוי נ״ט בר נ״ט ומ״מ במקום שאין הפסד יש לאסור[64] דחשבינן כאלו הנצוק הזה המקלח מכלי לכלי מחבר יחד ב׳ הפליטות ומתערבין זה בזה[כז] ואינו אלא חומרא[כח] אבל המערה מים מכלי איסור לכלי היתר אסור דבאיסור ל״ש נ״ט בר נ״ט כמבואר לקמן סי׳ י״ז ומ״מ אפי׳ בכלי של איסור אין אסור אלא אותו כלי שהקילוח של עירוי עליו[65][כט]

יד. ואם בשלו דבש במחבת של בשר ב״י והריקוהו חם בקערה של חלב ב״י מותר אלא דבזה אפילו בלא הפסד מותר אף למנהגנו בין הדבש ובין הקערה[66] ולא מבעיא במשקה מעד שנעשה מדבש דבזה לכולי עלמא השמנונית נ״ט לפגם אלא אפילו בדבש עצמו דלדעת רמ״א שמנונית אינו נ״ט לפגם מכל מקום מותר כיון די״א דגם בדבש נ״ט לפגם סמכינן על דעת הב״י דלעולם נ״ט בר נ״ט מותר.[ל][לא]

טו. כל זה שכתבנו בהדחה שאוסר דוקא אם הדיח במים נקיים אבל אם נתנו אפר במים חמין שבירורה קודם שרחץ הכלים

כז. שם ט״ז ס״ק י״ג.
כח. שם כו״פ ועי׳ בש״ך שם ס״ק ה׳ בשם מ״צ.
כט. ש״ך ס״ק י״ח ועיין לקמן כלל נ״ט.
ל. צ״ד סעיף ט׳ ובש״ך שם.
לא. ולפ״ז י״ל בקדירה שבשלו בה בשר היום ועבר עליו כל הלילה ולמחר בשלו בה ירקות ונתנו בה כף חולבת ב״י אע״ג שלא עבר עדיין על הקדירה כ״ד שעות מבישול הבשר מותר אפילו אין בו ס׳ כיון דל״א דלינת לילה פוגמת** סמכינן ע״ד ב״י דנ״ט בנ״ט מותר כנלע״ד.

יד אדם

63. In section 10, it has been explained that the *Rama* is strict and rules that when secondary emissions of meat and milk are entering into a liquid at the same time, the liquid, as well as the vessels in it, become forbidden. The case here, however, is different. We are taking water with secondary meat taste from a meat vessel and are pouring it into a dairy vessel. This is analogous to the fish which has been cooked in a meat pot mentioned in section 1—if it becomes mixed with milk, the mixture is permissible.

64. Even though according to the letter of the law, everything is permissible, it is customary to prohibit the vessel for the reason stated below. Thus, if the vessel can be kashered, it is proper to kasher it before using it again. This ruling applies only to the vessel upon which the water was poured. The vessel from which the liquid was poured is permitted in any case. (*Taz* 95:13) What is the status of the liquid itself? The liquid should be discarded unless there will be a great loss (*Maadanei Hashulchan* 95:62).

See also the end of section 1, where it is mentioned that in cases of urgency one may pour hot liquids from meat to dairy vessels, especially if one allows the liquid to cool off somewhat.

65. If the forbidden liquid falls on one vessel and splashes onto a nearby vessel, the latter remains permissible. Since it is considered to

is to prohibit [vessels in which] the two emissions [of meat and milk] are mixed together, this [prohibition] does not apply to pouring,[63] as it is secondary transmitted taste [in the water and the vessels remain permitted]. Even so, in a case where there is no loss, it is proper to prohibit [the vessel][64] for we regard it as if this stream that flows from one vessel to the other connects the two emissions and mixes them together,[כז] but this is only a stringency.[כח] However, if one pours [hot] water from a forbidden vessel into a permitted vessel, [the permitted vessel] becomes forbidden, because regarding forbidden taste [the leniency of] secondary transmitted taste does not apply as [explained] later on in section 17. Nevertheless, even with a vessel that is forbidden, only that vessel upon which the stream [directly falls] becomes forbidden.[65][כט]

14. If one cooked honey in a meat pot which was used that day [for meat] and emptied it out while hot into a dairy plate which was used that day [for dairy], it is permissible, but in this case it is permissible even without a loss, even according to our custom, both the honey and the plate.[66] And there is no question [that this leniency applies] with regard to the drink [called] mead which is made from honey—for in this case according to everyone the grease imparts a detrimental taste [to it]—but even regarding honey itself, where according to the opinion of the *Rama* grease does not impart detrimental taste [to it], nevertheless, it is permissible; for since some say that even in honey it imparts a detrimental taste, we [can be lenient and] rely on the opinion of the *Bais Yosef* that a secondary transmitted taste is always permissible.[לא][ל]

15. All this [which] we have written regarding washing which makes [vessels] forbidden [applies] only if one washed with clean water. However, if one placed ashes in hot water in the large pot

כז. *Taz* there (chapter 95, paragraph 13.

כח. *Kreisi u'pleisi* there. And refer to the *Shach* there (chapter 95) in paragraph 5 in the name of the *Masas Binyamin*.

כט. *Shach* (chapter 95) paragraph 18, and see later on, topic 59 [section 2].

ל. *Shulchan Aruch* 94:9 and *Shach* there.

לא. And according to this,* it is proper to say that if one cooked meat in a pot today and it was left over through the entire night and the next day he cooked green vegetables in it and inserted into it a dairy spoon used on that day, even though 24 hours had not yet passed since cooking the meat in the pot, [everything] is permissible, even if there is not sixty [times the spoon in the contents of the pot] for since some authorities say that staying overnight spoils [the taste in the pot],** [in this case] we can rely on the opinion of the *Bais Yosef* that secondary transmitted taste is permissible. So it appears according to my humble opinion.

Yad Adam

*That we are lenient and rely on the *Bais Yosef* to permit a secondary transmitted taste when there are other grounds to be lenient.

** I.e., we do not generally accept this lenient opinion. (Compare with topic 46, section 8.)

be a "second vessel" there will be no transfer of taste.

14. Honey Cooked in a Meat Pot

66. The reason for the leniency is explained below—that the taste of meat is detrimental to the honey. See topic 54, section 16.

15. Leniencies That Apply When Ashes Are Present in the Water

לב. ל״ה סעיף ד׳.
לג. שם ובט״ז.

אע״פ שהשומן דבוק בהן מותר דע״י האפר נ״ט לפגם[לב] ועיין לעיל כלל מ״ה סי׳ י״ז.

טז. אם נמצא כלי חולבת בין כלי בשר לא אמרינן מסתמא הודחו יחד[67] דהוי ס״ס שמא לא הודחו יחד ואת״ל שהודחו יחד שמא לא היתה ב״י[68] ולכן אפי׳ רגילין באותו בית להדיח תמיד בכלי ראשון[69] מותר.[לג]

קדרה של חלב שבשלו בה מים תוך מעל״ע ואחר כך בשלו בה בשר ועדיין הוא בתוך מעל״ע של בישול החלב ואם כן לכולי עלמא צריך שיהי׳ בו ס׳ בבשר נגד כל הקדרה אם אינו יודע כמה חלב בלע ואם יודע כמה חלב בלע[70] אין צריך ס׳ רק נגד החלב שבלע[71] כדלעיל כלל מ״ו[72] דאף על גב שבישל בו מים תוך מעל״ע ולא היה במים ס׳ נגד החלב לא אמרינן שנחשוב כל המים לחלב ויצטרך ס׳ נגד כל המים דכיון דאינו אלא נ״ט בר נ״ט החלב בקדרה והקדרה במים ועדיין כולו היתר ובדבר היתר ל״א חנ״נ כדלעיל כלל מ״ד[73] ולפיכך א״צ לשער בבשר רק שיהיה ס׳ נגד החלב שבלע הקדרה.

יד אדם

16. Dairy Vessels Found Among Meat Vessels; Laws Concerning a Vessel Used to Cook Meat and Dairy Foods Where a Pareve Food Was Cooked in Between

67. We do not conclude that the vessels have been washed together and have thereby become forbidden.

68. Perhaps the meat vessels were not used on that day so that they transmit only a detrimental taste. We have learned previously that in certain situations, it is proper to be lenient if a double doubt is present (topic 45, section 3).

69. The vessels are washed in hot water inside a vessel which was heated by the fire.

70. I.e., he knows how much milk he cooked in the pot during the past 24 hours; this will be the maximum amount of taste the pot could have absorbed.

71. For example, if he knows that only a few drops of milk were cooked in the pot, he needs only sixty times these few drops (and he will not need sixty times the material of the pot).

72. (Sections 1 and 2 there.) The fact that water was cooked in the pot in between the cooking of the meat and dairy food will not affect the situation, as the *Chochmas Adam* goes on to explain.

73. In this situation, the "piece" is the water: We do not say that the water became

לב. *Shulchan Aruch* 95:4.
לג. *Ibid.* (*Rama* 95:3), and in the *Taz* [paragraph 14].

before he washed the vessels [in it], even though there is fat adhering to them, they are permitted, for as a result of the ashes [each of them] imparts a detrimental taste,[לב] and see above, topic 45, section 17.

16. If dairy vessels are found among meat vessels, we do not say that they were probably washed together,[67] because there is a double doubt: Perhaps they were not washed together, and [even] if you say they were washed together, perhaps they were not used on that day.[68] Therefore, even if it is customary in that house to wash all the time in a "first vessel"[69] [the vessels] are permitted.[לג]

If one cooked water in a dairy pot within 24 hours [of cooking milk in it], and afterwards cooked meat in it and it is still within 24 hours of cooking the milk, as such, according to all authorities it is necessary that there be in the meat sixty times the entire pot if he does not know how much milk it absorbed; and if he knows how much milk it absorbed[70] he needs only sixty times the milk which it absorbed,[71] in accordance with [what was noted] above in topic 46.[72] Even though he cooked water in it during the 24 hour period and the water was not sixty times the milk, we do not say that we are to regard all of the water as milk and require sixty times all of the water. This is because there is only secondary transmitted taste [in the water–the taste of] the milk [is transmitted] into the pot and [then from] the pot into the water–and still all of it is permitted matter, and with something that is permitted matter we do not say that a piece becomes inherently forbidden, as [noted] above in topic 44.[73] Therefore, with regard to the meat, it is necessary that it measure only sixty times the milk that the pot absorbed.

Yad Adam

inherently forbidden and should be considered as if it were completely milk. If we did conclude this, then we would need sixty times the water if the amount of water cooked in the pot was more than the milk. ⟦Although the *Chochmas Adam* concludes there (in topic 44 section 6, and also in topic 46 section 7) that one should not rely on this leniency (to say that a piece does not become inherently forbidden when dealing with cooked mixtures of liquids) except where there is a great loss–in this case, where only secondary transmitted taste is involved, it is possible that one can be lenient even without a great loss. See the end of section 18 below, and the *Issur v'heter* 24:8.⟧

ואם חזר ובישל בו בשר לאחר מעל״ע מבישול החלב אע״פ שהוא בתוך מעל״ע של בישול המים המאכל מותר דחשבינן לקדרה כאינו ב״י ולא חשבינן מבישול המים[לד] ואפילו בישל דבר חריף בקדרה ב״י של בשר ואחר מעל״ע מבישול הבשר בישל בו חלב אע״פ שהוא עדיין בתוך מעל״ע מבישול החריף וקיימא לן דבדבר חריף עושה הבלוע לשבח[74] אפי׳ הכי מותר החלב שהרי גבי מים שחיממו בתוך מעל״ע היה נמי לשבח ואפ״ה מותר מטעם נ״ט בר נ״ט.[75][לה][לו]

וכן אם בישל דבר חריף בקדרה של בשר שאב״י ואחר כך[76] בישלו בה חלב בתוך מעל״ע המאכל מותר דלא אמרינן חריפות הראשון עושה שמפליט עכשיו לשבח[77][לז] אבל אם בישל דבר חריף בקדרה של בשר שאב״י ותחבו בו כף[78] של חלב ב״י צריך ס׳ לבטל הכף שהרי יש בו טעם בשר לשבח ונמצא ב׳ טעמים מתערבים יחד[79] ואם יש ס׳ בקדרה המאכל והקדרה מותר והכף אסור.[לח]

לד. סימן ל״ד סעיף ו׳.

לה. סימן קכ״ב בש״ך ס״ק ג׳.

לו. ואף על גב דהחריף מוליא גוף הטעם כדלקמן כלל מ״ט סימן א׳ מכל מקום מה שנבלע עתה בקדירה מן החריף אינו רק טעם קלוש אף על גב דבודאי אין במה שבקדירה ס׳ נגד הכלי מ״מ נקלש טעם הבשר הרבה. וכעין זה נזכר גם בט״ז.

לז. שם.

לח. וכללא הוא דדבר חריף משוי לשבח מה שנפלט מן הקדרה לתוכו אבל אינו עושה לשבח הבלוע בקדרה ואע״פ שעכשיו ג״כ נבלע החריפות בתוך הקדרה מ״מ אינו נבלע בתוכו רק טעם קלוש היינו נ״ט בר נ״ט.

יד אדם

74. The sharp food will change a detrimental taste (one that is more than 24 hours old) which has been absorbed in a vessel to a beneficial one. This concept is explained in topic 49, section 1. As such, the beneficial taste of meat will remain in the pot for another 24 hours.

75. In the case where water was heated in the pot, the water indeed absorbed beneficial taste from the milk cooked previously. Nevertheless, we do not say that any meat subsequently cooked in this pot must contain sixty times the water. Rather, it is permissible if it contains sixty times the milk. Why are we lenient to say this? It is because the water contains only a secondary taste from milk (the taste was first transferred to the pot and then into the water, and it is still in a permissible state), and when the milk taste will again be absorbed back into the pot, it will have been considerably weakened. The same reasoning will apply when sharp food is cooked in a meat pot and then milk is cooked in it. Even though the taste of the meat in the sharp food will be beneficial, nevertheless, the milk later cooked in the pot will not have to be sixty times the sharp food, but only sixty times the meat which was present. (See also note לו. In the case of forbidden taste, however, the rule is different, as noted below in sections 17 and 18.)

76. After emptying out the sharp food.

77. It is true that the meat taste in the sharp

And if one went on and cooked meat in it after 24 hours from cooking the milk, even though it is within 24 hours of cooking the water, the food is permissible, for we regard the pot as if it were not used that day and we do not consider from [the time of] cooking the water.לד And even if one cooked a sharp food in a pot which was used that day for meat and after 24 hours from cooking the meat he cooked milk in it, even though it is still within 24 hours of cooking the sharp food—[although] it is established for us that a sharp food changes what is absorbed to make it beneficial[74]—even so, the milk is permissible; for with respect to the water [in the previous case] which he heated within 24 hours [of cooking milk, the milk taste] was also beneficial and even so [the meat] is permissible because there is [only] secondary absorbed taste [of milk].[75]לה לו

And similarly, if one cooked a sharp food in a meat pot which was not used that day [for meat] and afterwards[76] he cooked dairy in it within 24 hours, the [dairy] food is permissible, as we do not say that the original sharpness causes that it should now emit beneficial [taste].[77]לז However, if he cooked a sharp food in a meat pot which was not used on that day and inserted a dairy spoon into it[78] which was used on the day, it is necessary to have sixty [in the pot] to nullify the spoon, for [the sharp food] contains beneficial taste of meat, and it is found that the two tastes mix together.[79] And if there is sixty [times the spoon] in the [contents of the] pot, the food and the pot are permissible and the spoon is forbidden.לח

לד. *Shulchan Aruch* 94:6.
לה. Chapter 122 in the *Shach* paragraph 2.
לו. And even though the sharp food causes the emission of the "embodied taste" as [explained] further on in topic 49 section 1, nevertheless, what [remains] absorbed now in the pot from the sharp food (while cooking the milk) is only a weakened taste. Even though certainly the contents of the pot are not sixty times the vessel, nevertheless, [the milk is permissible if it is sixty times the meat, since] the taste of the meat has been weakened very much [after being transferred from the pot into the sharp food and back into the pot]. And something similar to this is mentioned in the *Taz*.
לז. *Ibid.* (*Shach* 122:2)
לח. [This is in accordance with topic 46, section 8.]
The rule is that a sharp food makes beneficial what was emitted from the pot into [the sharp food], but it does not make beneficial what [remains] absorbed in the pot; and even though now also the sharpness is absorbed in the pot, nevertheless, only weakened taste [of meat] is absorbed in it, that is, secondary absorbed taste. [Therefore, once the sharp food is removed, the pot will no longer emit a beneficial taste of meat.]

Yad Adam

food will be beneficial, due to the property of sharp food to change a detrimental taste into a beneficial taste. However, after the sharp food is removed from the pot, the sharp taste which remains absorbed in the pot is not sufficient to cause the absorbed meat taste (which has been considerably weakened) to be emitted as a beneficial taste. (See note לח.)

78. The spoon was inserted directly into the sharp food.

79. And a forbidden mixture results in accordance with section 10 above. Even though the taste of meat which is absorbed into the sharp food is more than 24 hours old, the sharpness makes the taste absorbed

לט. כו"פ סי' ל"ד ועיין כ"ז כלל כ"ה.

יז. כל מה שכתבנו להתיר מטעם נ"ט בר נ"ט זה שייך דוקא בבו"ח כדגים שנתבשלו ביורה של בשר ב"י לאכול אותם בחלב דכיון דנקלש טעמו של בשר כ"כ מתחלה ביורה ואחר כך בדגים וא"כ כשמניח הדגים אח"כ בחלב רותח אין בו כח שיחול עליו שם בו"ח שטעם הבשר נקלש אבל בשאר איסורין ל"ש כלל לומר נ"ט בר נ"ט ואסור ולכן קדירה של איסור ובתוך מעל"ע חימם בו מים[80] ואחר כך בישל בו היתר[81] אם היה בתוך מעל"ע של חימום המים אע"פ שכבר עבר מעת לעת מבישול האיסור אסור[82] דכיון דנפלט האיסור במים בתוך מעל"ע הוא משובח וחוזר ונבלע בכלי[83] ולכן חשבינן משעת החימום.[לט]

יח. ולכן לדעת רמ"א דבכל איסורין נ"נ[84] א"כ נעשו כל המים נבלה[85] וכשחוזר ובישל בתוך מע"ל של חימום המים צריך ס' נגד כל המים[86] ואין לך כלי שיהיה בו ס' נגד הכלי והכל אסור אבל לדעת הב"י דלא אמרינן חנ"נ בשאר איסורין אע"ג דל"ש נ"ט

יד אדם

into it beneficial. When the dairy spoon is then inserted into the food, a forbidden mixture results and everything will be forbidden.

17. Transmission of Forbidden Secondary Taste

80. If a pot was used to cook unkosher meat and within 24 hours it was used to heat water. (See also topic 55, section 4 that one can be lenient if the pot was left overnight.)

81. The water was emptied out and permissible food was cooked in the same pot.

82. The permissible food now in the pot is forbidden, even after the fact.

83. If the absorbed taste was milk or meat, we would be lenient with regard to the taste reabsorbed into the vessel, as noted in the previous section. This leniency does not apply here where a forbidden taste is absorbed. This is because the water here is not regarded to be merely water with absorbed forbidden taste. Rather, the water is considered to be a primary forbidden substance with a strong taste, and it is as if a new forbidden substance is being absorbed into the vessel. The discussion of this concept continues in section 18.

18. Stringencies Which Apply to Transmission of Forbidden Secondary Taste According to the Rama

84. The principle applies to forbidden mixtures, as well as to mixtures of meat and milk. Refer to topic 44, section 7.

85. I.e., we must regard the entire volume of water which was cooked in the forbidden

לט. *Kreisi u'pleisi* chapter 94, and see all of this [covered below] in topic 55.

17. Wherever we have written that one can permit [a vessel or food based on] the reason that the taste is secondarily transmitted, this is applicable only to meat and milk. For example, if fish were cooked in a meat pot which had been used on that day, [it is permissible] to eat them with milk. Since the taste of the meat has weakened so much, first [being transmitted] into the pot and afterwards into the fish, as such, when one places the fish afterwards into hot milk, there is not a strong enough [taste of meat] in the fish such that the name of "meat and milk" should apply to it, because the taste of the meat has weakened. However, regarding other forbidden foods it is not applicable at all to say that a taste is secondarily transmitted [and use this as grounds for leniency], and [food absorbing such taste] is forbidden. Therefore, if a forbidden pot was used within 24 hours to heat water[80] and afterwards one cooked permissible food in it,[81] if it was within 24 hours of heating the water, even though 24 hours already elapsed since cooking the forbidden food, it is forbidden,[82] for since [the taste of] the forbidden food was emitted into the water within 24 hours, it is beneficial, and it goes on and is reabsorbed into the vessel [from the water].[83] Therefore, we figure [the 24 hours] from the time of heating [the water].[לט]

18. Therefore, according to the opinion of the *Rama* that with regard to all forbidden foods [we say that whatever absorbs forbidden taste] becomes inherently forbidden,[84] as such, all of the water becomes forbidden[85] and when he goes on and cooks within 24 hours of heating the water, it is required to have sixty times all of the water;[86] and there is no vessel which will have in [its contents] sixty times the vessel, and everything will be forbidden. However, according to the opinion of the *Bais Yosef* that we do not say that a piece becomes inherently forbidden with regard to other forbidden foods, even though

Yad Adam

pot (mentioned in section 17) as consisting entirely of forbidden substance.

86. If he later cooks permissible food in the same pot, it will not be sufficient for the pot to contain sixty times the forbidden food which had been present. Rather, if the volume of the water was greater than the volume of the forbidden food, then sixty times the water will be required. This would be the case if the volume of water was less than (or equal to) the substance of the pot. If

מ. ועיין כו״פ שם. מא. סי׳ ק״ג בש״ך ס״ק כ׳ ועיין היטיב בבל״י סימן קכ״ב ס״ק ב׳ חילוקי דינים בזה ומה שמגיה ג״כ בש״ך.

בר נ״ט באיסור וא״כ נאסרו המים מ״מ אם היה האיסור כזית ואחר כך חימם מים רק נ״ט זית וא״כ נאסרו המים[87] אבל לא נעשו נבלה לשיטה זו אלא שאסורים מטעם דל״א נ״ט בר נ״ט באיסור מ״מ כשחוזר ונבלע בקדירה אינו נבלע אלא לפי שיעור וא״כ אע״ג דחשבינן מע״ל משעת החימום[88] מ״מ נ״מ דלדעת המחבר א״צ בתבשיל רק ס׳ נגד האיסור ולרמ״א צריך ס׳ נגד כל המים.[מ]

וה״ה אם היה קדירה של איסור ובשלו בו לאחר מע״ל דבר חריף דקיימא לן דאגב חורפיה משוי ליה לבלוע לשבח ואחר כך בתוך מע״ל לבישול השני[89] בישל בו דבר היתר שאסור אע״ג שכבר עבר מע״ל מבישול הראשון כן משמע בש״ך סימן קכ״ב דבישול דבר חריף לאחר מע״ל נעשה כבישול מים בתוך מע״ל.

ומ״מ במקום הפסד קצת יש להקל בכל זה ולחשוב מע״ל רק מבישול איסור כיון דלא בלע מגוף האיסור[90] ובלא״ה לרוב הפוסקים ל״א חנ״נ בשאר איסור וכ״ש בלח בלח כדלעיל כלל מ״ד סימן ט׳.[91][מא]

יד אדם

the volume of water is greater than this amount, then sixty times the substance of the pot will be required. However, THERE IS NO VESSEL...

87. Unless the volume of water is sixty times the size of an olive.

88. Both according to the *Bais Yosef* and the *Rama*, the 24 hour period should be measured from the time the water was cooked, and not from the time the forbidden food was cooked in the pot. This is because water which contains forbidden taste is like a primary forbidden entity, and when cooking such forbidden water, the time must be measured from the time of this cooking.

89. Within 24 hours of cooking the sharp food in the pot. (We are more strict here than in the case of section 16, because there we are cooking a permissible sharp food in a pot with absorbed meat or dairy taste, whereas here, the sharp food itself has become a forbidden entity.)

90. Rather, the water absorbed only the taste of the forbidden food which had been absorbed into the pot. As such, as long as the forbidden food was cooked in the pot more than 24 hours ago, there are grounds to permit the food presently in the pot.

91. It is explained there that some authorities do not say that "a piece becomes inherently forbidden" when a taste is dispersed throughout a liquid. As such, there are grounds to be lenient here when the absorbed forbidden taste in the pot is dis-

מ. And refer to the *Kreisi u'pleisi* there.
מא. *Shach* 103:20. And look carefully in the *Bais Lechem Yehudah*, chapter 122, paragraph 2 regarding different laws in this matter, and what he corrects in [the text of] the *Shach*. [The correction to which the *Chochmas Adam* is referring is also mentioned in the current edition of the *Shulchan Aruch* in the *Nekudas Hakesef* there. The *Aruch Hashulchan* (122:9), however, explains that it is not necessary to make this correction.]

[the leniency of] a secondary transmitted taste does not apply to forbidden food and as such the water becomes forbidden, nevertheless, if the forbidden food [cooked in the pot on that day] was the size of an olive, and afterwards he heated water [in that pot], it emits only an olive-size of taste [into the water]. As such, the water becomes forbidden,[87] but does not become inherently forbidden according to this opinion, but it is forbidden due to the reason that we do not say secondary transmitted taste [is permissible] with regard to a forbidden food. Consequently, when [the taste] goes on and is re-absorbed into the pot, it is absorbed only according to the measure [of forbidden food]. As such, even though we figure the 24 hours from the time of heating [the water],[88] still, there is a [practical] difference [between the two opinions] in that according to the *Bais Yosef* it is necessary to have in the cooked food only sixty times the [olive-size of] forbidden matter, [whereas] according to the *Rama* it is necessary to have sixty times all of the water.[מ]

And the rule is the same if the pot was forbidden and one cooked a sharp food in it after 24 hours [following the cooking of the forbidden food], as it is established for us that because of its sharpness, [a sharp food] makes what is absorbed beneficial. [Therefore,] if afterwards, within 24 hours of the second cooking[89] he cooked permissible food in it, it becomes forbidden, even though 24 hours had elapsed since the first cooking. So it is implied in the *Shach* chapter 122, that cooking something sharp after 24 hours is like cooking water during the 24 hours.

Nevertheless, in cases involving a little loss, one can be lenient with all this and figure the 24 hours only from the cooking of the forbidden food, since [the water] did not absorb from the forbidden food itself.[90] And [even] without this [reason we can be lenient, since] according to most authorities we do not say that a piece becomes inherently forbidden with other forbidden foods and certainly where it involves liquid with liquid [we can be lenient], as [noted] previously in topic 44, section 9.[91][מא]

Yad Adam

persed into water and rule that in the final cooking, only sixty times the original unkosher food (mentioned in note 80) need be present.

כלל מט

דין מאכל חריף שנחתך או שנתבשל בסכין של בשר או של איסור

(סימן צ"ו)

א. נ"ט בר נ"ט[1] ונטל"פ[2] לא שייך בדברים החריפים דאגב החריפות עושה מה שבלוע בכלי לשבח וגם עדיף מנ"ט בר נ"ט דמחמת החריפות ודוחקא דסכינא מוציא מן הכלי גוף הטעם שבו[3] ועדיף מאלו נתבשל בו[4] דאפילו לדעת המתירין נ"ט בר נ"ט ע"י בישול כדלעיל בכלל הקודם[5] מ"מ בדברים חריפים מוציא עיקר הטעם ואפי' בדיעבד אוסר אם חתכו בסכין של בשר צנון וכיוצא ונתנו בחלב[6] ומ"מ אם טעמו ישראל ואמר שאין בו טעם בדיעבד מותר וסמכינן על טעימתו.

יד אדם

1. Stringencies Which Apply to Sharp Foods

1. In certain instances we say that a secondary transmitted taste will not make a food or vessel forbidden because the taste has been weakened. For example, if eggs were cooked in a meat pot and they are later mixed with milk, the mixture will be permissible. The reason for this leniency is that the eggs did not absorb the meat taste directly from the meat; rather, the taste was first transmitted from the meat into the pot and then from the pot into the eggs. (See topic 48, section 1.) However, when sharp foods are involved, this leniency does not apply due to the increase in transmission of taste into sharp food (see below).

In section 4 below, the *Chochmas Adam* will mention which foods are to be regarded as sharp.

2. Ordinarily, we say that an absorbed forbidden taste which has been present in a vessel more than 24 hours becomes spoiled (detrimental). As such, if it is transmitted into another food it can no longer make that other food forbidden. (See topic 54.) This leniency does not apply to the taste transmitted into sharp foods, since sharp foods change a detrimental taste and make it beneficial.

The *Rambam* rules differently—although sharp foods do cause an increase in transmission of taste, they do not generally change a detrimental taste into a beneficial taste. Rather, according to the *Rambam*, only the

Topic 49

Laws Concerning Sharp Food Which Was Cut with a Meat Knife or Forbidden Knife, Or Which Was Cooked [in a Meat Vessel or a Forbidden Vessel]

(based on *Shulchan Aruch—Yoreh Deah* chapter 96)

1. [The leniencies normally allowed with] secondary transmitted taste[1] and transmission of a spoiled taste[2] are not applicable with [regard to] sharp foods. [Rather,] due to their sharpness, [any taste] which had been absorbed into a vessel becomes beneficial. And [sharp foods] also supersede [the leniencies allowed with] secondary transmitted taste, since [their] sharpness and the pressure of the knife [while cutting them] causes emission from the utensil of the "embodied taste" that is in it.[3] And the [emission] is more than if [ordinary food] were cooked with it;[4] for even according to those who permit secondary transmitted taste which occurs through cooking, as [noted] previously in the above topic,[5] nevertheless, sharp foods cause emission of the main component of the taste, and will cause a prohibition even after the fact if, [for example,] one were to cut radish or something similar with a meat knife and place [the radish] in milk.[6] Nevertheless, if a Jewish person tasted it and stated that there is no taste [of meat] in it, it is permissible after the fact and we rely on his tasting.

Yad Adam

sharp food known as *chiltis* (discussed in section 4 below) has this property. (See the *Aruch Hashulchan* 96:2-3.)

3. Therefore, we regard the taste emitted by the vessel as if it were emitted directly by the food itself.

4. The *Chochmas Adam* is explaining that cutting a sharp food, such as a radish, with a meat knife will result in more absorption into the food than cooking an ordinary food (such as fish) in a meat pot.

5. It is the opinion of the *Bais Yosef* in the *Shulchan Aruch* (mentioned in topic 48, section 1) that to begin with, one may take fish which had been cooked in a meat pot and mix it with milk.

6. A radish which was cut with a meat knife contains secondary taste of meat, as the taste

וה"ה אם בישל דבר חריף בקדירה[7] אפילו אב"י[8] וכן אם דכו תבלין או שחתכו בסכין של בשר ונתנו בחלב[9] וה"ה בחתכו בסכין של איסור או שדכו מלח במדוך של בשר או במדוך של איסור[10] ובזה כ"ע מודים כיון שהמדוכה והסכין בלעו מהאיסור בעין.[11]

ב. מדינא אינו אוסר רק כדי נטילה דמחמת החריפות אינו מתפשט הטעם יותר מכדי נטילה[12] וכן סתם הב"י בש"ע אבל אנו נוהגין כרמ"א לאסור לכתחלה כשחתך בסכין של בשר צנון וכיוצא בו אסור לאכלו כולו בחלב דחיישינן לדעת הפוסקים דס"ל דהטעם מתפשט בכולו ומ"מ בדיעבד אם כבר נתבשל[13] סמכינן על

יד אדם

is first transferred from the meat into the knife and then from the knife into the radish. Nevertheless, when dealing with sharp food, such secondary transmitted taste can make it forbidden, and therefore, one may not take a radish which was cut with a meat knife and mix it with milk.

There are some authorities who rule that we can be lenient under certain circumstances and permit a secondary transmitted taste in a sharp food. See section 7 below.

7. A sharp food cooked in a pot is to be treated with the same stringencies as sharp food which has been cut with a knife.

8. Since the detrimental taste absorbed in the pot is made beneficial.

9. The mixture will be forbidden if the spice is a sharp food (such as pepper or ginger) even though everything is cold. See section 4 below for other examples.

10. A mortar is a bowl used for crushing spices. We are dealing with a mortar or knife which had been used with hot meat (or hot forbidden food) at some time in the past. Such a mortar or knife will contain absorbed taste of meat (or forbidden food).

11. All agree that the meat taste (or forbidden taste) will be transmitted to the salt or other sharp food. As such, the sharp food processed with the meat utensil may not be mixed with milk, and if processed with a forbidden utensil it will become altogether forbidden. (According to the opinion of the *Rambam* mentioned in note 2, this applies only if the utensil had been used for hot meat or hot forbidden food during that day.)

In summary: Sharp foods are to be treated more stringently than ordinary foods under two different circumstances: One situation involves a sharp food that is cut with a knife (or other utensil) which contains absorbed taste. When this occurs, the pressure from the knife together with the sharpness of the food causes the taste to be emitted from the knife and absorbed into the food, even though the food is cold. The sharpness also causes detrimental taste absorbed in the knife to become beneficial. If sharp food is crushed in a bowl or ground in

And the rule is the same if one cooked something sharp in a pot,[7] even if it had not been used on that day.[8] The same [applies] if one crushed spices or cut [them] with a meat knife and placed them in milk.[9] And the rule is the same if one cut them with a forbidden knife or crushed salt in a meat mortar or with a forbidden mortar;[10] and all authorities agree [to these rulings], since the mortar or the knife have absorbed from intact forbidden food.[11]

2. According to the letter of the law, [absorbed taste in a knife] will prohibit only the outer thickness [of a sharp food which is cut with it]. [When taste is transmitted] due to sharpness the taste cannot spread more than the outer thickness,[12] and this is the conclusion of the *Bais Yosef* in the *Shulchan Aruch*. However, our practice is in accordance with the *Rama* to prohibit [the entire sharp food] to begin with, such that if one cut a radish or something similar to it with a meat knife, it is forbidden to eat all of it with milk, for we are concerned about the opinion of the authorities who rule that taste spreads through all of it. Nevertheless, after the fact, if [the sharp food] was already cooked[13] we rely on the *Shulchan Aruch* and we require only

Yad Adam

a grinder, it has the same status as if it were cut with a knife. The second situation involves a sharp food that is cooked in a pot which contains absorbed taste. In this case, the cooking and the sharpness of the food combine to make any detrimental taste absorbed in the pot become beneficial. (See topic 48, end of section 16.)

In the case of cooking a sharp food in a pot, the effects of sharpness occur only if the sharp food is the main food being cooked. If one adds a little bit of sharp food (such as pepper) to a pot of meat and soup, the stringencies of cooking a sharp food will not apply. (Section 6 below. See also topic 55, section 2.)

2. Penetration of Taste When Cutting a Sharp Food

12. When taste is transmitted due to the presence of sharpness and pressure from a knife, the taste extends only through the outer layer of the food along the cut surface and no deeper than this. We have already mentioned that the thickness of this layer is equal to the width of the thumb at its widest portion.

13. For example, the radish cut with a meat knife was cooked in a pot of milk, and the pot does not contain sixty times the entire radish. When the mixture is cooked, the meat taste in the radish is transmitted into

א. מנ״י כלל ס״א ס״ק י״ח.

הש״ע ואין צריך ס׳ רק כנגד הנטילה[14] ואם הסכין קטן מכדי נטילה או אפילו הסכין גדול אלא שיודע בבירור שלא נגע בכל הסכין רק בקצת ממנו א״צ ס׳ רק נגד מקום הסכין[15] רק מן הסתם אמרינן שחתך בכל הסכין וכן אם חתך הערינג וצנון בסכין של איסור[16] ויש קצת הפסד הסומך לזרוק כדי נטילה ולאכול השאר לא הפסיד[17] דזה נקרא דיעבד[18] דדוקא בחתך בסכין של בשר נוהגין לכתחלה לאסור כולו לאכלו בחלב כיון דאפשר לאכלו עם בשר[19] אבל בסכין של איסור הוי כדיעבד.[א]

ג. בד״א דסגי בנטילה בחתך רק במקום א׳ כגון שהצנון והבצל עדיין שלם ולא חתכו רק במ״א אבל אם חתכו דק דק וא״כ כל חתיכה וחתיכה נאסרה כדי נטילה וצריך ס׳ נגד כל הצנון[20] ואם הסכין קטן מן הצנון א״צ ס׳ אלא נגד הסכין אם הוא בבו״ח אבל אם חתכו דק דק בסכין של איסור להנמשכין אחר רמ״א דאמרינן בכל איסורין חנ״נ[21] וא״כ כל חתיכה וחתיכה נעשה נבלה[22] וא״כ

יד אדם

the milk (and the taste of the milk in the pot is transmitted into the radish). The question now is how much milk must be present in order to nullify the meat taste in the radish. (See also note 25.)

14. It is not necessary for the pot to contain sixty times the entire sharp food. Rather, if the pot contains sixty times the outer thickness along the cut surfaces of the radish, this will be sufficient to nullify the meat taste. This ruling has already been mentioned in topic 44, section 12.

15. This is because the maximum amount of taste transmitted into a sliced food cannot be more than the volume of that portion of the knife-blade which was in contact with it. As such, if it known that only the middle third of the blade was in contact with the radish, then the maximum amount of taste transmitted into the radish will be the volume of the middle third of the blade.

16. Such as a knife which was used to cut hot unkosher meat.

17. He has not acted improperly.

18. It is "after the fact" because the only alternative would be to discard the entire food. One may therefore rely on the lenient authorities in this instance.

19. Thus, a radish cut with a dairy (or meat) knife has the status of "to begin with," as follows: "To begin with" he may eat the entire radish as long as he does not mix any part of it with meat (or milk, respectively). But "after the fact," if the radish is mixed into a pot of meat (or milk) and loss would result, we permit the mixture if sixty times the outer thickness is present.

א. *Minchas Yaakov* 61:11.

sixty times the outer thickness.[14] If [the volume of the blade of] the knife is smaller than the outer thickness [of the food], or even if the knife is large but we know with certainty that [the sharp food] did not come into contact with the entire knife but only a part of it, we require only sixty times that portion of the knife.[15] However, in general, we say that one has cut with all of [the blade of] the knife [unless it is known otherwise]. Similarly, if one cut herring or radish with a forbidden knife[16] and there would be some loss [if the entire food were to be prohibited], one who relies [on the lenient authorities] to throw away the outer thickness and eat the rest does not lose out,[17] as [such a situation] would be called "after the fact";[18] as only when one cut with a meat knife is the practice to prohibit all of it to be eaten with milk, since it is possible to eat it with meat,[19] but with a forbidden knife it is like a case of "after the fact."א

3. When is it so that it is sufficient to remove [the outer thickness]? This is only where he sliced in one place, such as where the radish or onion is still complete except for the one place where he cut it. However, if he sliced it very thinly, and as such, each and every piece becomes forbidden by its outer thickness, we require sixty times all of the radish.[20] But if the knife [blade] is smaller than the radish, we require only sixty times the [volume of the] knife [blade] if there is [absorption of] meat or milk. However, if he sliced it very thinly with a forbidden knife, then according to those who follow the *Rama* who say with regard to all forbidden foods that a piece becomes inherently forbidden,[21] as such, each and every piece becomes inherently forbidden,[22] and therefore we always need sixty times the entire radish if he

Yad Adam

3. A Sharp Food Which Has Been Thinly Sliced by a Forbidden Knife

20. If the radish was sliced like this with a meat knife and it falls into a hot pot of dairy food, we require that the pot contain sixty times the entire radish.

(The *Chochmas Adam* goes on to say that if the knife blade is smaller than the radish, then only sixty times the knife will be required, in accordance with note 15 above. See also note 100 on topic 44 where it is mentioned that according to Rabbi Akiva Eiger, even if the blade is smaller than the radish, sixty times the entire radish will be required. This is because the entire radish will be permeated with the meat or dairy taste.)

21. Topic 44, section 7.

22. The pieces are to be viewed as if they

ב. ט״ך ס״ק ט׳.
ג. פ״ח סק״ח.
ד. ט״ז ס״ק ט׳.

לעולם צריך ס׳ נגד כל הצנון בחתך דק דק[ב] ועיין בכלל מ״ד סי׳ י״ב[23] ולפי מ״ש שם סימן י״ג דלא אמרינן חנ״נ רק דוקא ע״י בישול וא״כ בסכין של איסור נמי אם הסכין קטן אין צריך ס׳ רק נגד הסכין.[ג]

אך זה דוקא לענין התבשיל[24] אבל הבצלים נשארים באיסור מטעם דאפשר לסוחטו אסור[25] כדלעיל כלל מ״ד סי׳ י״ב וילקט הבצלים מהתבשיל מה דאפשר.

ד. לדעת מקצת פוסקים ראשונים לא מקרי דבר חריף רק דוקא קורט של חלתית[26] וי״א גם צנון דזה איתא בגמרא בהדיא דמקרי חריף[27] ודעת הרבה פוסקים וכן סתם בש״ע דאפילו תרדין ושומין ובצלים וכרישין ותמכא (שקורין חריין) וכן חומץ אפילו אינו חזק ובארשט[28] ואפילו אינו חמוץ הרבה עדיין כיון דאיתא לקיוהא דפירי[ד] ודגים מלוחים שקורין הערינג וכן תבלין כגון אינגבער ופירות חמוצים וכיוצא בו כ״ז יש להם דין חריף לכל החומרות ולפיכך אם חתך צנון ושאר דברים מהנזכרים בסכין של

יד אדם

consist entirely of forbidden food. As such, if a radish is thinly sliced with a forbidden knife and it falls into a pot of forbidden food, it will not be sufficient for the pot to contain sixty times the knife blade. Rather, sixty times the entire radish will be required.

23. Additional rules applying to a cut sharp food are discussed there.

The *Chochmas Adam* now goes on to mention that when using a forbidden knife to thinly slice a sharp food, there are grounds to be lenient and permit it if sixty times the knife blade is present. Refer also to the end of section 7 for leniencies which apply in cases of great loss.

24. If the radish or onions were thinly sliced by a forbidden knife and then were mixed into a hot pot of food, then the food in the pot remains permissible if sixty times the sharp food is present (or according to some authorities, sixty times the knife blade if the blade is smaller than the radish).

25. (See note 25 on topic 44 regarding the translation.) However, in the case where a radish was thinly sliced with a meat knife and cooked in milk, then, according to the *Chochmas Adam*, it is not necessary to remove the radish from the mixture if sixty is present. See topic 44, section 12.

4. Which Foods Are Sharp?

26. *Chiltis* is a spice which is commonly used

ב. *Shach* [chapter 96] paragraph 9.
ג. *Pri Chadash* paragraph 8. [Note: The *Pri Megadim* (*Sifsei Da'as* 96:9) discounts this leniency, since the radish will become *nevelah* when it is present in the hot pot of permissible food and thereby becomes cooked.]
ד. *Taz* [chapter 96] paragraph 9.

sliced it very thinly.ב And refer to topic 44, section 12.[23] And according to what is written there in section 13 that [according to some authorities] we do not say that a piece becomes inherently forbidden except by means of cooking, as such, with a forbidden knife also—if the knife is small we will require only sixty times the knife [blade, since the taste entered the radish without being cooked].ג

However, this is only regarding the cooked food,[24] but the [radish or] onions remain in their forbidden state because it is not possible to extract [the forbidden taste from them],[25] as [noted] previously in topic 44, section 12. [Therefore,] one should gather up [and discard] the [radish or] onions as much as possible.

4. According to some early authorities, the term "sharp food" refers only to particles of *chiltis*.[26] And some say also radish [is a sharp food in all respects] as it is explicitly called a sharp food in the *gemara*.[27] But the opinion of many authorities, and also the conclusion of the *Shulchan Aruch*, is that even beets, garlic, onions, leeks, and horseradish (which we call *chrain*) [are all sharp foods] as well as vinegar, even if it is not strong. And borscht[28] [is considered sharp] even if it is still not very fermented, since it has the acrid taste of the "fruit."ד And salted fish which we call herring, and also spices such as ginger, and sour fruits and similar things—all of these have the status of a sharp food with respect to all of the stringencies. Therefore, if one cut radish

Yad Adam

today in Persia, and is called asafetida in English. The particles of *chiltis* are formed by extracting a milky resin from the *chiltis* plant and drying it out.

According to these authorities, only particles of *chiltis* have all the properties of sharp food: They cause an increase in the transmission of taste, and they also change a detrimental taste into a beneficial taste. These authorities rule that there are other foods which are called sharp, but their sharpness is limited: Such sharp foods do cause an increase in the transmission of taste, but they do not change a detrimental taste into a beneficial taste. (This is the opinion of the *Rambam* which is mentioned in note 2.)

27. According to this opinion, radish also has the ability to change a detrimental taste into a beneficial taste, but the other foods mentioned below do not have this property. This is the opinion of Rabbi Yechiel as quoted by the *Bais Yosef*.

28. A drink made from bran and vinegar (topic 55, section 2). Other items which are not mentioned here but which are to be treated as sharp foods include lemon juice, and sour fruits and vegetables (see section

ה. ועיין נב״א סי׳ מ״ע.
ו. ת״ח.

בשר אב״י והוא מקונח אסור לאכלו בחלב וכן אם חתכו בסכין של איסור ודינו כדלעיל[29]ה ובהפ״מ יש להתיר בחומץ שכר או יין שאינו חזק[30] כדעת המ״א בסימן תמ״ז ס״ק כ״ח ונ״ל דלפ״ז ה״ה בארשט שאינו מחומץ הרבה וכ״כ בח״ד שאם יכול לשתותו חי דינו כפירות מחומצים.[31] ואף בדבר שהוא חריף לכ״ע אם לבנו בביצים או נתנו בו מים בטל חורפיה.

ה. ודוקא הצנון עצמו הוא חריף אבל אם חתך הירק מן הצנון[32] וכן זנבות השומים והבצלים ר״ל השרשים שלהם לא נקרא חריף ואפילו לא נשאר מן הירק רק כרוחב קש של חיטים מותר הצנוןו והמנהג לקנות חריין אף שנראה שנחתך דמסתמא תלינן שלא נחתך בסכין אלא במרא וחצינא[33] שכן הדרך ואם ספק שמא נחתך בסכין או ספק אם היה הסכין ב״י או לא[34] וא״א לקנות אחרים שאינם נמצאים קונין אותן וחותכין כדי נטילה שהיא כעובי אצבע[35]

יד אדם

8). Olives are also to be regarded as sharp (as mentioned in note 55). It has been mentioned at the end of section 1 that salt is to be treated as a sharp food.

29. See section 3 above.

30. I.e., that the stringencies of a sharp food need not be applied to them unless the vinegar is very strong.

31. And one need not apply the stringencies of a sharp food to them in cases of great loss, in accordance with section 7 below.

5. Cutting the Roots of a Sharp Food; A Sharp Food Which Was Cut with a Utensil Whose Status Is in Doubt

32. The green stem which grows from the top of the radish plant.

33. Literally, a hoe or a spade.

34. I.e., a forbidden knife had definitely been used but it is uncertain whether the knife was used with forbidden food during the past 24 hours.

It is implied here that if we were certain that the knife had not been used for forbidden food in the past 24 hours, then the horseradish would certainly be permitted if its outer layer is removed (and if no other horseradish is available). In section 1, however, we have learned that most authorities rule that with regard to sharp food, it does not matter whether or not the knife was used during that day, as the food will be forbidden in any case. Why then can we be lenient here? The answer is that here there are other grounds to be lenient: If the knife had definitely not been used for forbidden food in the past 24 hours, the *Rambam*

ח. Refer to the *Binas Adam*, section 49.
ו. *Toras Chatas*

or other things that are mentioned [here] with a meat knife which was not used on that day and it had been wiped clean, it is forbidden to eat it with milk. And similarly, if one cut it with a forbidden knife the rule is as above.[29]ח And in a situation involving a great loss, one can be lenient with beer vinegar or wine vinegar which are not so strong,[30] in accordance with the *Magen Avraham* in chapter 447, paragraph 28. And it is my opinion that accordingly, borscht should have the same rule if it is not strongly fermented, and such is written in the *Chavos Daas* that if one is able to drink it undiluted it has the same rule as sour fruit.[31] And even with something that is sharp, according to everyone, if one whitened it with eggs or placed water into it, its sharpness is nullified.

5. [The stringencies of a sharp food apply] only to the radish itself which is sharp but if one cut the green portion of the radish[32]—or similarly, [if one cuts] the "tails" of garlic or onions, that is, their roots—they are not called sharp. And even if nothing is left from the green portion [after being cut with a forbidden knife] except for the size of the width of a stalk of wheat, the radish is permissible.ו The custom is [to permit one] to purchase horseradish even though it appears to have been cut, because we assume that it probably was not cut with a knife but with a garden tool[33] as this is the usual way [it is cut]. And if there is a doubt whether it was cut with a [forbidden] knife, or there is a doubt whether the knife was used that day or not[34] and it is impossible to purchase others since they are not available, one may purchase them and cut off their outer thickness, which is the thickness of a finger.[35] For since there is a doubt, we rely on the

Yad Adam

would rule that the sharp food is completely permissible, since only *chiltis* is sharp in all respects (as mentioned in note 2). Furthermore, even if we are not to accept the *Rambam's* opinion, there is another authority (Rabbi Yechiel, mentioned as the second opinion in section 4) who rules that vegetables such as horseradish are not sharp in all respects. (He rules that only *chiltis* and radish fit this category, and they alone have the ability to change a detrimental taste into a beneficial taste.) When the knife has not been used for 24 hours and there are therefore already grounds to be lenient (based on the *Rambam* and Rabbi Yechiel), we can at least rely on the opinion of the *Shulchan Aruch* and permit the sharp food if its outer thickness has been removed.

35. Specifically, it is equivalent to the width of the thumb.

דכיון דיש ספק סמכינן על דעת הש״ע דאינו אוסר יותר מכ״נ[36] אבל אם אפשר לקנות שאינם נחתכים נוהגין לאסור כולו.[י]

וצנון שחתכו וידוע שהסכין היה ב״י אלא שמסופק אם חתכו בו[37] כתב הש״ך דאזלינן לחומרא דדוקא בחריין די״א דלא מקרי חריף[38] מקילינן ומשמע מדבריו דכולו אסור[ח] וצריך לדקדק בבצלים כי הרבה שחותכין הזנבות וזה ודאי נעשה ע״י סכין ולכן אסור לקנות א״ל שנשאר כרוחב קש.[39]

ו. הא דדגים מלוחים נקרא חריף דוקא הערינג אבל שאר דגים שנמלחו לא מקרי חריף ולכן אם חתכם בסכין של איסור סגי בגרירה בעלמא[40] וכן בכל החריפים לא נקרא המאכל חריף בשביל מעט מלח או תבלין שיש בו אלא דוקא אם כולו או רובו הוא חריף.[ט]

ז. פירות החמוצים אע״ג דכתבנו דהוי חריף מ״מ במקום הפסד יש להקל דהא י״א דדוקא חלתית הוי חריף[41] ועכ״פ נ״ל דיש להקל בדברים שאינם חריפים וחמוצים הרבה אם חתכו בסכין שאב״י ולסמוך על הפוסקים דס״ל דאפילו בצנון אינו אוסר רק דוקא ב״י[42] ובמקום הפ״מ אפשר דיש לסמוך אפילו בב״י ולסמוך

ז. מה שהק׳ הכו״פ נעמיד הצנון על חזקת היתר צ״ע שהרי בסימן קי״א בקדרה א׳ וב׳ אחי׳ באיסור תורה אסור דע״י נפילה אתרע חזקתו.

ח. וצ״ע דהא עכ״פ דעת הש״ע דאפי׳ בצנון אינו אוסר יותר מכ״נ וא״כ בספק אם חתכו בו ג״כ יש להתיר עכ״פ לאחר שיעור כ״נ שהרי לדעת הש״ע מותר.

ט. סי׳ צ״ה סעיף ב׳.

י. ט״ז ס״ק ח׳ ט׳.

יד אדם

36. Another case where we can be lenient with horseradish is where the knife in question was definitely forbidden but we are unsure whether or not the horseradish was cut with this knife. In such cases the horseradish may be eaten after its outer thickness has been removed. Again, the reason for these leniencies is that we are not certain whether or not horseradish is to be regarded as a sharp food in all respects.

37. It is not known whether or not the knife in question was used to cut the radish.

38. This is the opinion of the *Rambam* and Rabbi Yechiel. However, with regard to radish we should be more stringent, since Rabbi Yechiel rules that it is sharp in all respects.

39. Nevertheless, if no others are available, the same leniencies that apply to horseradish should also apply here.

6. Salted Fish; Lightly Spiced Food

40. It is sufficient to scrape off the place where the fish was cut. (See also note 48.) Thus, the stringencies of a sharp food apply only to foods (such as herring) which are heavily salted.

opinion of the *Shulchan Aruch* that more than the outer thickness does not becomes forbidden.[36] However, if it is possible to purchase [others] which are not cut, we are accustomed to forbid all of it.[ז]

If radish was cut and it is known that the [forbidden] knife was used that day but it is uncertain whether it was cut with it,[37] the *Shach* writes that we are to be stringent, for it is only with horseradish, where some say that it is not called sharp,[38] that we are lenient. And it is implied from his words that all of it is forbidden.[ח] And it is necessary to be careful with onions, because there are many who cut the "tails" and this is certainly done with a knife, and therefore it is forbidden to buy [such onions] unless there is remaining the width of a stalk [of wheat].[39]

6. Regarding salted fish—only herring is called sharp, but other fish which are salted are not called sharp. Therefore, if one cut them with a forbidden knife it is enough with mere scraping.[40] And regarding all sharp substances, a food is not called sharp because of a little salt or spices that are in it, but only if all of it or most of it is sharp.[ט]

7. If fruits are sour, even though we have written [in section 4] that they are sharp, nevertheless, in case of a loss one can be lenient, since some say that only *chiltis* is sharp.[41][י] At least, it is my opinion that one can be lenient with things that are not very sharp and fermented if they were cut with a knife which was not used on that day, and rely on these authorities who hold that even with radish it is forbidden only [if the knife] was used on that day.[42] And in a situation of great loss, it is possible that one can rely [on lenient authorities] even if the knife was used on that day, by relying on those authorities [who rule] that secon-

ז. Regarding what the *Kreisi u'pleisi* asks, that we should presume that the radish remains permissible, requires investigation, because in chapter 111 regarding one pot and two pieces [of food, one permitted and one forbidden and one fell into the pot]—where there is a Torah prohibition, [the pot of food] is forbidden, because when [this piece] falls [into the pot] its presumed status [of being permissible] is spoiled.

ח. And this [decision of the *Shach*] requires investigation, for at least the opinion of the *Shulchan Aruch* is that even with radish it does not become forbidden more than its outer thickness, and as such, if there is a doubt if one cut with it, also there is reason to be lenient at least after he removes the outer thickness, as according to the *Shulchan Aruch* it is permissible.

ט. *Shulchan Aruch* 95:2.

י. *Taz* [chapter 96] paragraphs 8 and 9.

Yad Adam

7. Sour Fruits; Leniencies Which Might Apply to Sharp Food Cut with a Knife

41. I.e., that only *chiltis* has enough sharpness to make a detrimental taste into a beneficial one.

42. This is the opinion of the *Rambam*, as we have noted above.

יא. סימן ל״ו.
יב. שם ועיין בש״ך.

על הפוסקים דאפילו בדברים חריפים מותר נ״ט בר נ״ט[43] אבל בסכין של איסור בן יומו אין להקל כלל[44]יא ועיין בפ״ח ובב״א סימן מ״ט.[45]

ח. מי לימוניש שמביאים נכרים וכן תפוחים חמוצים וכיוצא בהן מותר לקנות מהם דאפי׳ את״ל שנחתכו בסכינן כיון שחותכין הרבה מאד נתבטל טעם הסכין בראשונים והראשונים נתבטלו באחרים הנחתכין אח״כ[46] וגם להרבה פוסקים לא מקרי חריף אבל צנון ובצלים שהם חריפים בודאי אפילו חתך הרבה הכל אסור.[47]יב (מ״ט)

ט. פירות שאינם חמוצים שחתכן בסכין של בשר מותר לאכלן בחלב ובלבד שיגרור מקום החתך דסתם סכין אין נקי[48] אבל הדחה לא מהני וכן בכל דבר שיש בו לחות דמכח הלחות אדרבה נדבק בהם השמנונית.

יד אדם

43. I.e., we can be lenient with sharp food when there is a secondary transmission of a permissible taste of meat or milk. For example, radishes were cut with a meat knife used that day and were then cooked with cheese. (These radishes contain secondary absorbed taste of meat—the taste is first transmitted from the meat to the knife and then from the knife into the radishes.) In such a case, where a great loss can be involved, there are grounds to permit eating the cheese after the radish has been removed. (Regarding the term "great loss," see the additional note on topic 40, section 5.)

44. Since the leniencies of secondary transmitted taste apply only to a taste which is permissible while it is being transferred. (topic 48, section 17)

45. It is noted there that there are a number of authorities (quoted in the *Bais Yosef*) who rule that under certain circumstances we can permit secondary taste even where sharp food is concerned. It is concluded there that if a great loss would be involved and the food is needed for a meal involving a precept, it is possible to permit a radish cut with a meat knife even if it was used that day (or a radish cut with a forbidden knife if it was not used that day) as long as the knife was free of grease.

8. Lemon Juice

46. These few pieces are nullified because

יא. Chapter 96 [in the *Bais Yosef*].
יב. *Ibid. (Shulchan Aruch* 96:4), and refer to the *Shach*.

dary transmitted taste is permissible even with regard to sharp foods.[43] However, with a forbidden knife [which was used that day], one may not be lenient at all.[44יא] And refer to the *Pri Chadash*, and the *Binas Adam* section 49.[45]

8. [Concerning] lemon juice which gentiles bring, and also sour fruits and similar things—it is permissible to purchase from them, because even if you say that [the fruits] were cut with their [forbidden] knives, since they cut a very large amount, the taste [absorbed] in the knife is dissipated into the first ones, and these first ones are nullified with regard to the others which are cut afterwards.[46] And furthermore, according to many authorities these are not called sharp. However, radish and onions which are certainly sharp, even if one cut many [of them], all are forbidden.[47יב] (See *Binas Adam*, section 49.)

9. If fruits which were not sour were cut with a meat knife, it is permissible to eat them with milk, but only if one will scrape the place of the cut, because an ordinary knife is not clean.[48] However, washing will not help. Similarly, anything which has moisture in it [requires scraping], for due to the strength of the moisture, contrary [to what you might think], grease will stick to it.

Yad Adam

they are not recognizable and the permissible pieces of lemon are in the majority. The fruits (as well as juice squeezed from them) are therefore permissible. The principle that a forbidden piece becomes nullified when there is a majority of permissible pieces has been mentioned in topic 43, note 64.

47. They are much sharper than lemon juice or sour fruits. Due to their high degree of sharpness, they continue to extract taste from the knife even after the first pieces are cut. (*Maadanei Hashulchan* 96:63)

9. Ordinary Fruits Cut with a Meat Knife; the Special Status of Turnips

48. We are concerned that grease from meat was present on the knife. "Scraping" involves scraping away the place of contact with the knife, and is less stringent than *k'lipah* (peeling off a thin layer) and it is certainly less stringent that *netilah* (removal of a thicker layer). In this case, since the food being cut is not sharp and it is cold, there is no significant penetration of taste and scraping is sufficient.

ואם חתך בו לפת[יג] די בהדחה[49] ולא עוד אלא אפי' צנון שחתכו אחר הלפת שרי בהדחה לפי שטעם הלפת משונה ומבטל טעם הנפלט מסכין ודוקא לפת אבל אם חתך ירק או לחם לא מהני לחתוך אחריו צנון[50] ואפילו לפת אין להתיר אא"כ שחותך תמיד בין כל חתיכה של צנון יחתוך לפת ובסכין של איסור יש להחמיר דאפילו בחותך הלפת ואח"כ הצנון[51] ואם נתערב הצנון אח"כ בתבשיל יש להתיר בדיעבד.[יד]

י. מדוכה שדכין בה זנגביל ושום וכיוצא בו מדברים החריפים שחתכו אותם בסכין של בשר[52] הרי נעשה המדוכה של בשר דע"י דוחקא וחורפא בלע ואסור לדוך בו דברים חריפים לאכלם בחלב כיון דל"ש נ"ט בר נ"ט בחריף[53] ובדיעבד צ"ע ועיין לעיל סימן ז' (מ"ט) ואם חתך דברים חריפים בסכין של חלב וחזר ודך אותם במדוכה זה הרי נבלע בו בשר וחלב וצריך להגעילו וכן הדין במדוך של נכרים במקום שדוכין בו דברים חריפים הנחתכין בסכין של איסור.[טו]

יא. ריב אייזין שגוררין בו חריין שנחתך בסכין של בשר אסור לגרור בו גבינה ודינו כדין מדוכה אך בזה אפי' לחם אסור לגרור עליו לאכול עם חלב[54] דא"א לנקותו יפה והא דאמרינן דאגב

יג. שקורין ריבין כ"כ הש"ך בשם מהרי"ל וכ"ל דל"ד ריבין דה"ה (מערין) ושאר לפתות וכ"מ מלשון רמ"א שכ' אבל חתך ירק משמע דוקא ירק אבל אין חילוק בין לפתות.
יד. ת"ח כלל ס"א ומנ"י שם ס"ק ל"ד.
טו. א"ח סי' תנ"א במ"א ס"ק ל"א. ועיין במנ"י כלל ס"א וא"ר בסימן תנ"א דזנגביל מקרי חריף כדעת רמ"א בת"ח ודלא כש"ך ס"ק י"ז.

יד אדם

49. Since it does not have much moisture, scraping is not required. (*Aruch Hashulchan* 96:21)

50. In such a case, washing will not help and the radish cannot be eaten with milk. This is because green vegetables do not have the turnip's power to nullify absorbed taste in the knife.

51. And we should be lenient only with regard to eating a radish with milk if it was cut with a meat knife (or vice versa). (The *Aruch Hashulchan* [96:21] rules differently, that cutting turnip after forbidden food will also help to permit the radish.)

10. Sharp Food Crushed in a Mortar

52. The ginger or garlic was cut with a meat knife, thereby transmitting meat taste from the knife into it. Subsequently, the ginger or garlic was crushed in a mortar (bowl).

53. Thus, although a far removed secondary absorbed taste is involved (the taste first goes

If one cut a turnip[יג] with [a meat knife], it is sufficient with washing.[49] And not only this, but even if a radish was cut after the turnip, it is permissible with washing because the taste of the turnip is different and nullifies the taste that is emitted from the knife. But [this applies only to] turnips, but if one cut a green vegetable or bread, it does not help to cut radish afterwards.[50] And even [with] turnips one may not permit [radish which is cut after it] unless when cutting each time he [alternately] cuts turnip between every cut of the radish. But with a forbidden knife, one should be strict [and not permit a radish] if he cuts turnips and afterwards the radish.[51] But if the radish is mixed afterwards with a [hot] cooked food, one can permit [the cooked food] after the fact.[יד]

10. If one crushes in a mortar [either] ginger or garlic or a similar sharp food which had been cut with a meat knife,[52] the mortar becomes a meat [utensil], since due to the pressure [in the mortar] and the sharpness [of the taste, the mortar] has absorbed [the taste of meat]; and it is forbidden to crush sharp foods in it to eat them with milk, since the [leniency of permitting] a secondary absorbed taste is not applicable to a sharp food.[53] But after the fact [if such sharp food is mixed with milk] it requires investigation [whether one can be lenient]—refer above to [the end of] section 7 [and note 45 there]. (See also *Binas Adam*, section 49.) And if one cut sharp foods with a dairy knife and he went on and crushed them in this mortar, there is absorbed in [the mortar the tastes of] meat and milk and it is required to kasher it with boiling water. And so is the rule regarding the mortar of a gentile in a place where they crush sharp foods in it which are cut with a forbidden knife.[טו]

11. If a grater was used to grate horseradish which had been cut with a meat knife, it is forbidden to grate cheese with it and the law is the same as the mortar. But with this, it is even forbidden to grate bread on it to eat with milk,[54] because it is impossible to clean it

יג. Which we call *ribin*. This is what the *Shach* writes in the name of the *Maharil*. And it is my opinion [that this applies] not only to turnips but also to carrots and other such vegetables. And so it is implied from the language of the *Rama* (96:5) who wrote: "But if one cut a green vegetable," implying only a green vegetable [will not help], but there is no difference among the turnip-like vegetables.

יד. *Toras Chatas* topic 61, and *Minchas Yaakov* there, paragraph 34.

טו. *Orach Chayim* chapter 451 in the *Magen Avraham*, paragraph 31. [Note: Some authorities rule differently—that pressure on a cold sharp food will not cause its taste to be transferred into a vessel. See *Darkei Teshuvah*, 96:1.]

And refer to the *Minchas Yaakov* topic 61, and the *Eliya Rabbah* in chapter 451, that ginger is called sharp according to the opinion of the *Rama* in *Toras Chatas*, but not according to the *Shach* in [chapter 96] paragraph 17.

Yad Adam

from the knife to the ginger, then from the ginger to the mortar, and then from the mortar to the next sharp food), we nevertheless are stringent to prohibit eating that sharp food with milk.

11. Using a Grater with Sharp Food

54. This differs from the mortar, where only sharp food may not be crushed in it for this purpose.

טז. ט"ז ס"ק ג'.

חורפא בלע היינו כשיש ג"כ דוחקא אבל בלא דוחקא לא בלע ולא מפליט ולכן אם גררו חריין על קערה חולבת נקיה אפילו אם היא ב"י מותר לאכול החריין עם בשר.[טז]

יב. דין דבר חריף שבישל בקדרה ותחב בו כף חולבת מבואר בכלל מ"ח סי' ט"ז ועיין לקמן בכלל נ"ה ס"ס ב' מ"ש בשם ח"י.[55]

כלל נ
דין פת שאפה עם בשר או גבינה
(סימן ל"ז)

א. דאם היה סתום מבואר בכלל ס"ג.

א. אין לאפות שום פת עם פלאדן של גבינה או פשטידא בשר בתנור אחד[1] אפילו פי התנור פתוח[2][א] ואפי' התנור רחב ואינו משופע דחיישינן שמא יזוב מהם אל הפת ואפי' הם במחבת

יד אדם

12. Miscellaneous Rules

55. The *Chok Yaakov* (in *Orach Chayim* 447:42-43) discusses the case of one who pickles olives in a *chometz* pot containing salt water, where the pot was not used that day for *chometz*. He concludes that the olives, even though they are sharp, will be permitted, since they absorb only detrimental *chometz* taste. One may ask: Since they are sharp, why do we not say that the taste of *chometz* which is absorbed into them becomes beneficial? The answer is that the water in which they are soaking removes their sharpness.

He further mentions that even though the olives will later become sharp again after they remain in salt water and become pickled in this vessel, this will not change the situation. The reason is that most of the absorption of taste occurs when the olives are first placed into the pot, and since they were not sharp when being placed in the pot (due to the presence of the water) and the *chometz* taste was detrimental at that time, the fruit will not become forbidden.

טו. *Taz* [chapter 96] paragraph 3.
[Note: See topic 56, section 2 regarding sharp food which is cut while it is on a forbidden plate. Further discussion about placing sharp food on a forbidden plate can be found there in sections 1 and 3.]

well. And when we say that as a result of sharpness [a utensil] absorbs, this applies when there is also pressure, but without pressure [a utensil] will not absorb [taste] nor will it emit [taste]. Therefore, if one grated horseradish onto a clean dairy plate, even if it was used that day [for dairy], it is permissible to eat the horseradish with meat.[טו]

12. The rules of a sharp food which one cooked in a pot and into which one inserted a dairy spoon are explained in topic 48 [at the end of] section 16. And refer below to topic 55 at the end of section 2 what is written in the name of the *Chok Yaakov*.[55]

Topic 50
Laws Regarding Bread Which Has Been Baked with Meat or Cheese

(based on *Shulchan Aruch—Yoreh Deah* chapter 97)

א. If it was closed, the rules are as explained in topic 62 [section 4, that even the *Bais Yosef* would not permit this].

1. One may not bake any bread [together] with a cheese pie or a meat pudding in one oven,[1] even if the door of the oven is open.[2א] Even if the oven is wide and it is not slanted, we are [still] concerned that [material] might flow from them to the bread. And even if they

Yad Adam

1. The Prohibition to Bake Bread with Meat or Cheese in the Same Oven

1. We will learn below that it is forbidden to bake bread which contains dairy or meat ingredients. This is because one might mistakenly come to eat dairy bread with meat, or vice versa. We are now learning that it is even forbidden to bake bread on the floor of an oven if dairy or meat food is present there. The reason is that the dairy or meat ingredients might come into contact with the bread and be absorbed into it, thereby making the bread forbidden.

2. Even though in such a case the cooking odors from the meat or milk are able to escape, it is still forbidden. (See topic 62, section 4.)

ב. ש״ך סס.
ג. עיין כו״פ.

נהגו להחמיר לכתחלה[3] ונהגו לשום אותם בפי התנור[4] וכ״ש דאסור להעמיד קדרה עם החלב לבשל דטבע החלב להעלות רתיחה לחוץ. ואם זב הפשטידא (הפלאדן) לחוץ דינו כאלו נלוש עמו ויתבאר בסמוך.[5]

ובדיעבד[6] אם אין התנור משופע או שהפת עומד למעלה מהפשטידא לא מחזיקינן איסור שמא זב דאפי׳ את״ל דזב שמא לא הגיע לתחת הפת והוי ס״ס[7] אבל אם ראינו שזב מפשטידא לחוץ אע״פ שהפת רחוק מהפשטידא אסור דהא קיי״ל דמספקא לן אם מפעפע בכל הכלי כדלעיל כלל מ״ה[8] וא״כ אין כאן אלא ספק אחד [9] ואם התנור משופע מסתמא זב תחת הפת עצמו[10]ב ובהפ״מ נ״ל אם לא זב תחת הפת ממש יש לסמוך להתיר הפת דהוי נ״ט בר נ״ט[11] השומן בתנור והתנור בפת וא״כ עכ״פ אין לדמותו לנלוש עם החלב ומותר לאכול הפת עכ״פ במלח.[12]ג

יד אדם

3. The *Aruch Hashulchan* (97:11) permits baking a meat or dairy pudding in the oven with bread if the pudding is in a covered pan.

4. It is customary to allow placing the pudding (even without a pan) by the oven door (rather than inside the oven). This will prevent the cooking odors of the pudding from entering into the bread which is baking in the oven. It will also prevent fatty material from flowing under the bread. (*Aruch Hashulchan* 97:11)

5. Bread kneaded from such dough is forbidden altogether except under the circumstances mentioned in section 3.

6. If meat or cheese puddings were cooked on the floor of an oven with bread.

7. It is doubtful if there was any flow at all, and even there was a flow, it is doubtful whether the flow reached the bread. We have already explained that the presence of a double doubt such as this can serve as grounds to be lenient. Compare topic 45, section 3. Nevertheless, although this bread is permissible to be eaten due to the double doubt, one should avoid eating it with meat if dairy was present in the oven, and vice versa. (See topic 62, section 4.)

8. (Section 14 there and in the *Binas Adam* section 42.) We are concerned that the taste of the flowing material is absorbed by the oven floor and will spread through the oven floor and then into the bread.

9. There is only one doubt—whether or not the fat reached the bread; this could happen either by flowing under the bread, or even without flowing under the bread, the taste of the fat might spread through the oven floor and thereby enter the bread.

ב. *Shach* there (97:2).
ג. See the *Kreisi u'pleisi*.

are in a pan—we are accustomed to be stringent to begin with.[3] And we are accustomed to place them at the opening of the oven.[4] And certainly, it is forbidden to place a pot with milk to cook [in the oven with bread], because it is the nature of milk to boil over outside [the pot]. And if [material from] the meat pudding (or the cheese pie) will flow outside [of itself to the bread], the rule is as if [the bread dough] had been kneaded with it and [the laws that apply to it] will be discussed shortly.[5]

After the fact,[6] if the oven is not slanted, or if [it is slanted and] the bread was standing higher than the pudding, we do not presume any prohibition [to be present to say] that perhaps [material from the pudding] flowed [to the bread]. For even if you say that it did flow, perhaps it did not reach under the bread and [as such] there is a double doubt.[7] However, if we saw that [material] flowed from the pudding outside [of it onto the oven floor], even though the bread was far from the pudding, it is forbidden, for it is established that we are in doubt if it spreads throughout all of the vessel as noted previously in topic 45.[8] As such, there is only one doubt.[9] [Moreover,] if the oven is slanted [and the bread is lower than the pudding, the material] probably flowed under the bread itself.[10][ב] And in cases of great loss, it is my opinion that if it did not actually flow under the bread, one may be lenient to permit the bread, because it is a secondary absorbed taste[11]—the fat [was first absorbed] into the oven [floor] and [from] the oven [floor] into the bread. As such, at least one need not regard it as kneaded with milk and it is permitted to eat the bread at least with salt.[12][ג]

Yad Adam

10. I.e., if the bread was lower than the pudding, then if a flow had occurred, we are to assume that the material would reach the bread. Therefore, there is only one doubt—whether or not a flow has occurred. The bread is therefore forbidden if it is lower than the pudding even if a flow was not observed.

11. Even though the taste may spread through the oven floor, it will be absorbed only in a secondary way into the bread, as the *Chochmas Adam* goes on to explain. Although it is proper to avoid eating such bread with meat (in accordance with the *Rama*— see topic 48, section 1), nevertheless, it need not be judged with the stringencies of bread kneaded with milk.

12. Or with other pareve food or with milk. See also section 5 for leniencies which might apply when bread becomes forbidden due to

ד. ט״ז ס״ק ג׳.
ה. פ״ח.
ו. הגהת ש״ד סי׳ ל״ב.
ז. פ״ח.

ב. ואם זב חלב או שומן בתנור ואח״כ העמיד על אותו מקום קדרה של בשר או חלב הקדירה אסורה דאע״פ שנבלע בתנור מ״מ ידוע שהשמנונית של בשר או חלב עדיין נשאר בעין והמאכל שבקדירה אם יש בו ס׳ נגד השמנונית מותר[13] ואם נתן על אותו מקום לחם דינו כנלוש עמו אבל אם אפה פלאדין בתנור בלא מחבת[14] וה״ה קיכלך שנלושו בחמאה או בשומן ידוע שלא נשאר בתנור שמנונית בעין אלא שנבלע בתנור ואז גם הקדירה מותר דכיון שכבר נבלע בתוכו ואין שם ממשות שומן או חלב בתנור הוי כשתי קדרות הנוגעות זו בזו ומותר.[15][ד]

ג. אין לשין עיסה בחלב או בשומן אפילו לאכלו לבדו גזרה שמא יאכלנו עם הפוכו[16] ואם לש אסור לאכלו אפי׳ במלח ואפילו אם נתפרסם בעיר שכל הלחם נלוש בחלב מ״מ אסור משום אורחים הבאים לשם[17][ה] ואם היה דבר מועט כדי אכילה פעם א׳ או כלחמי שבת שאוכלין באותו יום או ששינה צורת הפת[18] שתהא נכרת שלא יאכל בה בשר מותר[19] וי״א דסימן מהני[20][ו] ודוקא פת שעומד לאכול עם בשר ועם חלב אבל מה שאין דרך לאכלו רק לקינוח או עם משקה מותר ולא חיישינן שיאכלנו אחר שאכל בשר או גבינה דכולי האי לא חיישינן.[ז]

יד אדם

flowing material and a great loss would be involved.

2. A Pot of Food on an Oven Floor Which Has Absorbed the Taste of Meat or Milk

13. Even though the pot will have to be kashered, the food will be permissible if sixty is present. This is in accordance with topic 45, section 14.

14. Rather, it had been placed directly on the oven floor.

15. A dairy pot and a meat pot which come into contact with each other while hot remain permissible as long as they are dry. Refer to topic 45, end of section 19.

3. The Prohibition to Knead a Bread Dough with Dairy or Meat Ingredients

16. For example, if a dough is kneaded with milk and baked into bread, one might mistakenly eat this bread with meat.

17. Guests from another location will buy this bread and not realize that it was made with milk or meat.

ד. *Taz* [chapter 97,] paragraph 3.
ה. *Pri Chadash*
ו. Notes of *Shaarei Dura* section 35 [paragraph 4].
ז. *Pri Chadash*

2. If milk–or meat fat–flowed on an oven [floor] and afterwards, on that same place, a pot of meat–or milk–was placed there, the pot is forbidden. Even though it was absorbed into the oven [floor], nevertheless, it is known that the grease of the meat or milk still remains intact [on the oven floor]. And with regard to the food in the pot–if there is sixty times the grease, it is permissible.[13] And if one placed bread on that place it is to be judged as if it were kneaded with it. However, if one had baked a dairy pie in an oven without a pan,[14] or similarly, [if one baked] cookies which were kneaded with butter or meat fat, where it is known that no intact grease remained in the oven but it had been absorbed into the oven [floor], then also the pot will be permitted. Since [the grease] was already absorbed into it, and there is no intact meat fat or milk in the oven, it is like two pots that touch each other and it is permissible.[15ד]

3. One may not knead a dough with milk or with meat fat, even to eat it by itself. This was decreed lest one eat it with the opposite [food].[16] And if one did knead [such a dough], it is forbidden to eat it even with salt. And even if it is publicized in the city that all of the bread is kneaded with milk, nevertheless, it is forbidden because of guests who come there.[17ה] But if it a small amount which is eaten at one time, or it is like the *challos* of the Sabbath which one eats [and finishes] on that day, or if one changed the shape of the bread[18] so that it should be recognizable in order that he should not come to eat meat with it, it is permissible.[19] And some say that a sign [on the bread] will help.[20ו] And [the prohibition to knead a dough with milk or meat applies] only to bread that stands to be eaten with meat or with milk. However, what is normally eaten only as a dessert or with a drink is permissible, and we are not concerned that one might [mistakenly] eat it [soon] after he ate meat or cheese, for we are not concerned to that extent.[ז]

Yad Adam

18. He formed the dough into a special shape while kneading the dough (before it was baked).

19. It is permissible to knead such doughs to begin with.

20. For example, placing a piece of cheese on a dairy bread. (In this case, the change in the bread is not made during the kneading, but only after the bread is baked.) In section 5, the *Chochmas Adam* rules that one should not rely on this method to begin with.

ח. סי׳ ל״ז.
ט. עיין כלל ס״ה סי׳ ג׳.

ד. ודוקא שהיה בו כ״כ חלב שאין בעיסה ס׳ כנגדו אבל אם אין בו רק מעט חלב עד שיש בעיסה ס׳ כנגדו מותר לאכלו לבדו או עם חלב ולא גזרינן שמא יבא לאכלו עם בשר[ח] ונ״ל דאם אינו יודע אם יש בו טעם חלב מותר לטעמו ואם אין בו טעם חלב מותר לאכלו לבד.[21] (נ׳)

ה. במקום הפ״מ יש לסמוך להורות בפת שזב תחתיו חלב או שומן[22] אז יחלק הפת לבתים הרבה לכל בעל הבית ככר אחד דמ״ש מאפה תחלה דבר מועט דמותר[23] וה״ה עכשיו שמחלק לכל אחד דבר מועט ועוד אפשר להקל שיעשה ג״כ סימן בכל ככר וככר דהיינו אם זב תחתיו שומן יתחוב בכל ככר עצם לסימן ואם זב חלב אזי ימשה מלמעלה בגבינה[24] וכיון שעושה ב׳ דברים יש להתיר וכן הורה הרב מהר״ש הזקן מ״ץ דק״ק ווילנא (נ״א) ודוקא בזב תחתיו אבל לכתחלה לא יסמוך על זה כיון שהוא מפורש בגמרא.

ו. התנור שזב תחתיו שומן או חלב[25] צריך היסק כדין[26] עד שילכו הגחלים על פני כולו ועד שיתלבן.

ז. ודוקא בפת וכיוצא בו שעיקר חיות אדם תלוי בו[27] גזרינן[ט] אבל מדוכה של בשר שדכו בו בשמים[28] או שהמדוכה אינו לא

יד אדם

4. A Dough with a Small Amount of Dairy Ingredients

21. Or with milk. In the *Binas Adam* it is explained that it might be permissible to eat this bread even with meat.

5. Leniencies Which Apply When a Large Amount of Bread is Involved

22. The bread in question thereby became forbidden because it contains meat or dairy ingredients. If a large amount of bread is involved, one need not discard the bread, but he may act in accordance with one of the following procedures.

23. See section 3 above.

24. Or he may write on the loaf the type of material which it has absorbed.

6. Kashering an Oven Floor for Baking Bread

25. And one desires to bake bread on the oven floor.

26. See topic 74, section 10 for further discussion.

ח. *Shulchan Aruch* chapter 97.
ט. See topic [65], section [2].

4. [The above stringencies apply] only when there is so much milk such that there is not sixty times it in the dough. However, if there is only a little bit of milk such that there is sixty times it in the dough, it is permissible to eat it by itself or with milk, and we do not decree that it is forbidden [out of concern] that perhaps one will come to eat it with meat.[ח] And it is my opinion that if one does not know whether it has in it the taste of milk, it is permissible to taste it, and if there is no taste of milk in it one is permitted to eat it by itself.[21] (See *Binas Adam*, section 50.)

5. In situations involving a great loss, one may rely [on lenient authorities] and rule that if milk or meat fat flowed under bread,[22] then the bread can be divided among many houses, with one loaf for the master of each house. This would be no different than baking a small amount, which is permissible [to begin with],[23] and the rule is the same now that we distribute a small amount to each one. Furthermore, it is possible also to be lenient by making a mark on each and every loaf, that is, if meat fat flowed under it he should insert a bone into each loaf as a sign, or if milk flowed [under the loaf] then he should smear the top with cheese.[24] And since he does [both of these] two things one can permit [the bread]. And this is how the teacher Rabbi Shimon the elder, rabbi of the Vilna community has decided. (See *Binas Adam* section 51.) And [this leniency applies] only where [the material accidentally] flowed under it. However, to begin with, one should not rely on this since [the prohibition] is explicit in the *gemara*.

6. If meat fat or milk has flowed on the floor of an oven[25] it is necessary to burn it out according to the law[26] until coals go over the entire surface and until they are heated to glowing.

7. It is only with bread and similar things upon which the essentials of the life of man depends[27] that we decree [that they may not be eaten if made with meat or milk].[ט] On the other hand, if a meat mortar was used to grind spices,[28] or [if there is] a mortar which is not [used

Yad Adam

7. Foods Other Than Bread Which Have Absorbed the Taste of Meat or Milk

27. Bread is a staple food commonly eaten with all meals, and it is eaten with meat as well as with dairy.

28. Such spices absorb the taste of the meat

י. פ"ח ומנ"י בת"ח כלל ס' דלח כט"ז.

של בשר וחלב ודכו בו עם בשר[29] מותר לאכול עם אותו מין[30] ולא גזרינן גזירות מה שלא נמצא בש"ס.[י]

ח. דין דגים שאפה עם בשר בתנור א' עיין כלל ס"ח סי' א'.

יד אדם

and may not be eaten with milk, as explained in topic 49 (section 10).

29. The other food will thereby absorb the taste of meat.

30. It remains permissible to eat the spices or other foods in these examples as long as they are eaten with meat (or pareve food). We do not say that it is forbidden to eat such things altogether lest one mistakenly eat them with milk.

8. Fish and Meat Baked Together in One Oven

'. *Pri Chadash* and *Minchas Yaakov* in *Toras Chatas* topic 60, not in accordance with the *Taz*.

for] meat or milk and one crushed [food together] with meat in it,[29] it is permissible to eat [them] with the same type,[30] and we do not make decrees [to forbid such practices] if they are not found in the Talmud.'

8. Regarding the rules concerning fish which were baked with meat in the same oven, see topic 68, section 1.

לח (כח) לאחוז אם בסכין של בשר לאכול בו גבינה נ"ל דמותר וכ"כ בהדיא הפ"ח וכ"מ מכל הפוסקים והש"ך בסימן פ"ט ס"ק כ"ב כתב בשם יש"ש דאסור ועיינתי ביש"ש ושם מבואר לאחוז בו גבינה ע"ש ואפשר דנוסחא מוטעת נזדמנה לש"ך ומה שהקשה הש"ך על רש"ל בסי' צ"ו נ"ל דלק"מ דכוונת רש"ל הוא כמו שכתב המ"א בסי' תק"ע דלכן אסור להגעיל מחלב לבשר שיבוא לטעות וזהו שכתב רש"ל דאינו נכון:

לט (כז) **שאלה** מידי דבעי הדחה ולא הדיח מה דינו:

תשובה הט"ז כתב סי' צ"א משמע דסבירא ליה דמותר כמו בקליפה דפסק רמ"א שם סעיף ד' דאם א"א לקלוף מותר וכר"ת ונ"ל דכ"מ להדיא מש"ע סי' צ"א ס"ד שכתב ואם נפלו זה לתוך זה וכיון מדיח הבשר מנכה דהחלב מותר וכ"כ המנ"י בהדיא בסי' ס"א ס"ק ל"ז ונ"ל דבאמת אם נחפוס דכל קליפה שהצריכו חכמים אינו אלא מדרבנן וא"כ בודאי ה"ה גרירה והדחה ובאמת כן משמע פשטא דלישנא דאו"ה כלל כ"ט דין ב' דאפי' קליפה אינו אלא מדרבנן אבל בחולין ח' ע"ב בפלוגתא דרב ואמר קולף פרש"י כיון דהוא דאורייתא אזלינן לחומרא וכן הכריע הרשב"א מטעם זה בריש חולין כיון דהוא דאורייתא אזלינן לחומרא וכן מוכח מדהצריכו חכמים קליפה בקדשים כדאיתא נטף מרוטבו כו' ונ"ל בכוונת או"ה כמו שהבין הכו"פ בסימן צ"א דכוונתו כמו שכתב המ"א בסי' תמ"ז במקום שהקליפה אינו אלא מדרבנן ועכ"פ נ"ל דה"ה הדחה וגרירה הוא דאורייתא במקום שיש לחוש שנדבק בו איסור קלה ולמאן דמתיר בקליפה כר"ת ה"ה בהדחה ומאן דאוסר כריב"א ה"ה בהדחה ורש"ל דפוסק כריב"א הביאו הש"ך סי' צ"א ס"ק א' ה"ה בהדחה קיים וא"כ האי מלח דל"ש בו הדחה אסור כולו ולא ידעתי. מה שכ' ע"ז הט"ז דבת"ח כתב שעת הדחק כגון שנתאכסן בבית נכרי כדיעבד דמי ונ"ל דהט"ז ס"ל לחלק בין קליפה להדחה שהרי בס"ק ז' מסיק למעשה כריב"א וכן בס"ק א' כתב דבהדחה בדיעבד מותר ולא ידעתי מה ענין ת"ח לדברי יש"ש דכי ס"ד בבית נכרי מותר לבשל בקדירות של נכרי דהוי כדיעבד וכן יהיה מותר לבשל בקדירות של בשר שאב"י חלב וח"ו ובת"ח שם כלל י"ז כתב זה רק לפי מ"ש שם דאם רחץ הכלי יפה מותר בדיעבד אם נשתמשו וע"ז כתב דבבית נכרי כדיעבד דמי וא"כ במקום דבעי הדחה מדינא כגון שהכלי אינו נקי בודאי אין חילוק אם הוא בבית נכרי או בביתו וכמו שנכתוב לקמן ותמהו ג"כ דעת הראב"ד שהביא הת"ח כלל ס"א דין י"א דאם חתך בשר דק דק בסכין של איסור כולו אסור דלא יכול לגררו או להדיחו ובודאי גם הת"ח מודה לדינא דרש"ל לשיטת ריב"א ודלא כמנ"י שם כלל י"ז שסובר דרש"ל חולק על ת"ח וע' במנ"י כלל כ"ב ס"ק ע"ו שכתב דבדבר לח צריך ס' ועיי' לעיל סי' י"ד:

מ (כח) **שאלה** תרנגולת שמנה טרפה שנמלחה עם בשר ומקצת חתיכה נוגעת בתרנגולת ושאר החתיכות נוגעות זו בזו והוא הפ"מ מה דינו:

תשובה לכאורה אין למלוח היתר כמו שכתב רמ"א בסי' ק"ה סוף סעי' ט' דבפס"מ יש להתיר במליחה בקליפה בכחוש אבל לא בשמן ומי יבא אחר הכרעת רמ"א:

ואמנם אחר העיון נ"ל דיש הרבה צדדים להקל החתיכות שאינם נוגעים בטרפה גופה. דהנה במליחה אם אוסרת כ"ק כדעת הרשב"א ודעימיה והיא דעת י"א שכתב רמ"א או עד ס' כדעת רשב"א ור"ן כבר הכריע המחבר ורמ"א דבשמן אוסר עד ס' ואמנם כ"ז הוא בחתיכה שנגעה בחלב עצמו ואמנם אחתיכה נוגעת רק בחתיכה שנוגעת בחלב היא פלוגתא מוהר"ם ור"כ במרדכי הביאו הב"י ודעת מהר"ם דחלב אינו מפעפע מחתיכה לחתיכה ומה שאינו נוגע בחלב מותר אף בלא קליפה ור"כ מספקא ליה ומצריך ס' בין הכל נגד החלב והמחבר הכריע להדיא כמהר"ם ובודאי משמע דדעת המחבר אפי' לקולא אינו מפעפע לשאר חתיכות כמו שכתב הט"ז ס"ק כ"ב ואמנם מה שתמה הט"ז שהרי בכלי פסק דאם בלע דבר המפעפע אוסר חברתה וכתב וא"ל דכלי חמור ממליחה דהא מסקינן בגמרא דמליחה כרותח דכלי עכ"ל אני בעניי לא זכיתי להבין תמיהתו שהרי הרא"ש וכל הפוסקים כתבו להדיא דאף דס"ד בגמרא דמליחה חמור מכלי אבל לפי האמת קי"ל מכלי וכן פסק המחבר דכלי הכחוש בעי נעיצה ובמליחה די בקליפ' והרי גדולי הפוסקים ס"ל דמליחה אפילו בשמן אינו אוסר יותר מכ"ק ומה שכתב הש"ך בנקה"כ דהב"י הכריע כמהר"ם רק לחומרא אבל באמת אפילו חתיכות שאינם נוגעות באמת אסורין דלקולא ל"א דאינו מפעפע המעיין בב"י יראה דליתא שהרי כתב על האי פלוגתא של מהר"ם ור"כ שנ"ל להכריע כמהר"ם דלא שבקינן פשיטותא דמהר"ם מחמ' ספק דר"כ ומהר"ם אפי' לקולא ס"ל

דאינו מפעפע כמ"ש בהגה' ש"ד שער ל"ז בהגה"ה המתחלת פסק מהר"ס וכ"כ שם בהגהת ש"ד וכן יש לדון וע"ש כמ"ש שכן דעת הר"ש מקולי' ועוד דאי איתא כדברי נקה"כ למה לא הזכיר המחבר דין של שאר חתיכות בידוע שלא נגעו באיסור והיתר א"ו דדעת המחבר לגמרי כמהר"ס דאינו מפעפע אפילו לקולא ואמנם רמ"א כתב דאין לשנות המנהג לשער בכל מליחה בס' ואח"ל הכל אסור דדיינינן למליחה כבשול ואח"ז כ' הרמ"א י"א דבהפ"מ יש להקל בקליפה והיא דעת מהר"ס פדווא בתשו' רמ"א והביאו בד"מ ור"ל דאפי' לפי המנהג ומוכח שם דדעתו דבהפ"מ יש לסמ"ך אסברת ראב"יה ודעמי' דאפי' בשמן מליחה אינו אוסר רק כ"ק וכ"ל שע"ז כתב רמ"א שיש לסמוך עליו בכחוש אבל לא בשמן דלדינא צריך ס' ור"ל שאותה חתיכה שנגעה באיסור שמן אין להתיר אפי' בהפ"מ ע"י קליפה דבזה צריך ס' מדינא לשיטת הרשב"א ודעמיה וכהכרעת הב"י אבל משאר חתיכות לא איירי רמ"א כלל שהרי בד"מ כתב והאריך כשיט' הרשב"א לשער הכל בס' אם אין דבוק ואח"ז כתב וז"ל אבל לא משמע כן מדברי או"ה דמשמע דאין מצטרפין כל החתיכות ומ"ש כ"ל כי מדינא לא היה צריך במליחה רק כ"ק שהיא דעת רוב הפוסקים אלא שאנו מחמירין לשויה כבשול ודי לנו בחומרא זו ולא להחמיר בו יותר מבשול ומטעם זה השיב לי מהר"מ פדווא דמנהגנו להתיר ע"י קליפה במקום הפ"מ עכ"ל ודעת מהר"ס פדווא הוא אפילו בשמן ואיך כתב הרמ"א בהגה"ה דמדינא צריך ס' אע"כ דר"ל לשיטת המחבר צריך ס' מדינא והיינו דוקא באותה חתיכה שנגעו אבל בשאר חתיכות לא הכריע רמ"א כלל וכן כתב בהדיא בתשובי' רמ"א ס"י קי"א דמדינא מליחה כ"ק וכ"ל דע"כ גם הש"ך ס"ל בפירוש דברי רמ"א שהרי בסי' ל"ב ס"ק י"ז כתב הש"ך דגם התו"ח דאף לפי מנהגנו לשער כל מליחה בס' מ"מ בהפ"מ עכ"ס לא אמרי' חנ"נ וכתב הש"ך דמשמע שם אפי' בשמן ודבריו ל"ע שהרי רמ"א כתב בסי' ק"ה דצריך ס' נגד איסור דבוק וידוע דא"א לומר איסור דבוק אלא כדבר שי"ל חנ"נ ולדעת הש"ך איך אפשר לומר דבוק ואח"ז מלאתי במנ"י והכריע משום זה דלא כש"ך וכתב כיון שרמ"א חזר בו בש"ע ממה שכתב בת"ח ואחר המחילה לא עיין יפה שהרי המנהג הזה הוא דוקא בלא הפ"מ ואז אמרינן חנ"נ ודבוק אבל בהפ"מ כבר הכריע רמ"א דאינו אוס' רק כ"ק וא"כ פשיטא דלא אמרי' חנ"נ ופשיטא דבוק וא"כ דברי רמ"א ודברי ת"ח עולין יפה בקנ"ן אחד ואמנם הא תינח בכחוש אבל הש"ך שכתב דת"ח איירי אף בשמן ל"א חנ"נ והרי הרמ"א כתב דבשמן אף בהפ"מ בעינן ס' ומשמע דלמנהגנו מחמירינן אף בדבוק אע"כ ל"ל דס"ל לש"ך דמה שכתב רמ"א בשמן היינו דוקא לענין אותה חתיכה כיון דדעת הרבה פוסקים דבעינן ס' מדינא אבל שאר חתיכות שאינם נוגעות בחלב יש לסמוך אדע' מהר"ס והמחבר דאינו מפעפע מחתיכה לחתיכה והוי כעין ס"ס דפלוגתא דשמא הלכה כראב"י וא"כ אף אותה חתיכה שנגעה בחלב מותר ע"י קליפה ואת"ל כרשב"א שמא עכ"פ אינו מפעפע מחתי' לחתיכה וע' במנ"י בכללי ס"ס ובמחודשים סי' ו' וכעין זה כתב הש"ך בסי' פ"ז ס"ק ל"ב בכשרה שינקה מן הטרפה ולפ"ז יש מקום להתיר שאר חתיכות שאינן נוגעין בתרנגולת וע' בפ"ח שכתב ג"כ כעין זה ותב"ש שכתבתי דגם דעת ר"ש מקולי' כמהר"ס ולא הוי יחידאי ומה שכתב הפ"ח דהרשב"א בתה"א דף ל"ה חולק על מהר"ס אמת שמדבריו משמע הכי אך מה שהביא מדברי הרשב"א בת"ה שם אדרבה מוכח מדבריו דס"ל דדוקא באותה חתיכה מפעפע בכולה אבל לא מפעפע מחתיכה לחתיכה וכ"מ עוד מדבריו שכתב שם אם נמלא חלב מפעפע כו' ולא נודע באיזה מהן נגע מוכח דאם ודאי לא נגע בהלב גופה אלא בחתיכה שנגע בחלב אינו מפעפע אח"ז ראיתי בתשו' אמ"ו נודע ביהודה סימן ל"ב דמצרף ג"כ סברא זו דאפשר דרמ"א לא כתב דנוהגין לאסור במליחה בשמן רק באותה חתיכה אבל לא באלו שנגעה בה ומצרף ג"כ דעת ראב"י לזה אלא דשם היה תב"ת וכשהצעתי הדברים להגאון בית מאיר הודה לדברי לפסוק כן בהפ"מ וסעודת מצוה ואמר לי דהוי ספיקא דדינא ודוקא שלא נגע ודאי בטריפה אבל אם יש לספק שמא נגע הנה שיש ג"כ ס"ס שמא לא נגע ואת"ל נגע שמא הלכה כראב"י ז"א דיש ג"כ ס"ס להחמיר שמא נגע ואת"ל לא נגע שמא הלכה דמפעפע מחתי' לחתיכה:

אח"ז בא לידי ספר כו"פ וראיתי שכ"כ בסי' ס"ט בספק אם נמלא חלב עם בשר והתיר ע"י קליפה מטעם זה ע"ש ודע דאין ללמוד מזה להתיר החתי' שנגעה בס"ט מטעם ס"ס שמא הל' כראב"י ושמא אינה טרפה דלא יהא אלא איסור דרבנן דקיי"ל דצריך ס' וכבר דחה זה בתשובת אמ"ו בנ"ב ואי משום הא נראה לי דלק"מ דכיון דאנן קיי"ל מליחה בס' ולכן אף באיסור דרבנן נהיגין כן דכל מה דתקון רבנן כעין דאורייתא תקון ומ"מ יש להחשיב דעת ראב"י לספיקא דדינא וכן איתא בתשובת שבות יעקב במעשה דמין עגל שנמלא קוץ תחוב עד החלל ומלחו עמו עוד בשר ופסק להיתר מטעם ס"ס שמא לא היה טריפה ואת"ל דטריפה שמא הלכה כראב"י בסי' ק"ה דמליחה אינו אוסר רק כ"ק ואפילו בשמן וא"כ אם אינו ידוע איזו חתי' נגעה בטל חד בתרי והנה שאמ"ו בנ"ב חולק ע"ז היינו דס"ל דהגיע לחלל טריפה ודאי ולא הוי ספק ובאמת לא זכיתי להבין כונתו שהרי מ"מ אינה טריפה

רק מספק שמא ניקב א' מאיברים הפנימים וגם לענין התערובת אפשר לצדד ולהחשיב דעת ראב״י לספיקא ודינא כנ״ל:

ואמנם כ״ז כשהתרנגולת מונח על דף שמולחין עליו לצד מטה והבשר מונח למעל' או שמולחין בכלי העשוי מקנים באופן שאין ציר הטרפה זב תחת שאר חתיכות אבל כשנמלח על דף והתרנגולת מונחת לצד מעלה וא״כ בודאי שהציר זב תחת כולם וציר נבלה דאורייתא ואמנם מצאתי בש״ד שם שכתב דהציר נעשה כגדי כחוש וע״ש בהגה' דמיירי מציר מחלב שמן ואפ״ה חשיב ליה כחוש ומצאתי באו״ה כלל ד' דין ז' שכ' בשם סמ״ק כשים כשאיהן לבעל החלב אבל לא כא' מהן אותה שנגעה בו אסורה דשמא לא מפעפע והשני מותר מ״מ (וזה סברת ר״כ שבמרדכי) ואין לאסור השני אפי' את״ל שאינו מפעפע מחמת הציר הראשונה הסמוך שג״כ דציר מחתי' שנאסרה מחמת בלועת איסור אינו דאורייתא ואמרי' בי' שפיר משרק סריך אע״פ שנאסרה מהחלב דלא גרע מהחלב עצמו שאין מפעפע גם עכ״ל או״ה ודבריו צ״ע דהא ציר נבלה דאורייתא וגם משרק סריך נ״ש אלא כדם אבל ציר אדרבה מסריך וצ״ל דכונתו דכיון דהכ״ג בשאר איסורין אינו אלא מדרבנן וא״כ אין הציר יכול לאסור יותר מן החלב וכשם שהחלב אינו מפעפע לחתיכה שאינו נוגע בו כך הציר שלו הנבלע בחתי' ראשונה אינו נבלע בחתי' ומה שכתב משרק סריך ר״ל אינו נבלע ועוד צ״ע בדבריו שכתב דהשניה יאסור מציר הראשונה הסמוך וצ״ל דקאמר שיאסור מציר החלב גופה וצ״ל דס״ל כיון דמיירי שאינו נוגע בחלב וא״כ מסתמא כשמגיע הציר מן החלב לחתיכה ראשונה נבלע בו ואינו מגיע לחתיכה שתחתי' או דמיירי שמונחים החתי' לרוחב כמלא דאין הציר של חלב מגיע לחתיכה ב' והנלע״ד כתבתי:

ודע דגם בש״ד כתב דר״י הלבן הביא ראיה דמליחה כמ' מהא דאיתי' בחולין ל״ז ע״ב הנהו אטמהתא דאמלחו בגידא דנשיא ולא פירש בילד הוא הראיה וע״ש בתכ״ש מה שפירש דראיתו כיון דקיי״ל כרב הונא דף צ״ו בגדי שבשלו בחלבו אסור וא״כ ק' היאך התיר ר' אחא וע״כ דהוי ס' ודבריו תמוהים דא״כ האיך פ״ד דר' אחא לאסור וצ״ל דכך הוא הראיה שהרי קשי' דפריך התם לר' אחא מדשמואל דאמר בירך שנצלה בג״ה קולף כו' וקשיא דפריך משמואל לייתי ראיה מדרב הונא דאמר אסור לאכול אפי' מראש אזנו וצ״ל דשאני דרב הונא דהוי שמן כדמשני הש״ס שם שאני חלב דמפעפע ופריך מר' יוחנן ומשני כחוש הוי וא״כ פריך שפיר מדשמואל שהרי בג״ה דהוי כחוש קיי״ל כשמואל וכבר כתבו תוספות שם אדשמואל דאמר קולף כו' היינו דקליפה עכ״פ אסור וא״כ ר' אחא דאוסר משמע ודאי דאוסר כולו והיינו דס״ל דאין חילוק בין כחוש לשמן ולכן פריך מדשמואל עכ״פ יוכח דבשמן מליחה וצלי שוה עד ס':

מא (נח) טפת מרק של בשר שנפל על כלי שמבשלים בו קאווע ואין מבשלין בו חלב לעולם ואין ס' נגד הטפה מה דינו. נ״ל דאף דקיי״ל דהקדירה לעולם אסור היינו דוקא לבשל בו בשר אבל אלו כלים שלעולם מבשלים בו רק הקאווע נ״ל דמותר לבשל בו קאווע לשתות עם חלב דאף דקיי״ל דנ״ט בר נ״ט ע״י בישול אסור לכתחלה עם בשר מ״מ זהו רק מחמת ספק שמא מפעפע וא״כ הוי ס״ס שמא אינו מפעפע ואת״ל דמפעפע שמא העיקר כדעת הפוסקים וכהכרעת הש״ע דאפילו לכתחלה מותר אך ז״א שהרי לכ״ע אסור לבשל לכתחלה כדי לאכול עם בשר אך יש לצרף לפי מש״כ הפ״ח דבכלים דא״א לבא לידי נתינת טעם שמשתמשין בהן בשפע מותר וכדפסק בש״ע סימן קכ״ב וס״א דעת רשב״א ואף שהש״ך כתב דלא קיי״ל הכי מ״מ יש לצרף להיתר עוד סניפין מע״ל יש להקל (וכ״כ במנ״י כלל נ״ו ס״ק ה' ובכו״פ) לענין טפת חלב שנפל על קדרת של בשר דמותר מה״ט:

מב (נט) **שאלה** קדירה צוננת העומדת על הכירה ובא תחתיה חלב רותח מה דינו:

תשובה דין זה מבואר להדיא בסי' צ״ב בש״ך ס״ק ל״ב וביש״ש ובפ״ח שם ובכו״פ ובמנ״י דאף התבשיל אסור דקיי״ל תתאה גבר אך הגאון בעל ח״ד דיבר דבר גדול דלא יהא דמפעפע לפנים מ״מ אין הבלוע יוצא מחתיכה לחתי' שלמעלה ממנה בלא רוטב דהמים שבתוכה ודאי דאין לו דין רוטב כ״ז שהוא צונן ודבריו נראין מאד דבודאי א״א שמה שנכנס לפנים הוא מבשל המים שהרי אפי' בשבת מותר ליתן צונן להמין אם א״א לבשל בתוכו כדאיתא בא״ח סי' ש״ח אלא דצ״ל דמפעפע לפנים ונבלע בתוך המים או התבשיל וגם בחתי' שנוגע בשולי הקדרה אבל מחתיכה לחתיכה א״א שתצא בלא רוטב ומ״מ אין להתיר כ״א בהפ״מ דכיון דאמרינן מפעפע לפנים ה״ז דומה לבשר שנפל לתוך חלב צונן דלדעת מקצת פוסקים אם יש בו בקעים אסור אפי' הוא חי כמש״כ בש״ך סי' צ״א ס״ק כ' אך מה שרצה הגאון שם לחלק דוקא כשהיה החלב מכסה כל עובי שולי הקדרה דבסי' צ״ב בש״ך ס״ק ל״ב כתב לאסור התבשיל ובסי' קכ״א כ' דקיי״ל דאינו מוליך הבליעה בכולו ולזה מחלק בין הפוסקים וחולק על כל הגאונים הנ״ל והנה באמת לפי שיטת הש״ך שם תמיהתו תמי' קיימת. ואמנם לפי דעת המ״א בסי' תנ״א שהחליט דמוליך הבליעה בכולו אלא שאין מפליט מכולו דין הנ״ל הוא אמת

שהרי מוליך בליעתו בכולו אלא שראיתי שהגאון הנ"ל בסי' צ"ב דחה בשתי ידים דברי מ"א וכתב שנעלם ממנו דברי תוס' בזבחים שכתבו דכשהכלי מקצתו קר בזה בודאי לא תפשט בכולו ועוד כתב שהוא נגד הסוגיא דע"ז דקיי"ל כבכ"פ כבר האריכתי בזה בסי' ס"ב דהעיקר כדעת המ"א וס"ל הא דאמרינן כבכ"פ היינו דאינו שוה שהרי גם במליחה מצינו כן שמבליע בכלי ואינו מפליט מן הכלי וגם לענין עירוי דעת א"ז בשם מהר"ח דמבליע ואינו מפליט כדאיתא בתו"ה כלל כ"ח ססי' מ"א ובסימן י' בחום בית השחיטה דמבליע בסכין ואינו מפליט כדאיתא שם בש"ך ס"ק י"ז ומש"כ שנעלם ממנו דברי התוס' כבר כתבתי שם דלפי מה שסיימו התוס' וכתבו ואי מספקא ליה היה לו למיבעיא בשאר איסורים קאי על מש"כ לעיל דהיינו אם מספקא ליה בין שהכלי מקצתו קר בין שכולו חם בכולהו מספקא ליה אי מפעפע וע"כ צ"ל שכן דעת כל הפוסקים שהרי לא מצינו באחד מן הראשונים והאחרונים שכולם כתבו הדין מטיפת חלב שנפל על הקדירה ולא הזכירו שום רמז ורמיזא לחלק אם כל הכלי חם או מקצתו קר ועוד לפי הכלל שמסור בידינו שכל דברי תוס' שאינם נזכרים בפסקי תוס' לא קיי"ל הכי ודין זה לא נזכר כלל בפסקי תוס' לחלק בין מקצתו חם לקר א"כ דהפירוש בתוס' כמש"כ או דלא קיי"ל הכי וא"כ אם באנו לדחות דין מפני דין יותר טוב לדחות דינו דש"ך שכתב בסי' קכ"א כיון שהוכחתי בתשו' שם דדעת רוב הפוסקים כמ"א וכ"ש שהש"ך גופא אף שכתב בסי' קכ"א דאינו מוליך הבליעה בכולו' אפ"ה כתב כאן דהכל אסור דתתאה גבר וכבר פשטה הוראה זו על הש"ך שלא שמענו מעולם מי שחולק ע"ז וכ"ש לפי מסקנת הפ"ח בסי' קכ"א דבכלי קבר ודאי מוליך הבליעה בכולו וא"כ כ"ש ה"ה הכא כיון דתתאה גבר. ועוד צ"ל דגם הש"ך ועמי' דס"ל דאינו מוליך הבליעה בכולו היינו למעלה ממקום תשמישו אבל לכ"ע עכ"פ מפעפע כנגדו ובזה מיושב מטיפת חלב דהלכה רווחת לאסור משום ספק שמא מפעפע לפנים וכן משמע בפשיטות מלשון הטור שכ' ומפעפע לפנים וכ"כ הב"י בפירוש דברי הסמ"ג הביאו הש"ך ס"ק י"ח וא"כ ה"ה הכא:

ועוד צ"ל דמה שכתב הש"ך דאינו מוליך הבליעה היינו דוקא בשאר כלים אבל בכלי חרס מודה דעכ"פ מפעפע ובזה מיושב מה שהנחתי בצ"ע בתשו' הנ"ל סי' ס"ב דהסמ"ג סותר א"ע שכתב דאינו מוליך הבליעה בכולו ואיך כתב בשם ר"י דמדאמרינן בישול מפעפע ולכן אם נפל טפת חלב על כלי חרס מפעפע בכל החרס ולפ"ז לק"מ דשאני כ"ח ולכן דקדק לכתוב כלי חרס דוקא אבל בשאר כלים באמת אינו מפעפע וא"כ אין כאן סתירה כלל מש"ך דבסי' קכ"א מיירי משאר כלים ובסי' צ"ד בי ג"כ הש"ך דמוליך. פליטתו בכולו והיינו בתנור דהוא כלי חרס:

מג (ס) שאלה מי שבשלו דגים בחלב ביורה ועירו כך רותח לקערה של בשר ב"י מה דינו:

תשובה לכאורה לפי מה שכתב הש"ך בסי' ס"ט דמסתמא ליכא ס' בקערה נגד הקליפה וא"כ הכל אסור אך זה מצאתי בש"ג שמביא המרדכי בשבת דף ע"ח ע"א בשם הרב משאנץ וז"ל הכל הוא דפשיטי שיש במקפה ס' מכדי קליפה ע"ש ובאמת החוש יעיד ע"ז ודבר פשוט בעיני שאו"ה ואפ"ד שכתבו דאין ס' היינו בקדרה שהיו בימיהם ועדיין נראה בגליל פוזנא מן הקערות הישנות של נר"ע שכמעט אין להם תוך אלא דבר מועט וע"ז כתבו דאין ס' אבל בקערה שלנו אין ספק שיש ס' נגד הקליפה ועי' במנ"י כלל כ"ח ס"ק כ"ה:

מד (סא) שאלה הא דכתבו הפוסקים דתוחב כף איסור בהיתר שצריך ס' נגד מה שתחב בקדירה אם ר"ל מה שנכנס ברוטב דוקא או ר"ל מה שתחב בקדירה אף שלא היה רק מקצת ברוטב כמו חתי' שחציה ברוטב לשיטת ר"י בסימן צ"ב דאמרינן הכל הקדירה מסייע להפליט (כ) הא דקיי"ל כר"י דחתיכה שמקצתה ברוטב שהרוטב מבלבל הכל אם תחב חתי' בשר בחלב ולא נכנס בחלב ובקדר' רק חלק קטן דאם נשער רק מה שנכנס בחלב יהיה בחלב ס' נגדו ואמנם אם אמרינן שמפליט גם מה שחוץ לקדירה אין כאן ס' מה דינו:

דין זה מצאתי להדיא בתו"ה כלל כ"ח דין ג' בסופו וז"ל חתי' איסור חם שנפל מקצתו לקדירה צריך ס' אף נגד מה שחוץ דציר האיסור פולט מתוכו כנ"ל ול"ד לכף מתכת דא"צ לבטל כולו דיש חילוק בין דבר מאכל לכלי והיינו מטעמא דלעיל דע"י הרוטב פולט החתיכה לחתי' ואפילו איסור שבלוע ותתאה גבר ומרתיחו וה"ה כשהחתיכה האיסור לונן מק"ו מב' חתי' יבישות דאמרינן תתאה גבר ואוסרת כולו וכ"ש הכא שמבלעת ומסכים יותר ע"י הרוטב הרותח ודוקא דבר מאכל אבל כלי שנאסר מבליעת איסור ונפל מקצתה לתוך היורה א"צ לבטל כ"א אותו המקצת לבד עכ"ל הרי להדיא דבדבר מאכל אמרינן שפולט כיר וא"כ בודאי אף מה שחוץ לקדירה אסור אבל בכלי אינו צריך לשער רק מה שנכנס ברוטב ואף דאינו מוכרח בכלי מאו"ה דיי"ל דכוונתו למעט מה שחוץ לקדירה אבל ז"א דז"ל או"ה כלל ל"ז דין ב' אפילו אם ספק אם נתחב כולו או מקצתו צריך ס' נגד כולו דעכ"ע באורייתא כו' ודוקא מה שנסתפק שתחב מן הכף לתוך התבשיל כו' הרי להדיא דוקא מה שנכנס

בתבשיל וכן הוא לשון סמ"ק שהבאתי בסי' שאח"ז וז"ל נגד כל מה שנתחב בקדירה כו' אבל מה שלא נכנס ברוטב אין אוסר עכ"ל הרי להדיא אע"ג דפתח וכתב מה שנתחב בקדירה כוונתו ברוטב וא"כ כוונת כל הפוסקים כן הוא אע"ג שכתבו ומה שנתחב בקדירה כונתם ברוטב גם מבואר בא"ה דבאתי' אין חילוק אם האחי' הוא חם או צונן אחר שכתבתי כ"ז קניתי ס' כו"פ וראיתי שכתב ריש סימן צ"ד דלכן דקדק המחבר לכתוב כל מה שנתחב בקדירה וכוונתו אף שלא נתחב ברוטב דהבל הקדירה מסייע כמו חמי' מקלחה ברוטב לר"י דמה שחוץ לקדירה הינו מצטרף דאין הבל הקדירה מסייע ובלתי ספק שנעלם ממנו דברי או"ה שהבאתי שכתב להדיא להיפך דבאבל מפליט מכולו אבל כלי אינו מפליט רק מה שבתוך הרוטב ומה שהביא ראיה מסימן ק"ה דכלי נוח יותר לפלוט בקל יש לחלק בין הכא להתם:

עוד מבואר מא"ה שהבאתי שכתב אבל הכלי הנאסר מבליעת איסור ונפל מקלחת ביורה א"ל לבטל כ"א אותו מקלת מזה מוכח להדיא כדעת המ"א בסי' תנ"א ודלא כש"ך בסי' קכ"א והבאתי דבריהם בסי' הסמוך שהרי איירי כאן מכלי שנאסר כולו ע"י בליעה ואפ"ה בנפל מקלחה א"ל לבטל כ"א אותו מקלת ולדעת הש"ך משום דטעמא דאין מבליע בכולו הא ל"ש הכא אע"כ דאינו מפליט מכולו:

מה (כב) שאלה התוחב לד השני של כף חלב בקדירה של בשר מה דינו די"ל אכיון דאין דרך להשתמש אלא בראש הכף וא"כ מעולם לא הלך הבליעי בצד השני (ב) אם תחב פרור שדרכו להשתמש בכולו והוא של בשר ועכשיו תחב ממנו מקלת בחלב אם בעינן ס' נגד כל הכף דאמרינן מפליט בכולו או לא (ג) כלי שנאסר והגעיל מקלת וכישל באותו מקלת:

הנה דעת הש"ך בסימן ס"ט ס"ק ס"ג דאף דלא נשתמש רק במקצת כלי מפליט מכל הכלי ובסי' קכ"ב כתב דכלי שנאסר במקלת לא נאסר כולו דאינו מוליך הבליעה בכולו וכן כתב הפ"ח שם ואמנם לברר הדברים דעת הרא"ה בבד"ה דף קכ"ח בכלי מתכות מוליך הבליעה בכולו דאם מקלתו ח"כ ואם בישל במקלת נאסר כולו ואם הגעיל במקלת אסור להכשירו דבכבכ"פ ונראה שזה גם כן דעת הי"א בסי' צ"ד סעיף א' בתוחב כף חולבת בבשר בכלי מתכת דצריך ס' נגד כולו דאע"ג דאין דרך להשתמש בכל הכף מ"מ מוליך ומפליט הבלוע בכולו והרשב"א במשה"ב מספקא לי' ואמנם בתה"ק כ' בפשיטות כלי מתכת שנאסר מקלתו נאסר כולו לפי שהוא מתחמם ביותר כו' עכ"ל וכ' הב"י בי"ד סי' קכ"א שגם דעת הרא"ש כרשב"א ודעת הסמ"ק בסי' רי"ג דאפי' בכלי עץ דינו הכי וז"ל כשתוחבין כף חולבת בקדירה של בשר משערינן בכל מה שנתחב אבל מה שלא נכנס ברוטב אין אוסר ואפילו בכלי מתכת אבל לענין הגעלה צריך להגעיל כולו כדאמרי' בפ' דם חטאת בישל במקלת הכלי צריך הגעלה בכל הכלי עכ"ל ומדכתב ואפי' בכלי מתכת ש"מ דמיירי בשל עץ ואפ"ה מבליע בכולו ולא מטעם הם מקלתו ח"כ ונראה דילא לסמ"ק לשיטתו הביאו הש"ך סימן צ"ד ס"ק י"ח וז"ל כתב הסמ"ק ספה שנפלה על הכלי מספקא לן בפ' דם חטאת אי מפעפע בכל הכלי או לא ונ"א כי כלי מתכת ש"מ דס"ל אע"ג דאיבעי' שם בכלי מתכת מדאמר מריקה ושטיפה מ"מ מדאמר הש"ס שם דם אינו מפעפע בישול מפעפע ומדתלי טעמא בבישול דמפעפע משמע דאין חילוק בין מתכת לשאר כלים ונראה שגם דעת המחבר כסמ"ק שהרי בסימן צ"ב בדין טפת חלב שנפל על הקדירה פסק כסמ"ק ומדפסק בע"ש או שעת הדחק להכשיר אף שלא כנגד הרוטב ש"מ דס"ל דאפי' בכל הכלים אמרינן דמפעפע בכולו ע"ש בש"ך ס"ק י"ח מה שפירש ב"י בדברי הסמ"ק וא"כ צ"ל דהא דכתב הש"ע בסימן קכ"א הדין בכלי מתכות הוא לרבותא דאפי' בכ"מ לא אמרינן דמפליט מכולו (אמת לפי מה שפירש הט"ז ס"ק י"ט שיותר היתר אם נאמר דאינו מפעפע וא"כ י"ל דאנן קיי"ל בע"ש דודאי אינו מפעפע וכן משמע בא"ה שכ' בסי' ל"ח מספקא לן אי מפעפע בכולו או לתוך הכלי או לא עכ"ל ור"ל או לא שאיני מפעפע כלל) הרי ביארנו דדע' הרשב"א והרא"ש והרא"ה דעכ"פ בכלי מתכת כיון דאם מקלתו חם כולו מבליע בכולו והסמ"ג במל"ת סי' קמ"א סוף דף ל"ג כתב גרסי' בזבחים בשול מפעפע כלומר מתפשט בכל הכלי כתב מורי מכאן נוהג רבי שאם נפלה טפת חלב ע"ג קדרה רותחת באור שמפעפע בכלי חרס כו' ולפ"ז צ"ל מש"כ שם בדף ל"ד ע"ב סמוך לסוף הסי' וז"ל וכן הדין אם הכניסו כף חולבת בתוך קדרה בשר שבכל מה שנכנס מן הכף בקדרה כו' אבל מה שלא נכנס בקדרה א"צ לבטל אפי' היא של מתכת כו' מ"מ אין מוליך בליעתו בכולה וצ"ל דר"ל דאינו מפליט מכולו וגם צ"ל מש"כ שם בהל' חמץ סוף דף י"ד וז"ל אומר ר' אליעזר דבכל איסורין כשנבלע האיסור במקלת הכלי א"צ הגעלה כ"א במקום בליעתו חוץ מקדשים כדאי' בזבחים בישל במקלת הכלי טעון מריקה בכל הכלי ובתרומה א"צ כו' ע"כ והרי לעיל כתב מזבחים דבשול מפעפע וע"כ דזהו סברת ר' אליעזר דס"ל דלמסקנ' דגמ' כל איסורין דומה לתרומה אבל הסמ"ג לא ס"ל הכי ונמלא דלסמ"ג וסמ"ק וכן מוכח דעת המחבר וכן כ' הא"ה סי' כ"ח דין מ' וז"ל וכתב בסמ"ק ואפילו לא

נאסר כ"א במקלת מ"מ צריך הגעלה בכולו והיינו אפי' בכלי עץ עכ"ל ודעת הר"ן בפי' כ"ש בסכינא דספקא אינו מוכרע די"ל דס"ל ג"כ דמבליע בכולו רק דס"ל כבכ"ש ואפי' על ידי ליבון כרשב"א עי' ש"ך סי' קכ"א וע"ז שם ומה שאכתוב בסמוך:

ומעתה נבא לדין כ' אם מפליט מכולו דעת הש"ך בסי' קכ"א דאינו מבליע בכולו וראיותיו מסי' צ"ד בתוחב כף חולבת שא"צ לשער רק נגד מה שתחב והיינו משום דגם מתחלה לא הוליך הבליעה לשם וכתב דהש"ד והסמ"ג והמרדכי וא"ה וסה"ת כתבו הטעם דאע"ג דהם מקלתו ח"כ מ"מ צ"א דמוליך הבליעה בכולו ור"ל דהעיקרא כשנשתמש בכף לא בלע בו השני כלום וכן כתב הפ"ח בהדיא. ונ"ל דהטעם בתוחב כף חולבת משום דאינו מפליט מכולו אבל לעולם מבליע בכולו דו"א לפי פירשו שכתב הש"ך בסי' ס"ע ס"ק ס"ע דאדרבא מפליט מכולו וע"כ הטעם משום דאינו מוליך הבליעה בכולו ולדידי' אם תחב כף פרור שדרכו להשתמש בכולו או שתחב אלי מראש הכף שדרך להשתמש בכל ראש הכף כמש"כ הש"ך בשם רש"ל בסימן צ"ד אעפ"כ צריך ס' נגד כל כף הפרור ונגד כל ראש הכף ובסיפך אם תחב צד השני של כף שאין דרך להשתמש בו א"צ ס' כלל אפי' נגד מה שתחב וזה צ"ע שהרי כל הפוסקים כ' סתמא דצריך לשער נגד מה שתחב ולא חלקו בין אם תחב מקלת מראש הכף או כולו וכן לא חלקו בין סתם כף דאין דרך להשתמש רק בראש הכף ובין כף הפרור דדרך להכניסו כולו דלעולם משערינן נגד מה שתוחב וכן פי' הש"ע בסי' צ"ד בסכין אף דדרך להשתמש בכולו והיאך סתמו כולם ולא פרשו וכי יש גבול והרי בהדיא מבואר בא"ה שהעתקתי לשונו סי' ס"א דצריך לשער נגד מה שנסתפק שתחב דעכ"פ דאורייתא וא"כ ניחוש שמא פ"א תחב יותר ואם כן בלע הכף ועכשיו אף שלא תחב כ"כ מ"מ מפליט אע"כ כמש"כ המ"א בסי' תנ"א דמבליע בכולו אבל אינו מפליט מכולו ובזה אתי שפיר כל פסקי המחבר בסי' צ"ב בטפה שנפל על קדירה חשש לדעת סמ"ק שמא מתפשט בכולו אפי' בכ"א וכלי עץ ובסימן צ"ד בכף חולבת דלעולם צריך לשער נגד מה שתחב בין בסתם כף בין בפרור וכן אין חילוק אם תחב כל ראש הכף או מקלתה דלעולם אינו מפליט יותר רק מה שתחב ובסי' קכ"א כתב דאפי' בכלי מתכת די"ל כיון דהם מקלתו ח"כ וה"א דג"כ מפליט מכולו ולהכי כתב דאפ"ה אינו מפליט מכולו ומכ"ש אחר כלים ומה מאד אני תמה על מאורן של ישראל הפ"א שכתב שנעלם מבי"י כשכתב סי' קכ"א מה שכ' בסי' צ"ד בתוחב כף חולבת דא"צ לשער רק נגד מה שתחב וע"כ הטעם משום דאינו מוליך בכולו ובסי' קכ"א כ' דצריך להגעיל כולו וע"ז סמכו להקל דא"צ להגעיל כל הכלי ואם תחב צד השני אינו אוסר והם דברים קשים לשמוע על מאור עינינו הב"י שישכח דבריו ולדעתם שכח ג"כ מה שפסק בסי' צ"ב דמתפשט בכולו ומה יעשה בדברי הסמ"ק סימן רי"ג שכתב וז"ל כשתוחבין כף חולבת בקערת בשר משערינן בכל מה שנתחב אבל מה שלא נכנס ברוטב אין אוסר ואפי' בכלי מתכת אבל לענין הגעלה צריך להגעיל כולו כדאמרי' בישל במקלת הכלי צריך הגעלה בכל הכלי עכ"ל הרי להדיא דאע"ג שכתב דא"צ לשער נגד כולו מ"מ כתב תיכף דצריך להגעיל כולו וא"ל דלחומרא בעלמא כ' ז"א שהרי כ' כדאמרינן בישל במקלת הכלי כו' אע"כ דכוונתו דאע"ג דא"צ לשער אלא מה שתחב והיינו דאינו מפליט בכולו וה"א דה"ה דאינו מבליע בכולו ע"ז כתב דלענין הגעלה אינו כן אלא כלי שנאסר במקלת אסור כולו משום דמבליע בכולו ולכך צריך להגעיל כולו ומביא ראיה מבישל במקלת כו' והיינו דמבליע בכולו ואינו מפליט מכולו והש"ך שם בקכ"א כתב ועי' לעיל סימן צ"ב ס"ק ע"ו (ע"ש וצ"ל י"ח) ומדמה לדין טפת חלב דמפעפע ולא זכיתי להבין כוונתו במה מתרץ זה ומה שכתב הש"ך דכל הפוסקי' כתבו דאין מוליך הבליעה בכולו עפר אני תחת רגליו ואדרבה נ"ל דמוכח להיפך אלא דכולם ס"ל כטעם המ"א ומה שכתב מסה"ת עיינתי בו ולא נזכר שום טעם רק כתב שאין צריך לשער רק נגד מה שתחב וא"כ י"ל דס"ל כרשב"א דאינו מפליט בכולו וכמש"כ המ"א וסמ"ג וסמ"ק אדרבה מוכח דס"ל הכי כמש"כ וז"ל או"ה בסימן ל"ז ואפי' בכף ש"מ דאע"פ דה"מ ת"כ מאחר שחיממו רק על ידי חמין ולא על ידי אור עצמו אינו מוליך ומפליט בליעתו בכולו עכ"ל ומזה למד הש"ך דלאו"ה אינו מוליך בליעתו בכולו וא"כ קשה למה הזכיר או"ה כלל ומפליט ודוחק לומר לדייק דעל ידי אור מפליט כמי ועוד דא"כ ה"ל לכתוב דידוע שלא הכניס כל הכף ומדסתם משמע אע"פ שהכניס כולו מ"מ א"צ ס' אלא נגד מה שנתחב ועוד ק' דא"כ יהיו דברי או"ה סותרים זא"ז דבסי' כ"ח ד' מ' כתב בשם סמ"ק דאפי' לא נאסר רק במקלת צריך להגעיל כולו כדמוכח מדם חטאת דבישל במקלת הכלי צריך הגעלה בכל הכלי וע"כ צ"ל דמבליע בכולו אע"כ דודאי מבליע בכולו ומש"כ בסימן ל"ז ה"פ כיון שאין חימומו על ידי אור צ"א בי' אם מקלתו ח"כ לענין זה שיפליט מכולו דוקא כמו שפוד של פסח שצללה הפסח על ידי אור אמרינן דמוליך הבליעה בכולו ומפליט מכולו וס"ל כרשב"א או כמו שכתב הש"ך בסי' קכ"א אבל על ידי חמין אינו מפליט מכולו אבל בודאי דמוליך בכולו דהא

אפי' בכלי עץ לאו"ה מוליך בכולו אע"ג דל"ש אם מקלתו א"כ ומש"כ מוליך ומפליט י"ל אינו ר"ל להוליך האיסור ולהבליע שהרי איירי מן הפליטה ואם כוונתו כש"ך הי' לו לכתוב שהרי מתחלה לא בלע צד השני אלא דלא איירי כלל מן הבליעה אלא מן הפליטה ור"ל שאינו מוליך מה שבלוע מצד השני להפליט ועיין באו"ה ותראה שדברי כנים וכן מוכח להדיא מדברי או"ה כלל כ"ח דין ג' שהעתקתי לשונו בסי' ס"א וע"ש מה שכתבתי ומה שהביא הש"ך מאו"ה כלל כ"ח דין מ"ג וז"ל כתב המרדכי וצריך להגעיל אף הבית יד של מחבת ול"א שיספיק בהגעלת המחבת דבכב"פ ומיהו נראה דבדיעבד מותר עכ"ל וס"ל להש"ך דכוונתו דבדיעבד אם נשתמש ביד המחבת בלא הגעלה, מותר וא"כ ע"כ הטעם דאינו מוליך הבלוע בכולו ודבריו לא משמע הכי שהרי לא נזכר כלל בדבריו תשמיש ועוד דאין דרך להשתמש ביד המחבת אלא כוונת האו"ה כפשוטו דצריך להגעיל גם היד שהרי אסור שמוליך הבליעה בכולו אך בדיעבד שהשתמש במחבת ולא הגעיל היד מותר משום דאינו מפליט מכולו וכן מוכח להדיא בהגהת או"ה דכוונת או"ה שהשתמש במחבת (אך דשם בהגה"ה מוכח דטעמא משום דבכב"פ ע"ש) ושם מוכח מאו"ה דין מ"ד להדיא דס"ל דמוליך בליעתו בכולו אמת מדברי תה"ד שהביא הש"ך משמע שמפרש כסמ"ג כדבריו וראיה ברורה לזה מהא דאמרי' בפי' דם חטאת דם אינו מפעפע בישול מפעפע ומה בכך דמפעפע הא בכב"פ ודי במריק' במקלת הכלי אע"כ כיון דמפעפע ומוליך בכולו אבל אינו מפליט מכולו ולפ"ז במכניס כף פרור א"צ ס' רק מה שתחב וכסתימת לשון כל הפוסקים דאינו מפליט בכולו ואם הגעיל רק במקלת ותחב צד שלא הגעיל צריך ס' דמוליך הבליעה בכולו ולפ"ז נסתר ג"כ מה שכתב הש"ך בסי' ס"ט דאם עירה הקערה במקלת אעפ"כ צריך ס' נגד כל קליפת הקערה ליתא דהא לדעת כל הפוסקים אינו מפליט מכולו כשיטת רשב"א ומ"א ואפשר כיון דהקערה חמה מפליט אך קי' דא"כ ה"ל להפוסקים לכתוב ,הדין בכף חולבת לחלק בין חם לצונן:

ועדיין צריכין אנו לבאר דברי הטור ורמ"א בסי' קכ"א משמע איפכא שהרי כ' אהא דכתב המחבר דכלי שנאסר במקלת צריך הגעלה בכולו וז"ל ודוקא שנשתמש בכל הכלי אבל אם ידוע שלא נשתמש אלא במקלתו בכב"פ כבר כתב המ"א שם לתרץ זה אך דבריו צריכין ביאור שכתב ובהכי מתיישבת קושית הב"י על הטור ר"ל שהב"י כתב בי"ד דדעת הרא"ש כרשב"א מדכ' הרא"ש שיספיק אם ילבן חודו של סכין לפי שרגילין הנכרים להשתמש בו באור אע"ג דח"מ א"כ מ"מ כיון שהישראל אין משתמש בסכין ע"י אור סגי בהכי משמע אבל להשתמש ע"י אור אסור דח"מ א"כ אמרינן לאיסור אבל לא לענין הכשר עכ"ל הב"י (ודברי רא"ש אלו כתב ג"כ רשב"א במשה"ב) ר"ל דאיך יחלוק הטור על אביו וכתב המ"א דלפ"ז לק"מ דהטור איירי שרוצה להשתמש רק באותו מקלת שהגעיל ולכן ד"ד כשמכשיר המקלת והרא"ש איירי להשתמש בכולו וא"כ גם דברי רמ"א מתפרש הכי דר"ל דוקא להשתמש באותו מקלת כך כונת מ"א אך עדיין צריכין ביאור דא"כ מ"ש אם נשתמש בכולו כיון שעכשיו אינו רוצה להשתמש רק במקלת שהגעיל ונ"ל דכונתו לפרש דברי הטור ורמ"א דקאי על מה שהביא הטור והמחבר דברי רשב"א שכתב דלא עלה לו הכשר עד שיכשיר כולו ומשמע דאפי' באותו מקלת שהכשיר לא עלה לו ההכשר ואסור להשתמש בו ע"ז כ' הטור ורמ"א ודוקא אם נשתמש בכולו אז אסור לכתחלה להשתמש אפי' במקלת שהכשיר דחיישינן שמא ישתמש במקלת האחר ואז אסור אפי' בדיעבד כיון דאינו מפליט מכולו והכלי נאסר כולו דהא נשתמש בכולו אבל אם לא נאסר רק במקלת ואותו המקלת הכשיר וא"כ אף אם ישתמש במה שלא הגעיל אינו אסור בודאי דהא מספקא לן אי מפעפע בכולו וא"כ שפיר נוכל לומר בכב"פ ומותר עכ"פ להשתמש באותו מקלת שהכשיר כנ"ל כונת המ"א וא"צ דהא כתב שם המ"א דדוקא דיעבד מותר במחבת י"ל דמחבת וכיוצא בו בידות הכלים וכן כף דקרוב הדבר שקבלו טעם ע"י תשמיש והוי כאלו נשתמש בכל הכלי כמש"כ הט"ז שם בא"ח ובזה מתורץ קו' הב"ח שהביא הט"ז והש"ך [שהק'] דברי הטור אהדדי ובזה מדויק דברי רמ"א שכ' אבל אם ידוע שלא נשתמש רק במקלתו מותר לכתחלה ור"ל באותו צד שהגעיל לאפוקי היכא דאינו ידוע בודאי כגון ידות הכלים וכפות דזה דוקא דיעבד מותר ואף שהרשב"א כ' בהדיא שאפי' לא נשתמש רק במקלת צריך להכשיר כולו כבר כ' הדרישה שהטור לא ראה תה"א ולכן מפרש הטור שדעתו בנשתמש כולו באיסור אז לא עלה הכשר אפי' להשתמש במקל' שהכשיר וע' בדו"פ שדחק עצמו מאד לתרץ דברי הטור. ועוד היה נ"ל לפרש דברי רמ"א דהק' דמה שכתב רשב"א והם דברי המחבר דלא עלה לו הכשר דמשמע דאם נשתמש אסור אפי' בדיעבד ע"ז כתב המ"א ודוקא כשנשתמש בכולו ר"ל שנשתמש עכשיו בהיתר בכל הכלי אזי אסור המאכל אבל אם לא נשתמש עכשיו עם ההיתר רק במקלתו שהגעיל מותר המאכל וכן י"ל לשון הטור אף שבלשון הטור הוא קצת דחוק יצא לנו מכ"ז דמבליע בכולו ואינו מפליט מכולו כשיטת הרשב"א והש"ע:

(סג) **ועדיין** חוב עלינו לתרץ סוגיא דזבחים ל"ו דאיתא התם בעי מיניה בישל במקלת בכלי

צריך מריקה ושטיפה. בכל הכלי או לא א"כ מסתברא דא"צ דתנן א"צ כבוס אלא מקום הדם א"צ דם אינו מפעפע בשול ועוד תני' בישל במקצת צריך מו"ש בכל הכלי ואמרי' התם דוקא בקדשים אבל בתרומה בישל במקצת א"צ מו"ש בכל הכלי ומזה הוכיח הר"ן פ' כ"ש והרא"ה ד' קכ"ח דכלי שנאסר במקצת א"צ להגעיל רק אותו מקצת דילפינן כל איסורים מתרומה דאמרינן בכב"פ ולא כשיטת רשב"א ומה שתי' רשב"א ומחלק בין היתירה בלע בתרומה לשאר איסורין כבר דחה הפ"ח ומסכינא דפיסחא נמי אין ראיה כמש"ה הר"ן בפ' כ"ש יע"ל בהקדים לתרץ מה שכתב הסמ"ק הביאו הש"ך סי' צ"ב ס"ק י"א וז"ל מספקא לן בפ' דם חטאת אם בישול מפעפע בכל הכלי עכ"ל ול"ע שהרי להדי' אי' התם דר"י דאבעי' ליה ידע הברייתא דתניא בישל במקצת צריך מו"ש בכל הכלי רק שאלה זאת האיבעיא לרמי בר חמא לנסותו אם יוכל לפשוט מסברא ע"ש ואדרבה בהדיא משמע בגמ' דקאמר כפשיטות בישול מפעפע ובאמת הסמ"ג כתב אמרי' בפ' דם חטאת בשול מפע"ע משמע דפשיטא ליה ואמנם תוס' שם הקשו תימה מאי קא מבעיא ליה ומאי ס"ד דר"י אי כשמקצת הכלי על האש שמבשל בו ושאר הכלי צונן א"כ מאי קאמר בישול מפעפע הא לא מפעפע ואי בכל הכלי חם פשיטא דמפעפע ואי קא מיבעי' ליה אי מפעפע בכולו או לא א"כ תיבעי ליה בשאר איסורין (ולכאורה מתוס' זה מוכח דהא דאמרינן מבליע בכולו הוא דוקא שכבר נתחמם כל הכלי אבל כ"ז שהצד הב' צונן אינו מבליע בכולו וכ"כ כו"פ אך מדברי הפוסקים שאין אי מחלק בכך משמע דאין חילוק וכן מוכח מדברי סמ"ג שהבאתי לעיל שכתב דתוחב כף חולבת א"צ לשער רק נגד מה שתחב אבל לענין הגעלה אינו כן ולדברי תוס' אין חילוק בין הגעלה לתוחב דאם גם מתחלה בשעת תשמיש היה מקצתו קר א"צ להגעילו אע"כ דאין חילוק ואפשר דכונת התוס' מש"כ אם מקצת הכלי קר הרי אנו רואין שלא פעפע ואי כולו חם הרי אנו רואין שפעפע ואי מספקא ליה ר"ל בין בחם ובין בקר) וצ"ל דזה היה ק' גם לסמ"ק וגם הוחק שנאמר דלא כיון ר"י באיבעיא זו רק לנסות רבו ולכן ס"ל לסמ"ק דבאמת מספקא ליה אי מפעפע ובאמת ה"ה בכל האיסורין מספקא ליה. אי מפעפע בכולו וא"כ כלי שנאסר במקצתו צריך הגעלה בכולו או לא והא דמיבעי' ליה בקדשים דוקא היינו משום דגלי קרא גבי קדשים דטעון מו"ש בכל הכלי ואוקמה למעט תרומה כדאיתא בברייתא ור"י ידע לברייתא ע"כ והנה לאביי התם דס"ל דאוקמה למעוטי תרומה דאם בישל במקצת הכלי אין טעון מו"ש בכל הכלי ומו"ש דקרא היינו הגעלה וע"כ צ"ל דאינו מפעפע דא"כ מ"ש תרומה אע"כ דאינו מפעפע וחידוש שחדשה תורה בקדשים ואע"ג דאינו מפעפע גזה"כ דטעון מו"ש בכל הכלי אבל לרבא התם דס"ל דאוקמה למעוטי תרומ' דאפי' ביין וקדשים דוקא במים וא"כ י"ל דמפעפע ואף בתרומה צריך הגעלה בכל הכלי רק דגזה"כ בקדשים שיהיה דוקא במים ור"י איבעיא ליה בקדשים אם בישל במקצת הכלי ואינו רוצה להשתמש עכשיו רק בצד שמגעיל אם טעון הגעלה בכולו או אינו צריך רק אותו מקצת והיינו דבשאר איסורין ממ"נ מותר דאת"ל דמפעפע בכולו עכ"פ אינו מפליט מכולו וא"כ פשיטא דמותר להשתמש באותו מקצת שהגעיל אבל בקדשי' מבעיא ליה די"ל דברייתא דתניא בה דטעון מו"ש בכל הכלי מיירי כשרוצה להשתמש בכל הכלי וס"ל לברייתא דמפעפע וקדשים דומה לשאר איסורין ומריקה ושטיפה דקרא במים ואוקמה למעוטי תרומה ממים אבל כשאינו רוצה להשתמש רק במקצת שמגעיל אין חילוק בין קדשים לש"א וכיון דגלי קרא בקדשים דטעון מו"ש בכל הכלי משום דמפעפע בכולו ממילא ידעינן דה"ה לשאר איסורין דמ"ש או אפשר דברייתא ס"ל אינו מפעפע וע"כ חידוש שחדשה תורה גבי קדשי' ואע"ג דאינו מפעפע אעפ"כ טעון מו"ש בכל הכלי ואם נתמעט תרומה לאביי וא"כ אפי' אינו רוצה להשתמש רק באותו מקצת שהגעיל אעפ"כ בקדשים אסור דכיון דחזינן דלא משום בלוע קפדה תורה שהרי אינו מפעפע ואעפ"כ הצריכה תורה מו"ש בכל הכלי וא"כ ה"ה כשאינו רוצה להשתמש רק במקצת אפ"ה טעון מו"ש בכולו ולכן מיבעיא ליה דוקא בקדשי' משא"כ בשאר איסורין אם אינו רוצה להשתמש רק באותו מקצת ודאי אין צריך הגעלה בכולו ממ"נ ופשט ליה דומיא דדם וה"ה הכא דא"צ מו"ש רק באותו מקצת ואפילו רוצה להשתמש בכולו וע"ז א"ל בישול מפעפע ר"ל דודאי לא דמי לדם דשם לא"ש פעפוע ואין שם חידוש דין כלל אבל בישול אפשר דמפעפע ועוד הא תניא בהדיא דצריך מו"ש בכל הכלי ועכ"פ צ"ל דברייתא מיירי כשרוצה להשתמש בכולו ועכ"פ נדחה סברת הב"ח דרוצה לדמות בישול לדם דאפי' כשרוצה להשתמש בכולו אין טעון מו"ש אלא באותו מקצת שבשל בו דזה בודאי מוכח מברייתא דליתא וא"כ בשאר האיבעיא ברוצה להשתמש רק באותו מקצת שהגעיל אי מפעפע בכולו או לא ושפיר כתב הסמ"ק דמספקא לי' אי בישול מפעפע ולפ"ז מתורץ קו' התוספות דודאי מספקא ליה אי מפעפע או לא ודוקא בקדשים קא מבעיא ליה באינו רוצה להשתמש רק במקצת שהגעיל ומדאמר בישול מפעפע משמע ליה לסמ"ק והדבר תלוי בבישול ולא משום שהוא כלי מתכת דשייך בו חמח"כ ולכן כתב בכל הכלים דמספקא לן אי מפעפע ולפ"ז שפיר י"ל כשיטת רשב"א דכלי שנאסר במקצת צריך הגעלה בכולו ומה שהקשה הרא"ה שהרי בהדיא אמרינן

אותה ולא בתרומה ז"א די"ל למעט ביין ובמזג אבל לעולם דמפעפע בכולו ואינו מפליט מכולו כיון דהוא אבעיי דלא איפשיטא:

ולכאורה לפי מה שכתבתי דתליא בפלוגתא דאביי ורבא וא"כ קשה דלודאי קי"ל כרבא וקשיא להנך דס"ל דאינו מפעפע אך בר"ן פ' כ"ה בסופו כתב הגירסא להיפך וא"כ הר"ן לשיטתו כתב שפיר בפ' כ"ש דאין טעון הכשר בכל הכלי והסמ"ג כתב דלא פליגי אביי ורבא דהלכה כשניהם. יצא לנו מכ"ז (א') אם תחב צד שני מן הכף צריך ס' נגד מה שהתחב דמתחלה בלע בכולו ואין להתיר אלא בהפ"מ (ב') דלעולם אין צריך לשער רק נגד מה שתחב דאינו מפליט מכולו (ג') כלי שנאסר בין כולו או מקצתו צריך להגעיל כולו ולא מהני מה שהגעיל המקצת דאינו מפליט מכולו ובדיעבד אם נשתמש באותו מקצת שהגעיל מותר אבל אם נשתמש במקצת שלא הגעיל אפילו לא נאסר רק אותו מקצת שהגעיל מ"מ אפילו בדיעבד אסור שהרי מתחלה הלכה הבליעה בכולו וע"י הגעלה לא פלטה אם לא בהפ"מ. וא"ל דהא קיי"ל לענין הגעלה בכב"פ ז"א דדוקא במקום שהשתמש אמרינן כשם שע"י חימום זה נבלע כך ע"י חימום זה יפלוט אבל שתפליט מקצה האחר י"ל שפיר דאף שהיה בו כח להבליע מ"מ אין לו כח להפליט ודוגמא לזה במליחה דאע"ג דמבליע קיי"ל דאין בו כח להפליט ובפרק כל הבשר אמרינן מבלע בלע מפלט לא פליט ובסימן י' בחום בית השחיטה בש"ך ס"ק י' דיש בו כח להבליע בסכין ולא להפליט ואף שדעת הרא"ה בב"ק הבית דף קכ"ח דבאמת דקי"ל גם לענין זה בכב"פ הא כבר הוכחנו מדכ' כל הפוסקים בכף דא"צ לשער רק נגד מה שתחב מוכח כשיטת המ"א בסימן תנ"א והוא המחוור. אחר כמה שנים שהיו כתובי' אצלי דברים הללו קניתי ספר כו"פ וראיתי בסי' ל"ד שהעלה ג"כ כמ"ה אך נעלם ממנו שהוא מבואר במ"א והעלה סברא זו מדעתו:

מן (סד) **שאלה** כף בשר ב"י שתחבו בקדירה של חלב ב"י שבשלו בו עכשיו מים או ירקות מה דינו:

תשובה דין זה איתא להדיא בסי' ל"ד סעיף ה' שכתב רמ"א או שיש במאכל ס' הכל שרי ור"ל אפילו שניהם בני יומן וכ"כ הר"מ בהדיא וז"ל ואפי' הכף שרי וכ"כ האו"ה בכלל ל"ה דין ז' וז"ל ואם יש ס' נגד הכף מותר הכל אע"פ ששניהם בני יומן כו' ואף הכף מותר בכאן מאחר שהתבשיל אינו של בשר עצמו וגם לא נאסר מעולם להיות חוזר ואוסר הכף שהרי יש בו ס' ומהקדרה לא קבל כי אם נ"ט בנ"ט דהתירא עכ"ל וכ"כ עוד בכלל כ"ז דין ע' וז"ל ואם יש ס' בתבשיל נגד הכף מותר גם כן שכל אפי' הכף לכתחילה כו' עכ"ל וע"כ צ"ל מה שכתב או"ה בכלל ל"ד דין ע"ו וז"ל כף הולכת שהודח בין כלים הרבה של בשר ב"י אם היה ס' במים נגד כל הכף ודאי שאר הכלים מותרי' אבל הכף אסור לשניהם דטעם הבשר שבמים לא נתבטל במצא שבלע עתה מבשר בן יומו עכ"ל וע"כ צ"ל דהתם שאני דמיירי שהיה שומן בעין על הכלים של בשר וא"כ המים הם של בשר ודומה לתוחב כף חולבת בן יומו בקדירה שמבשל בו בשר ויש ס' נגד הכף דהכף אסור משא"כ כשמבשל מים או ירקות אע"ג דיש טעם בשר במים מן הקדרה מ"מ חשבינן לנ"ט בנ"ט ולפ"ז צ"ע על הש"ך בסי' ל"ד ס"ק ח' דכתב לרמ"א אסור הכף והרי בד"מ ובאו"ה ב' פעמים כתב להדיא דהכף מותר והש"ך לא הביא דבריהם וצ"ע ואפשר שכוונתו לפי מה שכתב הש"ך סי' צ"ה סק"ח בשם הר"ן גבי הדחה בשניהם ב"י דאמן ליתא לן שלא יתערבו פליטת הבשר ופליטת החלב בעצמה שלא באמצעות המים וא"כ לא הוי נ"ט בר נ"ט א"כ ה"ה הכא וא"כ מדינא אסור ולפ"ז י"ל דמה דנוהגין לאסור הכלי שאב"י כמש"כ רמ"א בסימן צ"ד סעיף ה' היינו כמי דחוששין לטעם זה של הר"ן וא"ב ה"כ יש לנהוג כן ביש ס' וכמ"ש הש"ך:

מן ☞ (סה) **שאלה** בחג השבועות לאחר חלות היום שזמן סעודה לכל הוא והתחילה הקדרה עם בשר להרתיח הרבה לצאת לחוץ ולקח כף של חלב ב"י ושאב בו מן הקדרה והחזיר לתוכו כדרך שעושין כשמעפחין ע"פ קדרה מרותחת וכן עשה כמה פעמים וכנגד הכף יש בו ס' אך אם נצטרך ס' על כל החיבה אין בו. מה דינו:

תשובה לכאורה הי' נראה לאסור דזה גרע מדין תחיבת הכף ב"פ בסי' צ"ד דא"צ אלא פ"א ס' לדעת רמ"א היינו כמש"כ הש"ך בשם תה"ד דבכולע צ"א כ"כ משא"כ הכא דהתבשיל הוא בעין וכ"כ וגרע ג"כ מהא דכ' רמ"א בסי' צ"ח סעיף ד' באיסור שנפל לאותו קדרה כמה פעמים דא"צ אלא פ"א ס' דהתם הכל איסור א' משא"כ בזה דמתחלה הי' צריך ס' נגד החלב ועכשיו הבשר נ"נ בתוך הכף וא"כ הוא איסור אחר כמש"כ הש"ך שם לדעת הש"ע אך כיון שהי' שעת הדחק וביטול שמחת י"ט סמכתי א"ע על מה שכ' הכו"פ בדין הכף ב"פ דכיון דהחלב שבכף כבר נתבטל אך הבשר נ"נ וא"כ הוי מב"מ ומה"ת בטיל ברוב וכיון דאינו אלא ספק שמא נשאר בו חלב כקו' הרשב"א דלהוי כהגעלה וכמש"כ הט"ז שם סקי"ב ולכן הכריע הכו"פ לענין תחיבת הכף ב"פ לקולא ומצאתי כעין זה בסולין

ל"ז ע"ב בתוס' ד"ה אלא מעתה שני בכלא כיון דספיקא הוא אם יצא כולו הוי ספ"ד לקולא ולפ"ז אין חילוק אם הוציא הכף ריקן או עם תבשיל והחזיר התבשיל לקדרה דס"ס אינו אלא ספק דרבנן ואם נאמר דהוי ס"ס לחומרא שמא לא פלט הכף כלום בפעם ראשון ואת"ל שפלט שמא עכ"פ עדיין נשאר בו עד שלא הי' בתבשיל שבכף ס' ה"נ יש ס"ס להקל שמא פלט בפ"א הכל ואת"ל שלא פלט הכל מ"מ שמא לא נשאר רק מעט עד שהי' בתבשיל ס' וא"כ הספיקות שקולים ואדרבה י"ל דהס"ס להקל הראשון מתיר יותר דאם פלט הכל אף הכף הי' מותר אבל בס"ס להחמיר הכל שם א' ושיפי שה"ם הוי ספ"ד לקולא. ועוד מדלא הזכירו הפוסקים לחלק אם הוציא הכף ריקן או מלא ואין א' מן הראשונים והאחרונים שיחלקו בכך מוכח דאין חילוק וע"ז סמכתי להתיר כדין דרבנן שלדינן מוכח והדר אותבינן תיובתא:

אח"ז ראיתי במנ"י כלל פ"ח ס"ק ה' שכ' וז"ל ואם נקח עם הכף מהתבשיל לחוץ ואחר ושפכו לתוכו. צריך ס' ג"כ נגד אותו תבשיל שב"כ תוך הכף ויש ללמוד דין זה מדין זבוב כלל כ"א וכ"כ בתמים דעים סי' ק"ת עכ"ל הנה לשון זה סובל ב' פירושים א' דר"ל דאם מה שבכף הוא יותר מהכף כגון שדפנות הכף הם דקים והחלל גדול א"כ לא סגי ס' נגד הכף לבד עד שיהי' ג"כ נגד התבשיל אבל א"צ ב"פ ס' אלא כד"ת שהכף מחזיק כביצה והתבשיל מחזיק כביצה וחומש אזי צריך שיהי' בקדרה ל' ביצים לבטל וכענין זה כ' האו"ה כלל כ"ד סימן ע' הביאו במנ"י כלל כ"א ס"ק כ'. או"ל, מדלא כ' שהתבשיל יותר מהכף אלא כ' סתם צריך ס' ג"כ נגד התבשיל אפשר דכוונתו דצריך ב"פ ס', וכמו שראיתי בחיבורי אחרונים שכ' להדי' דאם החזיר התבשיל לקדרה צריך על כל פעם ס':

ואמנם להיות מיראי הוראה אני אם לא אדע מקור הדין מפוסקים ראשונים לזאת חקרתי על מקור הדין. והנה דין זה דשתי כפות נובע מסמ"ק והביא ראי' ממס' תרומות פ"ה מ' ז' סאה תרומה שנפלה לתוך ק' של חולין ולא הספיק להגביה עד שנפלה אחרת ה"ז אסורה ור"ש מתיר ואמרינן בירושלמי דידיעה מקדשתה דלר"ש אם לא נודע כראשון עד שנפלה ב' הכל אסור אבל השתא דנודע מותר ופסק הרמב"ם כר"ש וכתב בהגה"ה ש"ד סי' צ"ט ולא נתברר לי הראי' (וכוונתו כמש"כ שם הרב"ש כמ"ש ור"ל דיש לחלק דהתם יש ב' סאין של איסור והכא אין כאן אלא כף א' של איסור והיכא דאיכא ב' כפות או ג' דומיא דמתניתין) וי"ל דחד קעמא הוא כיון שאם תחב זה הכף לקדירה אחרת צריך ס' משום דהוי בחתיכה דאיסור ה"ה נמי לאותה קדירה וחוזר וניעור עם הראשון כיון שלא היתה ידיעה בנתים וכ"כ במרדכי פרק הגוזל קמא דכן הדין אם נפל אחרי' איסור כגון חזיר בתוך הקדירה דדינא הוא ככף ומצטרפין בס' ואם נפל ב' פעמים או יותר זה הדבר תלוי באם נודע לו בנתים כדפרשתי לעיל:

ולפ"ז בדין דתחב הכף ב' פעמים דהכריע הרמ"א דא"צ אלא פעם א' ס' צ"ל. כמש"כ הש"ך שם סק"ו בשם תה"ד כיון דאין שם אלא בלוע. ומש"כ הש"ך שם דאפי' באיסור שנפל, לפ"ז אין ענין לכף דאדרבה באמת צ"ע למה כי הרמ"א באיסור א' שנפל לקדירה ב"פ דאינו צריך אלא פעם א' ס' כיון דכי בפי' צ"ע דחוזר וניעור ובאמת דין זה תלוי בחוזר וניעור וכ"כ הכו"פ והניח דברי הרמ"א שם בצ"ע. והתימה על הכו"פ שלא הביא דברי המרדכי שהביא בהגהת ש"ד שהבאתי שכ' להדיא דאם נפל ב"פ תלוי באם נודע לו בנתים ולפ"ז כיון דדינא דב' כפות תלוי בדין חוזר וניעור וא"כ ע"כ מוכח דכוונת הראב"ד בתמים דעים כמש"כ דאם יש מה שבכף יותר מן הכף גופא אז צריך ס' נגד התבשיל, ולא נגד הכף דא"ל שכוונתו שצריך ב"פ ס' הרי לראב"ד אפי' בשני זיתי איסור שנפלו בזא"ז ואפי' שלא נודע בנתים אינו חוזר וניעור דקמא קמא בטל ואפי' בדבר שנותן טעם כמש"כ הש"ך בסי' צ"ט ס"ק כ"א אע"כ דכוונתו דלעולם אזלינן לחומרא דאם הכף יותר מן הרוטב שבתוכו צריך ס' נגד הכף ואם הרוטב יותר מן הכף צריך ס' נגד הרוטב. וליתר שאת העתקתי לשון הראב"ד מספר תמים דעים. וז"ל וכן עץ פרור של בשר ואם הוא בת יומא שבתכו בקדירה חולבת אם אין בה בכ"ע ואית קפילא ארמאה דיכול למטעמי' סמכינן עלי' ואי ליכא קפילא בששים ומ"מ עץ הפרור אסור משום הבלוע מן התבשיל אבל שמעתי מחכמי דורינו ששמעו מפי הרב ר' יעקב ז"ל דהיכא דהגביה עץ הפרור מלא מתבשיל הקדירה יש לנו לומר שמא מה שילא מפליטת הכף אינו יכול להתבטל בתבשיל שהגביה באותו הכף משום דלית בי' ששים באותו תבשיל שהגביה ואחר ההגבהה החזיר הכל לקדירה מה שהגביה עם עץ הפרור עלמו נעשה הכל נבלה ואוסרת כל הקדירה אם אין בה שיעור ס' כשיעור מה שהגביה עם עץ הפרור עכ"ל. הרי דבראב"ד לא נזכר תיבת ג"כ. וא"כ אין כאן ראי' מראב"ד. וצ"ל דע"כ גם דעת המנ"י הכי שהרי כ' ויש ללמוד מדין זבוב בכלל כ"א ושם לא נזכר רק, דהרוטב נעשה נבלה אבל לא נזכר שם כלל שילטרך ב"פ ס' אע"כ כמו שכתבתי:

ולפ"ז יצא לנו דאפי' לפי הכרעת רמ"א בסי' צ"ט בנפל איסור בין לא נודע בין נודע חוזר

וניער מ"מ בדבר שלא ע"י בלוע אין חילוק דבין בנודע בין בלא נודע בין בשאר איסורים אם לקח תבשיל בכף והחזיר התבשיל לקדירה א"צ אלא פעם א' ס' אלא דתלוי אם הכף גדול או התבשיל מרובה ואפי' בנו"ט דיש כאן ב' איסורים א' של חלב והשני' משום בשר בכ"ל מ"מ כיון דאינו אלא ספק הוי סד"ר ולקולא:

מח (סו) שאלה מעשה שחתכו בסכין של בשר מולייתא של גבינה אם שהיס"ב לאחר שהניחו אותו בכ"ש ונתערב הסכין בשאר סכינים ודין דבר גוש:

הנה דין זה דסכין והמולייתא מבואר בסי' צ"ד ס"ז ודין הסכינים הנערבים מבואר בסי' ק"ב סעיף ג' אך כל האחרונים ובראשם מהרי"ל חולקים על הרשב"א בזה וס"ל דבכלי לא בטיל ואכן כמאן נעביד והנה הפ"ח הק' דכשישתמש בזה הסכין בשר יטעום טעם חלב והוי מבשא"מ דבכ"ע דאורייתא ע"ש ואמנם נ"ל דזה תליא דאי אמרי' דכ"ש מבשל בדבר גוש וא"כ נאסר הסכין מדאורייתא אבל אי אמרי' דאינו אלא מבליע ומפליט וא"כ אינו אסור אלא מדרבנן דבנו"ט דוקא דרך בישול אסרה תורה והנה ממש כל האחרונים הסכימו לאו"ה ורש"ל דבדבר גוש אפי' בכ"ש כיון דליכא דפנות המקררות מבשל לעולם ע' סי' צ"ד וש"ך סי' ק"ה וכן מוכח דעת המ"א בא"ח סי' שי"ח ס"ק מ"ה דאסור לטוח שום על הכלי אם הוא רותח שהיס"ב דדבר גוש אפי' בכ"ש מבשל וכ"ש לכלי ע"ש והרי בשבת מותר ליתן בכ"ש (כדאי' בש"ס ופוסקים) ואף על גב דמבליע ומפליט דאינו אסור אלא מבשל וע"כ ס"ל דמבשל וה"נ מוכח מאו"ה שם כלל ל"ז שכתב דאם חתך בשר בסכין חולבת ב"י הבשר אסור בהנאה והרי קיי"ל בסימן פ"ז וכ"כ האו"ה כלל ל' דין ה' דנו"ט שאינו אלא מדרבנן מותר בהנא' אע"כ דס"ל דדבר גוש מבשל ממש והוי דרך בישול ולפ"ז יש בסכין הנ"ל איסור דאורייתא כקושית הפ"ח:

אך המנ"י כלל ס"א בסופו הקשה ע"ז מגמרא חולין פ' כ"ח דמקשה הש"ס סוף סוף כ"ש הוא והא התם איירי מדבר גוש ומאי פריך ומזה הוכיח דע"כ אינו רק מבליע ומפליט ויש לדחות כמש"כ התי"ט ר"פ כ"ה דלא גרסינן להאי קושי' כלל ע"ש עוד נ"ל ראיה גדולה מהא דאי' מעשרות פ"א מ"ז והנותן לחמיעה ולמחמוי כו' ופי' הר"ש ורע"ב חמיעה היא עוגה וכשמוציאין מן התנור רגילין להחליק פניה בשמן וקמ"ל דלא חשיב בישול דהאש קובעת למעשר אבל האי לא חשיב בישול ע"כ הרי בהדיא דאינו מבשל אע"ג דהוי גוש ואמנם ל"ע הרבה וכי גרע דבר גוש שנתבשל ע"ג האש מתבקעת ביצה ע"ג סודרין שהוחם ע"י האש דקיי"ל דאם גלגל בשבת דחייב דהוי תולדות אור והתוי"ט והמ"א שם סי' שי"ח כתבו באמת דאסור לטוח שום על הכלי אפי' אינו אצל המדורה וכ"כ רש"י בשבת ק"ט ד"ה שוריקא שמתנו הוציא הב"י דין זה דאפי' אינו כנגד המדורה אסור ובאמת שהרמב"ם כפי' כי חמיעה ומחמוי הם שמות לכלים ודלא כפי' ר"ש אע"כ דכוותי' דבר גוש כ"ז שהוא רותח מבשל ומה שהקשה המנ"י מגמרא דחולין דפריך סוף סוף כ"ש הוא נ"ל החילוק כמ"ש רמ"א בסי' ק"ה סעיף ג' דבאמת כ"ז שלא הניח הגוש בכ"ש יש לו דין כ"ר ומבשל אבל כשהניחו כבר בכ"ש הכלי גורם הקירור ואינו מבשל עוד רק מבליע ומפליט לקצת פוסקים ופריך שפיר הגמרא סוף סוף כ"ש הוא כיון שכבר מונח באלפס ולפ"ז ע"כ מוכח דלא מיבעיא הצד שמונח בכ"ש דאינו מבשל דהכלי גורם הקירור אלא אפי' מה שלמעלה ולצדדים אע"ג שאינו נוגע בכלי גם כן אינו מבשל דאל"כ עדיין קשה מ"פ הש"ס כ"ש הוא והא יש לגזור שיגעו הבשר והגבינה למעלה ולצדדין ולמה דחק הש"ס לתרץ שמא יעלה באלפס כ"ר שאין דרך להעלות על השלחן בכ"ר אע"כ שמקצת הבשר שנוגע בתבשיל גורם הקירור אף למעלה ולצדדים ופי' הר"ש והרע"ב ל"ע שהרי הוכחתי דע"כ כ"ז שאינו מונח בכלי הוא מבשל ולפ"ז אף דברי המ"א שהבאתי אינו מדוקדק אף שהדין שכ' הוא אמת דאף שלא כנגד המדורה אסור כ"ז שהוא רותח וכדאיתא בהדיא ברש"י אבל מה שסיים שכ"כ הפוסקים דדבר גוש אפי' בכ"ש מבשל וע"כ ז"א דכיון דמונח כבר בכ"ש אזי אינו אלא מבליע ומפליט אבל לא מבשל וזה אינו ענין לשבת. ולפ"ז ל"ע ג"כ על האו"ה שהבאתי שכתב דהבשר אסור בהנאה דכיון דכתבנו דאינו מבשל וא"כ בנו"ט אינו אלא מדרבנן וכל נו"ט שאינו מדאורייתא מותר בהנאה וא"ל דס"ל או"ה דכיון דאיכא נמי דוחקא וגוש מבשל נמי כדאמרינן דחומץ וציר גורם בישול אפי' בכ"ש ומגמרא דחולין לק"מ דהתם איירי בלא דוחקא ליתא מהא דאיתא בא"ח סי' שי"ח סעיף י"ח ובסי' שכ"א סעיף י"ט דמותר לגמור שחיקת הריפות בעץ פרור אפי' בכ"ר לאחר שהעבירו מן האש והא הוי גוש ודוחקא ומעשים בכ"י לחתוך בשבת דבר גוש שהיס"ב בסכין ואפי' כשמונח בכ"ר ול"א דיבשל הבלוע בסכין אע"כ דאינו מבשל הבלוע ולפ"ז נ"ל דס"ל לאו"ה דדוקא עוף בחלב או כבוש דאין בו שום צד דאורייתא בזה מותר בהנאה אבל כשהוא דרך בישול רק מחמת שנתקרר אינו מבשל כיון דעכ"פ מבליע ומפליט ס"ל דאסור בהנאה ג"כ ולפ"ז כיון שהוכחנו דבלוע זו שבסכין אינו אלא מדרבנן וא"כ יש כאן הרבה צדדים להקל חדא

שהרי הש"ע ורמ"א לא מחלקים בין גוש לצלול לעולם אינו אלא מבליע ומפליט בכ"ש וגם הש"ע ורמ"א והרבה אחרונים הכריעו כרשב"א דכלי בעל ברוב ומכ"ש לאחר ששהא מע"ל כמו שכתב הש"ך ולכן יש להתיר ואמנם בסכין של איסור לדעת המחמירים דגוש עכ"פ מבליע ומפליט וא"כ יש כאן איסור דאורייתא כקושית הפ"ח ל"ע ואמנם באו"ה כלל ל"ד סוף דין ט"ו מוכח דס"ל דדבר גוש אף בלא דוחקא ואפי' כשכבר מונח בכ"ש מבשל שכתב דעצל שהודח צריך ס' נגד כולו דלפעמים נוסכין עליו בשר רותח עכ"ל:

ואמנם מה שכתבתי והבאתי ראיה מהא דחותכין בשבת גוש ומסי' שכ"א זה תלוי בחקירה אי הא דקיי"ל אין בשול אחר בשול לענין שבת. אם הכונה דדבר מבושל ל"ש כלל בשול וא"כ אין לחלק בין שבת לבו"א כיון דל"ש בו בישול וא"כ שפיר יש ראיה דכמו דמותר בשבת לחתוך גוש ול"א דיבשל הבלוע מחמת דוחקא ה"נ בו"א ואמנם י"ל דבודאי שייך בשול אחר בשול רק בשבת דבעינן מלאכת מחשבת וא"כ כיון שכבר נתבשל וא"כ אין הבישול השני עושה פעולה משא"כ בבו"א יש לומר שפיר דיש בישול אחר בישול (והגאון בעל בית מאיר השיב לי על זה באריכות). ולכאורה יש ראיה דבבו"א יש בישול אחר בישול מחולין דף ק"ח ע"ב דמוקי להא דרב דאמר חלב מותר מכפל ליורה רותחת דמבלע בלע ונ"פ והא כיון דהחלב כבר נתבשל ל"ש בה בישול ולכן מותר משא"כ הבשר שנתבשל בחלב ויש לדחות דהא עכ"פ אסור מדרבנן ורב אמר חלב מותר ולכך הוצרך לשנות מבלע בלע:

והנה לכאורה מוכח דלעולם ל"ש בשול בגוש אף קודם שהניחו בכ"ש מהא דאיתא בפסחים פ' כ"ש אבל סכין ומטבילין בהם פרש"י סכין בשעת צלייתו והרע"ב כתב לאחר צלייתו וכ"מ מפי' רמב"ם ובהל' ק"פ פ"ח משמע דמפרש כרש"י ול"ע דבדף ע"ו איתא סכו בשמן תרומה יקלוף ופריך למ"ד תתאה גבר אמאי סגי בקליפה ומשני שאני סיכה דמשהו עבדו לי' וע"ש בתוספות שכ' דלדעת המקשן ע"כ איירי שסכו אחר צלייתו ולא נשתהא בתנור אחר סיכה כלל דא"כ על ידי רתיחת אור היה נבלע אפי' למאן דאמר עילאה גבר ע"ש ולפ"ז אי נימא דדבר גוש מבשל אף אי נימא כיון דמשהו הוא אינו מבשל יותר מקליפה ק' מאי איריא סכו בשמן תרומה הא אפי' בשמן חולין אסור משום מבושל בפסח דאפי' במי פירות אסור אע"כ דאינו מבשל ואמנם ע"כ ז"א דהא כתבנו דע"כ בשלא הניחו בכ"ש לכ"ע מבשל. וראיתי דהרמב"ם שם הל' ז' כתב דמותר לסוך במי פירות חוץ מן המים והכ"מ לא כתב מאין הוציא וראיתי שגם התוספות סוף כ"ש כתבו כן ולפ"ז לא ק"מ ושפיר י"ל דמבשל:

מט (קז) (קח) **שאלה** עלין חמוצין שקורין בל"א (שלאטויי) שחתכו אותם דק דק בכלי שקורין בל"א (האק מעסער) של נסר דהיינו שחותכים בו בשר ובצלים ביחד בעריבה של בשר ואחר כך בשלו השלאטויי בחלב מה דינו:

תשובה הנה צריכין אנו לבאר דין דברים חריפים. דעת הרי"ף והרמב"ם כפי מש"כ הב"י בסוף סימן צ"ו וכ"מ דעת הרשב"א בתה"א ובחידושיו והר"ן בפכ"ה דטעם צנון שחתכו בסכין של בשר אסור לאכלו בחלב הוא מטעם ששמנונית קרוש עליו ועל ידי החריפות הצנון בולע לדעת הראב"ד בכדי נטילה ולהרשב"א בכולו ולפ"ז אם היה הסכין מקונח יפה אע"פ שהוא ב"י מותר לאכלו בכותח מטעם דהוי נותן טעם בר נותן טעם והוכיחו כן מדגים שעלו בקערה דר"ל נתבשלו או צללו וידוע דע"י בישול או צלי מפליט ומבליע יותר מע"י חריפות ואפי' הכי מותר לאכלן בחלב מכ"ש ע"י חריפות דמותר מטעם דהוי נותן טעם בר נותן טעם. אבל דעת ספר התרומה והרא"ש דדוקא נתבשלו מותר דהוי ג' נותן טעם אבל דגים שעלו בקערה של בשר דאינו אלא ב' נותן טעם אסור לאכלו בכותח דב' נותן טעם אסור אף בכו"ה. ודברי הש"ע צ"ע שפסק בסימן צ"ה דאפי' בצללו מותר וכן פסק הרמ"א דעכ"פ בדיעבד מותר אפי' לדידן וא"כ מסייעא דעל ידי חריפות צנון מותר ובסימן צ"ו פסק דצנון שחתכו בסכין של בשר ב"י אפי' היה מקונח אסור לאכלו בכותח ומטעם קושיא זו פסק הפ"ח לאמת שאם היה המקונח אף שהיה ב"י מותר לאכלו בכותח וגם הכו"פ כתב דבמקום שיש עוד צד להקל יש לסמוך על הפ"ח:

אבל אם חתכו בסכין של איסור ב"י אע"פ שהוא מקונח כיון דלא שייך בו נותן טעם בר נ"ט דעל כל פנים דוחקא דסכינא והחריפות מפליט ומבליע ואף דהרא"ה בבד"ה דף ל"ה כתב דאינו מפליט כלל ומתיר לחתוך בסכין של איסור אם הוא מקונח יפה בטלה דעתו נגד כל הנך פוסקים:

עוד החמיר הרמ"א בדברים החריפים דאפי' אם חתכו אותם בסכין שאינו ב"י מקונח אסור מטעם דחורפיה מחליא ליה לשבח כדמצינו גבי חלתית בסי' קי"ד סעי' י'. ואפי' לענין נותן טעם בנ"ט כגון סכין של בשר שחתך בו צנון וכן התבלין שדכו אותם במדוכה של בשר ס"ל ב' חומרות דחשוי ליה לשבח ובולע גוף הבשר אבל דעת המחבר נ"ל דסבירא ליה דאף על גב דלענין איסור מחמירים

בכל דבר חריף כמו גבי חלתית דאמרי' משויה ליה לשבח כמו שכתב בהדיא בסי' ק"ג סעיף ו' ובסימן קי"ד סעיף א' מ"מ לענין בב"ח דעתו להקל דב' חומרות לא מחמירינן ולכן כתב בסי' ל"ו סעיף ג' דהבלין שנדוכו במדוך ב"י דוקא ובזה מסולק תמיהת האחרונים מסימן ק"ג דהשלמא באיסור דל"ש נותן טעם בר נותן טעם מחמירין לומר דהכל הוי חריף אבל בבו"ח דהוי נותן טעם בר נותן טעם לא מחמירינן כולי האי לומר גם כן מחליא ליה לשבח דאפי' אם הוא לשבח אינו אלא נותן טעם בר נותן טעם ונלערך לומר גם כן דעדיף מנותן טעם בר נותן טעם כולי האי לא מחמירינן. עוד כתב בש"ע שם סעיף ב' דפירות חמוצים דינם שוה לחתך בו לנון. אבל הט"ז שם כתב בשם הת"ח שכתב בשם איסור והיתר דתפוחים חמוצים לא מקרי דבר חריף וכתב הע"ז דבמקום הפסד יש לסמוך על זה עוד כתב הע"ז שם בס"ק י"ח ובעין זה כתב הש"ך שם בדין מי לימונים כיון שאינם חריפים כמו בצון לא מחליא ליה לשבח אלא מה שבלוע בדופני הסכין:

ולפ"ז כיון שעינינו רואות דשלאויי עכ"פ לא חריפי יותר מתפוחים חמוצים יש לומר אפי' לדעת רמ"א דאפי' לענין נותן טעם בר נותן טעם ואינו ב"י מחמירי' בדברים החריפים. היינו דוקא דברים החריפים המוזכרים בש"ע אבל פירות החמוצים כיון שאינם חריפים כ"כ עכ"פ יש לסמוך על דעת המחבר דדוקא בן יומו או סכין של איסור אבל סכין של בשר ואינו ב"י יש להתיר בפשיטות ומכ"ש לדעת רוב הפוסקים ראשונים דאפי' בב"י ומקונח מותר בבו"ח דהוי נ"ט בר נ"ט וכמו שכתב הפ"ח וכו"פ וא"כ יש לסמוך עליהם באינו ב"י בדברים חריפים כתפוחים חמוצים וע' בחבורי נ"א על א"ח בהל' פסח סי' ע' שבזה ישבתי דברי המ"א בסי' תמ"ז ס"ק כ"ח ואפשר דבמקום הפסד וסעודת מצוה גם כן יש להתיר אפי' בב"י בסכין של בשר ובסכין של איסור שאינו ב"י:

ועוד אני אומר דלפענ"ד כלי (האק מעסער) שחתכו בו בשר עם בצלים אינו בלוע מבשר כלל שהרי לא חתכו בו מעולם בשר רותח ואינו בלוע מבשר אלא מה שבלע מבשר ובצלים שחתכו בו וכבר כתב הרשב"א בתשובה הביאו הב"י בסי' ל"ו וז"ל מכתשת חולבת שאב"י וכתשו בה בילים עם מרק בשר דמותר לפי שהמכתשת אינה ב"י ולא אסרו משום תבלין שמשימין בבילים דהתבלין שנתערב עם הבילים דבר מועט הוא ואין כ"כ חריפות בהם להחזיר לשבח פליטת המכתשת עכ"ל. וה"נ אין כח בבצלים המעטים שנתערבו עם הבשר להבליע בכלי (האק מעסער) טעם הבשר אך י"ל כיון שנחתכו הבצלים בסכין של בשר א"כ בלעו מבשר שנבלע בסכין ועכשיו נבלע טעם זה בהאק מעסר והארכתי בנידון זה בחבורי נ"א בהל' פסח ע"ש:

נ (סע) בכו"פ סי' ל"ז מביא ראיה דלא מהני טעימה לפת שלש בחלב דאל"כ למה אסרה רבה ה"ל למטעמיי וא"ל דבאמת טעם והוי ליה טעם חלב דא"כ מאי פריך מתנור שטחו כו' ומשיק מותר ומאי קושיא כיון שיש בו טעם היאך יועיל לו הסקה וכ"ל דודאי הא דאסר רבה ר"ל עד שיטעום אלא משום דאמר אסרה לעולם פרש"י אף לאחר שהוסק התנור וס"ל דלעולם צריך לטעום אם יש טעם וע"ז פריך מברייתא משיק מותר ר"ל דא"ל טעימה וא"כ אין חילוק בין טעימה ובין מש"כ מהרי"ט דאם יש בו ס' מותר ולפ"ז י"ל דמותר לאכול אפי' עם בשר דמ"ש מחלב שנפל למים בסי' ל"ט סעי' ו' אך הואיל וילא מפה כו"פ נ"ל כעין פשר ועיין באו"ה כלל ל"ט סי' י"ח שכ' להדיא וז"ל והא דאם עם כל הפת אסור היינו כשאין שם ס' כו' דלא גרע מאילו נתבשל עוד י"ל דבודאי אם עם התנור או לש העיסה לכתחלה אפי' בדבר מועט וכונתו לבטל החלב כדי לאכול עם בשר ודאי אסור לעולם כדין מבטל איסור לכתחלה. אבל אם בדיעבד שזב שומן תחת הפת או באומר מותר ודאי אם יש בו ס' בכל ככר כמש"כ באו"ה שם מותר:

נא (ע) כתב כו"פ בשם אני אמו שמותר לחלק לבתים הרבה וק' דא"כ למה אסרה רבה ה"ל לומר שיחלק לבתי' והיראה שהרב ר' שמעון זקני נ"ן דק"ק ווילנא הורה בשומן שזב תחת הפת בתנור שישימו בכל ככר עלם כדי שיהיה להיכר שהיא של בשר ונחלקו עליו חכמי העיר ואני א' מהם מחמת קושיא הנ"ל ועכשיו מלאתי בהגהת ש"ד סי' ל"ה וז"ל אמר לנו הרא"ש כשאופין קוסטיל או קוללא עם מולייתא דלכתחלה יש לעשות כ"י כפי מה שהם המולייתא אם הם של בשר ישימו עליו קלת עלמות ואם הוא של חלב ישימו עליו קלת גבינה דהוי כעין תורא לפי פירוש א' דפירש כעין שורא סי' עכ"ל וע' בר"ת סי' ל"ו בשם או"ה ולפ"ז ע"כ הא דכתב הרמב"ם שישנה לורת הפת לאו דוקא אלא ה"ה כל סי' ולפ"ז י"ל שפיר דאף לאחר אפיה מהני סי' וכ"ל דה"ה לפ"ל דמהני אם יכתוב עליו בשר או חלב שהרי ביומא דף כ"ה א"י שמה שהיו כותבין על השופרות חדתין ועתיקין היה לסי' ואפשר אם כלרף יחד שימכור לכל בע"ה ככר א' ויעשה בככר סי' בעלם או בגבינה וא"כ אף שהכו"פ כתב דלריך עוד לד להקל כ"ל דעל כל פנים בשניהן יחד מותר בהפ"מ. וא"ל דא"כ למה אסרה רבה בגמרא יש לומר דבאמת ה"ק אסרה עד שיעשה תיקון ודוגמתו מלינו בחולין קי"א ע"ב רש"י ד"ה האי

דכתב ומותר דקאמר כגון שטעמו כו' ושם בגמרא קערה שמלח כו' אסור כו' והיינו עד שיטעום קפילא כדאיתא שם בגמרא ובמנחות דף י"ו ע"ב אמר רב זר שקמץ יחזור ופריך והתנן פסול מאי פסול עד שיחזור וגם די"ל דהתם ברייתא והכא מימרא ויותר נ"ל לתרץ דבודאי אם יעשה כן לכתחלה דעת המטור באלי' או שלש עיסה בחלב כדי לאכול עם בשר או חלב אפי' נתן רק דבר מועט דהוי מבטל איסור לכתחלי' בודאי לא מהני שום תיקון להתיר דכיון דכבר נאסר מתחלה דומה למה שכתבתי לעיל סי' ה"ח בשם הגהת ש"ד במלח בכלי שא"מ דאסור מיד כולו אבל אם בדיעבד זב תחת הפת אע"פ דלכתחלה אסור להעמיד בתנור אחד דבר שיש לחוש שמא יזוב כדאיתא בש"ע סי' ל"ז היינו לכתחלה אבל בדיעבד מותר כמש"כ הש"ך סי' ל"ז סק"ב דבלא ראה שזב מותר מטעם ס"ס שמא לא זב ואת"ל דזב שמא לא זב תחת הפת ולכאורה י"ל דגם זה אסור מדינא וא"כ ק' דאפי' לא זב כיון שעבר על תקנת חז"ל יהיה אסור אפילו בדיעבד שהרי בחולין קי"ב בעי מהו לאכותי כדא דמלחא גבי כדא דכמכא א"ל אסור דהלא מאי מותר ומוכח שם ברש"י אפילו אם יש לחוש שיפול לתוכו רק מעט וזה דומה למלחא שלא יהיה האיסור ניכר נ"ל דהתם לא קאמר אסור ואם הניח אסור וכן העתיקו כל הפוסקים בסי' ל"ה אין נותנין משמע לכתחלה אבל על דיעבד היכא דלא חזינן ריעותא ל"ג חז"ל משא"כ באין לשין עיסה גזרו דאם לש כל הפת אסור כדאי' בגמרא בהדיא וא"כ ה"נ לא מצינו שתקנו חז"ל דאם הניח הלב עם פת שיהי' אסור בדיעבד וא"כ לא קנסו חז"ל וא"כ מצד תקנת חז"ל אין לקנסו אלא שיש לחוש שמא יאכל עם חלב י"ל שפיר דמהני סי' וכ"ז בזב אבל אם לש עיסה בחלב לא מהני שום תיקון ולכן אסר רבה כל הפת אפי' במלחא ולא מהני שום תיקון ושאני ההוא דש"ד שהבאתי שעשה הסימן קודם האפי' וא"כ עשה כתיקון חז"ל:

Bibliography

Authorities Cited in the Chochmas Adam and the Commentary

This section contains a listing of all the rabbinical sources which are quoted by the *Chochmas Adam* in *The Laws of Meat and Milk*, together with pertinent biographical material on each of them. The many sources which were used to prepare the English commentary have also been included in this listing.

We will begin with a discussion of the *Tur*, since this work provides the foundation for the *Shulchan Aruch* and its commentaries. All of the other sources are then divided into three categories depending on the historical era in which they fall. Within each category, they are listed in alphabetical order.

1. The Tur

The term *"Tur"* denotes the *Arba'ah Turim* (literally, four rows) written by Rabbi Yaakov Ba'al HaTurim. The *Tur* was written in Spain in the first half of the fourteenth century. It contains a comprehensive summary of the entire body of Jewish law as it applies nowadays. As implied by its name, the *Arba'ah Turim* is divided into four main sections:

Orach Chayim contains laws that pertain to one's daily activities (such as recitation of prayers and blessings) as well as the regulations that pertain to the Sabbath and holidays.

Yoreh De'ah deals with many varied topics. The first part includes laws pertaining to slaughtering animals, salting of meat, forbidden mixtures, and food or drink prepared by a gentile. It continues with laws pertaining to vows, charity, making a loan with interest, the *niddah* (a woman who is impure due to a flow of blood), and the laws that pertain to the mourner.

Even Ha'ezer contains laws of marriage and divorce.

Choshen Mishpat deals with Jewish civil law, such as settling disputes between neighbors, the proper way to conduct business, and compensating a person for damage or injury that he suffers.

2. Rishonim—Early Authorities

(Those who lived before 1492
when the Jews were expelled from Spain)

Issur v'heter This very important work, which serves as the basis for many of the laws of meat and milk, was written by Rabbi Yonah ben Yisroel. He lived in Germany during the fifteenth century.

Maharil The Maharil (Rabbi Yaakov Moelin) was a famous German authority who lived during the late fourteenth and early fifteenth centuries. ("Maharil" is the abbreviated form of Moreinu HoRav Yaakov haLevi.)

Mordechai This work was written by Rabbi Mordechai ben Hillel, who lived in Germany during the thirteenth century. This is an extensive work on Jewish law which is printed in many editions of the Talmud.

Raavad Rabbi Avraham ben David, great Talmudic authority of the twelfth century. He is best known for his critical notes on the *Mishnah Torah* of the *Rambam.*

Rabbenu Tam This is Rabbi Yaakov ben Meir Tam, who was a grandson of Rashi. He lived in France during the twelfth century. His comments on the Talmud provide the basis for a large part of the *Tosafot* commentary on the *Talmud* (see below).

Rabbi Isserlein See *Terumas Hadeshen.*

Rabbi Yechiel He is one of the authors of the *Tosafot* commentary on the *Talmud* (see below). Rabbi Yechiel was born in Paris, living in France and then in Eretz Yisroel in the early thirteenth century.

Ran Rabbenu Nissim, a famous Talmudic commentator who lived in Spain during the fourteenth century.

Ravan This refers to Rabbi Avraham ben Nasan, a student of the *Ri* (see below). He lived in the twelfth and early thirteenth centuries in Provence and Spain, and became renowned as a great scholar.

Rambam This is the very famous Rabbi Moshe ben Maimon, author of the *Mishnah Torah,* which contains a complete summary of Jewish law. He lived in Egypt during the twelfth century.

Rashi Rabbi Shlomo Yitzchaki, the most famous of all commentators, lived in France during the eleventh century. In addition to his well known Torah commentary, he also wrote a commentary on most of the *Talmud.*

Ri The *Ri* (Rabbi Yitzchak of Dampierre, France) was a nephew of *Rabbenu Tam* (see above), living in the latter part of the twelfth century. His comments provide a large part of the *Tosafot* commentary on the Talmud.

Riva Rabbi Yitzchak ben Asher. He was a pupil of Rashi who lived in Germany in the early twelfth century.

Shaarei Dura This work was written by Rabbi Yitzchak of Duren in Germany during the early fifteenth century.

Terumas Hadeshen This famous work, consisting of responsa, was written by Rabbi Yisroel Isserlein who lived in Germany during the fifteenth century. Rabbi Isserlein is also known for his notes which he wrote on the *Shaarei Dura* (see above).

Tosafot Commentary on the Talmud written by prominent French and German scholars during the generations following Rashi. A large part of the commentary was authored by Rashi's descendants and pupils.

Tur See above.

3. Achronim—Later Authorities

Bach Abbreviation of *Bayis Chadash*, a commentary on the *Tur* written by Rabbi Yoel Sirkes. He was a rabbi in Poland during the late sixteenth and early seventeenth centuries.

Bais Lechem Yehudah Commentary on the *Shulchan Aruch* by Rabbi Zvi Hirsch of Vilna, Poland. It was published at the beginning of the nineteenth century.

Bais Yosef This work consists of a very comprehensive commentary and analysis of all four parts of the *Tur*. It was written in Greece and *Eretz Yisroel* in the sixteenth century by Rav Yosef Karo, the author of the *Shulchan Aruch*.

Binas Adam Written by the author of the *Chochmas Adam*. It contains detailed discussions on certain topics covered in *Shulchan Aruch-Yoreh De'ah*.

Chayei Adam This work summarizes the laws of the *Shulchan Aruch-Orach Chayyim*. It was written by the author of the *Chochmas Adam*.

Chavos Da'as A commentary on the *Shulchan Aruch* written by Rabbi Yaakov Lorberbaum of Lissa (a city in Poland) during the end of the eighteenth century.

Chok Yaakov Laws dealing with *Pesach* written by the author of the *Minchas Yaakov* (see below).

Bibliography

Dagul Mei-r'vavah Notes on the *Shulchan Aruch* by the famous Rabbi Yechezkel Landau. He was rabbi in Prague during the eighteenth century.

Darkei Moshe Commentary on the *Tur* written by the *Rama* (see below).

Damesek Eliezer Commentary on the *Toras Chatas* (see below) written by Rabbi Eliezer of Shebrishin, Poland. It was published in the beginning of the eighteenth century.

Derisha and **Perisha** Commentaries on the *Tur* written by Rabbi Yehoshua Falk, a famous Polish rabbi who lived during the late sixteenth and early seventeenth centuries.

Eliya Rabbah Commentary on the *Shulchan Aruch—Orach Chayim* by Rabbi Eliya of Prague. He lived during the late seventeenth and early eighteenth centuries.

Kreisi u'Pleisi Commentary on *Shulchan Aruch—Yoreh De'ah* by Rabbi Yonasan Eybeschutz, a well known Rabbi in Prague, France, and Germany during the eighteenth century.

Magen Avraham Commentary on the *Shulchan Aruch—Orach Chayim* written by Rabbi Avraham Gombiner, who lived in Poland during the seventeenth century.

Maharshal He lived in Poland during the sixteenth century, being one of the greatest Torah scholars of his generation. His most famous work is the *Yam shel Shlomo*, a commentary on several tractates of the *Talmud*. (Maharshal is an abbreviation for Moreinu HoRav Shlomo Luria.)

Masas Binyamin Responsa written by Rabbi Binyamin Aharon Slonik. He was a Polish Rabbi who lived in the late sixteenth and early seventeenth centuries.

Minchas Yaakov Commentary on the *Toras Chatas* by Rabbi Yaakov Reisher, who served as a rabbi in Bohemia, France and Germany in the early eighteenth century.

Nekudos Hakesef This consists of comments written by the *Shach* in which he indicates his disagreement with comments of the *Taz*.

Pri Chadash Critical work on the *Shulchan Aruch* written by Rabbi Chizkiyahu da Silva, Rabbi of Yerushalayim, in the seventeenth century.

Pri Megadim This is the name of a *sefer* written by Rabbi Yosef Teomim which contains notes on the *Shach* (called *Sifsei Da'as*), notes on the *Taz* (the *Mishbetzos Zahav*), as well as other explanatory material. He served as rabbi in Germany during the eighteenth century.

Perisha See *Derisha.*

Rabbi Akiva Eger Renowned rabbinical leader in Germany during the early part of the nineteenth century. Among his many writings are glosses to the *Shulchan Aruch.*

Rama This refers to Rabbi Moshe Isserles, who lived in Poland during the sixteenth century. He is best known for the *mappah* (literally, tablecloth) which consists of notes on the *Shulchan Aruch* of Rabbi Yosef Caro. Specifically, he records the decisions of *Ashkenazic* authorities which conflict with the decisions of Rabbi Yosef Caro (who was of Sephardic descent). All current editions of the *Shulchan Aruch* consist of both the text written by Rabbi Yosef Caro, and the notes of the *Rama.*

The *Rama* is also the author of *Darkei Moshe* which is a commentary on the *Tur*, and the *Toras Chatas*, a work dealing with laws of meat and milk and other related topics.

Rashal See *Maharshal.*

Shach Abbreviation of *Sifsei Kohen*, commentary on the *Shulchan Aruch—Yoreh De'ah* by Rabbi Shabsai ben Meir Hakohen. He lived in Lithuania and Bohemia in the seventeenth century.

Shulchan Aruch (Literally, set table) This work, written by Rabbi Yosef Karo, summarizes all of the *halachic* decisions which were mentioned in his *Bais Yosef* commentary on the *Tur*. The organization follows that of the *Tur* (see above), being divided into four sections: *Orach Chayyim, Yoreh De'ah, Even Ha'ezer* and *Choshen Mishpat.*

Taz Abbreviation of the work *Turei Zahav*, a commentary on the *Shulchan Aruch—Yoreh De'ah* written by Rabbi David ben Shmuel Halevi. He was a rabbi in Poland during the seventeenth century.

Toras Chatas A *sefer* written by the *Rama* dealing with the laws of meat and milk and other related topics.

Tzemach Tzedek A collection of responsa written by Rabbi Menachem Mendel Krochmal, who lived in Poland and Moravia during the seventeenth century. He studied together with the *Taz.*

Yam shel Shlomo See *Maharshal.*

4. Contemporary Authorities

(Those who lived within the last century)

Aruch Hashulchan A detailed summary and analysis of the *Shulchan Aruch* by Rabbi Michael Halevi Epstein, rabbi in Novardok, Russia.

Badei Hashulchan Laws of Meat and Milk written in the style of the *Mishnah Berurah*, by Rabbi Shraga Feivel Cohen of Brooklyn, New York.

Chayei Avraham Commentary on the *Chochmas Adam* written by Rabbi Avraham Chayim Spitzer of Brooklyn, New York.

Chazon Ish Rabbi Avraham Yeshaya Karelitz, renowned leader of the Torah community in *Eretz Yisroel.*

Darkei Teshuva Commentary on the *Shulchan Aruch* written by Rabbi Zvi Hirsch Shapira, a rabbinical leader in Munkach, located in Hungary.

Guide to the Laws of Kashrus by Rabbi Moshe Morgan of Brooklyn, New York.

Igros Moshe The Responsa of Rabbi Moshe Feinstein, world renowned rabbinical leader who resided in the lower east side of New York City.

Biur Halacha See *Mishnah Berurah*.

Hilchos M'ieros Basar B'cholov Illustrated Guide to the laws of meat and milk by Ehud Rosenberg, based on the *Kitzur Shulchan Aruch* mentioned below.

Kaf Hachayim A detailed commentary on the *Shulchan Aruch* by Rabbi Yaakov Chayim Sofer, who lived in Baghdad and *Eretz Yisroel.*

Kitzur Shulchan Aruch Review of laws pertaining to various sections of *Shulchan Aruch-Yoreh Deah*, written by Rabbi Aharon Pfeifer of Johannesberg, South Africa.

Kuntres Bais Yisroel Notations on the *Chochmas Adam* written by Rabbi Yisroel Avraham Lerner, Rabbi of Moldavia.

Madanei Hashulchan Commentary on portions of *Yoreh Deah* written by Rabbi Levi Hakohen Rabinowitz, currently being published in *Eretz Yisroel.* Its organization is similar to that of the *Mishnah Berurah*, consisting of three parts. The basic commentary on the *Shulchan Aruch* is entitled *Madanei Hashulchan*. There is an extensive discussion of source material in the *Matamei Hashulchan*, and sources (with additional comments) are mentioned in the section called *P'eir Hashulchan*.

Matamei Hashulchan See *Madanei Hashulchan.*

Mishnah Berurah The well known commentary on the *Shulchan Aruch* by Rabbi Yisroel Meir Kagan of Radun, Poland (the *Chofetz Chayim*). Rabbi Yisroel Meir authored two other commentaries which are printed together with it: *Shaar Hatziyun* consisting largely of source material, and *Biur Halacha* which contains detailed discussions of various topics.

P'eir Hashulchan See *Madanei Hashulchan.*

Shaar Hatziyun See *Mishnah Berurah.*

Shaarei Isur V'heter Guide to laws of meat and milk and laws of forbidden mixtures, by Rabbi Moshe Mendel Brus of Brooklyn, New York.

List of Hebrew Abbreviations

א׳: אחד, אחת
א״א: אי אפשר
אא״כ: אלא אם כן
אב״י: אינו בן יומו
או״ה: איסור והיתר
א״ח: אורח חיים
אח״כ: אחר כך
אי׳: איתא
א״י: אינו יודע
אי״ה: אם ירצה השם
א״כ: אם כן
א״ל: אם לא, אין לומר
א״נ: אי נמי
אע״ג: אף על גב
אע״פ: אף על פי
אפ״ה: אפילו הכי
אפ׳: אפילו
א״צ: אין צריך
א״ר: אליה רבה
את״ל: אם תמצא לומר
ב״א: בינת אדם
באו״ה: באיסור והיתר
בא״ח: באורח חיים
ב״ב: בני ביתו
בב״א: בבינת אדם
בבו״ח: בבשר וחלב
בב״י: בבית יוסף
בד״א: במה דברים אמורים
בהכ״ס: בית הכסא
בהמ״ז: ברכת המזון
בהפ״מ: בהפסד מרובה
בו״ח: בשר וחלב
בח״ד: בחוות דעת
בט״ז: בטורי זהב

ב״י: בית יוסף, בן יומו, בני יומן
בי״ד: ביורה דעה
בכ״א: בכל אחד
בכה״ג: בכהאי גוונא
בכ״ח: בכלי חרס
בכ״ר: בכלי ראשון
בכ״ש: בכלי שני
בל״א: בלשון אשכנז
בלא״ה: בלאו הכי
בל״י: בית לחם יהודה
במ״א: במגן אברהם, במקום אחד
בס״ט: בספק טריפה
בסי׳: בסימן
בע״ש: בערב שבת
בפ״ח: בפרי חדש
בפ״ע: בפני עצמי
בש״ך: בשפתי כהן
בש״ע: בשלחן ערוך
ג״כ: גם כן
דאו״ה: דאיסור והיתר
דא״ל: דאין לומר
דאל״כ: דאם לא כן
דאע״ג: דאף על גב
דאע״פ: דאף על פי
דאפ׳: דאפילו
דא״צ: דאין צריך
דבו״ח: דבשר וחלב
דבכ״א: דבכל אחד
דבכה״ג: דבכה״ג
דה״ה: דהוא הדין
דחנ״נ: דחתיכה נעשית נבילה
די״א: דיש אומרים
די״ל: דיש לומר
דכ״ש: דכלי שני

דל״א: דלא אמרינן
דל״ד: דלא דמי, דלאו דוקא
דל״ז: דלפי זה
דל״ש: דלא שייך
דלכ״ע: דלכולי עלמא
ד״מ: דרכי משה
דמ״א: דמשק אליעזר
דנ״נ: דנעשית נבילה
דנטל״פ: דנותן טעם לפגם
דס״ל: דסבירא ליה
דע״י: דעל ידי
דעכ״פ: דעל כל פנים
דק״ל: דקיימא לן
דק״ק: דקהילה קדושה
דר״ל: דרוצה לומר
הב״י: הבית יוסף
הגה׳: הגהה, הגהות
ה״ה: הוא הדין
ה״ז: הרי זה
הט״ז: הטורי זהב
הי׳: היה
הי״ס: היד סולדת
היס״ב: היד סולדת בו
הכו״פ: הכריתי ופליתי
המ״א: המגן אברהם
המנ״י: המנחת יעקב
ה״נ: הכא נמי
הפ״ח: הפרי חדש
הפ״מ: הפסד מרובה
הצ״צ: הצמח צדק
הר״ל: הראויה להתכבד
הש״ך: השפתי כהן
הש״ע: השלחן ערוך
וא׳: ואחד

List of Hebrew Abbreviations

וא״א: ואי אפשר
ואב״י: ואינו בן יומו
ואח״כ: ואחר כך
וא״כ: ואם כן
ואע״ג: ואף על גב
ואע״פ: ואף על פי
ואפי׳: ואפילו
ואפ״ה: ואפילו הכי
וא״צ: ואין צריך
ואת״ל: ואם תמצא לומר
ובב״א: ובבינת אדם
ובבו״ח: ובבשר וחלב
ובהפ״מ: ובהפסד מרובה
ובכ״ח: ובכלי חרס
ובלא״ה: ובלאו הכי
ובש״ע: ובשלחן ערוך
וה״ה: והוא הדין
וה״ז: והרי זה
והיס״ב: והיד סולדת בו
וז״ל: וזה לשונו
וי״א: ויש אומרים
וכו״פ: וכריתי ופליתי
וכ״ז: וכל זה
וכ״ש: וכל שכן, וכלי שני
ול״א: ולא אמרינן
ולפ״ז: ולפי זה
ומש״כ: ומכל שכן, ומה שכתוב
ומ״מ: ומכל מקום
ונטל״פ: ונותן טעם לפגם
ונ״ל: ונראה לי
ונ״מ: ונפקא מינה
וס״ל: וסבירא ליה
ועכ״פ: ועל כל פנים
וע״ש: ועיין שם
וצ״ל: וצריך לומר
וקיי״ל: וקיימא לן
ז״א: זה אינו

זא״ז: זה את זה
ז״ל: זה לשונו
ח״א: חיי אדם
ח״ד: חוות דעת
חהר״ל: חתיכה הראויה להתכבד
חז״ל: חכמינו זכרונם לברכה
ח״י: חק יעקב
חנ״נ: חתיכה נעשית נבילה
חתי׳: חתיכה, חתיכות
חתיכ׳: חתיכה, חתיכות
ט״ז: טורי זהב
טכ״ע: טעם כעיקר
ט״ס: טעות סופר
י״א: יש אומרים
י״ד: יורה דעה
יהי׳: יהיה
י״ל: יש לומר
י״פ: י׳ פעמים
יש״ש: ים של שלמה
כ׳: כתב
כ״א: כל אחד
כ״ה: כל הבשר
כה״ג: כהאי גוונא
כו׳: כולו
כו״פ: כריתי ופליתי
כ״ז: כל זה, כל זמן
כ״ח: כלי חרס
כ״כ: כל כך, כן כתב
ככ״ר: ככלי ראשון
ככ״ש: ככלי שני
כ״מ: כן מצאתי, כן מוכח
כמ״ד: כמאן דאמר
כמש״כ: כמו שכתב
כ״נ: כדי נטילה
כנ״ט: כנותן טעם
כנלע״ד: כן נראה לעניית דעתי
כ״ע: כולי עלמא

כ״צ: כל צרכן
כ״ק: כדי קליפה
כ״ר: כלי ראשון
כ״ש: כלי שני, כל שכן
ל״א: לא אמרינן
לבו״ח: לבשר וחלב
לבהכ״ס: לבית הכסא
ל״ד: לא דמי, לאו דוקא
להדי׳: להדיא
לי׳: ליה
לכ״ע: לכולי עלמא
למש״כ: למה שכתוב
לנ״ט: לנותן טעם
לפ״ד: לפי דעת
לפ״ז: לפי זה
ל״צ: לא צריך
ל״ש: לא שייך
לשתי׳: לשתיה
מ״א: מגן אברהם
מ״ב: משאת בנימן
מבו״ח: מבשר וחלב
מבשא״מ: מין בשאינו מינו
מ״ד: מאן דאמר
מהרא״י: מורינו הרב איסרליין
מהרי״ל: מורינו הרב יצחק לוריא
מהר״ש: מורינו הרב שמעון
מה״ת: מן התורה
מכ״נ: מכדי נטילה
מכ״ק: מכדי קליפה
מכ״ר: מכלי ראשון
מכ״ש: מכלי שני
מ״מ: מכל מקום
ממ״נ: ממה נפשך
מנ״ט: מנותן טעם
מנ״י: מנחת יעקב
מס״ס: מספק ספיקא
מע״ל: מעת לעת

List of Hebrew Abbreviations

מעל"ע: מעת לעת
מ"ש: מה שכתוב, מה שנאמר
מ"ץ: מורה צדק
משא"כ: מה שאין כן
נ"ט: נותן טעם
נטל"פ: נותן טעם לפגם
נ"ל: נראה לי
נלע"ד: נראה לעניית דעתי
נ"מ: נפקא מינה
נ"נ: נעשה נבילה, נעשית נבילה
ס': ספק
ס"ט: ספק טרפה
ס"י: סימן
ס"ל: סבירא ליה
ס"ס: ספק ספיקא, סוף סימן
סס"י: סוף סימן
סס"ק: סוף סעיף קטן
ססעי': סוף סעיף
סעי': סעיף
ס"ק: סעיף קטן
סק"א: סעיף קטן א'
סק"ב: סעיף קטן ב'
סק"ח: סעיף קטן ח'
ע"ד: על דעת
ע"ז: על זה

ע"י: על ידי
ע"כ: על כרחך, על כן
עכ"ל: עד כאן לשונו
עכ"פ: על כל פנים
ע"פ: על פי
ע"ש: ערב שבת, עיין שם
פ': פירוש
פ"א: פעם אחת
פג"ה: פרק גיד הנשה
פ"ח: פרי חדש
פמ"ג: פרי מגדים
צ"ל: צריך לומר
צ"ע: צריך עיון
צ"צ: צמח צדק
קיי"ל: קיימא לן
ק"ק: קהילה קדושה
ראב"ד: רב אברהם בן דוד
ראב"ן: רב אברהם בן נתן
ר"י: רב יצחק
ר"ל: רוצה לומר
רמ"א: רב משה איסרלש
רמב"ם: רב משה בן מיימון
ר"ן: רבינו ניסים
רש"י: רב שלמה יצחקי

רש"ל: רב שלמה לוריא
ר"ת: רבינו תם
שא"א: שאי אפשר
שאב"י: שאינו בן יומו
שא"ה: שאני התם
שאפ': שאפילו
ש"ד: שערי דורא
שהי': שהיה
שהי"ס: שהיד סולדת
שהיס"ב: שהיד סולדת בו
שו"ע: שתי וערב
שיהי': שיהיה
שכ': שכתב
ש"ך: שפתי כהן
שכ"א: שכל אחד
ש"ס: ששה סדרים
ש"ע: שלחן ערוך
שע"ג: שעל גבי
שע"י: שעל ידי
שעי"ז: שעל ידי זה
שעכ"פ: שעל כל פנים
תה"ד: תרומת הדשן
תוס': תוספות
ת"ח: תורת חטאת
תע"ב: תבוא עליו ברכה

List of Halachos in This Work By Topic and Section

13. Using Meat Utensils with an Insufficiently Prepared Udder
14. Salting an Udder With Meat

Topic 42: Meat and Cheese (or Forbidden Food and Permissible Food) Which Come into Contact with Each Other While Cold

1. Forbidden Mixtures of Cold Food
2. Leaving Foods Together Which Will Have to be Washed; Placing Raw Meat in a Forbidden Vessel
3. Storing Meat and Dairy Foods (or Permissible and Forbidden Foods) Near Each Other
4. Placing Certain Pareve Substances Next to Milk
5. Bread Which Comes Into Contact With Meat or Milk
6. Mixtures of Cold Broiled Meat With Milk; Mixtures Involving Raw Meat Which Contains Cracks or Is Spiced
7. תתאי גבר (The Lower Substance Is Dominant)—Applying This Rule When the Lower Food is Cold
8. תתאי גבר (The Lower Substance Is Dominant)—Applying This Rule When the Lower Food is Hot
9. Food Is Considered to Be Hot When It Is יד סולדת בו
10. Food Which Requires "Peeling" But Was Used Without Being Peeled (Or Which Is Impossible to Be Peeled)
11. Definition of "Peeling" *(k'lipah)*

Topic 43: Forbidden Food and Permissible Food (or Meat and Cheese) Which Are Salted Together

1. A Salted Food Is Considered to Be Hot
2. The Liquid Flowing from Salted Meat (ציר)
3. Meat Which is Salted More Than 18 (or 24) Minutes
4. Meat Which Is Salted a Second Time
5. Mixtures of Kosher and Unkosher Food Where One or Both Are Salted
6. Does the Lower Food Dominate When It Is "Hot" Due to Salting?
7. Applying the Rule That "The Lower Substance Is Dominant" to Salted Food When There Are Other Grounds to Be Lenient
8. Salted Kosher Meat Mixed with an Unkosher Unsalted Liquid
9. Meat and Cheese Coming into Contact with Each Other, Where One or Both Are Salted

15. Definition of דבוק (Attached); Nullification of a Forbidden Substances in Cases of Doubt

16. The Stringencies of an Attached Forbidden Substance Apply Only to a Separate Entity

17. A Piece Becomes Inherently Forbidden Only When the Prohibition Is Clear Cut

18. Can a Vessel Become Inherently Forbidden *(nevelah)*?

Topic 45: Laws Concerning Milk Cook in a Meat Pot; Regulations Regarding a Dairy Spoon Inserted Into a Meat Pot (or Vice Versa)

1. Regulations Regarding Forbidden Liquid Which Has Splashed onto a Pot

2. One Who Cooked with a Pot Which Became Forbidden Due to Splashed Liquid

3. Leniencies Which May Apply to a Pot Which Always Contains a Large Quantity of Liquid When It Is Heated

4. Milk Falling on a Meat Pot Which Contains Pareve Ingredients

5. Stringencies Which Apply to Liquid That Splashes on a Pot Above The Level of Its Contents

6. Leniencies Which Apply to a "New Pot" or a Covered Pot

7. Leniencies Which Apply Under Difficult Circumstances

8. Leniencies Which Apply if Liquid Splashes on the Part of the Pot Which Is Near the Fire

9. Laws Concerning a Forbidden Drop Which Falls on a Pot Cover

10. Transmission of Taste Via Steam

11. Hot Milk Flowing Onto a Cold Pot of Meat

12. Cold Milk Flowing Onto a Hot Pot of Meat

13. Cold Milk Which Flowed Under a Hot Pot of Meat

14. A Pot of Meat Placed on Hot Milk Which Is Next to the Fire

15. Cold Milk Which Flowed Under a Hot Pot of Meat Next to the Fire

16. Pots of Meat and Milk Next to the Fire, Where Liquid Flows from One of Them

17. Leniencies Which Apply if Ashes Are Present

18. If a Pot Overflowed and the Circumstances Are in Doubt

19. A Pot of Meat Placed on Hot Milk Which Is Not Next to the Fire

20. Forbidden Fat from Candles Which Falls onto a Vessel

21. Rules Concerning the "Peel" of a Vessel Which Became Forbidden

Topical Listing of All Halachos

Topic 46: Laws Concerning Milk Cooked in a Meat Pot; Regulations Regarding a Dairy Spoon Inserted into a Meat Pot (or Vice Versa)

1. Milk Cooked in a Meat Pot (or Vice Versa); Kosher Food Cooked in a Forbidden Pot
2. Leniencies Which May Apply When the Amount of Absorbed Taste is Known
3. Stringencies Which Apply to a Pot Cover
4. Placing a Cover from a Meat Pot onto a Hot Dairy Pot
5. Placing a Cover from a Hot Meat Pot onto a Cold Dairy Pot
6. Inserting a Dairy Spoon into a Pot of Meat (or Vice Versa); Inserting a Forbidden Spoon into a Pot of Kosher Food
7. Inserting a Spoon with Absorbed Taste Twice into the Same Pot; Measuring Absorbed Taste in a Spoon
8. The Status of a Dairy Spoon Which Had Been Inserted into a Pot of Meat (and Vice Versa)
9. Inserting a Dairy Spoon into Pareve Ingredients Which Are Being Cooked in a Meat Pot
10. A Vessel Which Contains Tastes of Meat and Milk Where One of Them is Detrimental
11. The Difference Between Liquid in a Hot כלי ראשון ("First Vessel") and Liquid Which Is Poured from It.

Topic 47: Laws Concerning a Knife Used for Cutting Forbidden Food, or a Meat Knife Used for Dairy

1. Hot Meat in a כלי ראשון ("First Vessel") Which Was Cut with a Dairy Knife
2. Leniencies Which Apply if the Knife Had Not Been Used on That Day
3. Hot Meat in a כלי שני ("Second Vessel") or Cold Meat Which Was Cut with a Dairy Knife
4. Guidelines for Kashering a Knife
5. Using a Knife to Remove Forbidden Structures from Meat
6. Laws Concerning a Knife Which Was Used to Cut Meat Before Its Blood Has Been Removed
7. A Knife Used to Cut Salted Unkosher Meat
8. Using a Forbidden Knife After Insertion into the Ground or Sharpening It
9. Miscellaneous Rules Regarding a Forbidden Knife

Topical Listing of All Halachos

Topic 48: Laws Concerning Secondary Transmitted Taste (נ"ט בר נ"ט); Meat and Dairy Vessels (or Permissible and Forbidden Ones) Which Have Been Washed Together

Topic 49: Laws Relating to Sharp Foods

Index

Example: 44:14 denotes Topic 44, Section 14.

Index

About the Author

Dr. Yehoshua (Jeffrey) Cohen is already a known author. His publications include seven volumes of a Mishnah series which include an English translation of both the Mishnah as well as the commentary of Rabbi Ovadiah MiBartinura. These works have been well received by the Torah community.

Dr. Cohen is an alumnus of the Rabbi Yitzchak Elchanan Seminary, where he studied until 1968. He has since continued his Torah learning under Rabbi Jacob Bulka, Rabbi Avigdor Miller, and Rabbi Avraham Asher Zimmerman.

An M.D. degree was awarded to Dr. Cohen by the Albert Einstein College of Medicine in 1972. He then went on to specialize in the field of radiology, and is presently a practicing radiologist at Brookdale Hospital in Brooklyn, New York. He currently resides in the Flatbush section of Brooklyn with his wife Yosefa (Josie) and their sons and daughters.